Preface

In 2012 my first book on Digital Photography was published followed by 2nd revised edition in 2015. These two books were like a handbook on photography targeted for beginners and serious amateur photographers. In those books I discussed about Camera techniques, Shooting techniques, Aesthetic part of an image and post processing.

The readers desired to get a book on advanced technique of photography. I have tried to use my expertise and experience to describe various advanced in-camera technique with an aim to enhance the skill of the photographers across the globe. I am sure this book will be useful for serious amateur photographers and professional photographers too. In this book only advanced photography techniques have been described with sufficient illustrations.

I am thankful to all my teachers like Iqbal K Mohmed, LLA, Nathan Daniel Singman, LLA, Susan, Hong Kong, Rainy Chastine, USA . My sincere thanx to my better half Ritu Srivastava for supporting me in writing this book. I am also thankful to Ritu Srivastava for editing language part of the book.

Thanx to the models Priya Jha, Veronica, Bipasha Dutta, Sohini Dhar, Ami Namo, Madhumita, Preety Ghosal, Sakshi, Prity Kumari, Soumya Singh, Surabhi Singh, Shivani Kumari, Sushma Singh, Sunita Mondal, Surjeet Das, Diksha Singh, Prerna Hazra & RBP Sinha for supporting me in the content shoot for this book.

To make it more informative I have added youtube links and QR code in the end of important chapters.

As always, my friend Ganapati is a great source of strength for me

Mukesh Srivastava

FIE, EFIAP, FFIP, FDCC

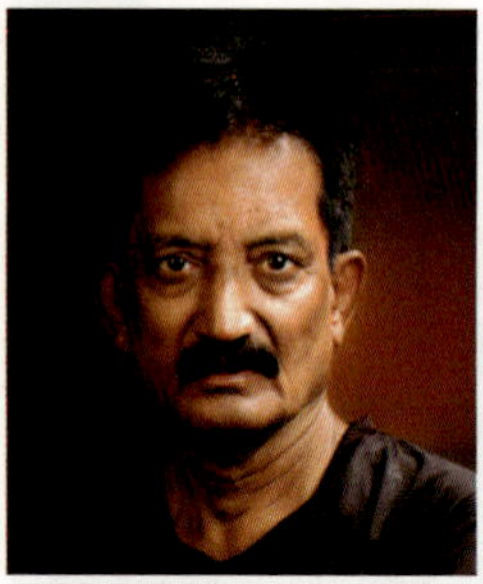

Mukesh is a qualified Engineer with Post graduate in Digital Electronics from Indian Institute of Sciences. He retired as Director from Govt. of India in 2012.

He has captured images in almost every genre of photography. He loves capturing raw expression of people around the world. He has more than 15000 images in stock. He has more than 150 National and International awards to his credit. To name a few he got 27 from Kodak, 4 from Natgeo, 1 from Savewater, Melbourne and 150 awards in International Salons accredited by FIAP and PSA.

To explore the world through his lens, he travelled to Australia in 2011, UK, Holland, Brussels, France, Switzerland, Germany, Italy, and Austria in 2013, South Korea in 2016, Iceland in 2018 & Nepal in 2020.

Few of his images are being sold in USA as Greetings cards. Some of his works have also been published in Lonely Planet, Syndic Literary Journal, USA, Better Photography, Smart Photography, Asian Photography, NatGeo Magazine and Outlook Business.

In 2008, his iconic image Thirst got displayed in Times Square, NYC for 24 hrs.

In 2011 he got first International award from Savewater, Melbourne, Australia.

In 2015 he was conferred with EFIAP honour from FIAP and FFIP from FIP, India

He got National Award for Photography in 2016

He has trained more than 8000 photographers through workshops under Center For Visual Arts, Nikon and IPA, Kolkata.

He was Nikon's Official Mentor from 2015 to 2017.

He is the first Indian author to write a book on Digital Photography published in 2012.

His website: www.mukeshphotography.in

Contact Nos.: +919470385811 & +917004184921

E-mail: *mailmukesh123@gmail.com*

Watch My intro on youtube:

My Intro 2021 updated 9th August - **YouTube**

ADVANCED PHOTOGRAPHY

Mukesh Srivastava, FIE, EFIAP, FFIP, FDCC

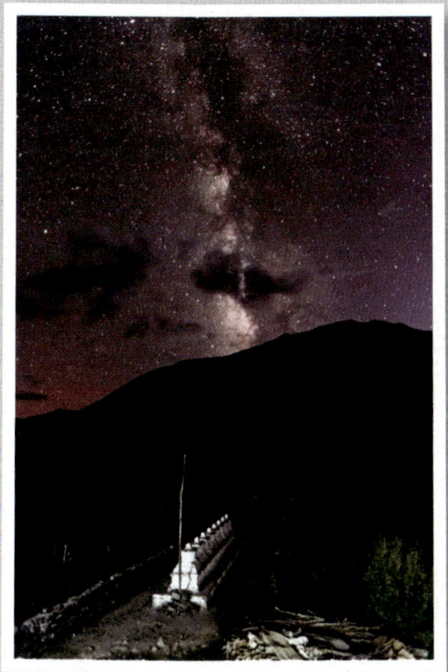

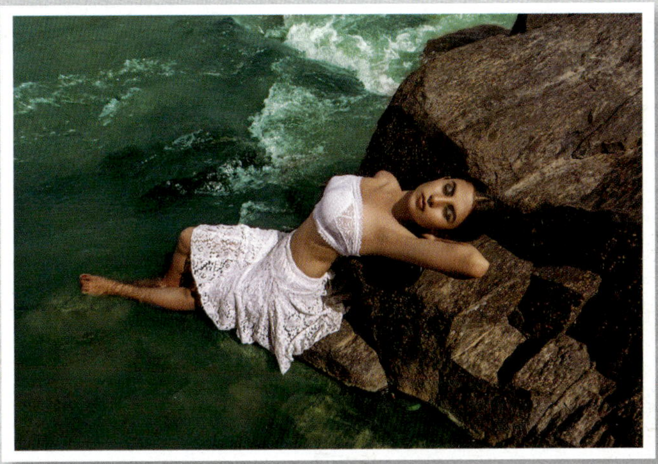

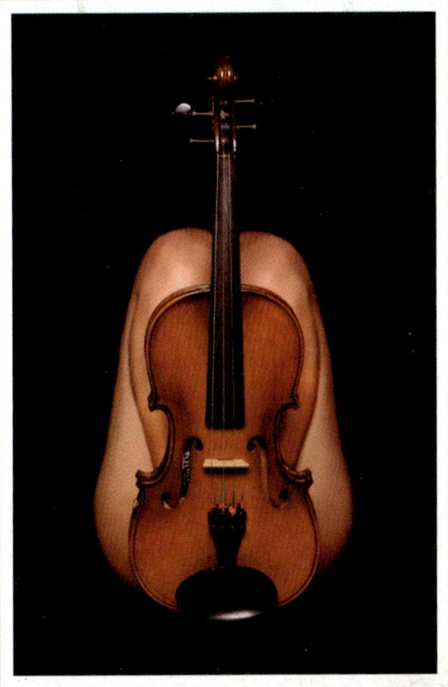

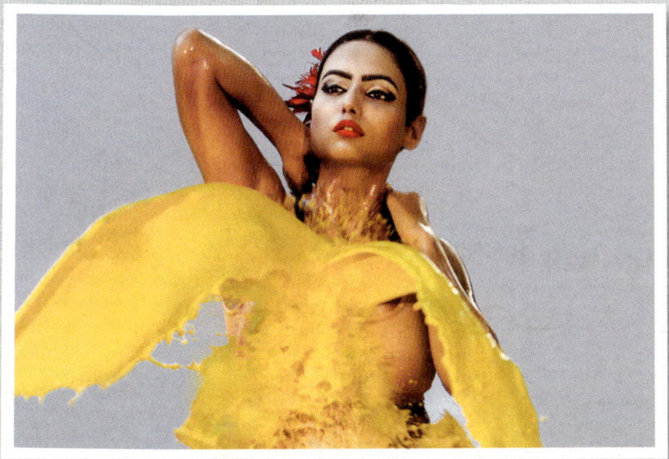

Publishers
UNICORN BOOKS
F-2/16, Ansari Road, Daryaganj, New Delhi-110002
☎ 23262683, 45644782, 23250704
E-mail: info@unicornbooks.in

Branch : Mumbai
23-25, Zaoba Wadi, Thakurdwar, Mumbai-400002
☎ 022-22010941, 022-22053387
E-mail: unicornbooksmumbai@gmail.com

Advanced Photography
ISBN: 978-81-7806-576-2
1st Edition: September, 2022

Printed at : Param Offsetters, Okhla, New Delhi-110020

Foreword

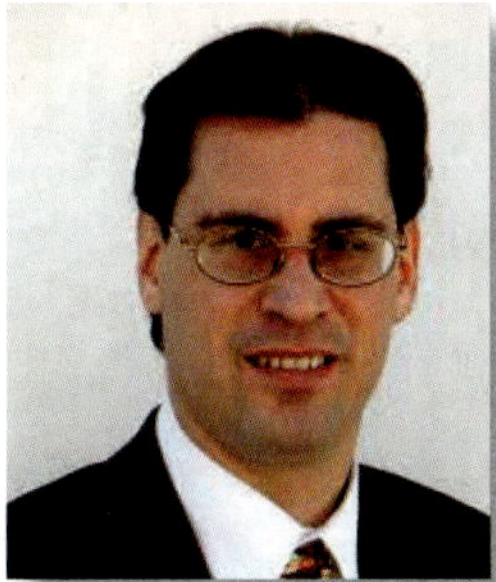

Although I knew that Mukesh was a very successful artist and a very competent teacher in the field of photography, I had never the chance to meet him in person. About 2 years ago, on the occasion of the pandemic that resulted in many online presentations, I had the opportunity to work with him and so I met him "up close" although still only online. I was immediately impressed by his responsibility and contagiousness, but also by his organizational skills.

A book written by such an author could only be characterized by the above qualities. Despite the fact that the author deals with many topics, which in principle are not related to each other, he divides them into small sections and manages to present them efficiently and methodically, in a completely informative way and even in just a few lines, without tiring the reader with excessive and often unnecessary information.

It is essentially a collection of tips for a variety of photographic subjects, which initially does not seem to address to the novice but to be limited only to the advanced photographer. These tips are accompanied by a series of explanatory photos or illustrations that help the reader better understand each topic. The variety of techniques is impressive. The tips range from screen calibration to astro photography and from panoramic photography to human body shapes!

If you wish to find information on these topics you either have to buy a series of specialized books and technical manuals or you have to spend countless hours in front of your screen searching for relevant articles or educational videos on the internet. But what made a special impression on me in Mukesh's book is that he manages to isolate through his experience and expertise the necessary advice on all these issues and offer them in a very understandable way. As a result, he succeeds in helping not only the photographer who is looking for advice on a specific subject but also the one who wants to discover a new path in the field of his favorite art and does not know where to start.

For this reason, I believe that it is a very remarkable book, full of concentrated knowledge, that will surely become an important tool in the hands of every photographer, whether the advanced one who is looking for a technical advice or the beginner who wants to discover something new.

Mukesh, congratulations on your new book!

Ioannis Lykouris EFIAP/s, MFIAP, HonEFIAP

FIAP Secretary General

Foreword

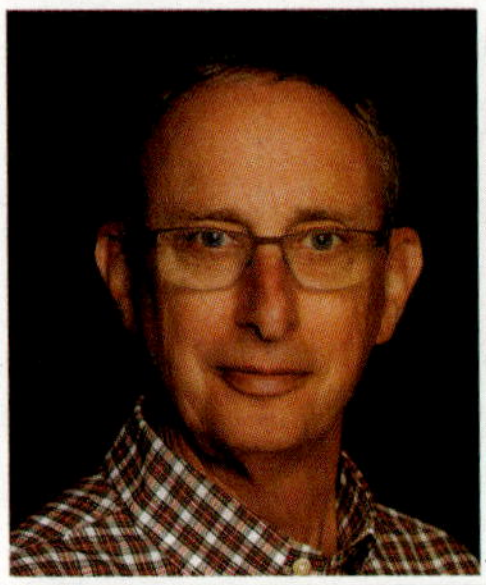

I was delighted and honored to receive a request from Mukesh Srivastava, FIE, EFIAP, FFIP to write a brief foreword to for his new book "Advanced Photography". I have been a fan of Mukesh and his photographic expertise, moreover, having been a guest speaker for him, I have gained appreciation for his editorial works. His first book on Digital Photography targeted for beginners has won wide acclaim. Now with this, his second book, he is targeting a more in depth look at how photography can be used for advanced photographers.

Looking through this stunning volume, I am absolutely amazed at how he articulates the complexity of calibrating your monitor with clear step by step instructions. explaining how to produce levitation composites and on to photo stacking, along with much more. I am sure the readers will find this and exciting and beneficial book to help the serious amateur advance in their photographic career.

J.R. Schnelzer

FPSA, MPSA2, EFIAP

Foreword

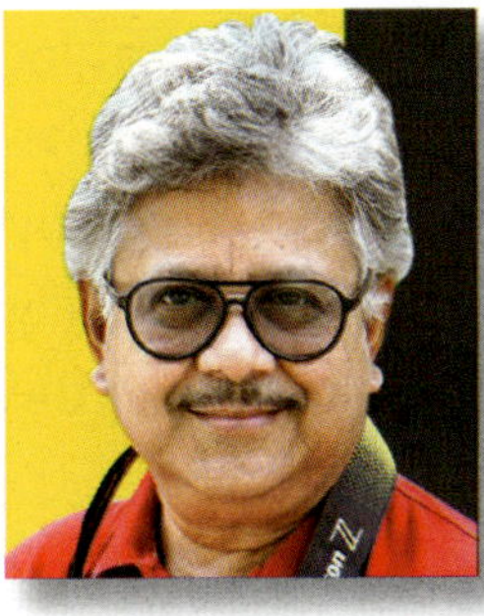

Mukesh Srivastava is a renowned and seasoned Pictorial photographer, having experience of so many years in the field of Portrait, glamour and Experimental photography.

I am very pleased to go through the pages of his 2nd book on the subject "Advanced Photography – Tips & Techniques". He has already a book to his credit on "Digital Photography" published in 2012 & had its revised edition in 2015.

He is an established teacher of photography, which is very much evident from his book. Each and every chapter has been dealt in detail in simple language. The adequate number of illustrations make the subject easy to understand. He has tried to cover all advanced aspects of photography like Levitation, Image stacking, art of wine glass etc.

I am very much impressed to find this book "Advanced Photography – Tips & Techniques", very informative. This book is a must for serious amateur and professional photographers.

Anil Risal Singh

MFIAP(France), ARPS (Great Britain), Hon.FIP (India)

Hon.LCC (India), FFIP (India), AIIPC, (India),

Former President

Federation of Indian Photography

Foreword

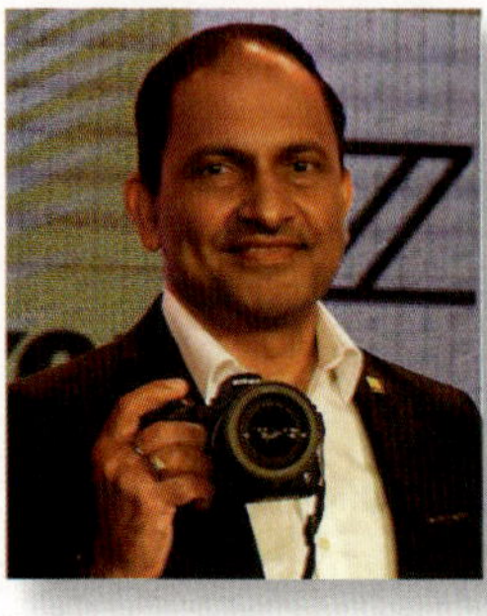

Technology in Photography equipment has changed a lot over the years. There are always new concepts to learn, creative techniques to explore – and there's no better way to do it than by picking up an inspiring book. A great photography book generally includes tips & Technics which can be very handy to enhance the photography skill.

If you'd like to take a masterclass in photography but can't afford the time or expense, pick up a copy of this book. This action-oriented book provides a "curriculum" to help photographers learn how to create images that offer deeper visual experiences for your audience. Mr. Mukesh Srivastava clearly explains from his rich experience each concept, adjustments and settings to make creative images within the book, he invites readers to play with them in a more hands-on kind of way.

Since compelling composition is one of the keys to create great images, this book can really help photographers take their work to the next level by taking images in an entirely new way.

I would like to Congratulate Mr. Mukesh Srivastava for bringing out a masterpiece once again. I am sure it is going to make a huge impact on the people who like to polish their photography skills and believe in attention to detail.

Sajjan Kumar

Sajjan Kumar

Managing Director Nikon India

Contents

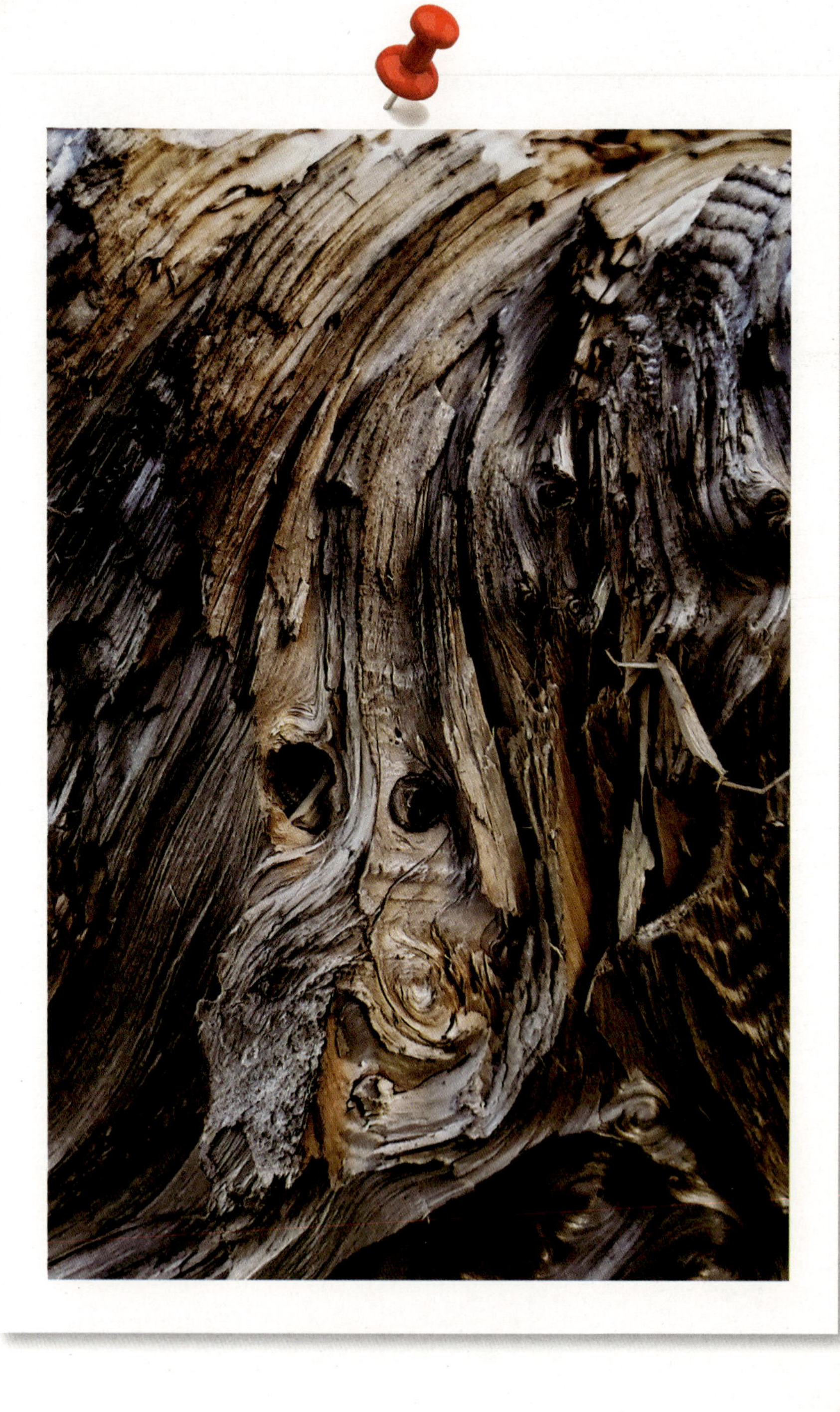

1. Monitor Calibration for Perfect Prints

Why to calibrate

Proper calibration of Monitor is very important to get perfect colours in your photographs. When you post process the image it looks good in terms of brightness and colours, but when it goes to colour lab for print, you do not get perfect colour and brightness. As a result customers become unhappy and we start losing customer's satisfaction.

Similar situation exists for online submission of images for any photo competition.

The reason is very simple. Your monitor is not calibrated to see black as black (RGB:0,0,0), white as white (RGB:255,255,255).

For example see the image Fig. 1 which is before calibration and compare with image Fig. 2 which is after calibration. You can see the difference.

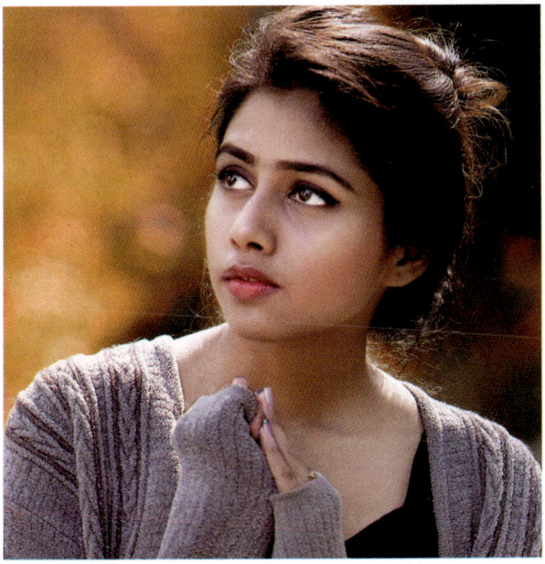

Fig. 1 Before calibration

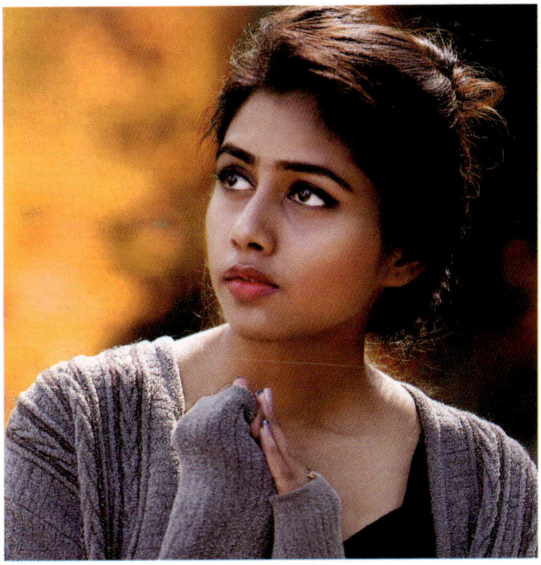

Fig. 2 After calibration

How To Calibrate

There are various methods to calibrate monitors:

1. Calibration using Built –In Windows & Mac tools
2. Calibration using Online tools
3. Calibration using Colorimeter Hardware

I will describe each method in detail below:

Before you begin calibration using any method mentioned above, you must do the following:

Turn on your monitor at least half an hour before calibration so that it can be warmed up to its normal operating temperature and conditions.

Set your monitor's resolution to its native default screen resolution.

Make sure you're calibrating in a room with moderate ambient lighting condition. The room need not to be pitch black, but should avoid the sharp glares and colour casts resulting from the direct light falling on your monitor.

Light should not fall directly on the monitor.

After calibration maintain the same room lighting while working.

Familiarize yourself with your monitor's display controls. They may be located on the monitor itself, on the keyboard, or within the operating system control panel.

1. Calibration using Built –In Windows & Mac tools

Both Windows and MacOS have built-in calibration tools. this process is particularly helpful if you are new to monitor calibration.

The terms like gamma, white point, etc. may seem a bit heavy and complicated, but you don't need to know the ins and outs of the jargon to calibrate your monitor.

Windows 10 display calibration tool

In the latest version of Windows 10, it's very easy to find the colour calibration tool in the control panel. Open the control panel you will get this screen:

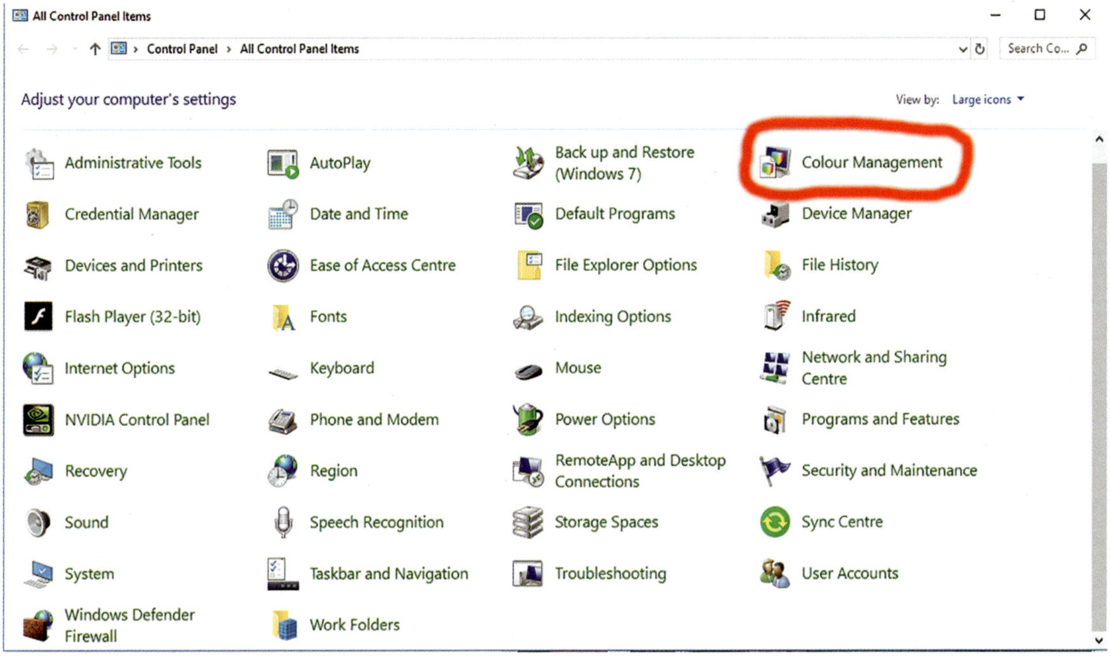

Fig. 3 Control Panel

In earlier versions of Windows, you can find the Colour Calibration utility in the Display section of the Control Panel, which is listed under Appearance and Personalization.

After clicking Colour Management you get this screen as shown in Fig. 4

In this screen click "ADVANCED" and then click "Calibrate Display".

Now You will get the welcome screen. Simply click "Next". On the next screen also simply click "Next". Now you will get How to adjust Gamma like shown in (Fig. 5)

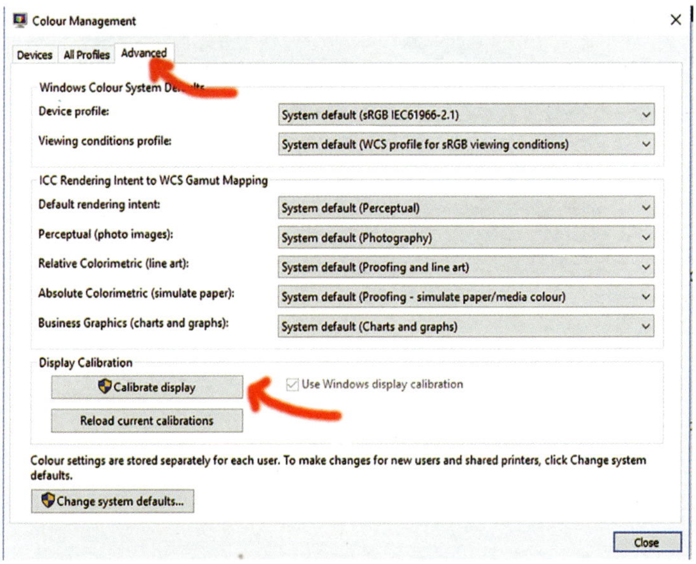

Fig. 4

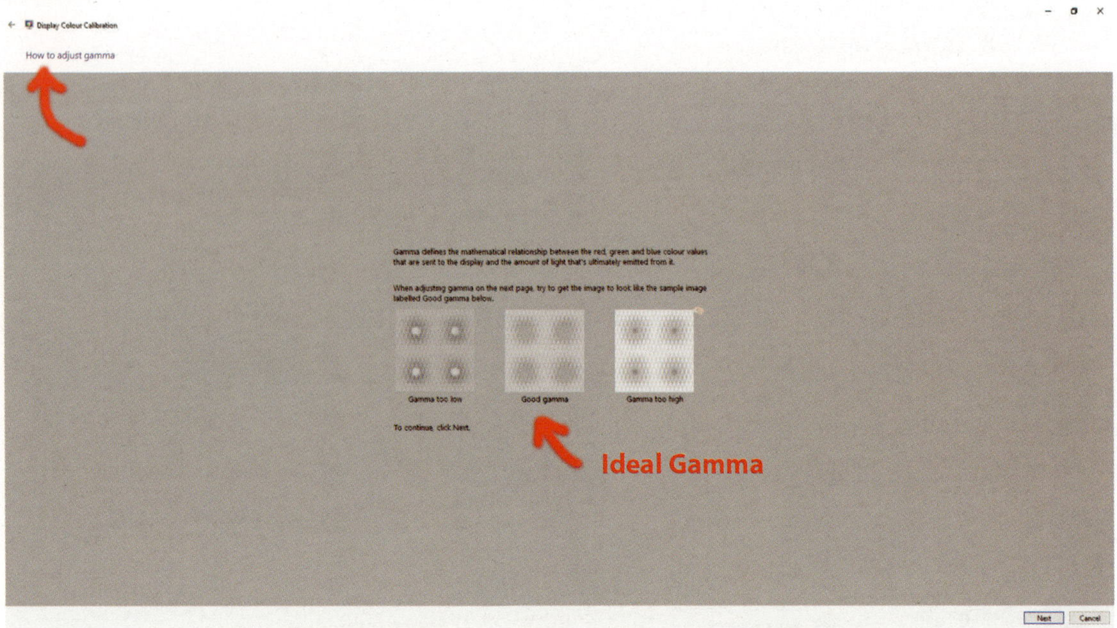

Fig. 5

Take a screen shot of your existing Monitor calibration, you may get like shown in (Fig. 1)

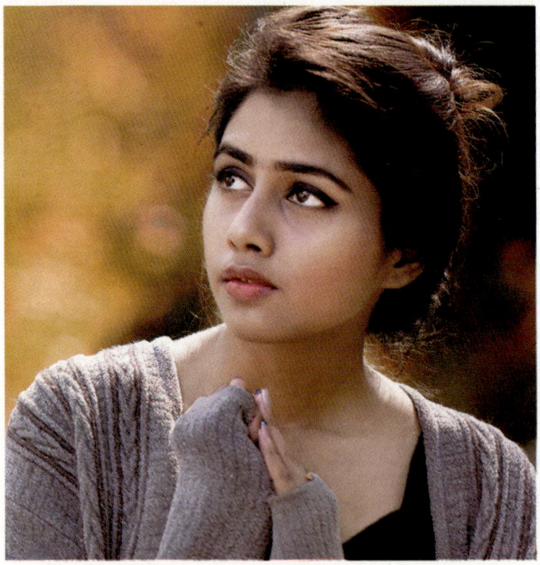

Fig. 1

After clicking Next in Fig. 5, you will get screen shown in (Fig. 6)

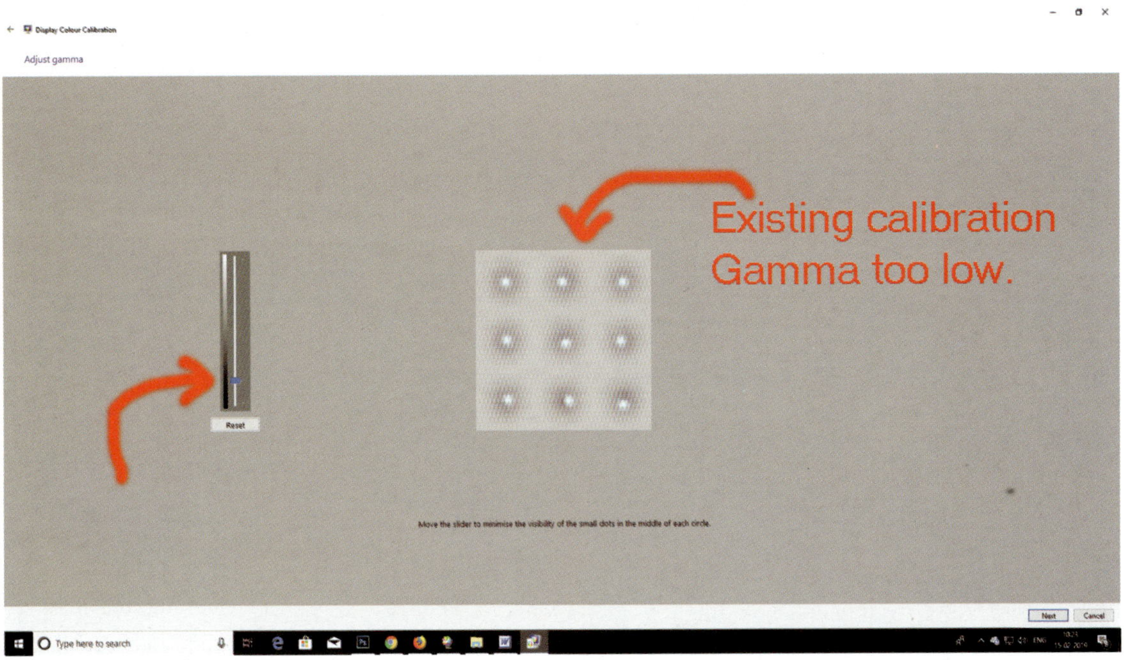

Fig. 6

These white dots in the centre indicates too low gamma i.e. low brightness.

You need to adjust slider in the left to get neither white nor black dot in the centre as shown in Fig. 7

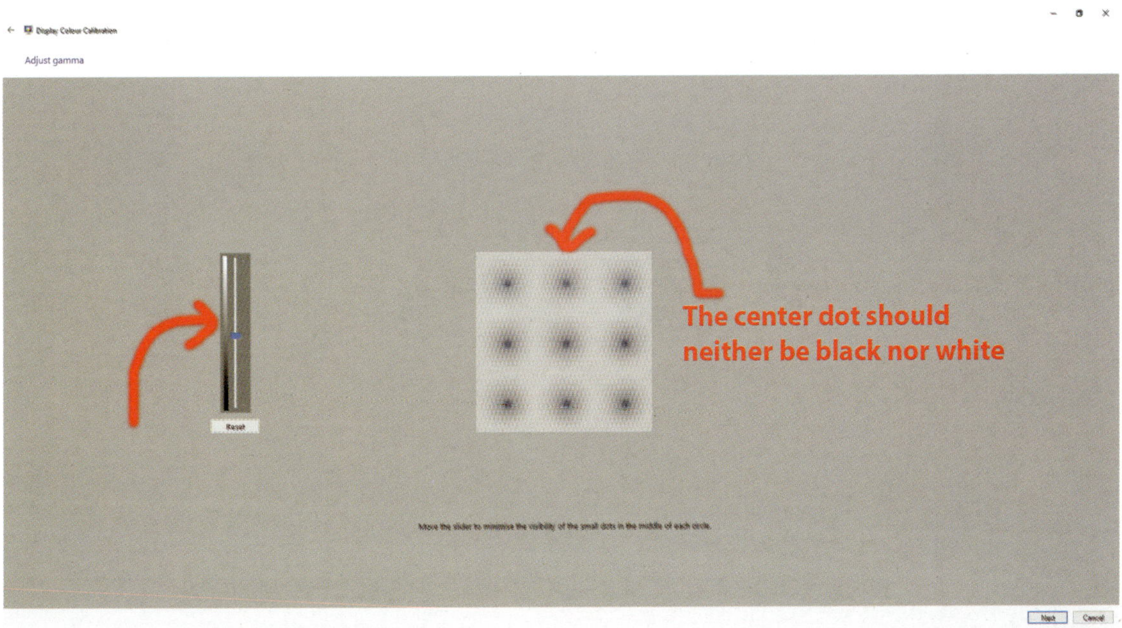

Fig. 7

Next screens in Fig. 8, 9 & 10 will ask you to adjust brightness and contrast of the monitor.

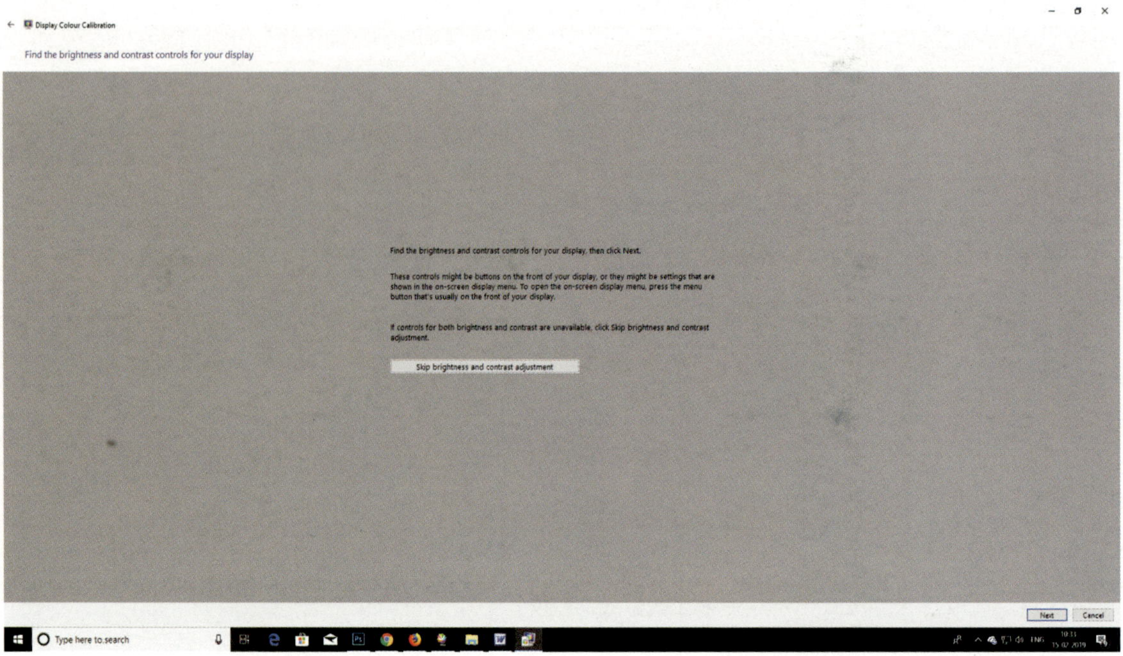

Fig. 8

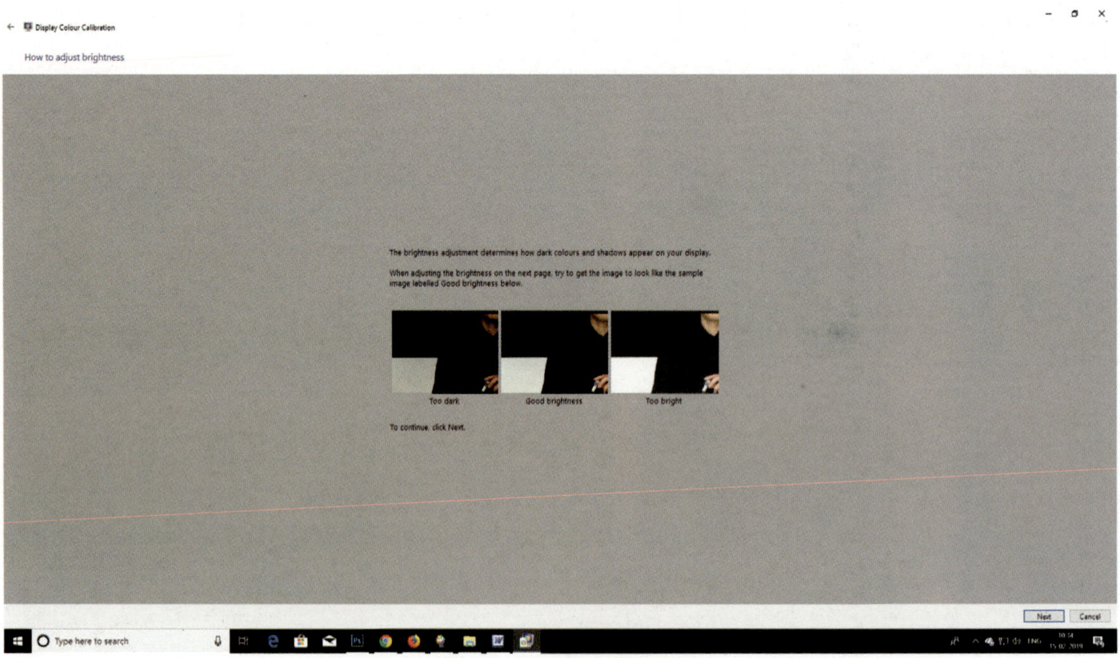

Fig. 9

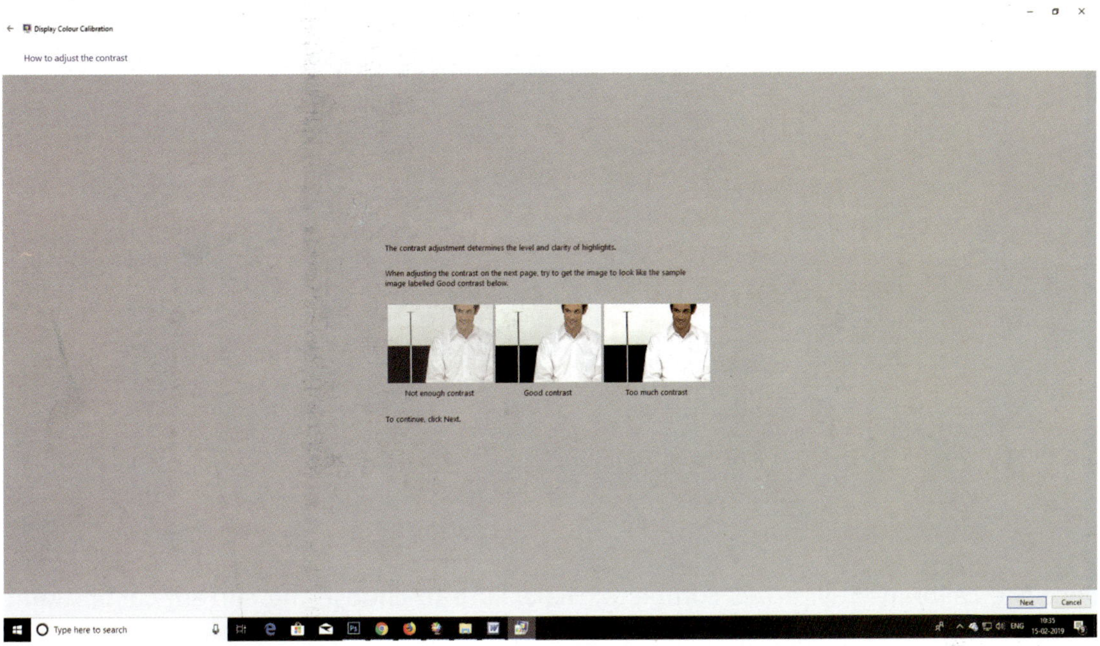

Fig. 10

Fig. 11 is the final screen where you can compare previous and current calibration of your monitor. Before clicking Finish, ensure to click current calibration.

You can also adjust clarity of text by checking bottom box or just uncheck and click finish.

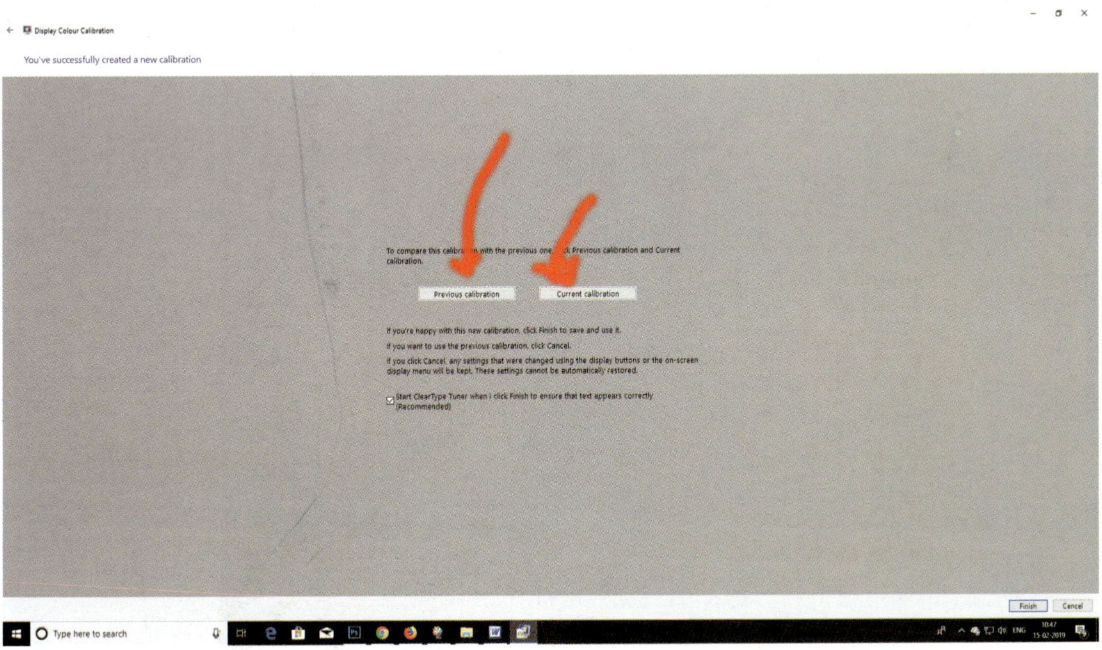

Fig. 11

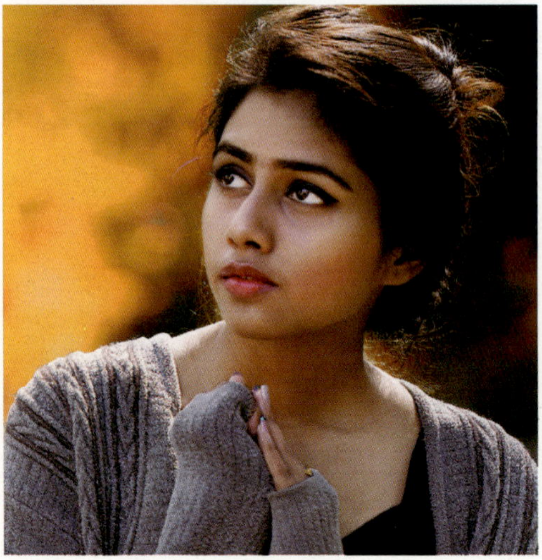

Fig. 2 After calibration

Once the calibration wizard is complete, make sure to choose the current calibration or return to the previous calibration if you are unsatisfied with the results.

The new calibration will be stored as an .ics file, or colour calibration file and will show up as a new International Colour Consortium (ICC) profile in the Colour Management settings app. The easiest way to open this app is to type colour management in the search box and choose the first result. Once it's open, you can select your monitor from the device list and see which ICC Profiles are available.

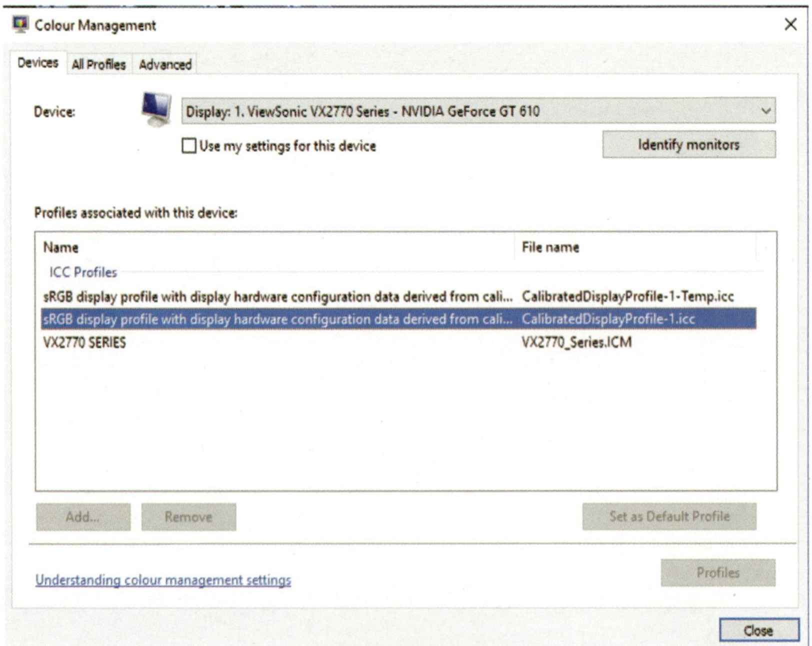

Fig. 12 ICC Profile

MacOS

1. Open System Preferences and go to the "Display" preference panel, then go to the "Colour" tab as usual.
2. Hold down the OPTION key and click on "Calibrate" to access the Expert Mode options in Display Calibrator

Proceed through the screen colour calibration process as usual in Mac OS

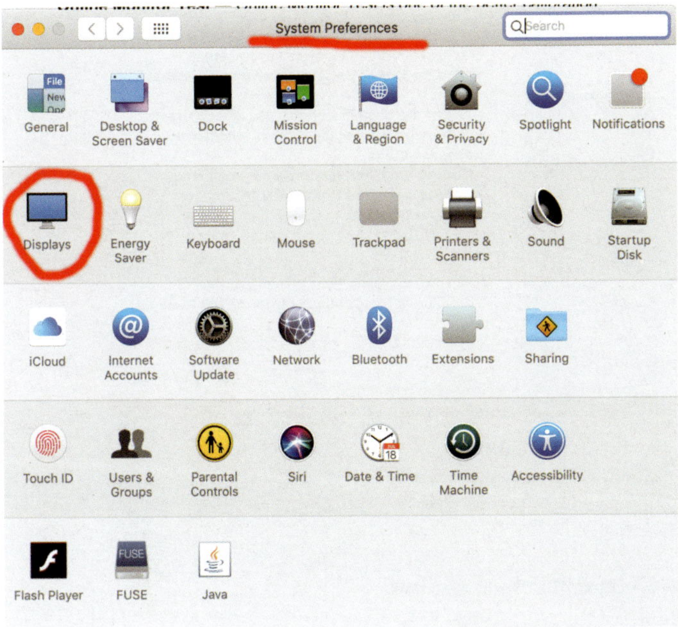

Fig. 13 Mac

Fig. 14 Mac 2

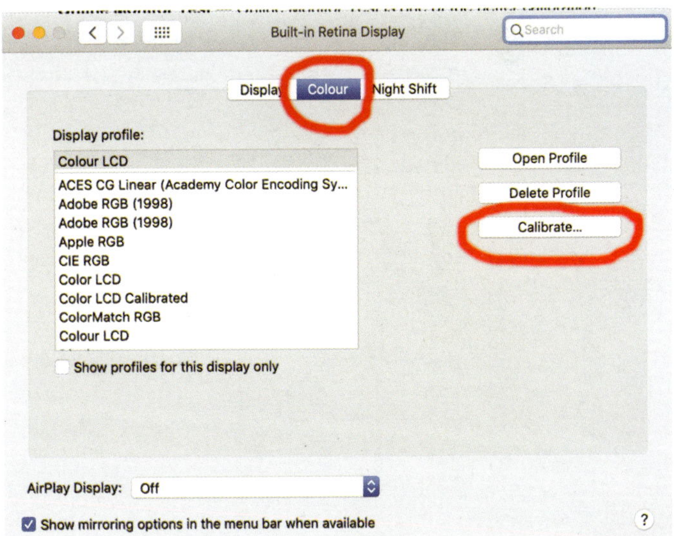

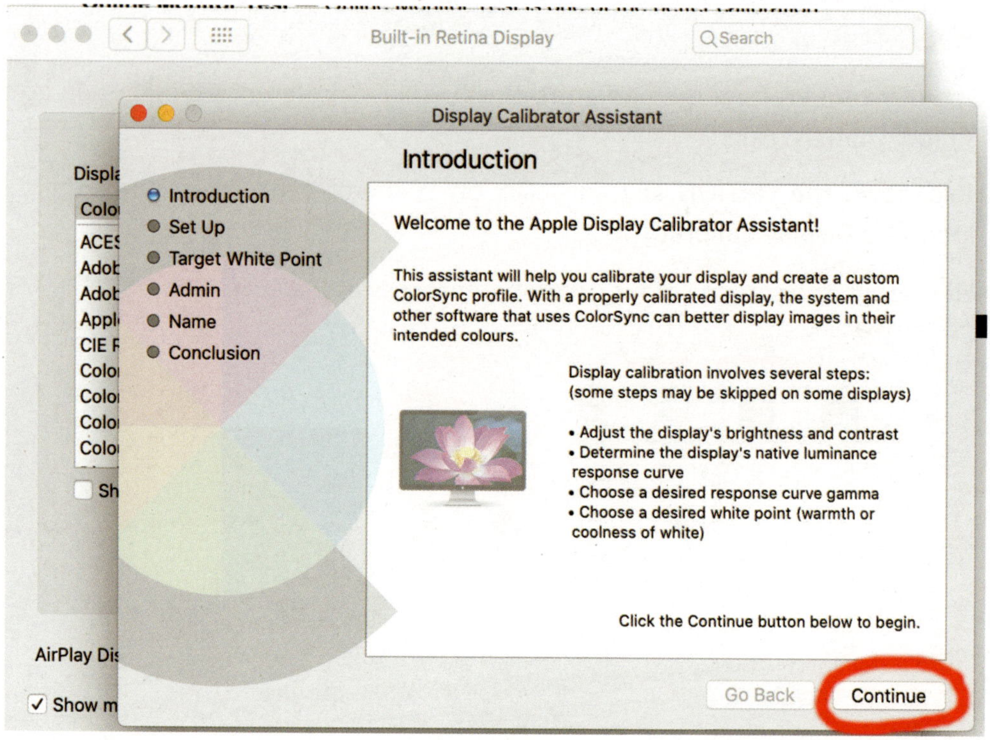

Fig. 15 Mac 3

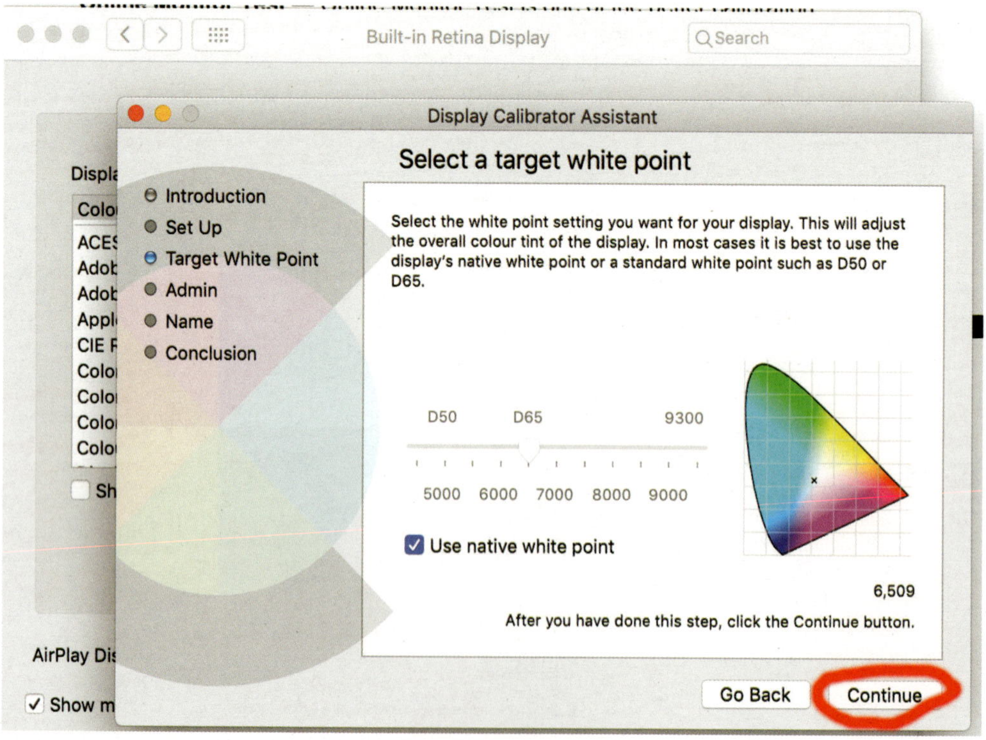

Fig. 16 Mac 4

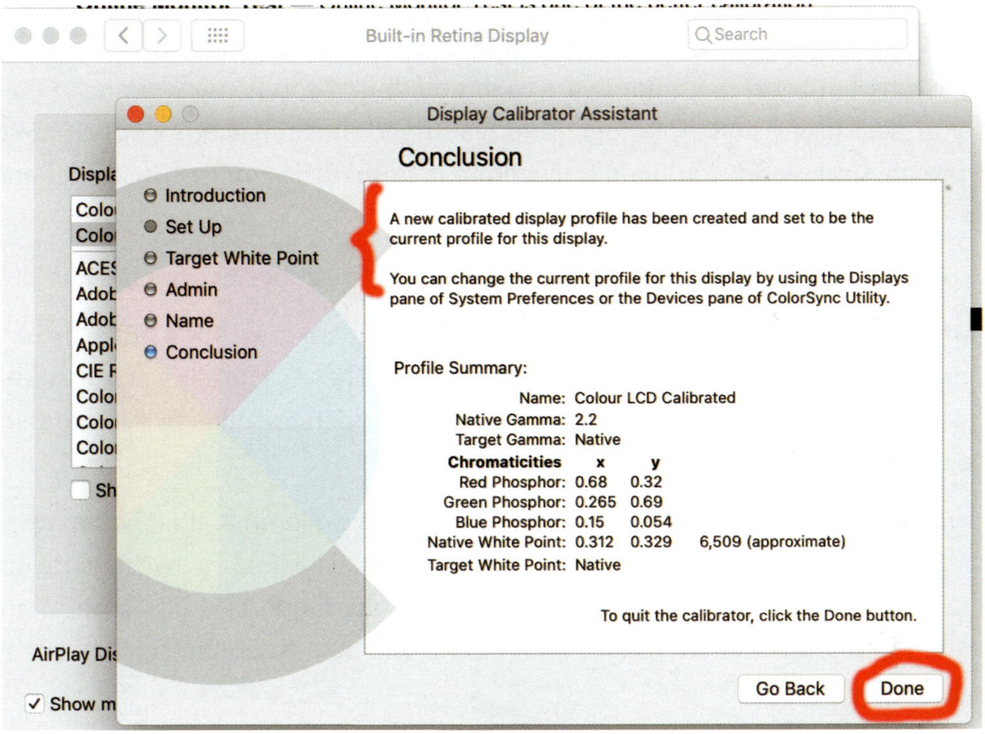

Fig. 17 Mac 5

Your Mac's step-by-step instructions will walk you through the calibration process

Just follow the on-screen instructions to choose your display's brightness, contrast, native gamma, target gamma and target white point. Click "Continue" and save the calibration profile once you have finished with the adjustments.

2. Calibrate Using Online Tools

There are a handful of web-based calibration tools that help you to manually adjust your monitor settings. They can provide more precise or more customized calibration than the built-in utilities.

Photo Friday — Photo Friday is a simple web page that is designed to help you to calibrate the brightness and contrast of your screen.

Online Monitor Test — Online Monitor Test is one of the better calibration websites out there.

3. Calibrate Using Colorimeter Hardware

Nothing is a true substitute for hardware calibration but if you're not working in the print industry or as a professional photographer, you need not to calibrate your monitor to match the physical world. You need to calibrate it so that the contrast is correct and you can use the monitor without straining your eyes.

This is the best system for professional photographers to get perfect colours and prints.

The built-in calibration utilities and web-based software are great for a quick fix but they are inherently imperfect because of one thing i.e. you. These calibration processes rely on an individual's perception of colour and are therefore open to subjectivity based on how you see different colours.

Purchasing a calibrating device is one way to bypass this dilemma. It is better to ensure that your monitor is calibrated to its true potential. You will need to invest some money if you're looking for greater precision and control but there are still some affordable alternatives that work well on a tight budget and will help to obtain colour consistency across all your monitors.

SpyderX Pro

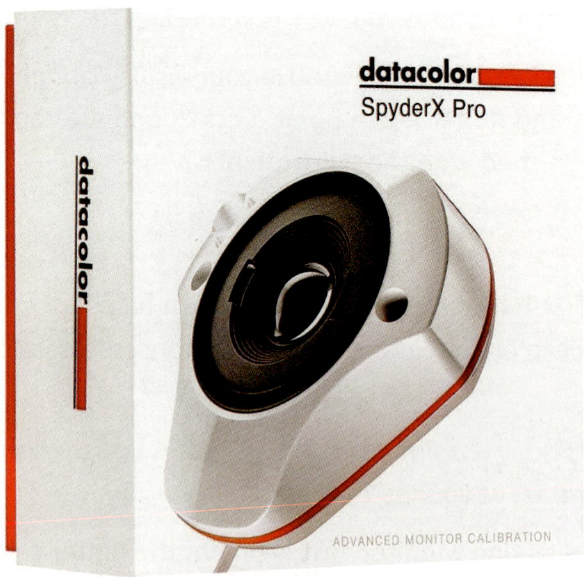

Fig. 18 SpyderX Pro

If you're looking to pick up a calibration tool, I recommend using the SpyderX Pro (₹17000) or the SpyderX Elite (₹25,000). All these devices feature a full-spectrum, seven-colour sensor to help accurately characterize a variety of wide-gamut and normal displays, but the more expensive versions are better equipped for the seasoned calibrator and are packed with more features. If you do decide to purchase one, all you have to do is attach the device to the screen, connect it to the USB port, and run the included calibration software. It will walk you through the process after that.

X-Rite's ColorMunki series (₹15000 to 19000) is also a good alternative. Like the Spyder series, all three devices come bundled with automated calibration software, with the more expensive versions touting more features and greater customization.

Most Important Note:

How often should you calibrate your monitor?

Most calibration software suggests that you calibrate your monitor every 2-4 weeks to insure that everything is accurate. This is because colour temperature and screen brightness will gradually change over time

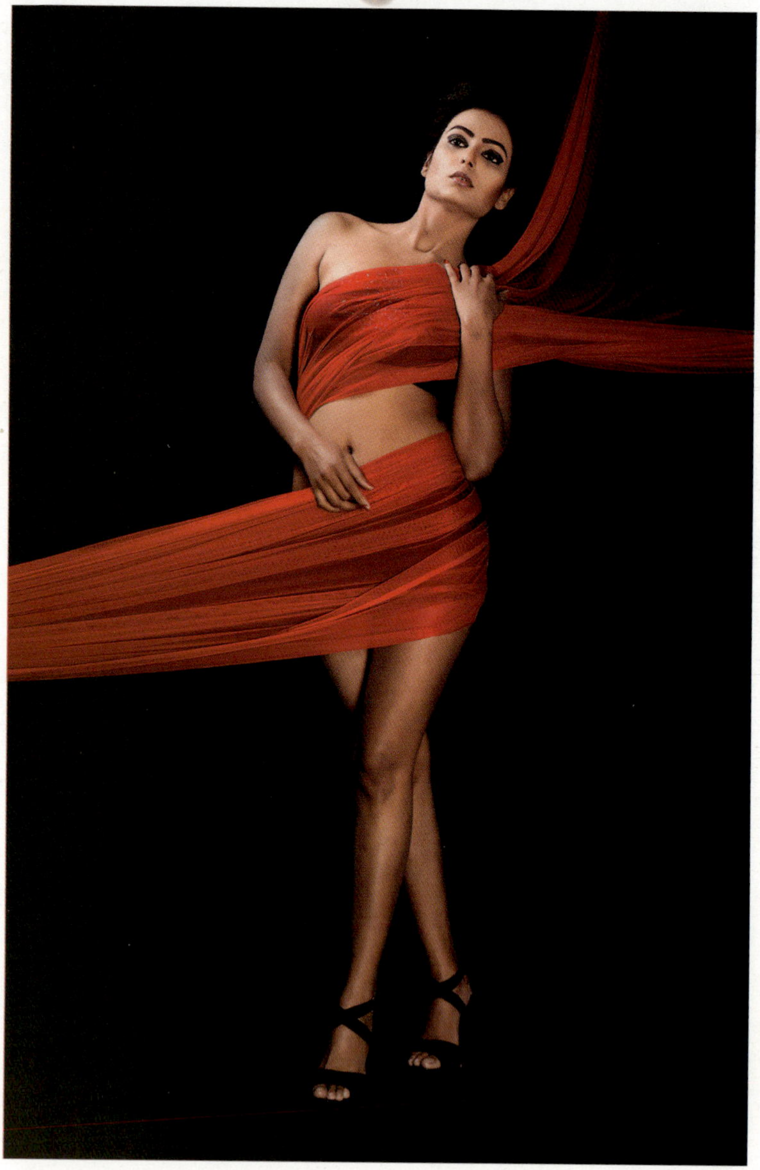

2. White Balance

Our eyes are very good at judging white as white and black as black under different light sources but digital cameras often have great difficulty with auto white balance (AWB) and can create sightly blue, orange or even green colour casts. White balance (WB) is the process of getting realistic colour casts, so that objects which appear white in the frame are rendered white in the photo. Camera white balance has to take into account the "colour temperature" of a light source. Understanding digital white balance can help you to avoid these colour casts, thereby improving your photos under a wider range of lighting conditions.

Selecting Right White Balance

There are various pre set options available in your camera. But to get perfect colour tone, use the white balance as per the light source. For example if you are shooting in direct sunlight select Direct Sunlight option. 'Direct Sunlight WB'. See the chart below Fig. 1:

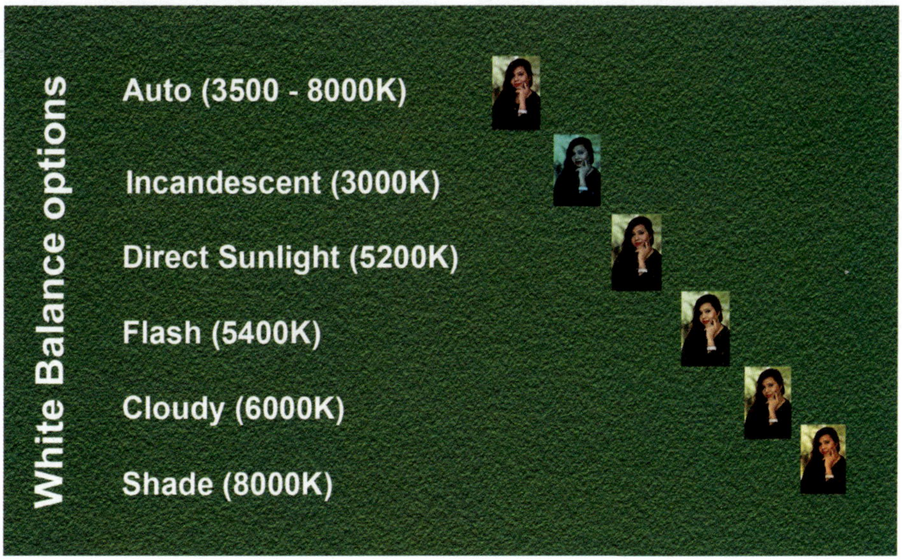

Fig. 1

In most of the situations Auto white balance works well, but not perfectly. If you are shooting in RAW you can set camera in Auto white balance. The colour can be corrected later on in the photoshop or any other editing software.

For shooting with studio light, do not use Auto white balance. It is better to use Flash white balance as the colour temperature of strobe light is very close to 5500 degree Kelvin.

While previewing your image in the camera, if you get more warm or bluish colour tone, you can fine tune the white balance as follows:

Select the white balance say Incandescent. Press right arrow from multi selector commander dial. You will get like this Fig. 2 & 3:

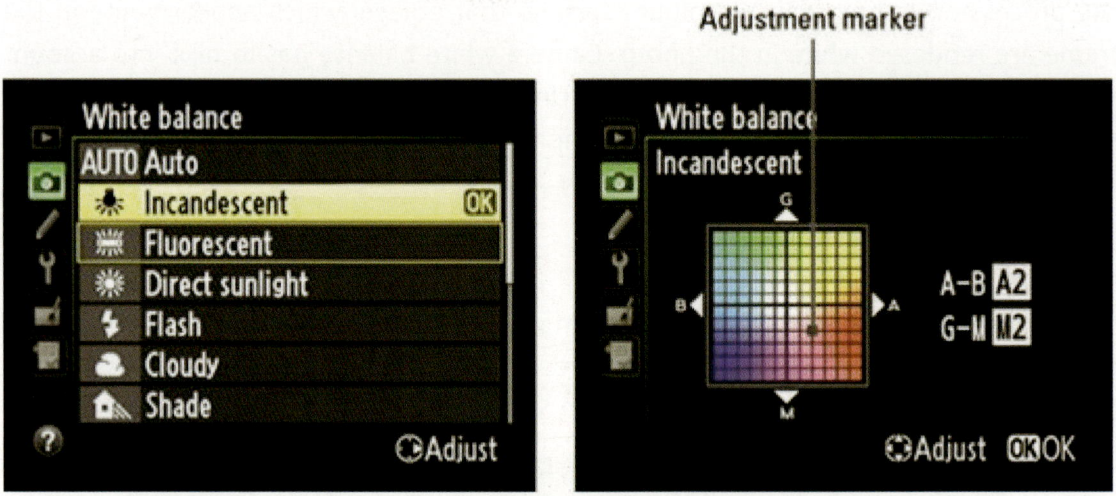

Fig. 2

Now you can adjust the required tone by tweaking the arrows A-B and G-M.

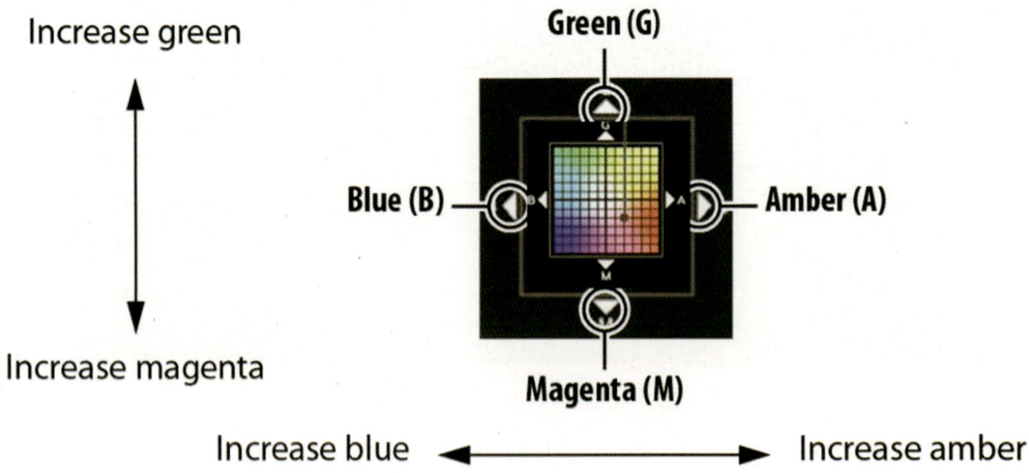

Fig. 3

Choosing Colour Temperature

For better professional quality, you can choose colour temperature as per your choice. To do this go to the white balance screen chose the Colour Temperature option' and select the desired value in Kelvin (Fig. 4).

For studio light, try to chose colour temperature 5000 degree Kelvin and see the result. Compare it with Flash white balance setting. Follow the better one.

Let's see the changes in colour tone by shooting a portrait in various options of White balance to know the difference.

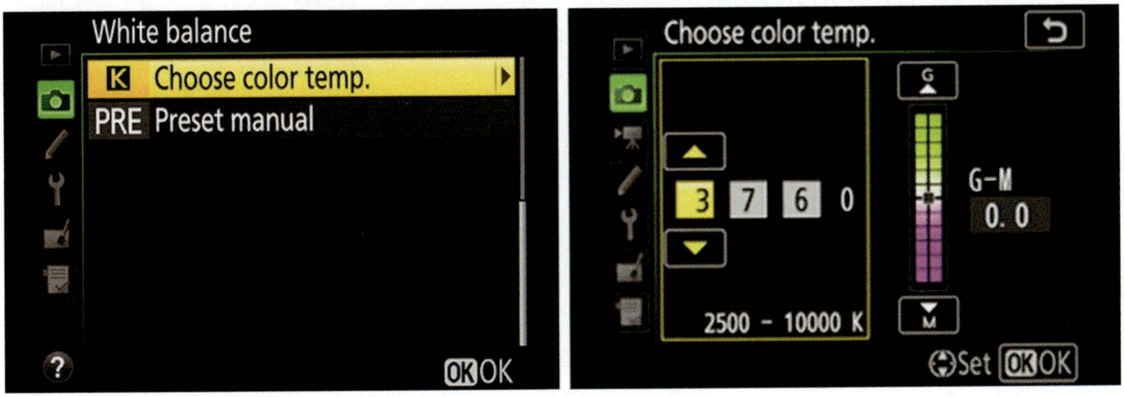

Fig. 4

Auto WB

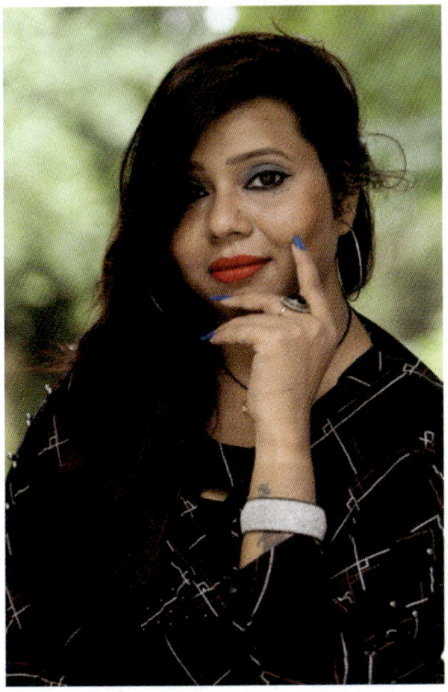

Fig. 5

Incandescent WB

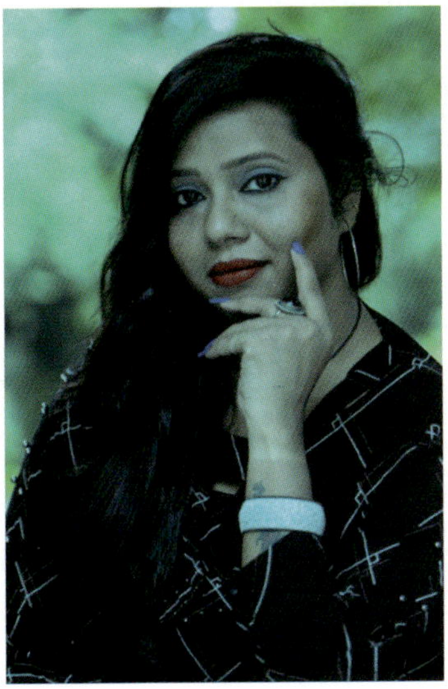

Fig. 6

Fluorescent WB

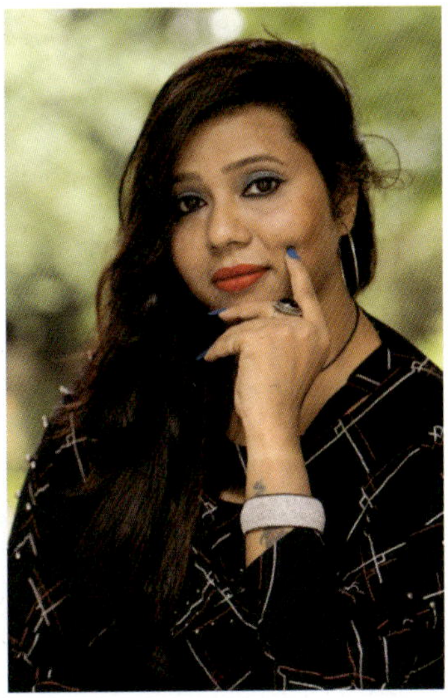

Fig. 7

Direct Sunlight WB

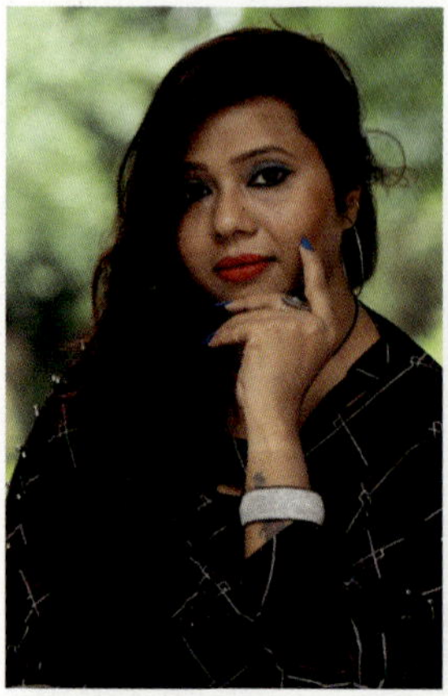

Fig. 8

Cloudy WB

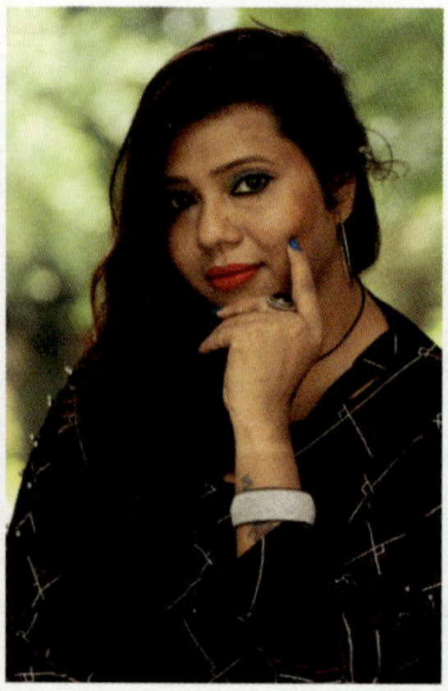

Fig. 9

Shade WB

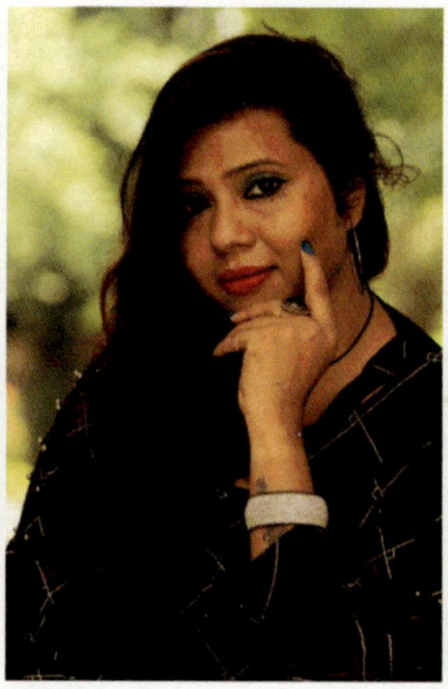

Fig. 10

Custom WB-5000K

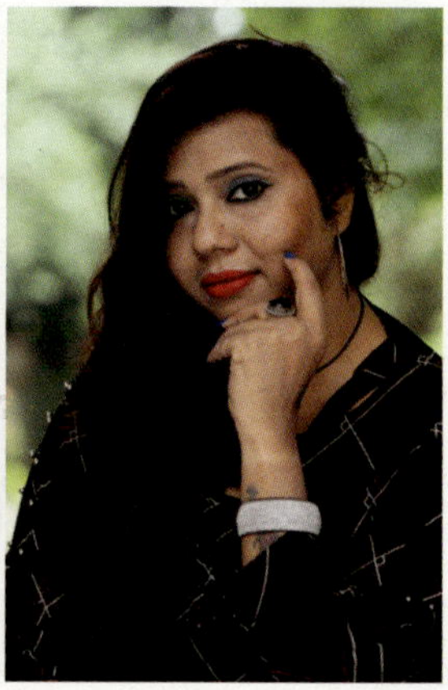

Fig. 11

You can set custom colour temperature. I normally set it at 5000 Kelvin.

With my experience I have noticed the 5000 kelvin colour temperature is more appropriate for outdoor shoot. And its my favourite setting. But still it's not perfect. For 100% perfection, you should use Neutral grey Card.

Using Neutral Gray Card

Here the model(Ms Namo Mitra) was asked to hold the neutral Gray card and shot in Auto WB mode. Further it was processed in photoshop by picking colour temperature using WB Tool in the RAW processor. You can see the change in the skin tone.

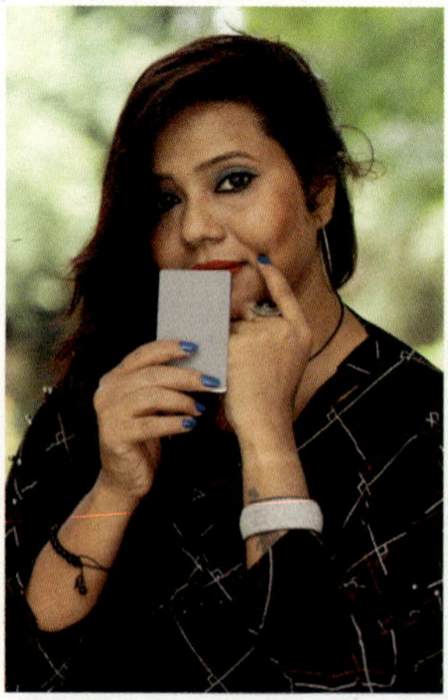

Fig. 12 With Neutral grey Card As Shot

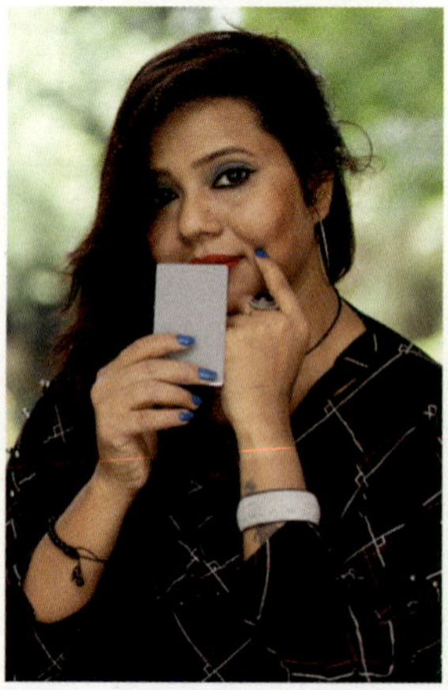

Fig. 13 With Neutral grey Card After Colour Correction

In Camera Pre-set Feature

You can also use neutral grey card to measure white balance by the camera as mentioned below:

Method	Description
Direct Measurement	Neutral gray or white object is placed under lighting that will be used in final photograph and white balance is measured by camera
Copy from existing photograph	White balance is copied from photo on memory card

Fig. 14

Flash

The image in Fig. 15 was shot using in camera flash with WB set in Flash mode.

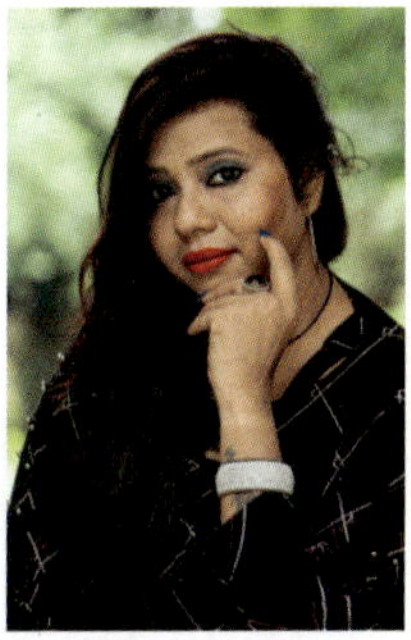

Fig. 15

Compare At a Glance

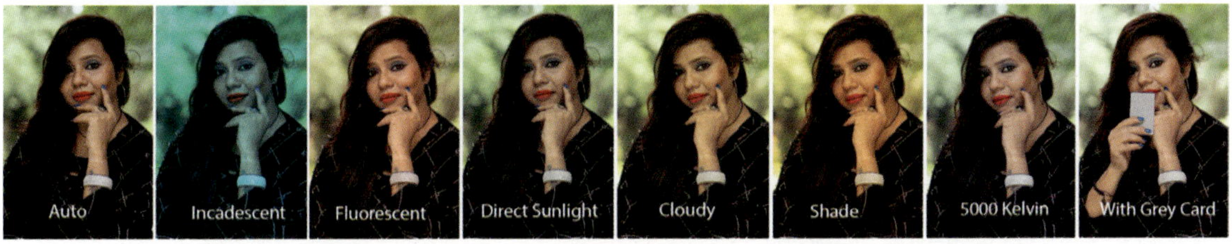

Fig. 16

Important Note:

Because of digital sensor, White Balance is very important with DSLR cameras. Some photographers prefer to set colour temperature after the preview of the image. But, for a wedding photographers, Travel Photographers and Press Photographers, it's not possible to get enough time to preview and set colour temperature in Kelvin, as you will miss the real time click of the moments.

So if you are shooting in RAW or RAW+JPEG, I recommend to set camera in Auto WB and you can very well fine tune the white balance in editing software to get desired colour tone.

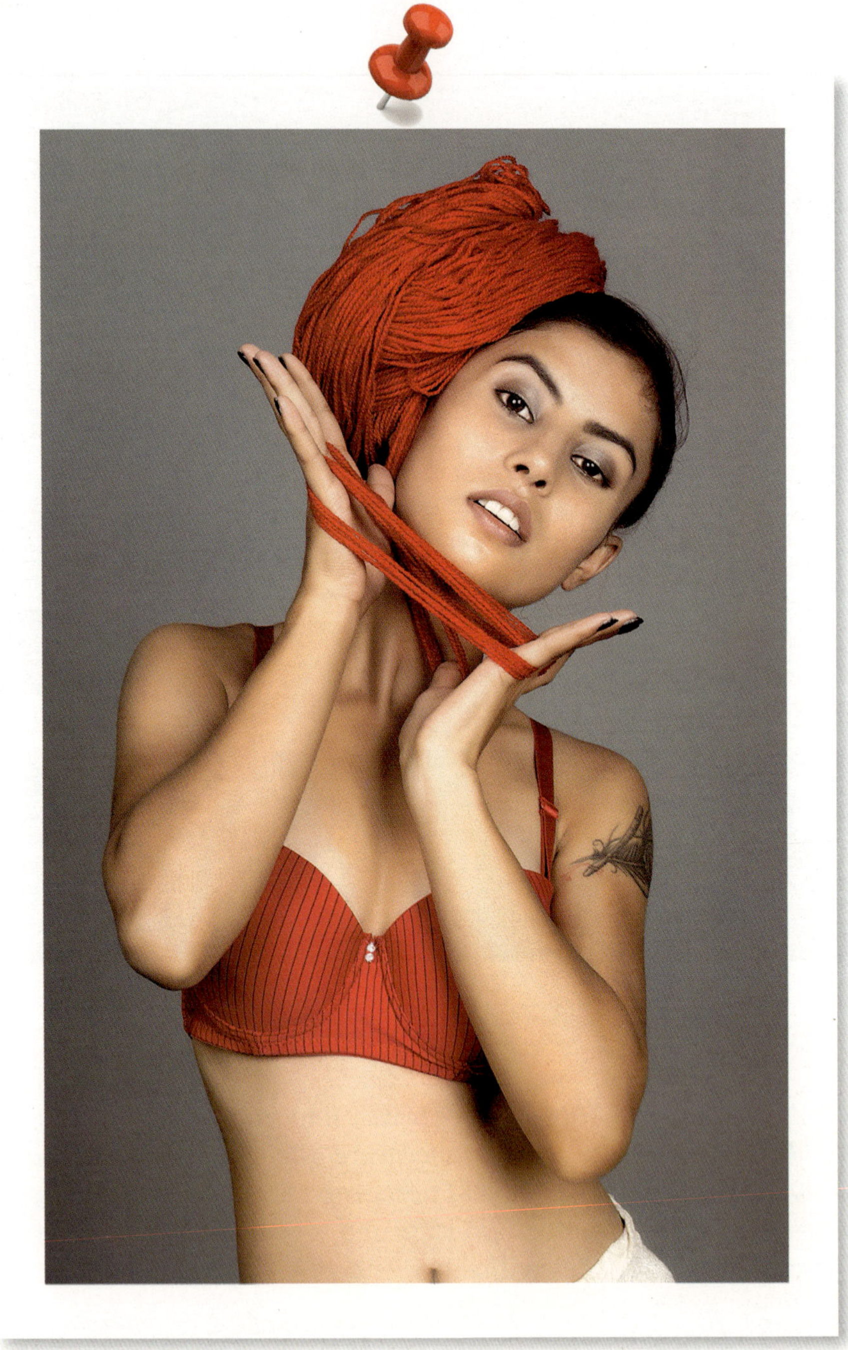

3. Levitation

Introduction

When You want to do creative editing to use two images to make the third image, You normally use collage method or by changing the background. You first select the main subject say a girl (Fig. 1) by using lasso tool etc then You paste on a landscape (Fig. 2) to get the third image (Fig. 3). This is not a perfect way. In this case it becomes un-natural and the size of the girl may vary from the original size. Even the lighting direction may vary.

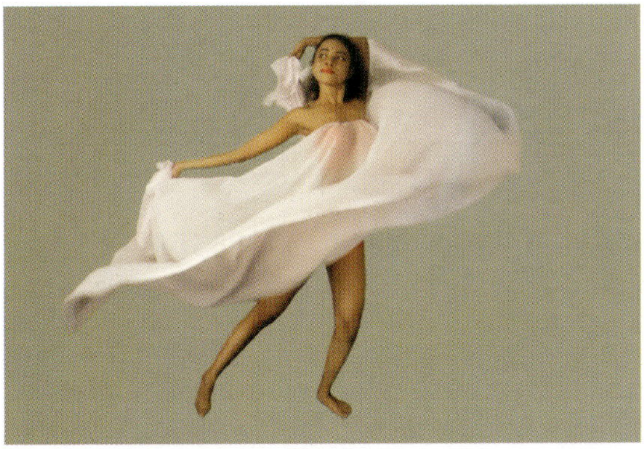

Fig. 1

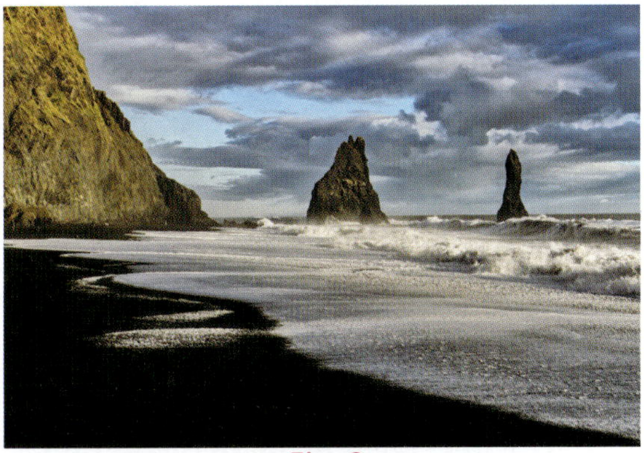

Fig. 2

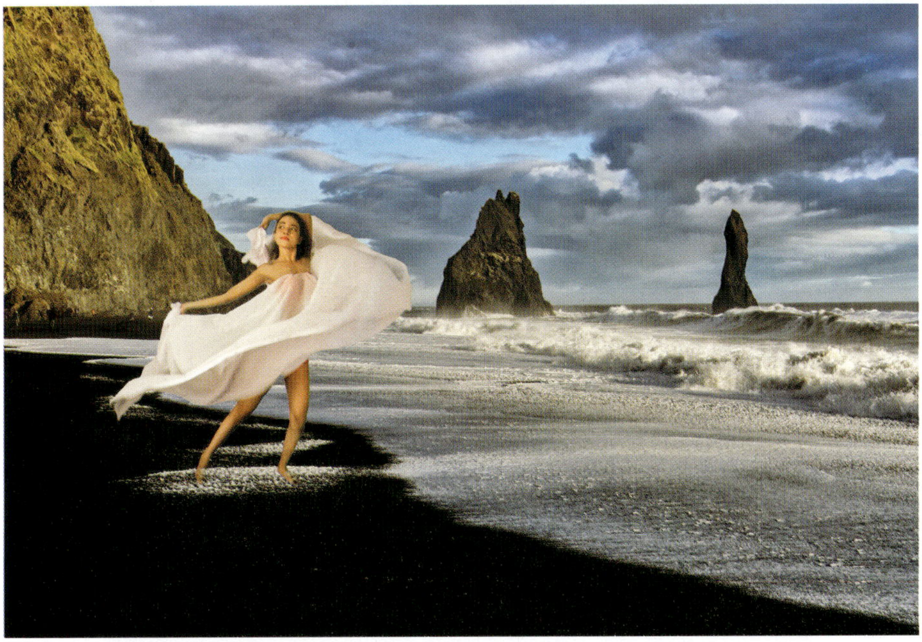

Fig. 3

To get a perfection in terms of Natural feel with exact human figure and light direction, You can use Levitation method.

Levitation Photography

In this method You first select a good location. Selection of location is very important. While selecting location, You should visualise the placement and posing of the model to match the background composition.

You also need a stable stool/table/ladder for posing of the model. You should take following care while selecting a location:

1. The weather condition should be such that the change in lighting condition remain similar for few minutes. Morning time is better than afternoon or evening hour.
2. If it's a cloudy day, the cloud should be stationary for few minutes.
3. The surface for keeping stool or the ladder should be flat to avoid unbalance and falling down the model.

I selected a location or the background facing sun at Maithon dam in morning hour (Fig. 4).

Setting up Camera

Mount the camera on tripod. Set Exposure mode to Manual. Adjust the exposure. Focus at the nearest point or 1/3rd point from the camera. Keep aperture value 8 to 11. Better to shoot in RAW.

Compose the frame keeping into mind the placement of human elements. The composition is very important. It should be in line with the background formation.

See the fig. 5. It was composed keeping in mind the formation of clouds.

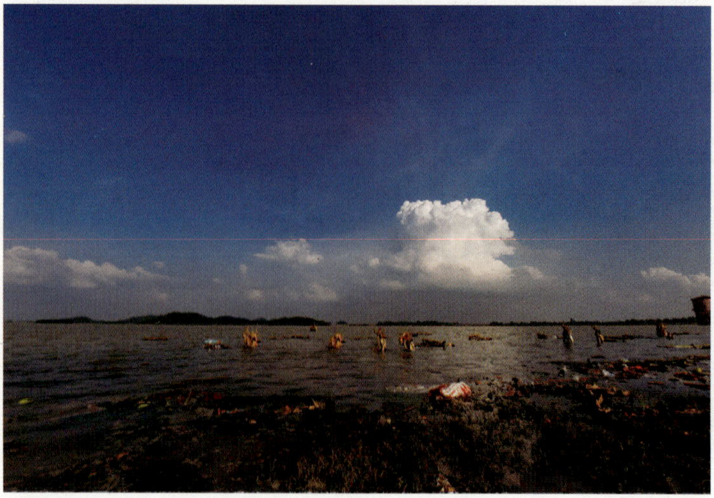

Fig. 4

Then you place a stool or ladder and ask the model to pose as if she is about to fly (Fig. 5). You use any probes such as umbrella, bunch of flowers, balloons etc. The colour of the probe should be contrasting with the background. Here I used white umbrella, but better to use red umbrella.

Preferably set the camera in continuous shooting mode to get the best pose and just click.

You can use external flash with small octa diffuser to fill the shadow on the model face.

Now you have got two images. Open both the images in photoshop and process to erase the stool using masking brush. The post processing technique will be described in another para. You can see the final image in fig.6

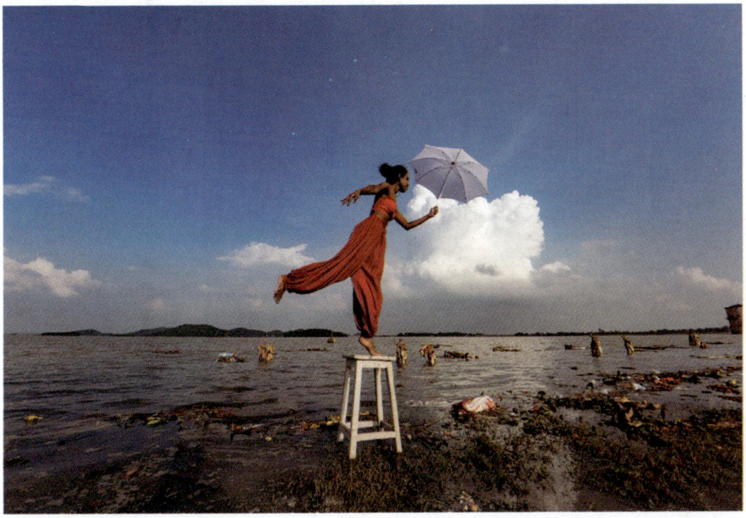

Fig. 5

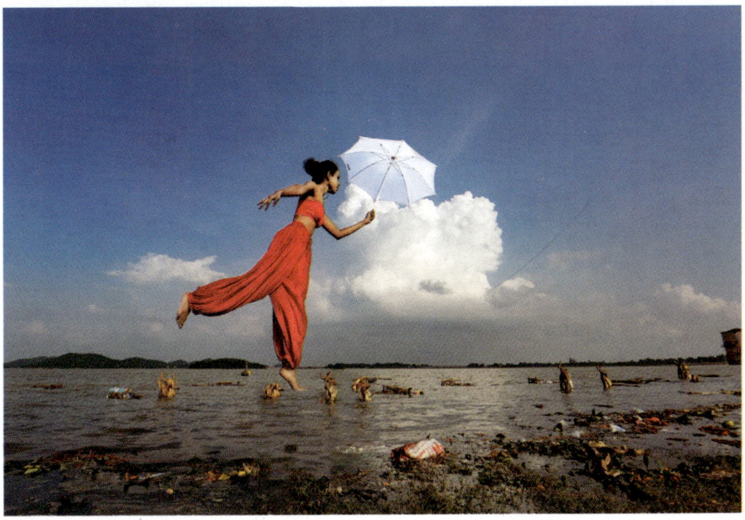

Fig. 6

Creative and Unique Idea for Pre-Wed Shoot

You can use this levitation technique for pre wedding shoots to give an edge over other wedding photographers in the market.

The process is same as described earlier. Here I selected a location at Topchanchi lake. Ashu Khan and Madhumita Soren performed as model.

It was a bad weather with dark clouds, but no matter you can do your job in any weather. See Fig. 7

This is all your creative vision to pose the male and female. Here in Fig. 8, I used one stool for female only. If you want both in flying pose you can use two stools or a wider single table.

You will get image as shown in Fig. 9. After Post processing you will get final image shown in Fig. 9A

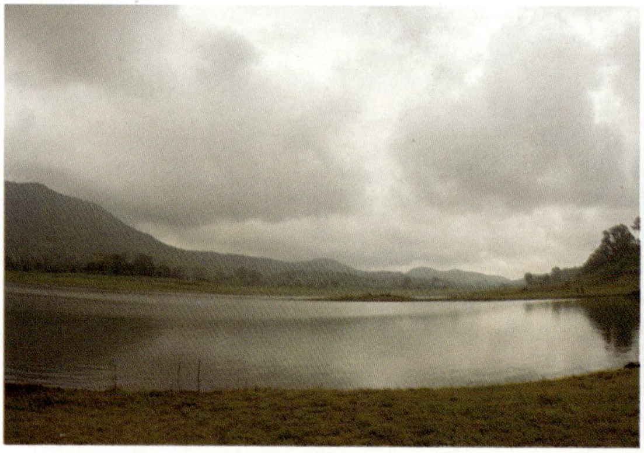

Fig. 7

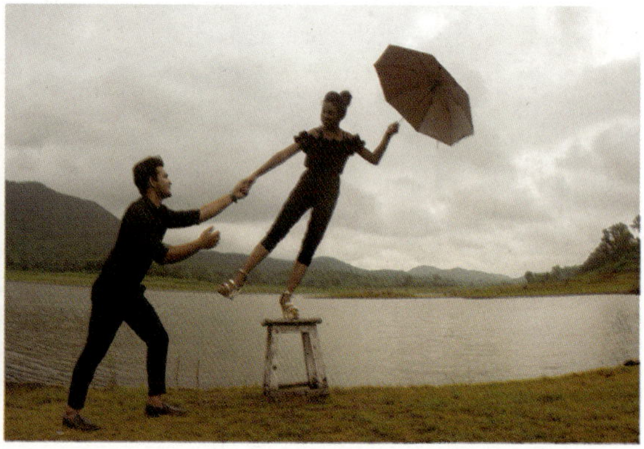

Fig. 8

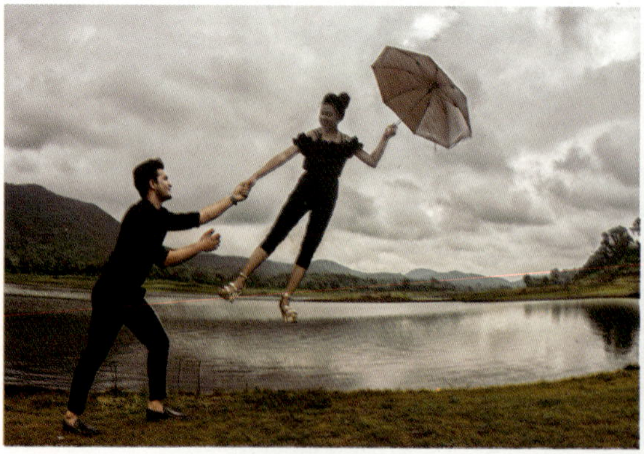

Fig. 9

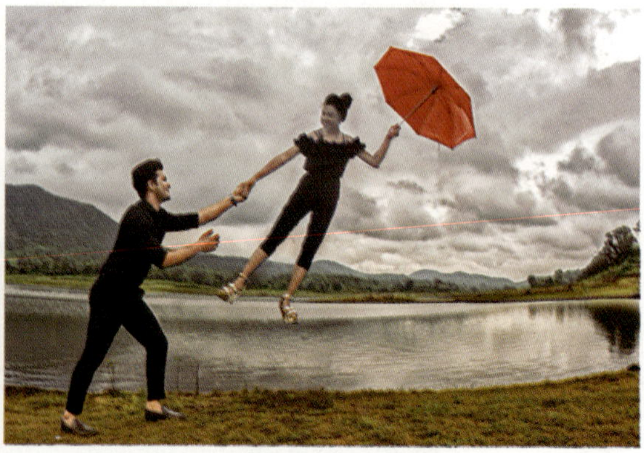

Fig. 9A

Post Processing

Post processing is very easy and can be done in just 5 minutes using any version of Photoshop. You have two images one as base background and another with stool and posing.

1. Open both the images in Photoshop as shown in Fig. 10.
2. Keeping the base image as background layer, select the 2nd image by pressing Control A&C and control V (Fig. 11)
3. Click add a mask and select a soft brush as shown in Fig. 11A

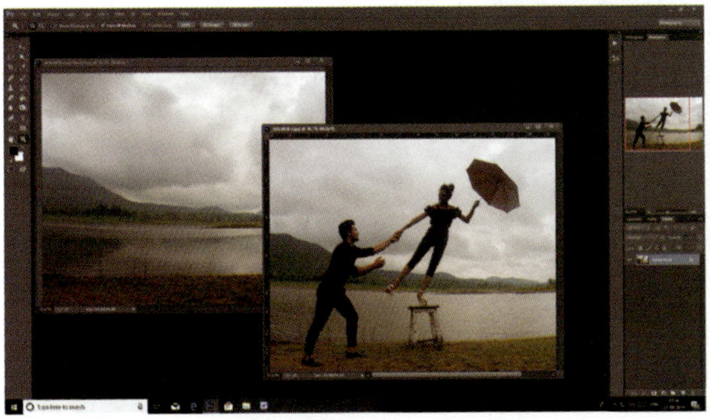

Fig. 10

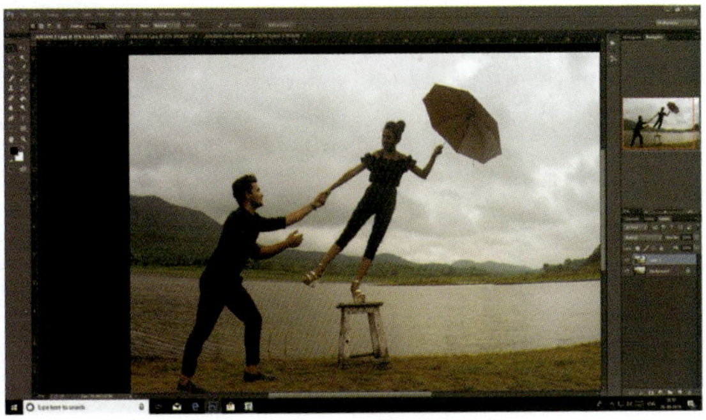

Fig. 11

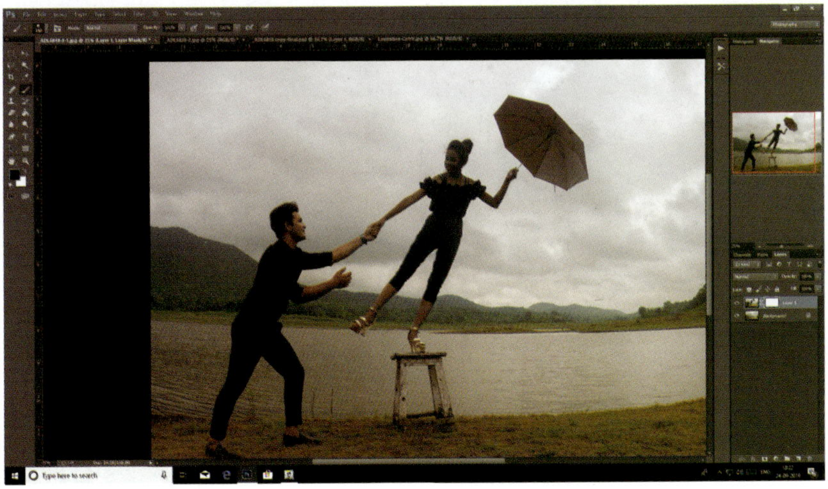

Fig. 11A

4. Simply erase the stool using this soft brush. While erasing do not forget to enlarge the image for flawless erase action.
5. After erasing, if required use spot healing brush or Clone tool to do minute correction. You will get Fig. 12.

6. Finally enhance the image for brightness, contrast and saturation etc. You will get final image as shown in Fig. 9A.

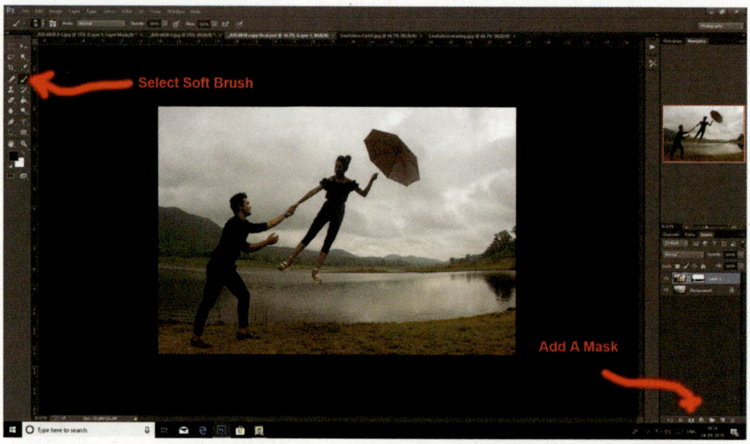

Fig. 12

Fig. 9A

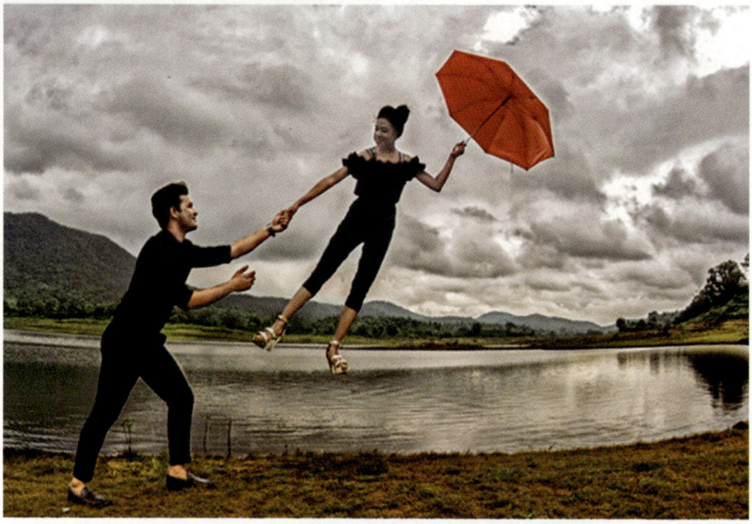

Watch youtube tutorial on this topic: *Episode 1- Through the Lens :* ***Levitation Photography-Levitation Photography - YouTube***

4. Photo Stacking

Except for special effect, you do not want out-of-focus (shallow depth of field) images. Whatever camera settings you use, every detail of an image can not be captured tack sharp. You can use smaller aperture i.e. higher f number to increase DOF, but moving the aperture farther from a lens's sweet spot introduces lens diffraction into the image resulting in some fuzziness. Also, with hand held situation, if you chose very high f number, like 16, 18, 22 etc, shutter speed will become very low resulting in blurry images. If you increase ISO to overcome the low shutter speed you will get digital noise in the image.

So, how to shoot with the best aperture, ISO and shutter speed combination, and get sharp images from front to back of an image? A technique called focus stacking can help to get such sharpness.

What You Need

A tripod.

A DSLR camera, capable of shooting in manual mode. It is possible to use a point and shoot camera, but it must have manual mode and manual focus capabilities.

Depth of Field iPhone app (helpful but not required).

Photoshop or another focus stacking software.

How to Shoot for Focus Stacking

Focus stacking is similar in principle to HDR. However, with focus stacking, images are captured with different focus points, and later combined in Photoshop, to create an image with more DOF than would be possible with a single exposure. Landscape and macro photography are two genres of photography that benefit most from using this procedure. Be warned – calm winds and reasonably stationary objects are a must!

Before beginning to shoot, it is always helpful to know a lens's sweet spot, defined as the aperture that the lens produces its sharpest image. (It is usually found about two to three stops from wide open.) Experiment until this important setting is determined.

Landscape

There are two basic situations while shooting landscapes, that may benefit from focus stacking. The first is when the subject is a close foreground object, with an interesting background, both desirable aspects to be in sharp focus. The second, is when using a telephoto lens (which typically has a shallow depth of field) and the subject covers multiple distances, that may be brought into sharper focus. If shooting a landscape with a wide angle lens, the DOF may be adequate enough to capture a sharp image that has no benefit in being processed by focus stacking.

Steps for Shooting Landscapes for Focus Stacking

1. Place the camera on **a sturdy tripod** – a must!
2. **Frame the subject** and compose the shot.
3. **Determine exposure** for the scene, and set the camera to manual mode, to ensure that the exposure is constant for every image.
4. **Set the camera to Live View** and aim the focus point on the nearest object desired to be in focus. Use the camera's zoom (+ button, not zoom on the lens) to preview the focus through Live View. Then switch to manual focus and use the focus ring to fine tune for sharpness if necessary.
5. **Take the first exposure**.
6. Without moving the camera or adjusting any settings, **move the focus point to an object mid-way in the image** and refocus.
7. **Take the second exposure**.
8. Again, without changing anything, **refocus on an object at the farthest point** of the intended image.

Take the third exposure. To capture landscapes, three images are enough to create sharp focus stacking images, but you can take extra images to make sure that the entire scene is covered. A rule of thumb would be to add more images for longer focal lengths. Be aware that extra images will take longer to process in post-production.

You can capture a landscape by focusing at different point. I captured 3 images of Estrahorn in Iceland using focus stacking technique.

The first image (Fig. 1) was focused on the left bottom, the second (Fig. 2) was focused mid-way into the image, and the third (Fig. 3) was focused on the mountain in the background.

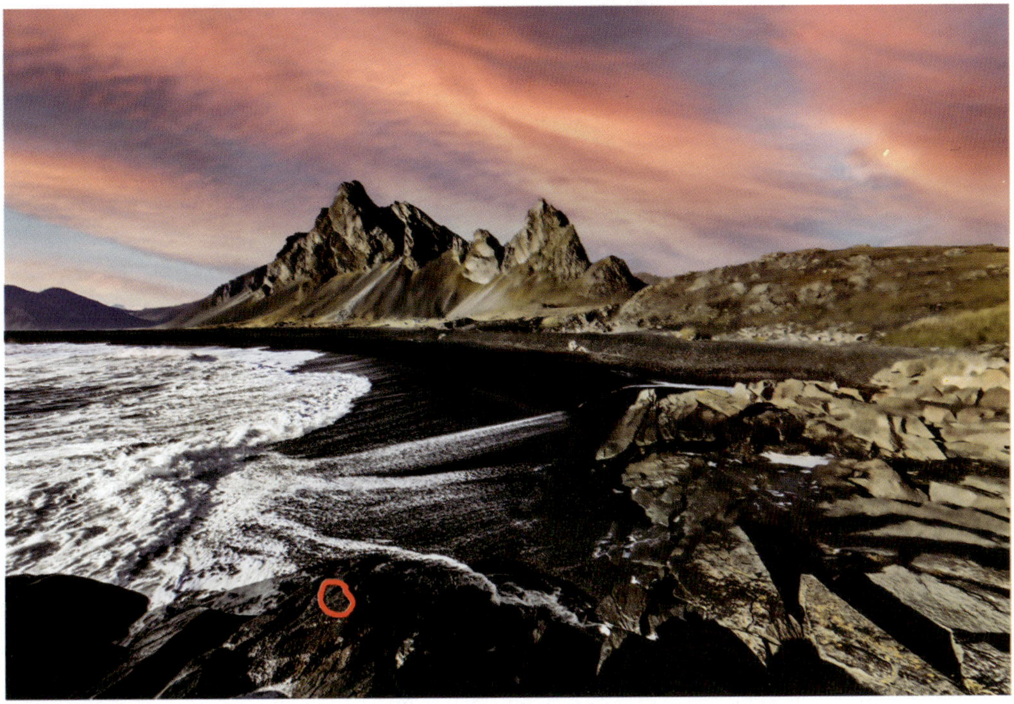

Fig. 1

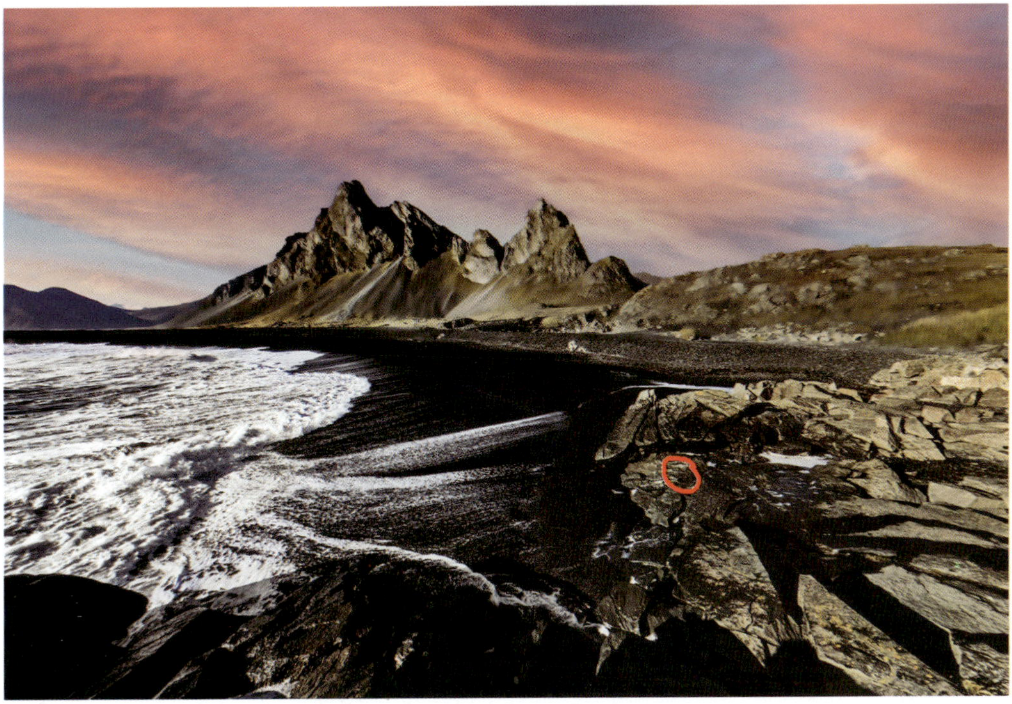

Fig. 2

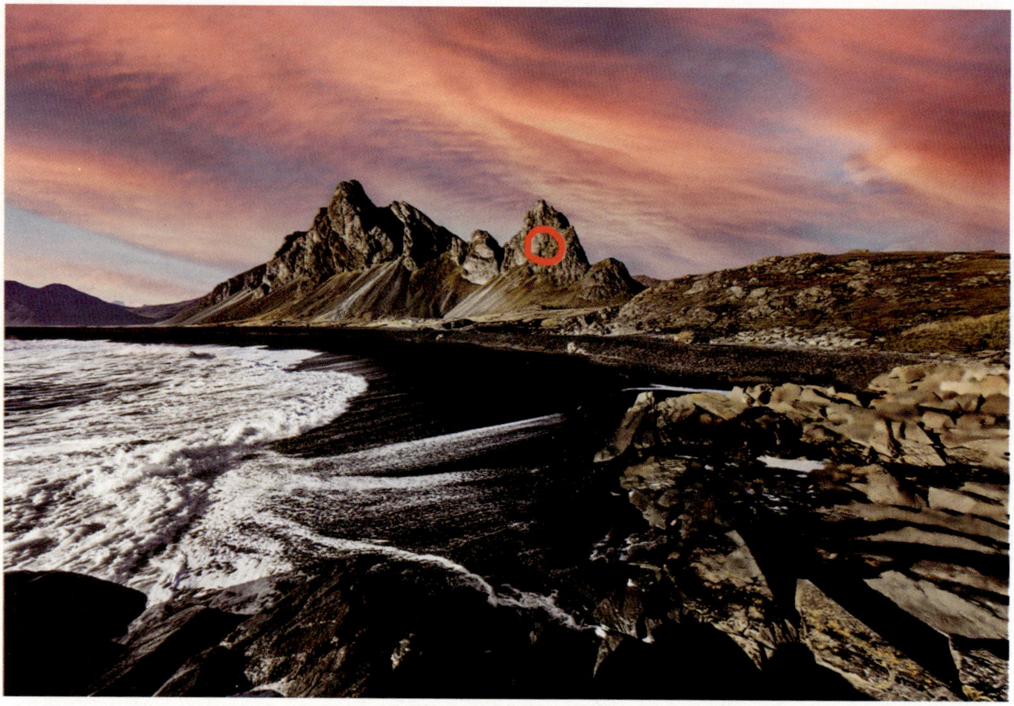

Fig. 3

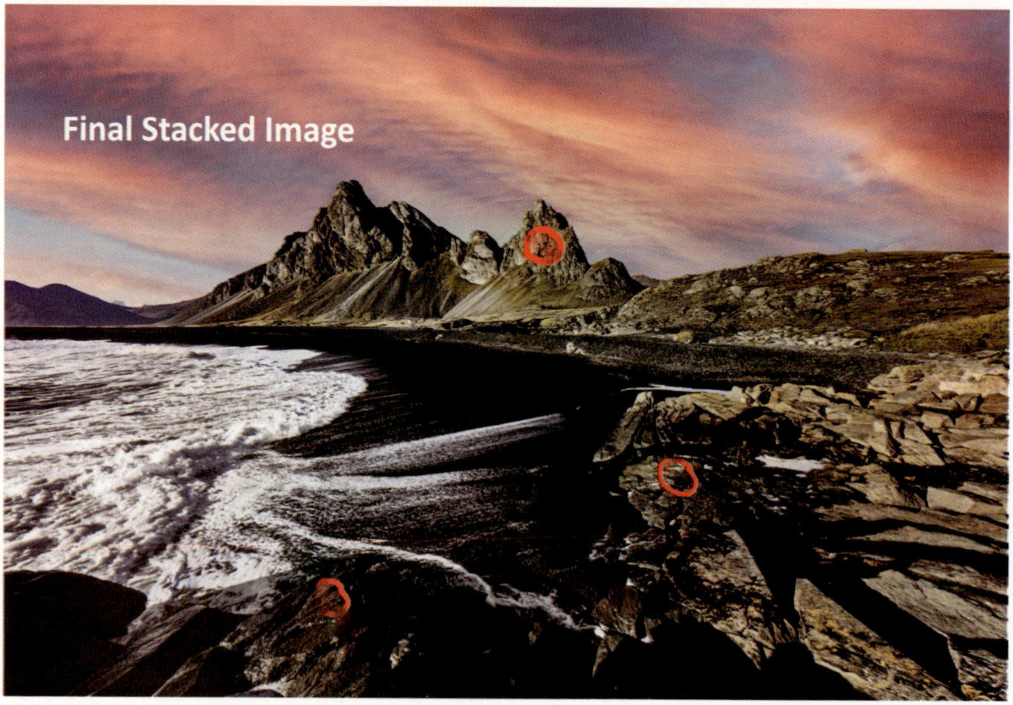

Fig. 4

Processing the Final Images

Processing the files to accomplish the final image may seem like the most difficult part of creating a focus stacked image, but it's really very simple to do in Photoshop. You can also do focus stacking by placing on layers and erasing unfocused part, but alignment of images will be a serious problem. So better to use in built technique of photoshop to do focus stacking perfectly. Here's how:

1. **Open Photoshop**
2. **Get each image on a separate layer:** Under File, choose Scripts and Load files into stack. See Fig. 5. Click Browse and select all the images.

Fig. 5

3. Check the box for Attempts to **Automatically Align Source Images** (Fig. 6).

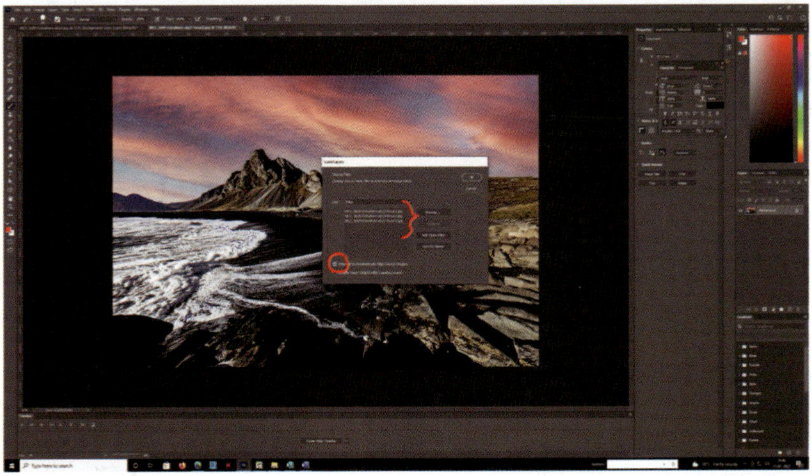

Fig. 6

4. **Click OK** and each of the images will open into a new layer in Photoshop. The computer will take some time to align the images.

5. Open the **Layer palette** and **select All Layers** or press shit key and select all three images (Fig. 7).

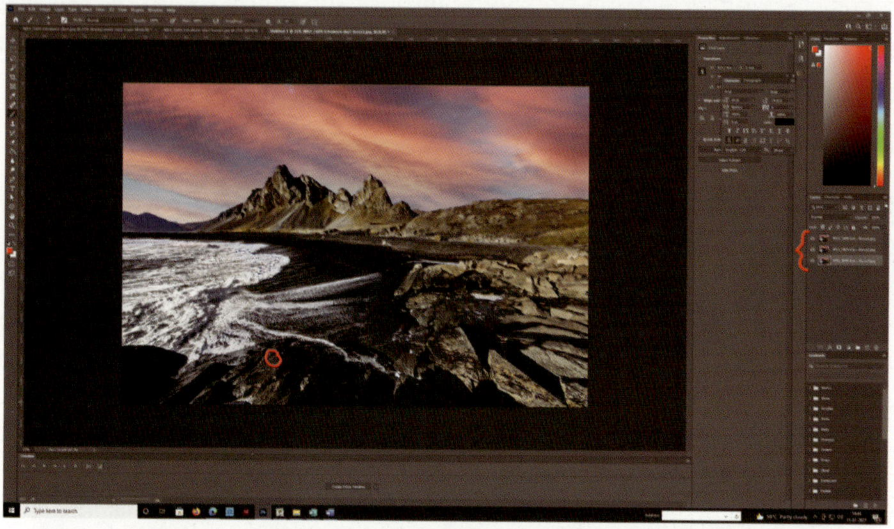

Fig. 7

6. Under Edit, select **Auto-Blend Layers (PP-4)**.

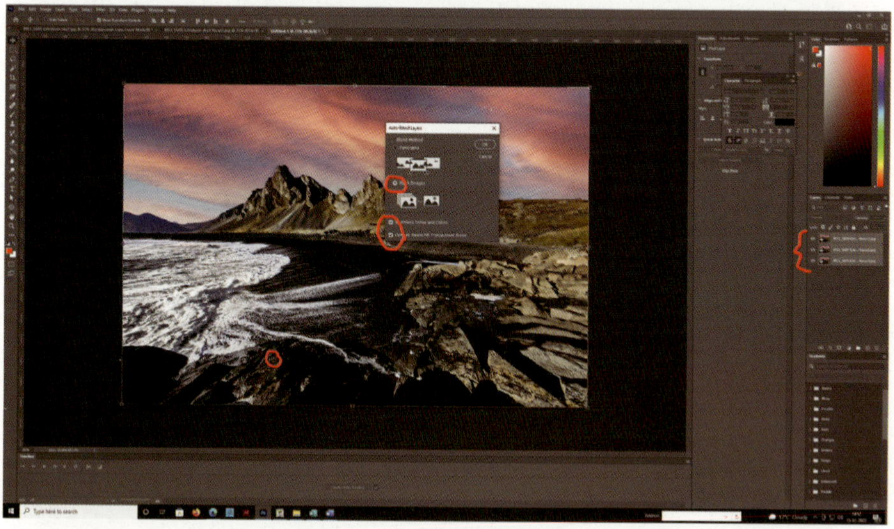

Fig. 8

7. Check the box for Stack Images and Seamless Tones and Colours. See Fig. 8. Click OK It will take some time to process the stacking and you will get image Fig. 9 and final stacked image as shown in Fig. 4.

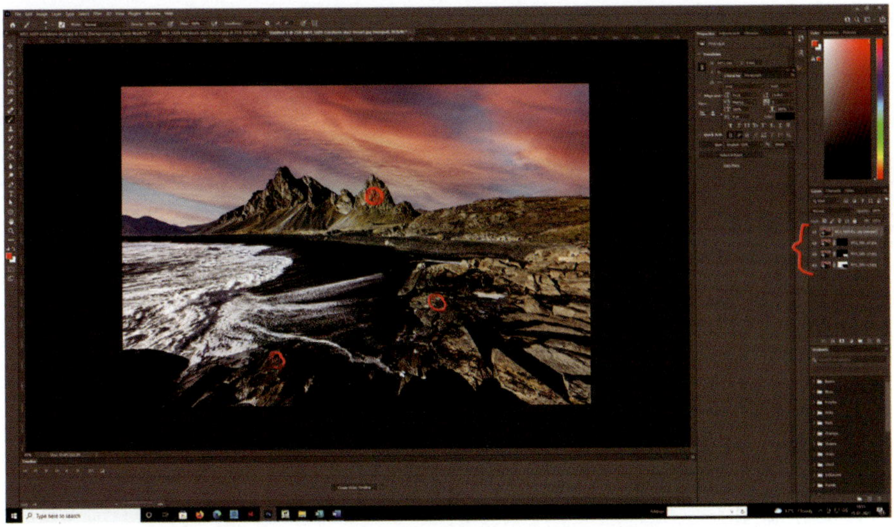

Fig. 9

Macro Photography (Stacking Technique)

Macro photography can benefit from focus stacking more than any other type of photography, because a macro lens has an extremely shallow depth of field.

1. Place the camera on **a sturdy tripod** – a must!
2. **Frame the subject** and compose the shot
3. **Determine the exposure** for the subject, and set the camera to manual mode to ensure that the exposure remains constant for each and every image.
4. **Set the camera to Live View** and aim the focus point on the nearest object desired to be in focus. Use the camera's zoom (+ button, not zoom on the lens) to preview the focus through Live View. Then switch to manual focus and use the focus ring to fine tune for sharpness if necessary.
5. **Take the first exposure**.
6. Without moving the camera or adjusting any settings, **move the focus point to a distance slightly farther away** from the lens. Remember that DOF in macro will be measured in fractions of an inch, instead of feet, as in landscape photography.
7. Repeat step 6 as many times as needed to cover every aspect of the subject's DOF. This could range from as few as six images to 30+ images. Make sure the entire subject is covered or the results may be unusable.

   If available, check the DOF with the iPhone app (www.setmycamera.com), in order to figure out how many images will be necessary to get every aspect of the photo in focus.

8. With this process macro of flowers images on Fig. 9, Fig. 10 and Fig. 11 were created.

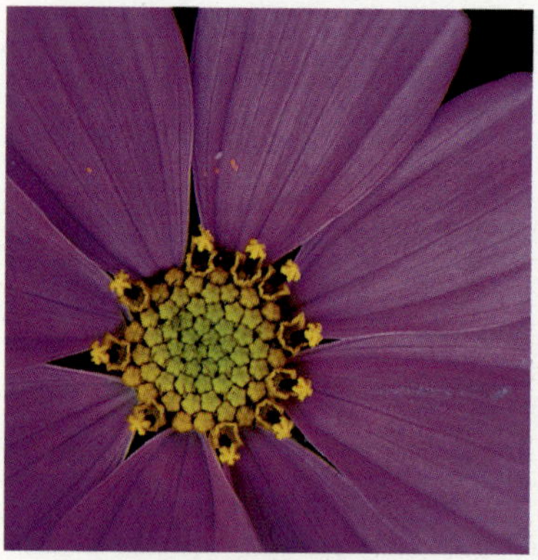

Fig. 10

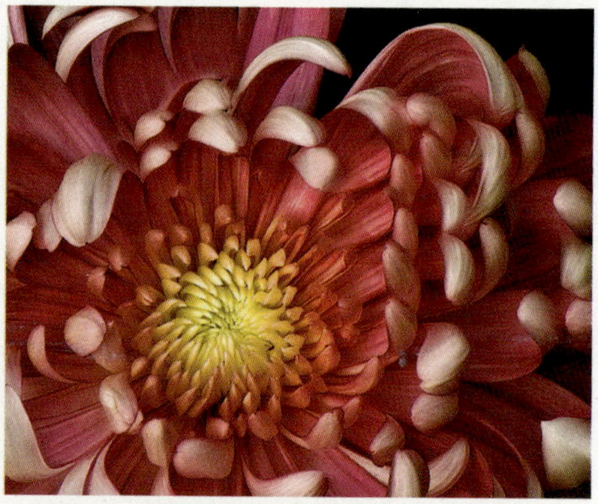

Fig. 11

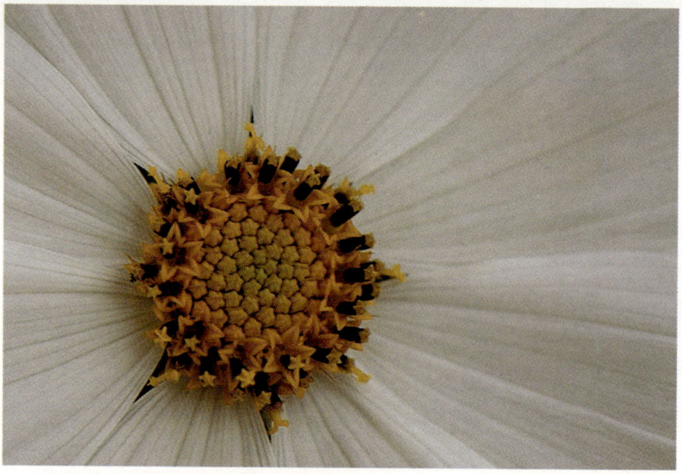

Fig. 11

Note:

Always every photographer's intention is to capture the sharpest images possible. Focus stacking is the best tool to achieve this goal. The more you click focused images, your final photo will be much better in focus from foreground to background. You will love the amazing result. Try to use this technique in pre wed shoots to be unique and different from other wedding photographers in the market.

Watch Youtube tutorial on this topic: *Episode 3- Through the Lens :* ***Photo Stacking - YouTube***

5. Product Photography

Product photography as such sounds very easy, but unless we do it perfectly the clients will never look back. I am describing the pro technique of shooting any product.

Most Important Factors

White Balance

Capturing TRUE colours and textures are most important. For this we need to use white balance perfectly. To get exact colours we need to use 18% grey card (Fig. 1), which is easily available in the market.

Exposure

To get correct exposure the use of light meter is advisable (Fig. 2)

Lighting set up

Setting of studio lights should be done in such a way that the product is evenly lighted without any dark shadows.

How To achieve it

We need to make a box with thermocol sheets. The size of the box will depend on the size of product. See the Fig. 3

Set image quality as **RAW**.

Set at least 2 soft boxes as shown in the Fig. 3. Shoot from top by using ladder (Fig. 4).

First of all take the value of right f number by using light meter. Set the camera accordingly.

Next put grey card just above the product and click. This image will be used in Photoshop for white balance correction for all the images clicked.

Fig. 1

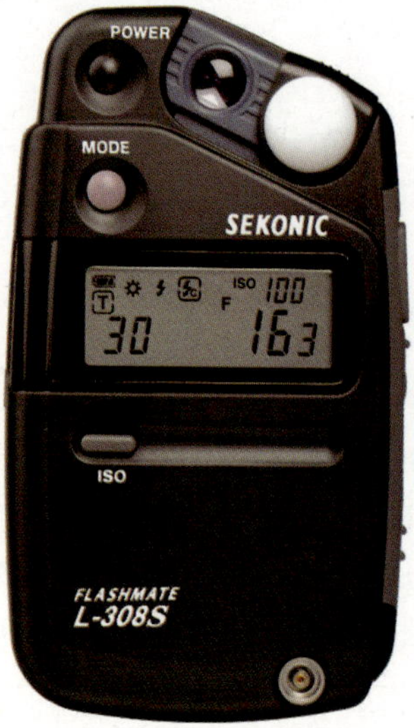

Fig. 2

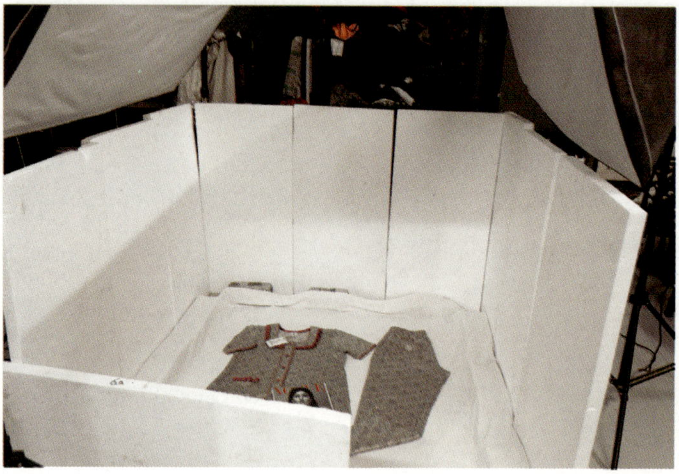

Fig. 3

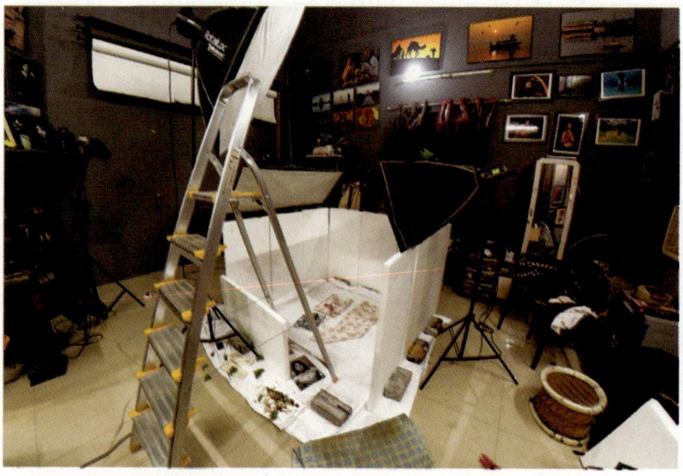

Fig. 4

Drag and drop all RAW files in the Photoshop (Fig. 5). Select the WHITE BALANCE TOOL from the top and click on the grey card image. You will see changes in the value of Temperature and the Tint. (Fig. 6)

Next click the Select All from left top menu bar. All images will be selected (Fig. 7). Further click SYNC SETTING and deselect all options except White Balance. Since you want to synchronise only white balance (Fig. 8) Click OK. Now all images will get perfect colour temperature as per grey card.

Further you have 2 options. Either you click SAVE IMAGE to get all WB corrected images saved as JPG or you click OPEN IMAGE to edit each WB corrected image as RAW. I recommend to opt second option. Be careful while editing so that natural colour should not change due to editing like contrast, saturation, sharpen etc.

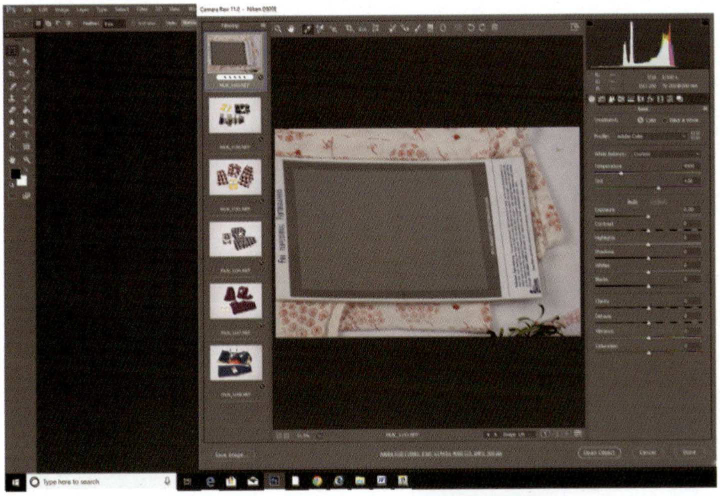

Fig. 5

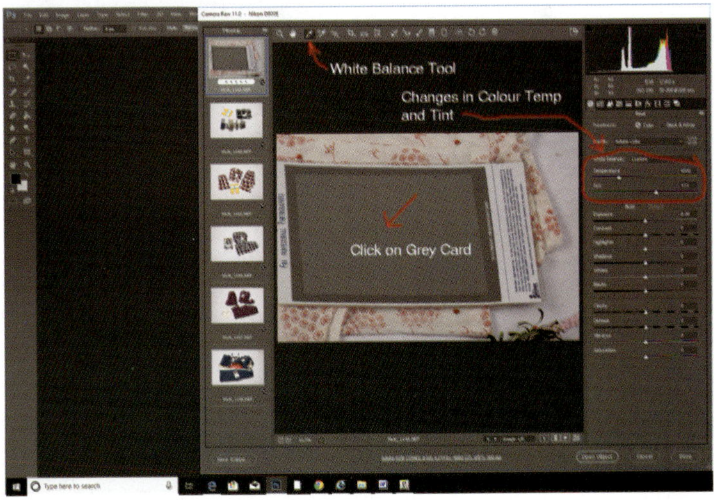

Fig. 6

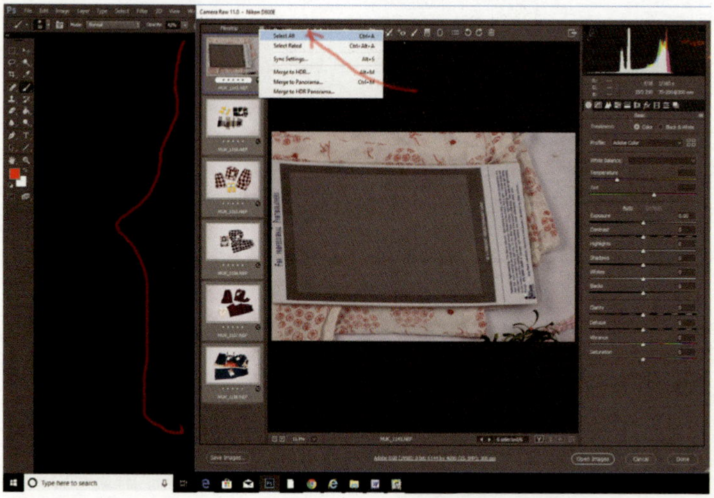

Fig. 7

Fig. 8

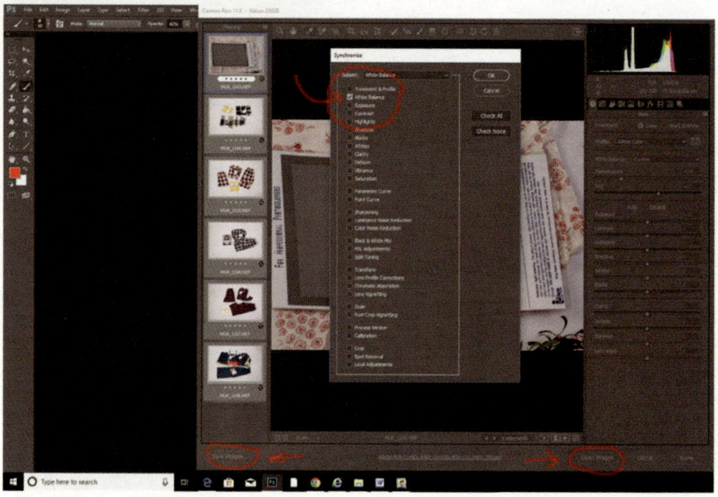

This method can be used to shoot products like Marble stone, Jewellery, Garments, Foods, etc.

See few night wear garments (P1. P4) shot recently for a client.

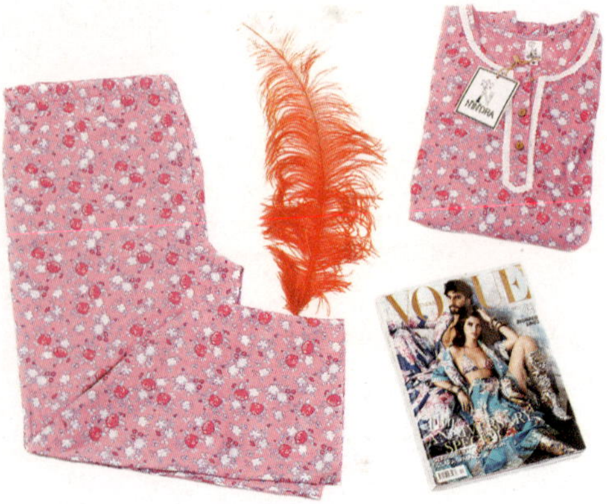

Fig. P1

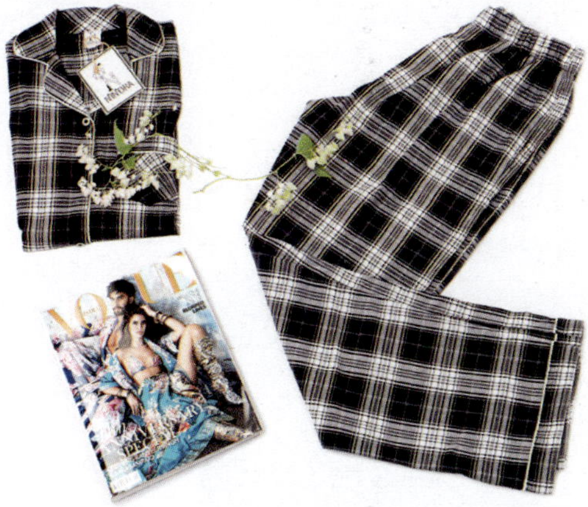

Fig. P2

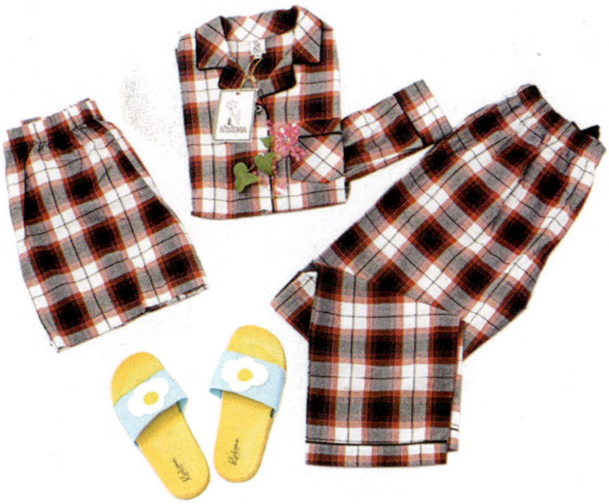

Fig. P3

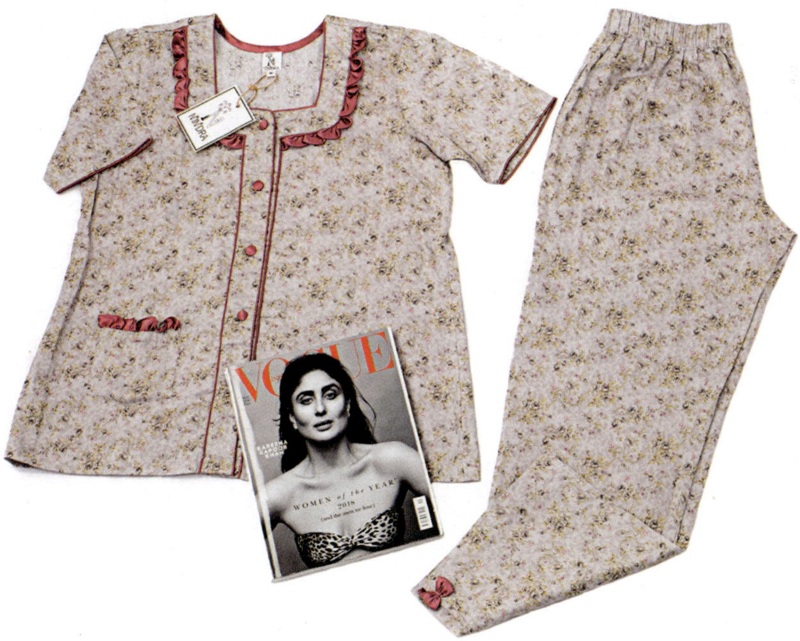

Fig. P4

Watch youtube tutorial on this topic:

Episode-5 : Product Photography-Part-1 - YouTube

Episode-7: Product Photography Part-2 - YouTube

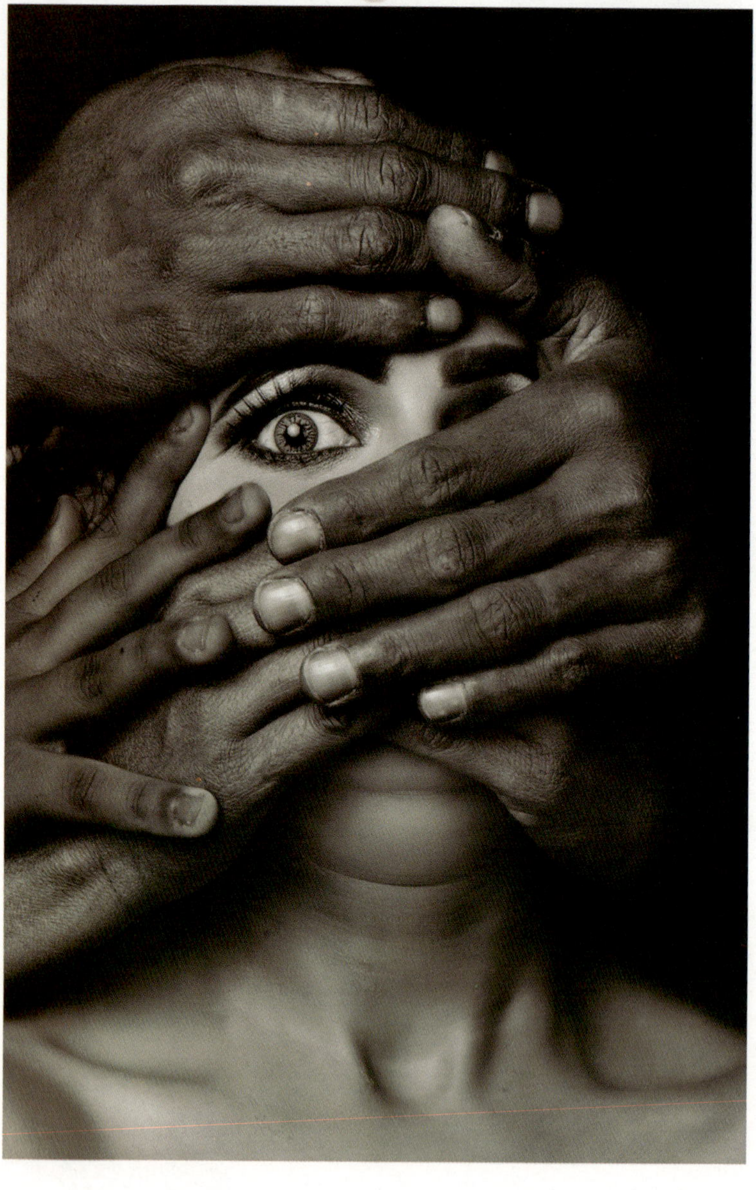

6. Astrophotography

Astrophotography is an advanced photography technique for capturing images of astronomical objects. The first photograph of an astronomical object i.e. moon was captured in 1840. With astrophotography techniques you can capture images of objects invisible to the human eyes such as dim stars, nebulae and galaxies.

In this article without going details into the theoretical aspects, you will concentrate on techniques to capture Star trails and Star galaxies or Milky way using DSLR camera.

Equipment Required

1. Sturdy tripod with ball head such as Manfroto 190XX.
2. DSLR camera with Time interval shooting feature or external timer like MC-36
3. Compass or app in the mobile to find the direction.
4. Wide angle lens such as 16-35mm, f/4 , 14-24mm, 11-16mm etc. And
5. High power torch.

Star Trail

Selecting Location

Since stars move around North star, so to get a perfect star trail you need to locate North star first. North Star is visible in North direction. So use compass to locate this direction with some beautiful fore ground.

Its very important to locate a beautiful fore ground such as Snow peak mountain, Hills with curves and sharp shapes, Historical buildings etc.

Care should be taken to select a location absolutely with no dust pollution and light pollution. Sky must be clear as stars will not be visible with cloudy sky.

Selection of Time Period

The best time period is on new moon day (Amawashya). But you can get good results even four days prior to and after the new moon night.

Set Up

Before you start shooting Star Trail make sure to have camera battery fully charged. Use a memory card with at least 32GB storage capacity. The memory card should be fast like 90MB/sec or higher.

Set up the camera on the sturdy tripod and set the camera as follows:

Camera Set Up
Focus Mode: Manual
Shooting Mode: Manual
Image Quality: RAW
Color Space: Adobe RGB
Picture Control: Standard
WB: Auto
ISO: 1200 or 1000
Shutter Speed: 30 sec.
Long Exposure Noise Reduction: OFF

Fig. 1

Important Note:

Make sure you turn off Long Exposure Noise Reduction. Otherwise, for each 30 second exposure the camera takes a 30 second dark image for subtraction. That makes the total time 60 seconds, which will leave large gaps in the star trails.

Set shutter speed at 30 sec. and aperture at wide open say f/1.4 to f/4 depending upon the lens attached. Say you are setting at f/4 for 16-35mm f/4 lens.

The most important part is the focusing during night time. Rotate the focusing ring to set just below the infinity point.

Take a trial shot. Enlarge 100% and check the sharpness of the stars. If it is not satisfactory, just rotate the focus ring little bit to get the sharp image.

Now the camera is set to record star trail.

Before you start shooting make sure that the view finder is closed (by Flip knob located by the side of view finder) to avoid any light entering into camera which can cause light flare.

Setting Number of Shots

With the above camera settings, you should click 100 to 250 frames. There are two ways to do it.

Interval Timer Shooting

1. By using Interval Timer Shooting feature of the camera. It's available in the Shooting Menu of the camera.
2. Go to the 'Interval timer shooting' options in the menu of your DSLR

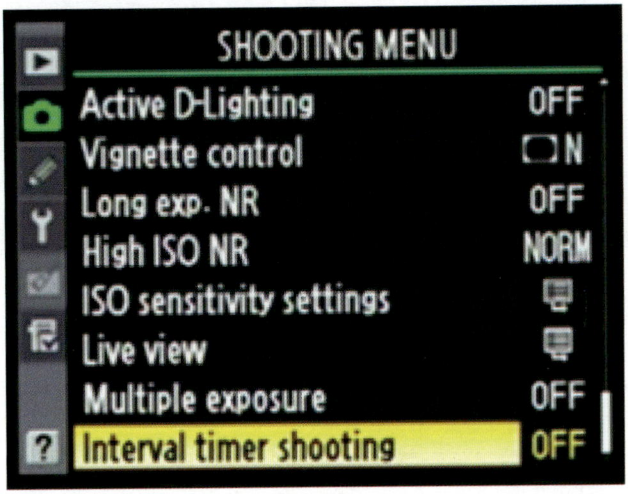

Fig. 2

3. For the sake of this example, let's assume you want it to start right away, so you highlight the 'Now' option and proceed to the next menu on the right.

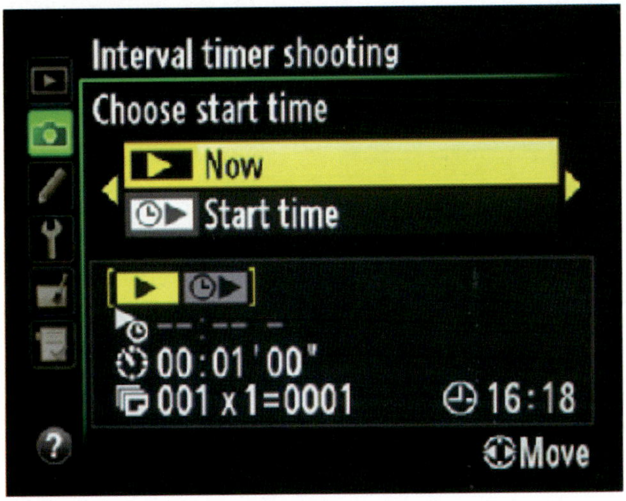

Fig. 3

4. This is where you set the interval, since you're shooting 30 second exposures, set the interval to 5 to 10 seconds (depending on the write speed of memory card). This way the camera has 5 to 10 seconds time to write every shot to the card in between shots. Say You have a XQD card with 200 MB/sec speed, then set it at 5 seconds. It also means you will see tiny gaps in the final star trail.

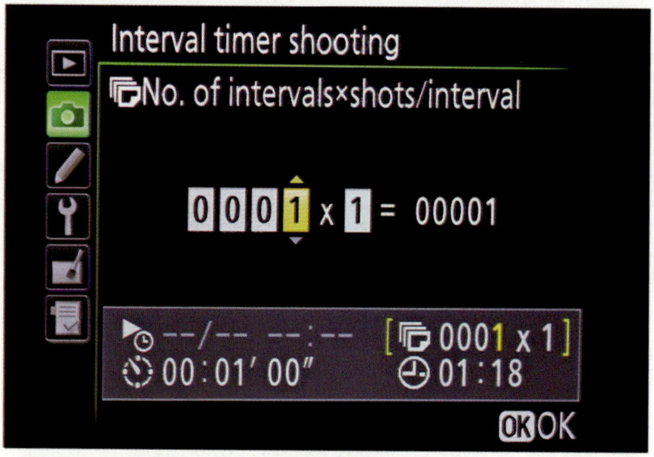

Fig. 4

5. Proceed to the next menu on the right again, now you select how much photos you want. Say you want 200 frames for the star trail, you set it to shoot 200x1 shots. This tells your camera to take 200 single shots.

6. Proceed to the next menu on the right again, highlight 'On' and press OK on your camera. The camera is now starting it's timed sequence. It will take 1 photo every 30+5 seconds, after 200 photos it will stop.

7. Alternatively you can use external timer such as Nikon MC-36.

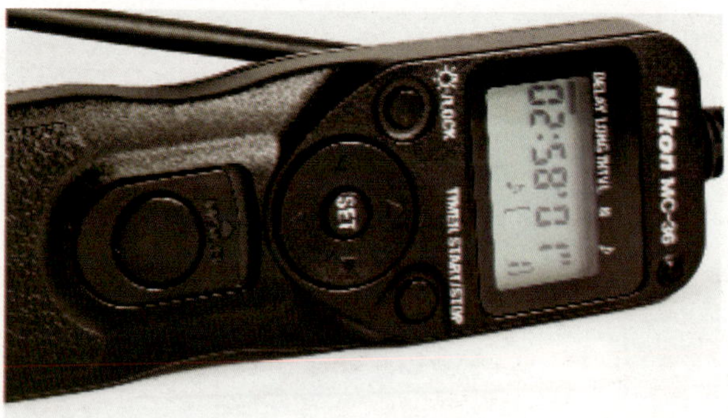

Fig. 5

This external timer is very useful. You can set time interval, no. shots like described above.

First select the appropriate exposure settings. The shutter at 30sec, aperture at something like f/4, depending on your light conditions. With 30sec shots method you will be using ISO 1200 or ISO 1600.

Now you are ready with 200 images with 30sec time interval.

Alternatively you can also go for long exposure like 15 minutes to 2 hours. But personally I prefer the techniques mentioned above.

Post Processing

Download the images in the computer. Open the images in Lightroom or Photoshop. Adjust the exposure, WB and Hue of one image to get visibility of stars clearly. Then select all and synchronize this settings for all images.

Download Starstax software. Open all these images synchronized in Lightroom or Photoshop in Starstax and process.

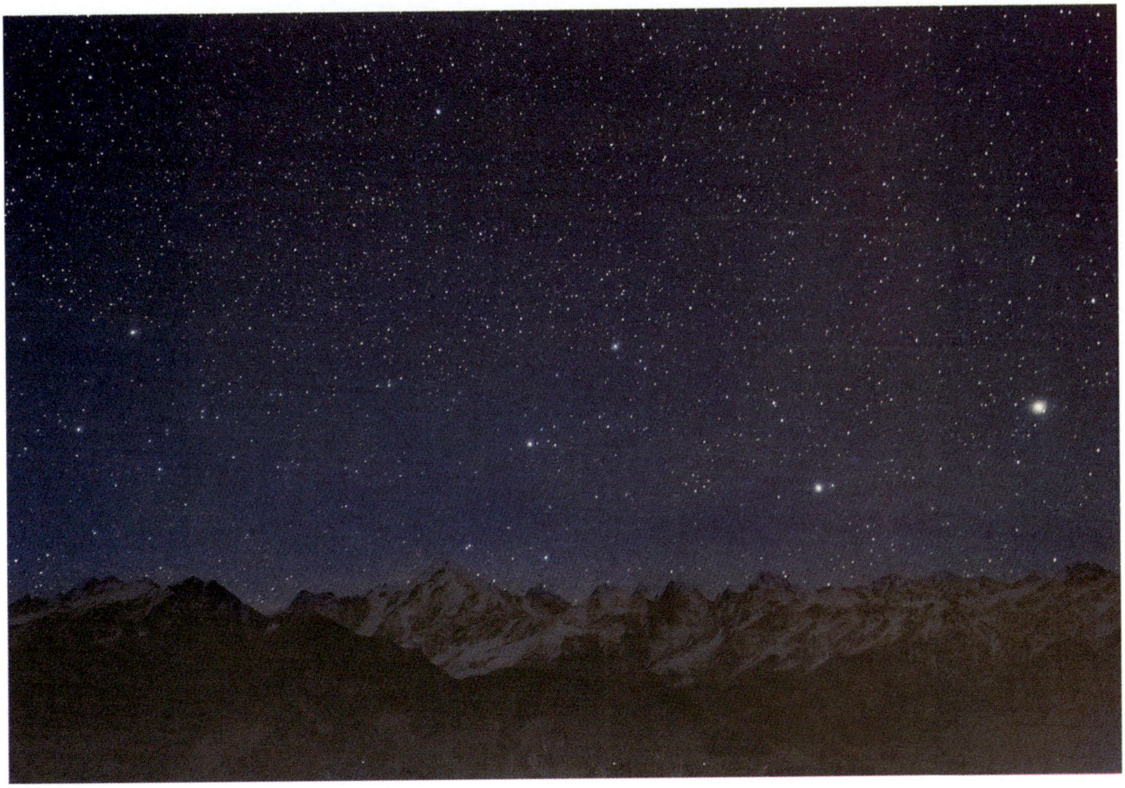

Fig. 6

This is the image after correction in Lightroom or Photoshop.

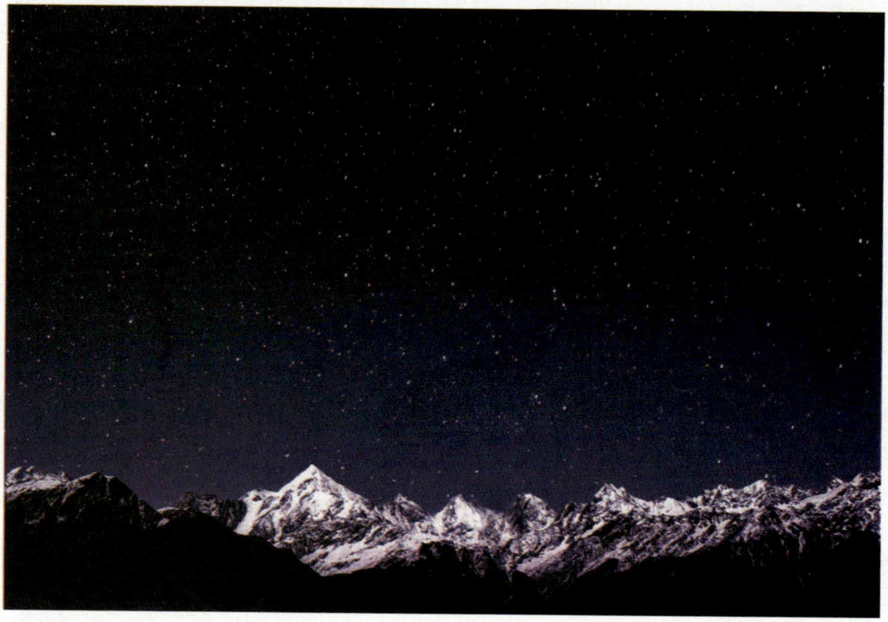

Fig. 7

I captured 150 frames. After stacking in StarStax, it was further edited in Photoshop to enhance Brightness, saturation etc and then converted to BW. See the final image below.

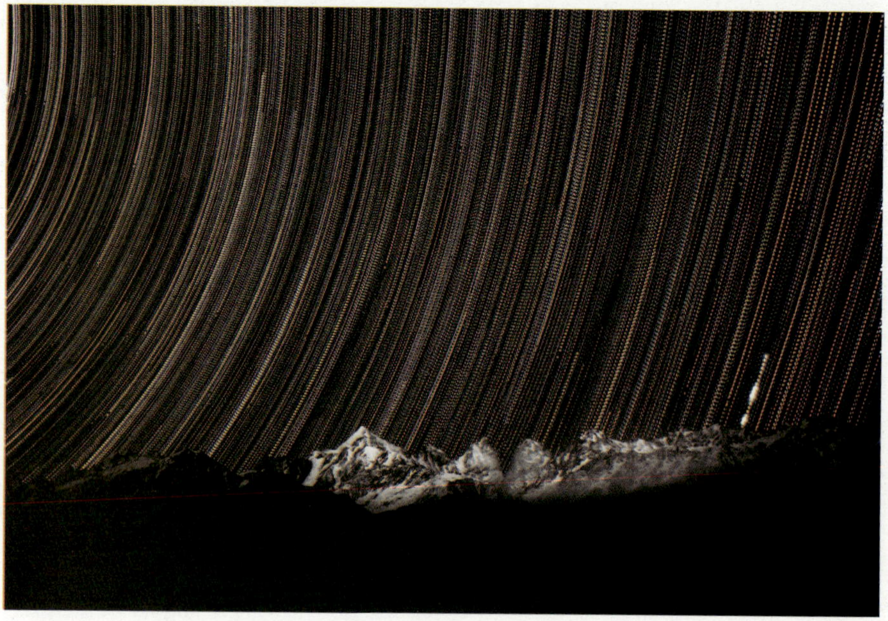

Fig. 8

With similar technique this image was captured in Pushkar, Rajasthan during my workshop on Astrophotography.

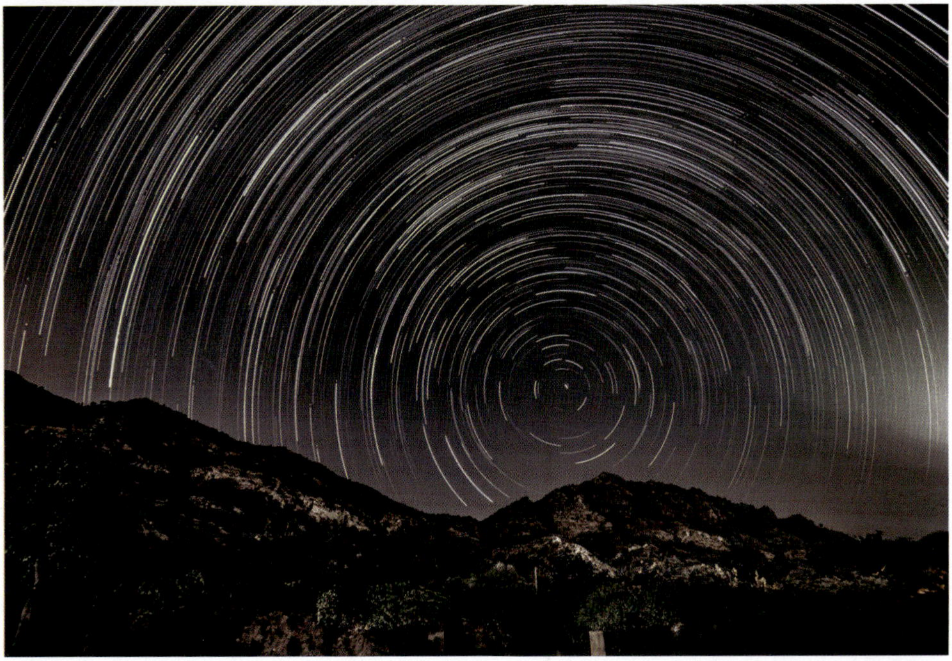

Fig. 9

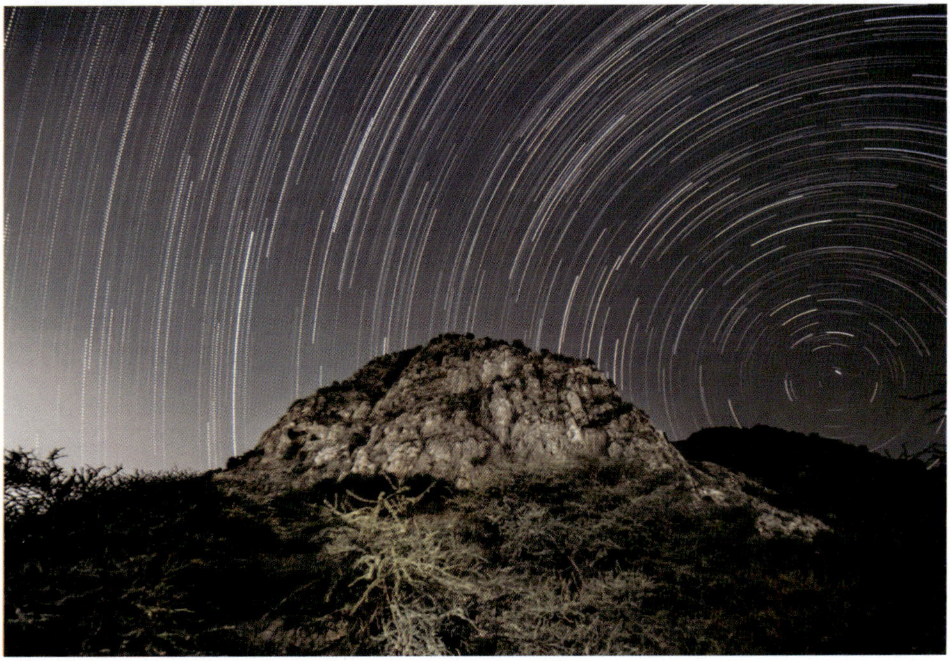

Fig. 10

Milky Way

What is the Milky Way?

The Milky Way galaxy is one out of at least 100 billion in the universe. And the Milky Way itself contains about 100 billion stars. Our galaxy stretches 100,000 light years wide. Every star you can see with the unaided eye is located within the milky way. The only object you can see (without optical aid) in the sky outside of the milky way is the Andromeda galaxy. Andromeda is over 2.5 million light years from earth; much too far to resolve individual stars without a powerful telescope. But when most people talk about "seeing the milky way", they are talking about the core of the galaxy. Located in the constellation Sagittarius, this is the brightest part of the milky way. Finding Milky Way: Northern Hemisphere: India is in Northern Hemisphere. So we can find milky way early morning (around 6AM) before sunrise in March until after sunset in October. It is visible in South West. Southern Hemisphere: Photographers who live in the southern hemisphere are lucky because they get to see the core from February right through to October, with peak visibility being in June and July. I'm rather jealous.

Mobile App

One of the favourite apps for locating milky way for iPhone is Photo Pills. Stellarium is another very powerful app for Window, Mac, Linux and Android. It's a very effective tool for looking of constellations, planets, sun, moon and Milky Way position for a particular location, date and time.

Camera Settings

Shutter Speed: 500/600 **Rule:** It's used to find ideal shutter speed to avoid trails. Shutter Speed = 500 or 600/Focal Length Say for 50mm focal length Shutter speed = 500/50 = 10 sec. or = 600/50 = 12 sec. So, set the shutter speed to 10 sec or 13 sec. Aperture (f value): Set f value to f/4.

White Balance

White balance setting examples for darker skies:

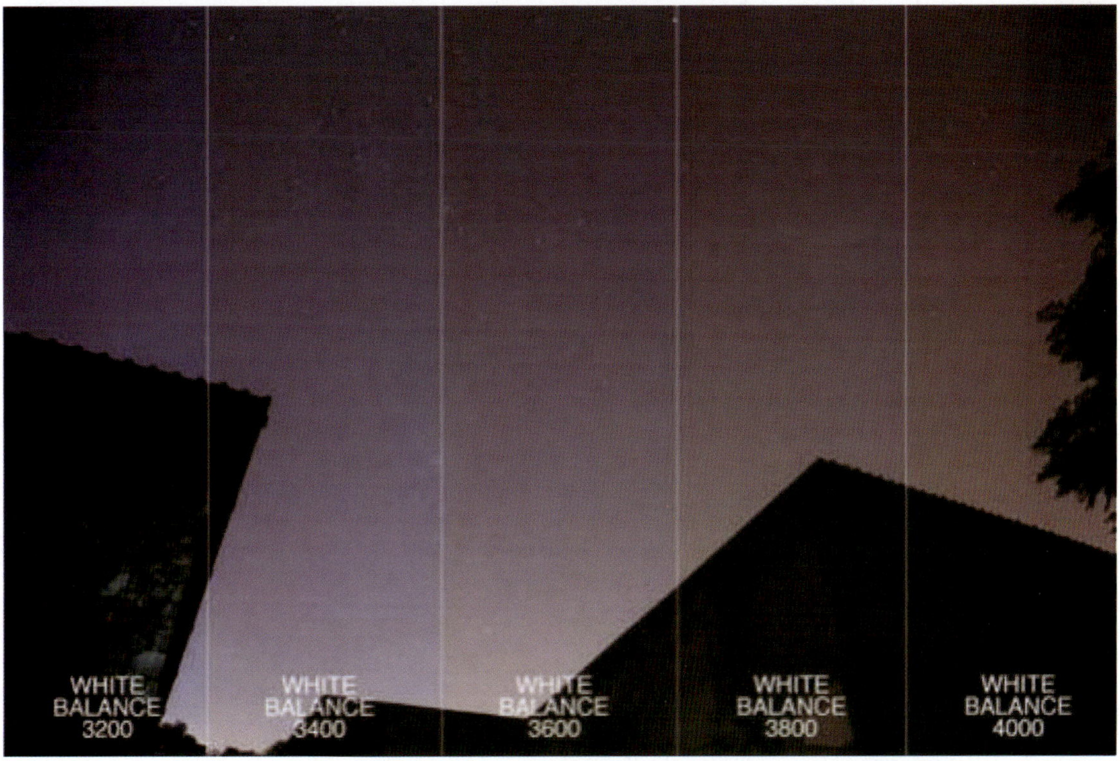

Fig. 11

When shooting The Milky Way I prefer to shoot with my White Balance set to Incandescent. I like the blue hue and it also displays a lot of contrast in my camera's view finder so that I can clearly see the Milky Way. When I process my images later I often reset the White Balance back to Auto (AWB) mode for a more realistic neutral colour temperature.

I advise you to experiment with different WB settings to get the colour temperature you like best. Shooting with the Incandescent/Tungsten pre set will almost always produce good, neutral results, which you can change later in Lightroom or Adobe Camera RAW. **ISO:** Start with 1200 and change after trial shot. It depends upon the darkness of the sky.

Noise Reduction

In-camera Noise Reduction Some cameras do a great job of processing and reducing noise reduction. But, this will double the amount of time it takes to complete your shot, so it's always a good idea to switch this function off, at least temporarily. If you like the results of your in-camera noise reduction you can always switch this function back on once you've finished all of your test shots.

Composition

Keep mountain or an architectural building in the foreground. You can keep a tent with some light inside it. You can also try light painting.

I captured this Milky way in Zanskar Valley at Purne. I composed by keeping Budhist Chortem in the foreground.

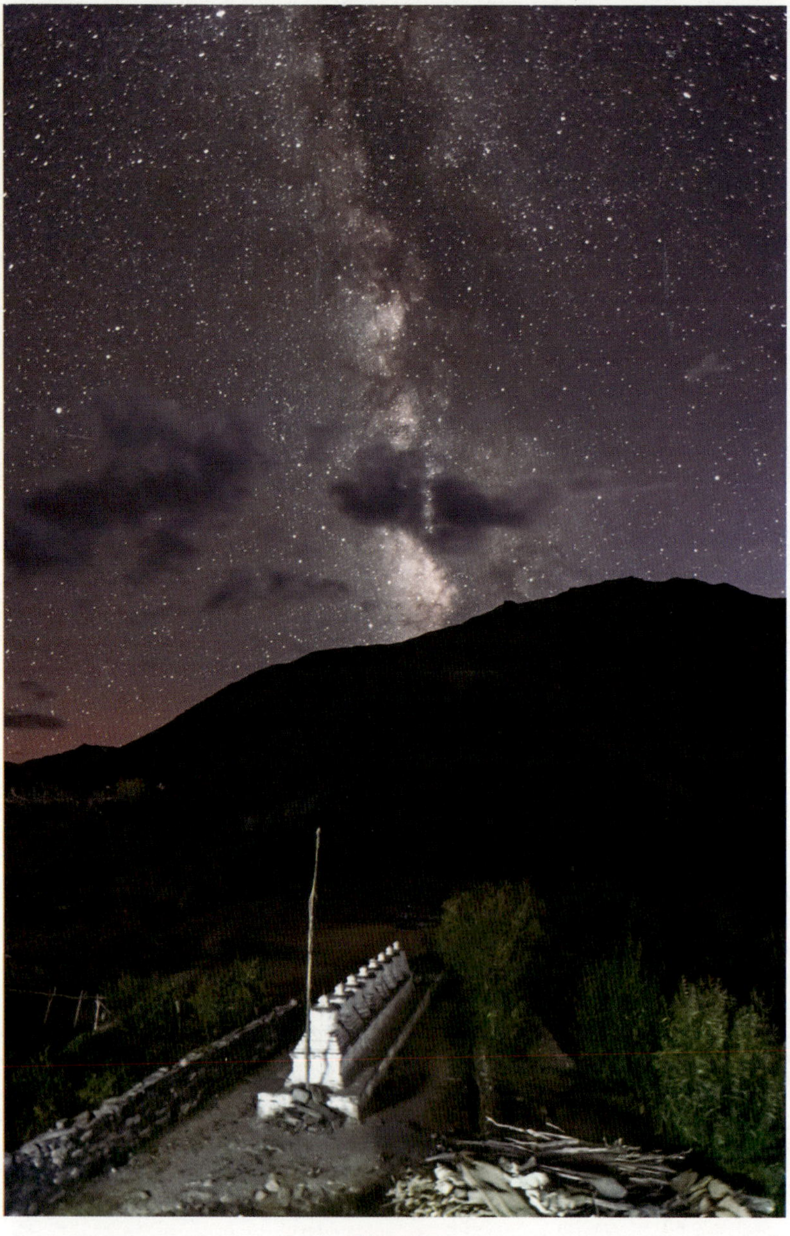

Fig. 12

I captured this Milky way in Zanskar Valley at Purtikchay. I composed by keeping lighted area in foreground.

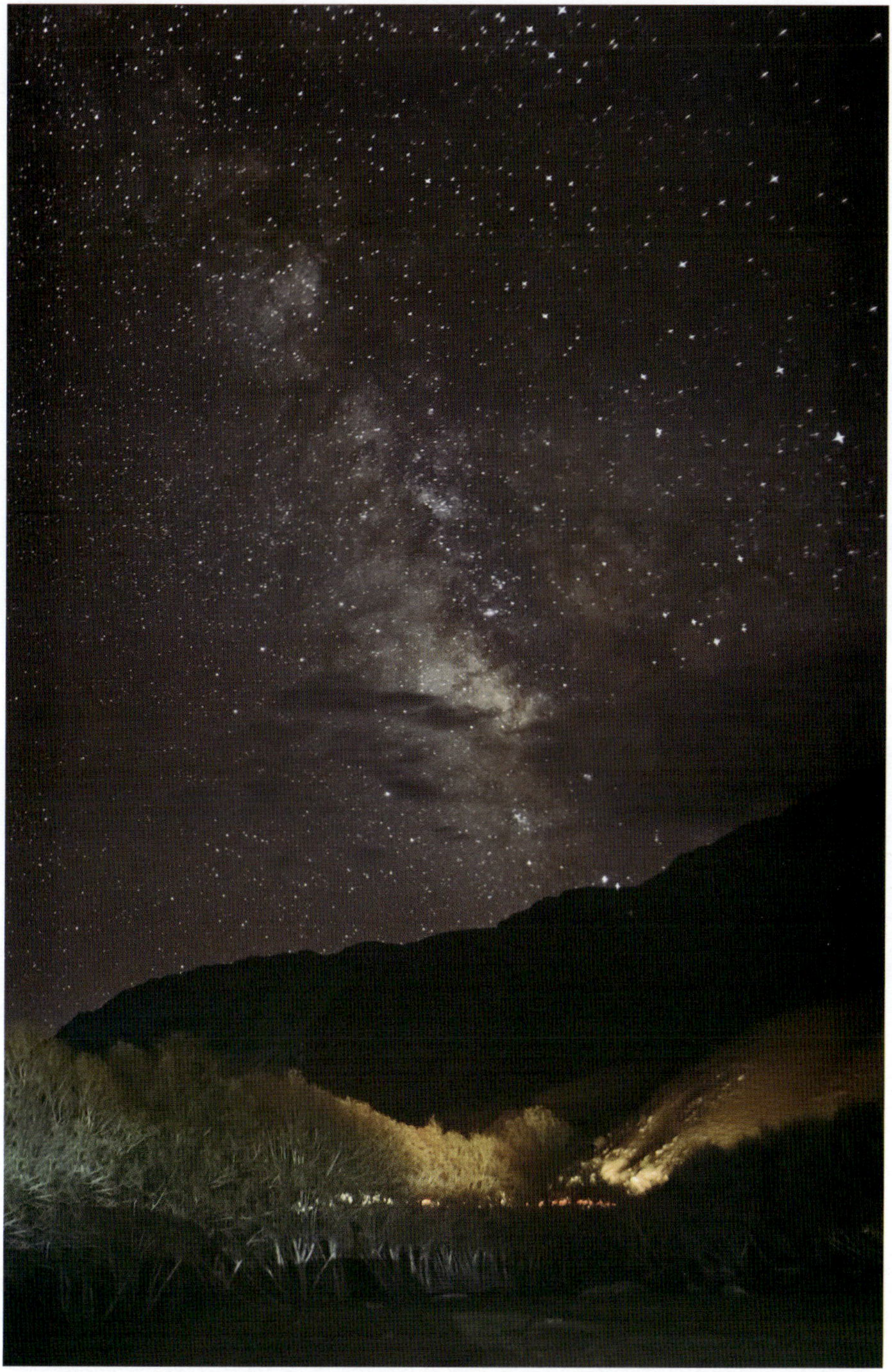

Fig. 13

I captured this Milky way in Zanskar Valley . I composed by keeping our tents in foreground. Composed with glacier in the foreground in next image.

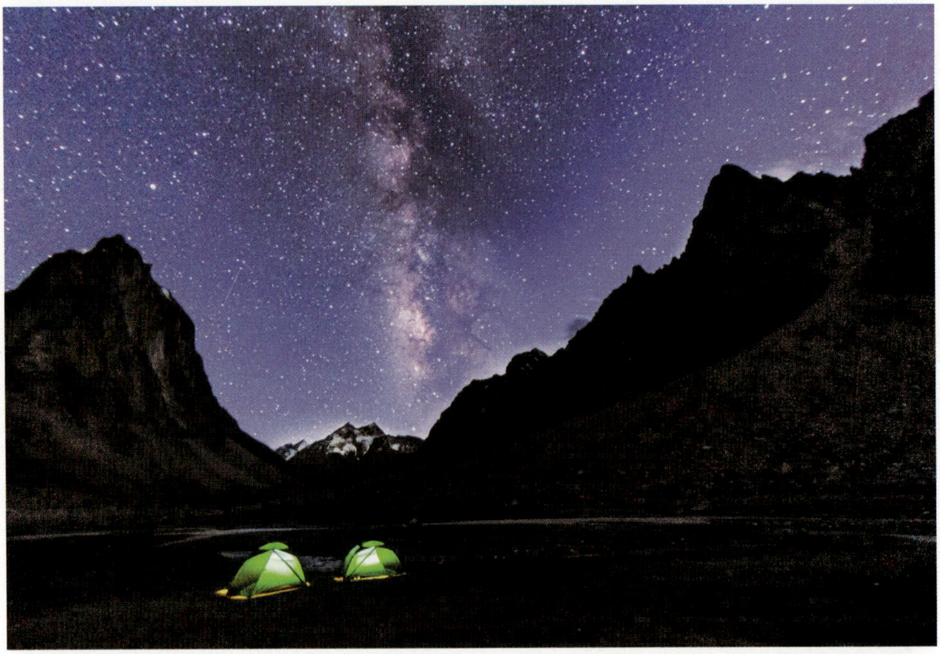

Fig. 14

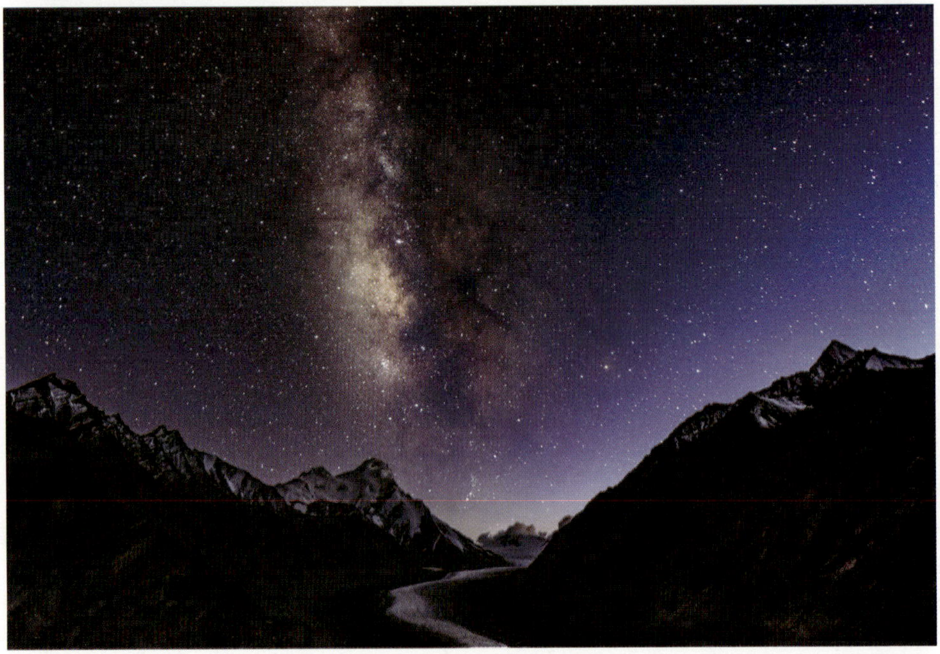

Fig. 15

I captured this Milky way in Zanskar Valley . I composed by keeping our colourful Chortems in foreground.

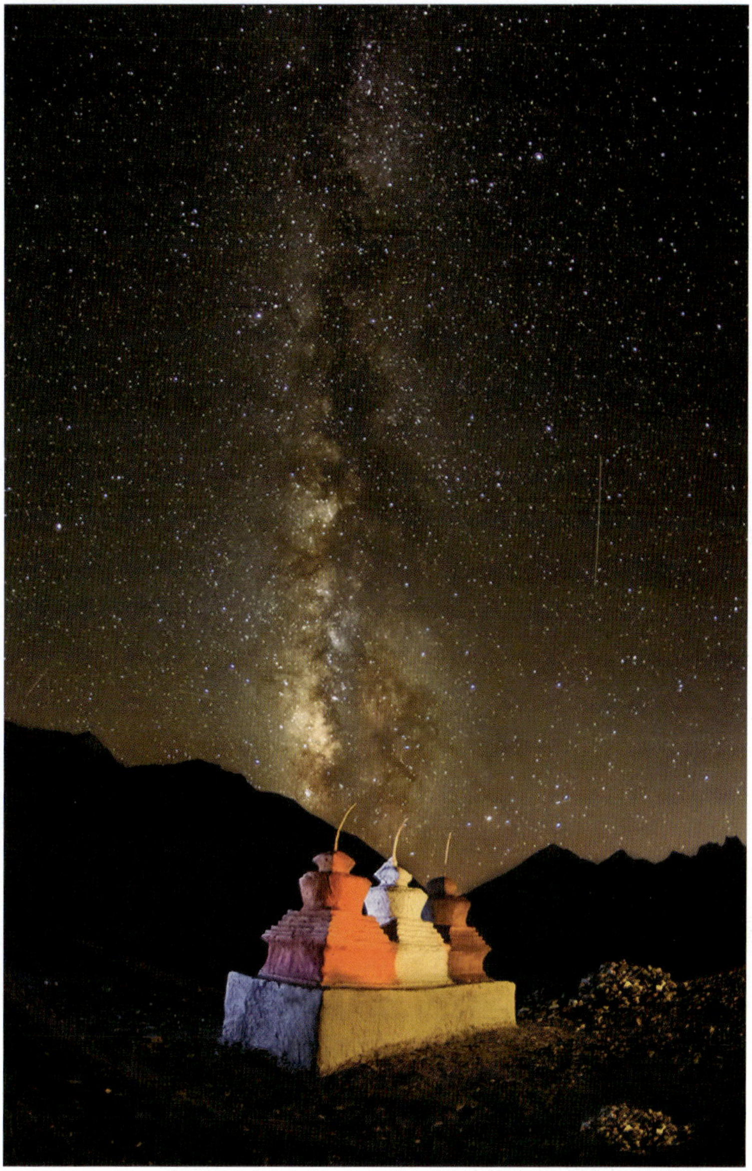

Fig. 16

Watch youtube Tutorial on the topic:

Episode 2- Through the Lens : Star Trail Photography - YouTube

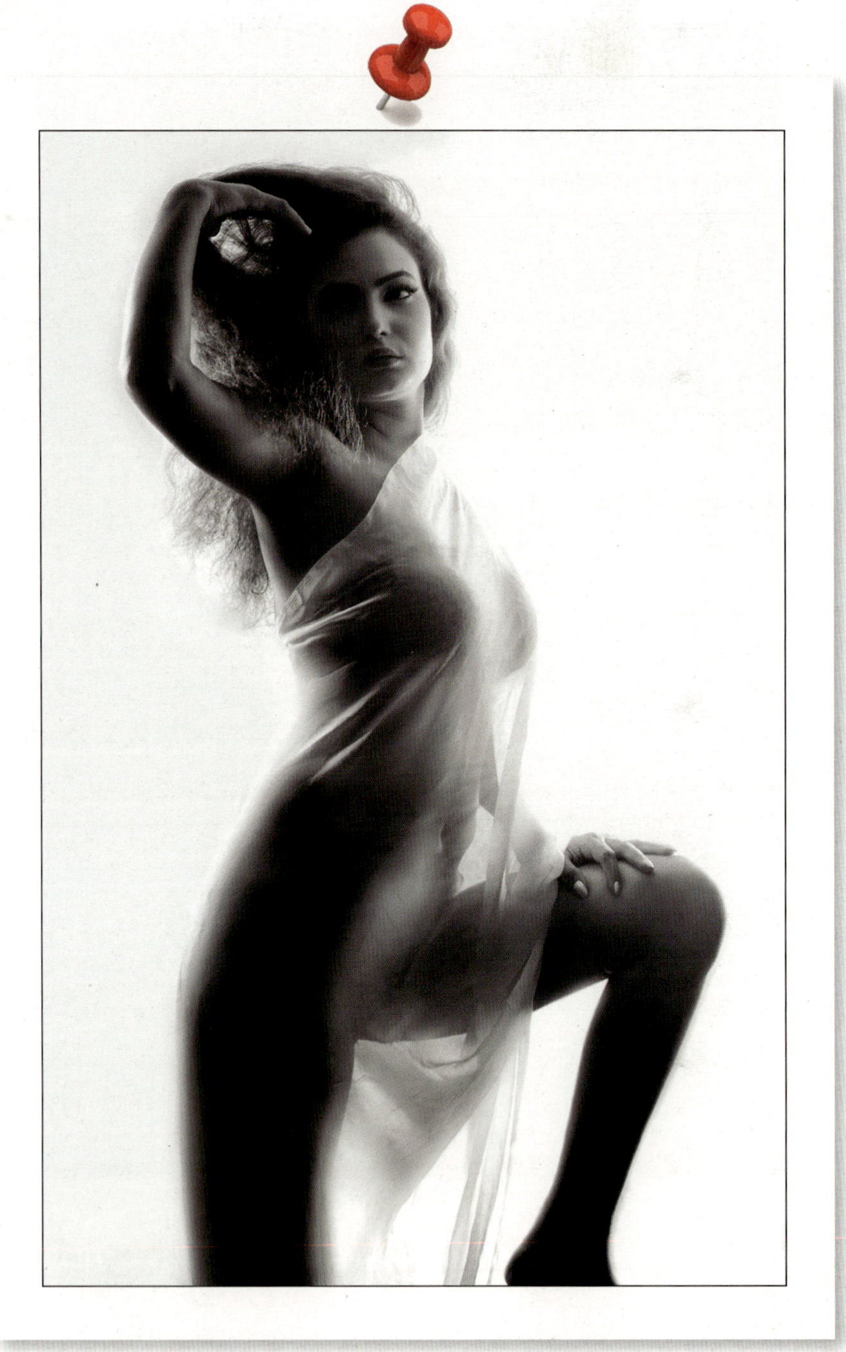

7. Flash Photography

This article will describe in detail about practical use of built in flash to get reasonably good photographs.

Benefits of Built-in Flash

Every photographer can not afford to buy costly external flash. If we master over built-in flash, we can get very good results without buying expensive external flash. We will analyse each situation in practical life, compare the results and come to a conclusion.

The most important factor in flash photography:

Guide Number:

You must know the value of Guide number of your camera built in flash. This will give you an idea about the working range of your flash in full power mode. You can increase the amount of light by increasing ISO, Aperture opening and flash compensation, but limited to the guide number.

The Guide number (m/ft at ISO 100) indicates the amount of light generated by the flash. Larger the number greater the flash output.

Guide Number (GN) = Shooting distance X Aperture/ISO sensitivity factor.

For built in flash it is around 12/39 (m/ft) at ISO 100, 20 degree cel. Depending on the model of camera. See the fig. 1 to know the range of built in flash

Aperture, Sensitivity, and Flash Range

The range of the built-in flash varies with sensitivity (ISO equivalency) and aperture.

Aperture at ISO equivalent of							Range	
100	200	400	800	1600	3200	6400	m	ft
1.4	2	2.8	4	5.6	8	11	0.7–8.5	2ft 4in.–27ft 11in.
2	2.8	4	5.6	8	11	16	0.6–6.0	2ft 0in.–19ft 8in.
2.8	4	5.6	8	11	16	22	0.6–4.2	2ft 0in.–13ft 9in.
4	5.6	8	11	16	22	32	0.6–3.0	2ft 0in.– 9ft 10in.
5.6	8	11	16	22	32	—	0.6–2.1	2ft 0in.– 6ft 11in.
8	11	16	22	32	—	—	0.6–1.5	2ft 0in.– 4ft 11in.
11	16	22	32	—	—	—	0.6–1.1	2ft 0in.– 3ft 7in.
16	22	32	—	—	—	—	0.6–0.8	2ft 0in.– 2ft 7in.

The built-in flash has a minimum range of 0.6 m (2 ft).

In exposure mode P, the maximum aperture (minimum f-number) is limited according to ISO sensitivity, as shown below:

Maximum aperture at ISO equivalent of:						
100	200	400	800	1600	3200	6400
2.8	3.5	4	5	5.6	7.1	8

If the maximum aperture of the lens is smaller than given above, the maximum value for aperture will be the maximum aperture of the lens.

Fig. 1

It is also important to understand the function of built in flash in different camera shooting modes. See the Fig. 2 below:

Shutter Speeds and Apertures Available with the Built-in Flash

Mode	Shutter speed	Aperture
P	Set automatically by camera ($^{1}/_{250}$ s–$^{1}/_{60}$ s) [1,2]	Set automatically by camera
S	Value selected by user ($^{1}/_{250}$ s–30 s) [2]	
A	Set automatically by camera ($^{1}/_{250}$ s–$^{1}/_{60}$ s) [1,2]	Value selected by user [3]
M	Value selected by user ($^{1}/_{250}$ s–30 s, bulb) [2]	

1 Shutter speed may be set as slow as 30s in slow sync, slow rear-curtain sync, and slow sync with red-eye reduction flash modes.

2 Speeds as fast as $^{1}/_{8,000}$ s are available with optional flash units when **1/320 s (Auto FP)** or **1/250 s (Auto FP)** is selected for Custom Setting e1

3 Flash range varies with aperture and ISO sensitivity. Consult table of flash ranges when setting aperture in A and M modes.

Fig. 2

Using the Built-in Flash-iTTL Mode

TTL is used to generically refer to automatic Through The Lens metering. iTTL meters a low power pre flash from the flash before mirror is raised, metered using the viewfinder RGB meter. Pre flash is with lens wide open, and pre flash calculation sets the power level in the flash to be appropriate for the aperture which will be used, with no additional attention or monitoring.

Let us see the difference in Spot and Matrix or Centre weighted metering mode while using iTTL feature of the built in flash.

ITTL with Matrix or Centre weighted metering

Choose a metering method . Select matrix or centre-weighted metering to activate i-TTL balanced fill flash. See Fig. 3 clicked using TTL fill flash in Matrix metering.

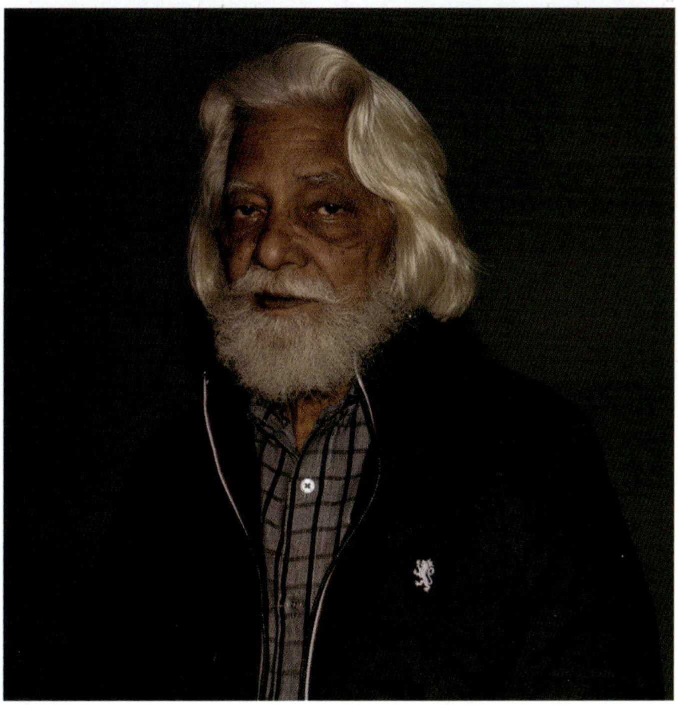

Fig. 3

ITTL with Spot metering

Standard i-TTL flash for digital SLR is activated automatically when spot metering is selected. See Fig. 4 clicked using standard TTL flash in Spot metering.

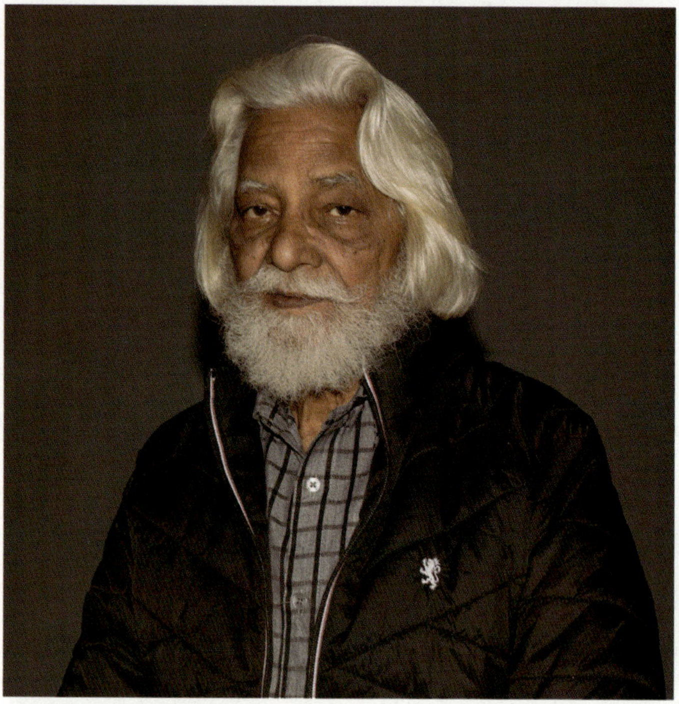

Fig. 4

It is very important to understand the function of different settings of built in flash such as flash modes and flash CONTROL MODES.

Flash Modes

The camera supports the following flash modes:

Front-curtain sync

This mode is recommended for most situations. In programmed auto and aperture-priority auto modes, shutter speed will automatically be set to values between 1/250 and 1/60s (1/8,000 to 1/60s when an optional flash unit is used with Auto FP High-Speed Sync).

Captured a portrait in Manual camera mode with f/8, 1/60s and ISO-200. See the Fig. 5 below:

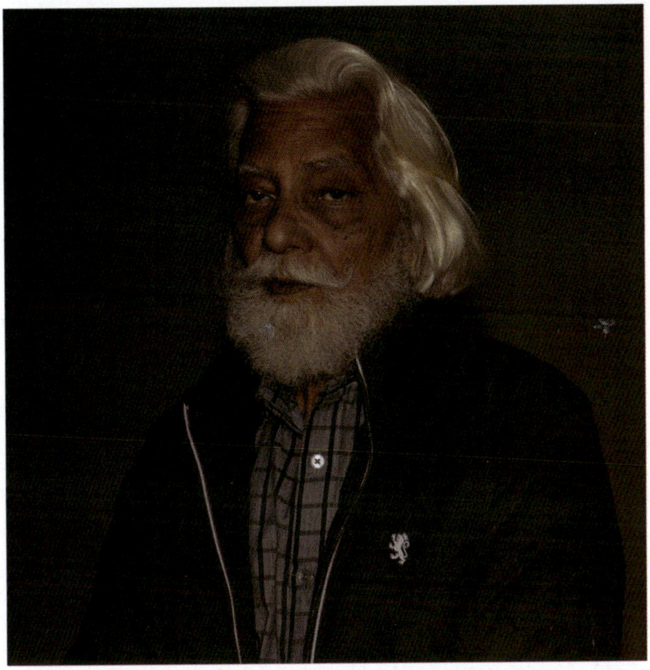

Fig. 5

You can use flash compensation to increase the amount of light. In the same setting I used +0.7 flash compensation in Fig. 6.

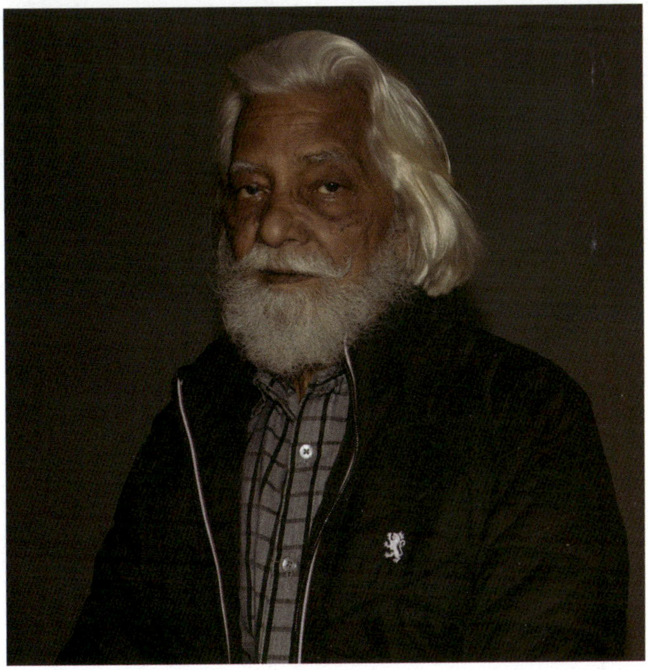

Fig. 6

Red-eye reduction

Red-eye reduction lamp lights for approximately one second before main flash. Pupils in subject's eyes to contract, reducing "red-eye" effect sometimes caused by flash. Owing to one-second shutter-release delay, this mode is not recommended with moving subjects or in other situations in which quick shutter response is required. Avoid moving camera while red-eye reduction lamp is lit.

Red-eye reduction with slow sync

Combines red-eye reduction with slow sync. Use portraits taken against a backdrop of night scenery. Available only in programmed auto and aperture priority auto exposure modes. Use of a tripod is recommended to prevent blurring caused by camera shake.

Slow sync (Fig.7)

Flash is combined with shutter speeds as slow as 30s to capture both subject and background at night or under dim light. This mode is only available in programmed auto and aperture-priority auto exposure modes. Use of tripod is recommended to prevent blurring caused by camera shake.

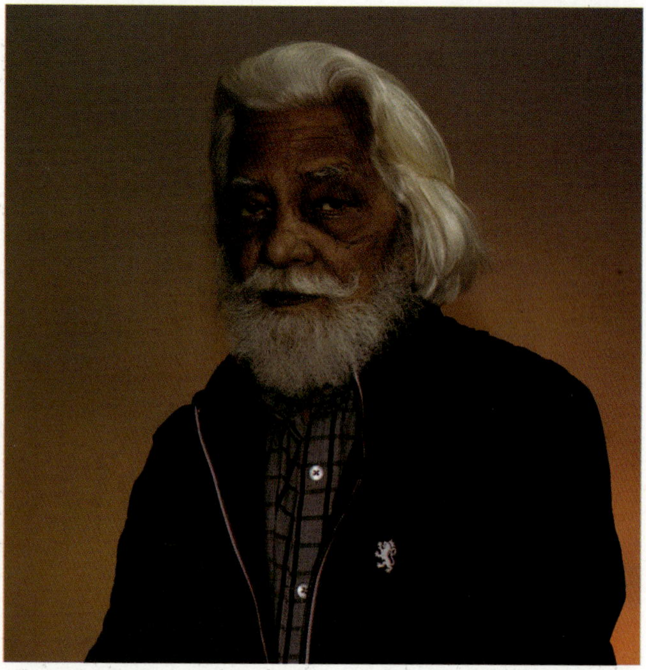

Fig. 7

Repeating Flash Control

In this mode, we get result like strobe light. You should practice to set the parameters mentioned below:

Output: You can adjust the amount of light depending upon the distance from the subject from ¼ to 1/128

Times: set number of times you want to fire.

Frequency: You can set from 1 to 50HZ.

The image in Fig. 8 was shot with ¼ output, 2 times firing of flash and with 2HZ frequency.

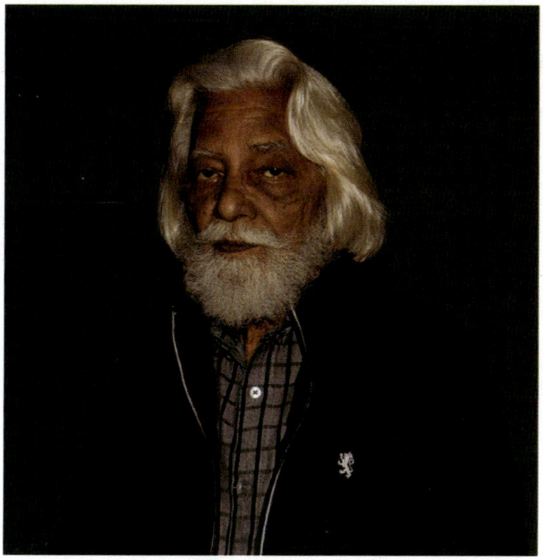

Fig. 8

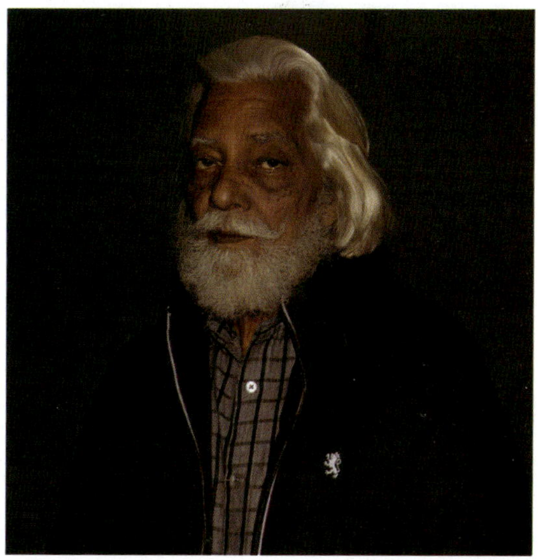

Fig. 9

The image in Fig. 9 was shot with ¼ output, 2 times firing of flash and with 50HZ frequency.

Diffusing and Bouncing

One of the main disadvantages of your camera's pop-up flash is the harshness and intensity of the light. This is due to the fact that the flash originates from such a small area. The smaller the area that the light originates from, more harsh the light source will be. Because your camera's flash is designed to fit compactly inside of the camera, it is one of the harshest light sources you can come by. There are special tools designed to alter and diffuse this light, but you may not always have these tools at your side. In this case, it is useful to know a few tips and tricks for creating a softer light using just your pop-up flash.

One of the ways in which you can soften the light is by diffusing it. A diffuser works to increase the size of your light source, thus softening it. This is why you will see photographers shooting with umbrellas or soft boxes. But these tools are cumbersome, and not always at our disposal. In cases where you are stuck with just your camera, you can improvise a diffuser using tissue paper, thin cotton, velum paper, or any similar material. You should notice an instant difference when shooting with a diffused flash as opposed to a direct flash.

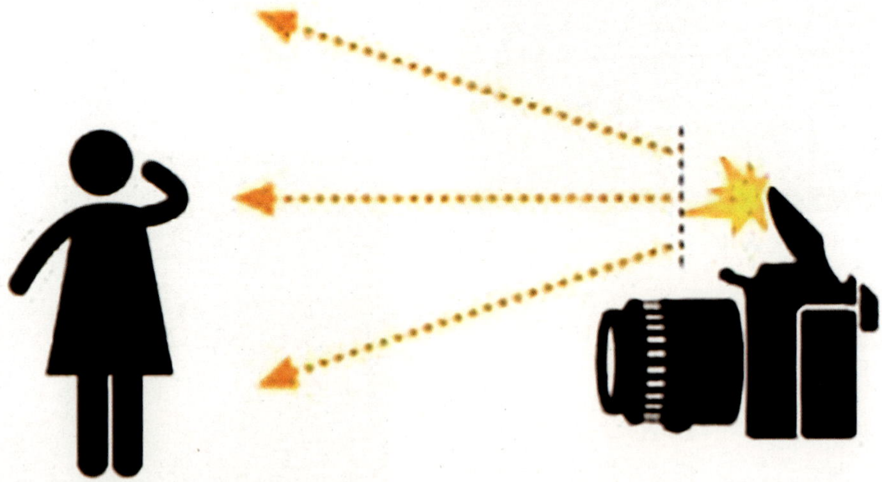

Using a material to diffuse the light

Fig. 10

I used a diffuser (Fig. 11) to get the image in Fig. 12

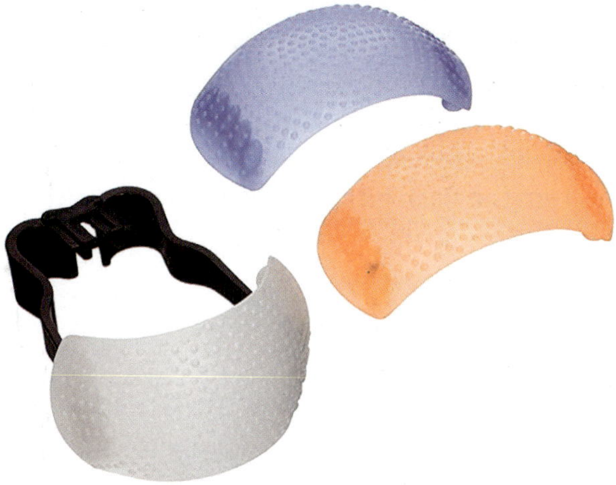

Fig. 11

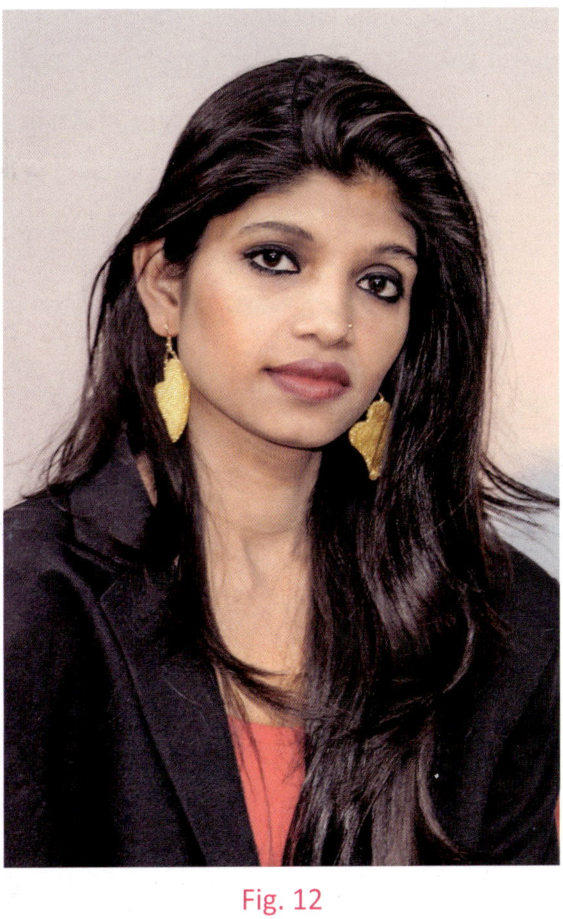

Fig. 12

When shooting with diffused light, it is important to note that because the light is being decreased, so is your range. Any diffuser you use will dim the light, so you will need to experiment with the flash compensation to get the results you want.

Another way to soften the flash is by bouncing it off of the ceiling, turning the room into a giant soft box. The light from the flash hits the ceiling, which softens the light by spreading it throughout the room. Note that this technique will only work indoors and in smaller-sized rooms.

While the pop-up flash on your camera is stationary, you can still bounce the light using a small white card. Hold the card at a 45 degree angle in front of your flash, and take your shot. The light should hit the card, bounce to the ceiling, and spread out into a nice soft light. Experiment with the light intensity and card angle until you get the best results. This technique isn't perfect, but most times will work.

Using bouncer shown in Fig.13 and captured the image shown in Fig. 14.

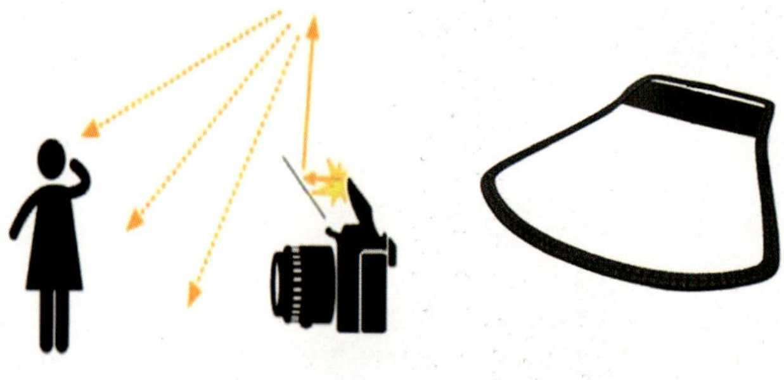

Using a material to bounce the light

Fig. 13

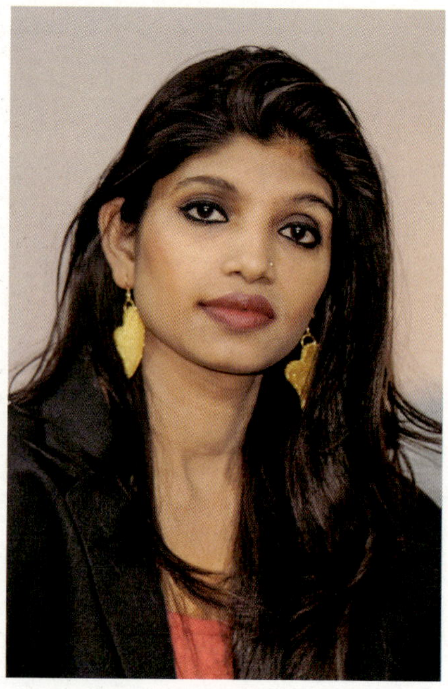

Fig. 14

Flash in Manual Mode

Against Light

We face the most difficult situation to shoot against light. The main subject becomes dark. Here the manual mode of built in flash is very useful. Depending upon the distance of camera from the main subject choose flash intensity of ¼, 1/8, 1/16 etc and shoot.

See the lighting condition in Fig. 15 which was clicked without using flash. Since the light is coming from the back, the subject is dark.

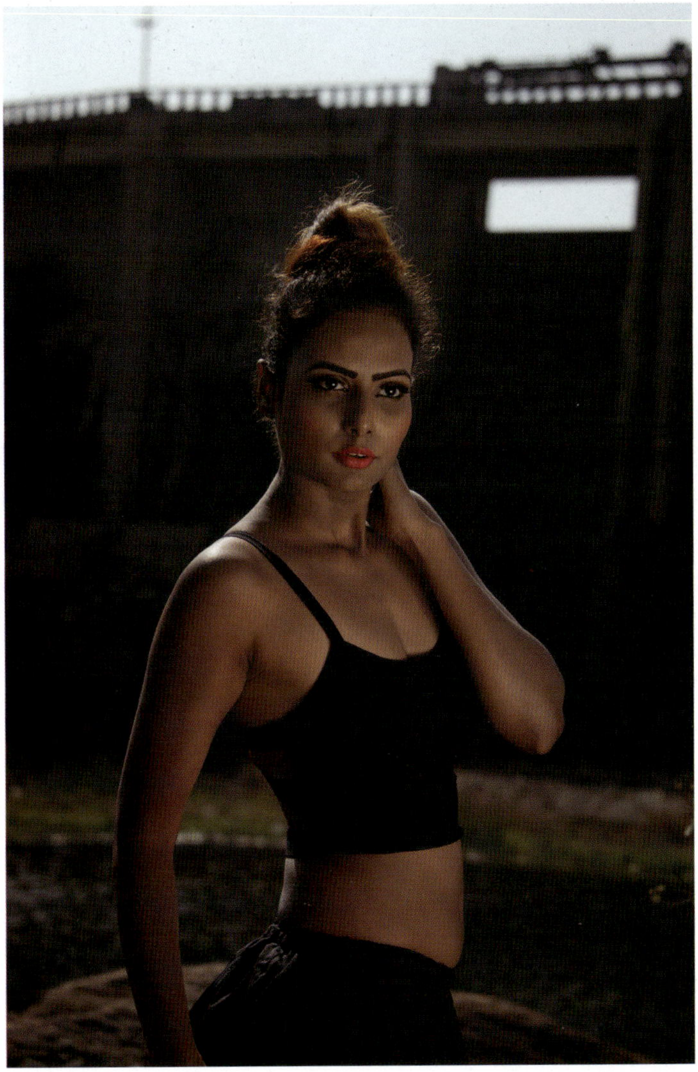

Fig. 15

Now we can use built in flash in manual mode and adjust the lighting depending on the distance from camera. I used ¼ flash intensity and got well illuminated subject as shown in Fig. 16.

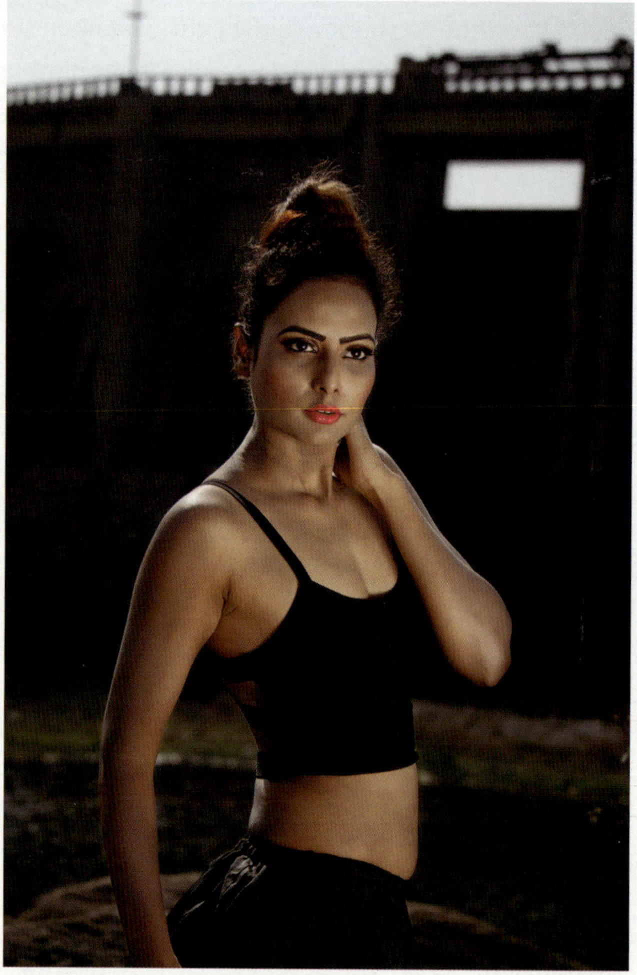

Fig. 16

My recommendations:

1. In normal lighting condition the best method is use of repeating flash mode, but it needs time to set the parameters. If you have time go for this option.
2. Using TTL fill flash feature in Matrix or centre weighted metering mode is the best option for every situation.
3. To shoot against light, the best option is to use flash in manual mode.

External Flash

To get profession output, it is recommended to use external flash as fill flash. It gives punch on the model.

Technique

Set exposure as per the lighting condition of the background. Under expose by 2 to 3 stops. Place the external flash (like AD 400) to fill the shadow. Put flash in manual mode. Adjust the flash intensity to get punch on the subject.

See the set up in Fig. 17. Without and with Fill Flash in Fig. 18, 19, 20 & 21. With Fill Flash in Fig. 22 , Fig. 23 & Fig. 24.

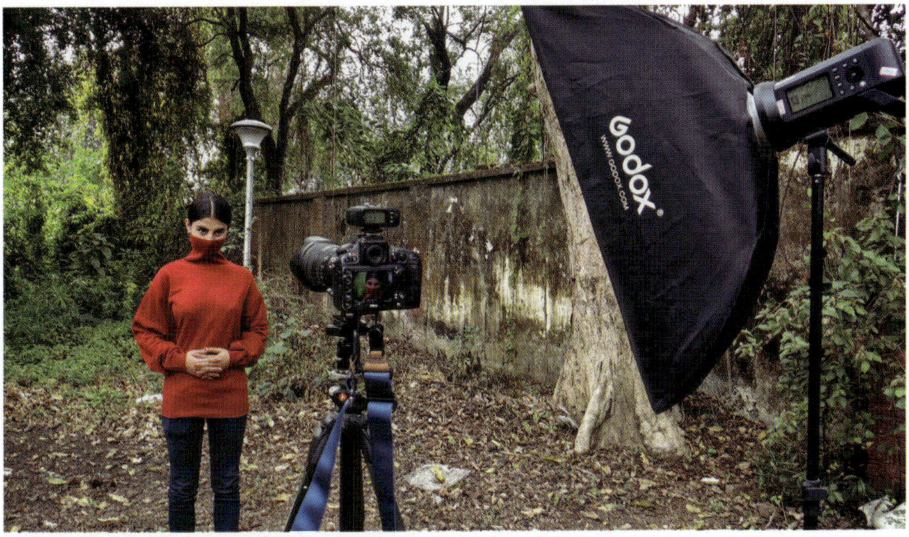

Fig. 17

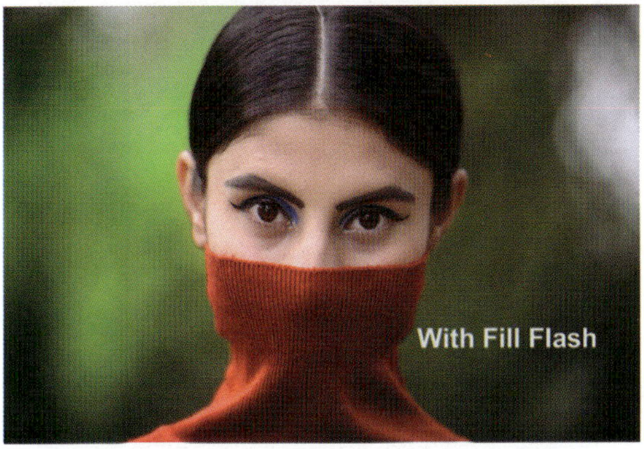

Fig. 18

Fig. 19

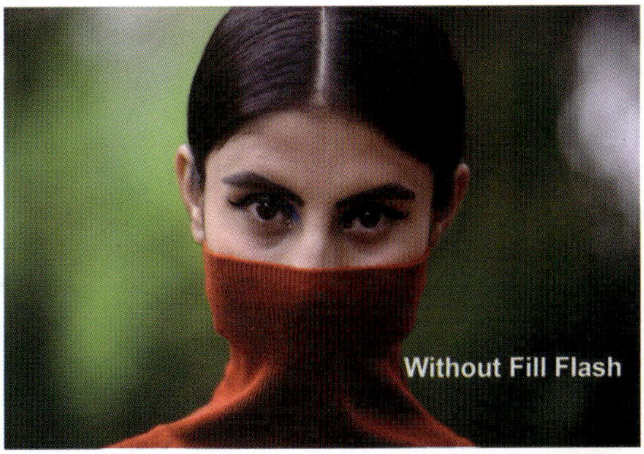

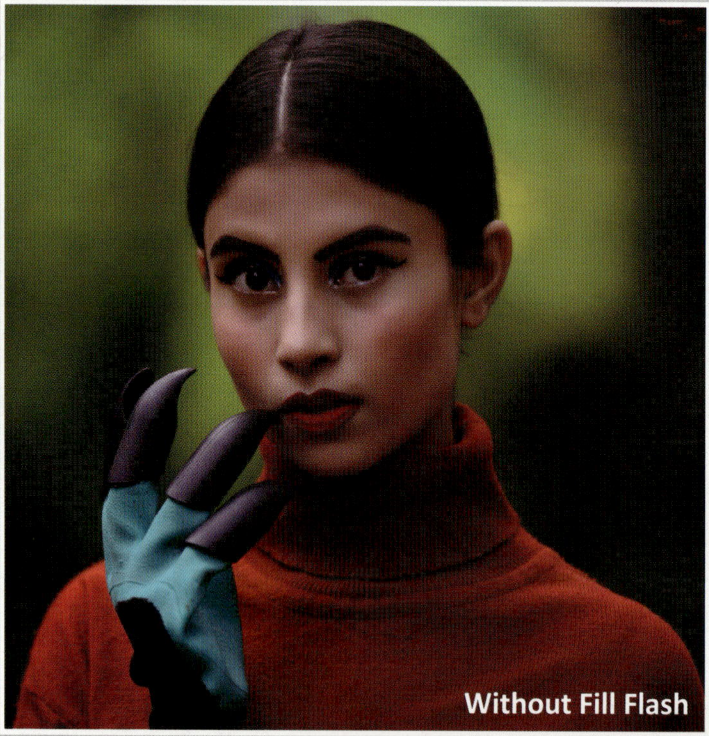

◀ Fig. 20

Fig. 21 ▶

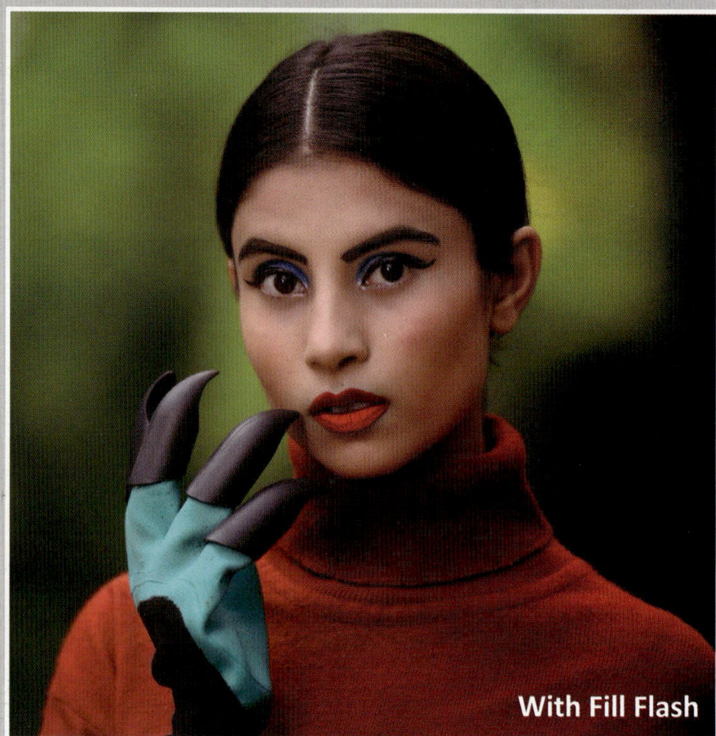

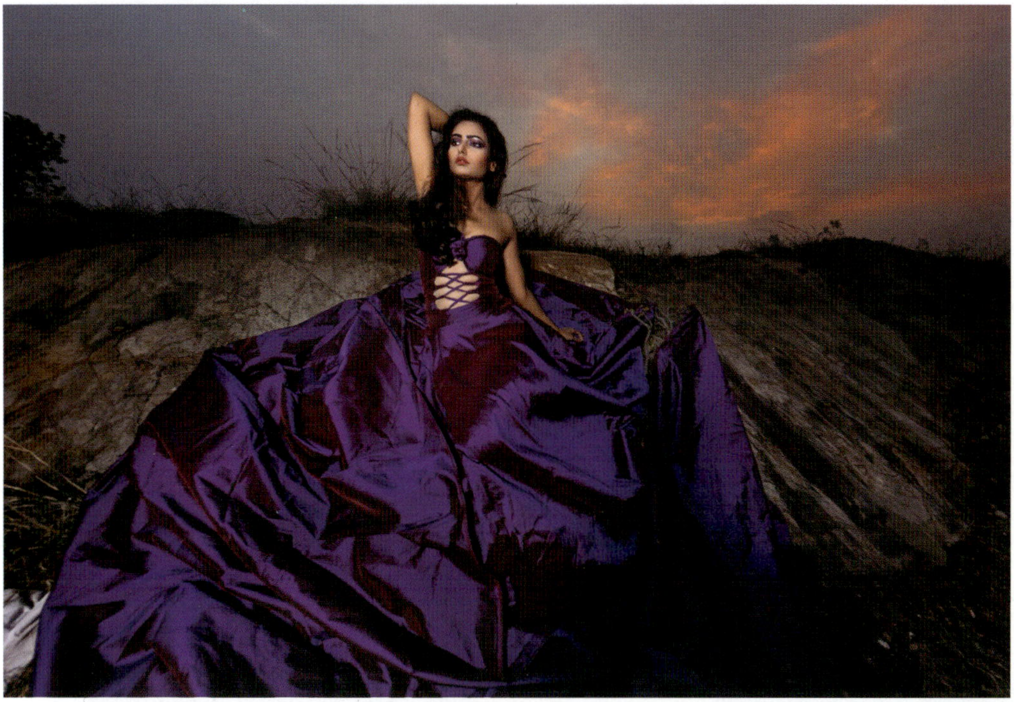

Fig. 22

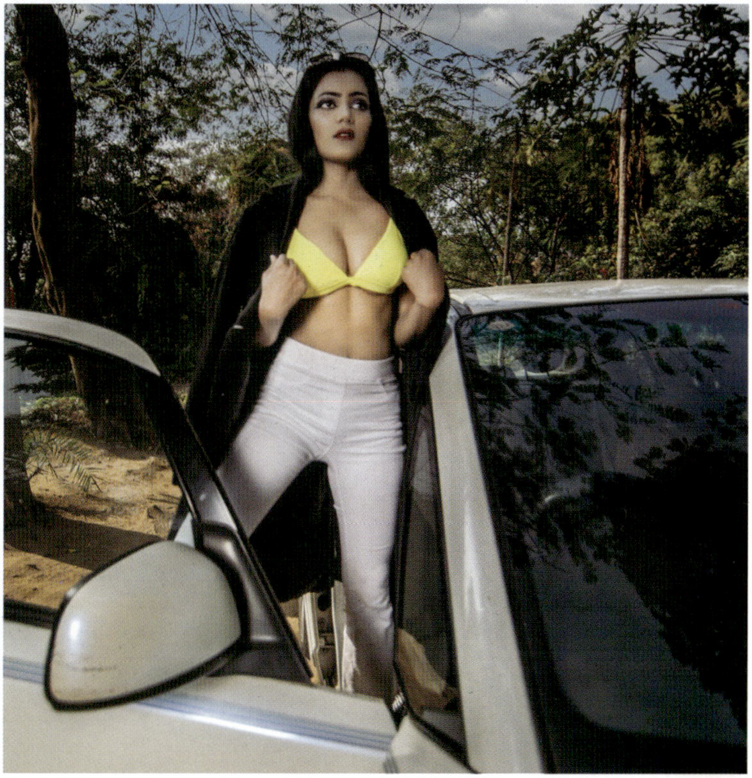

Fig. 23 ➤

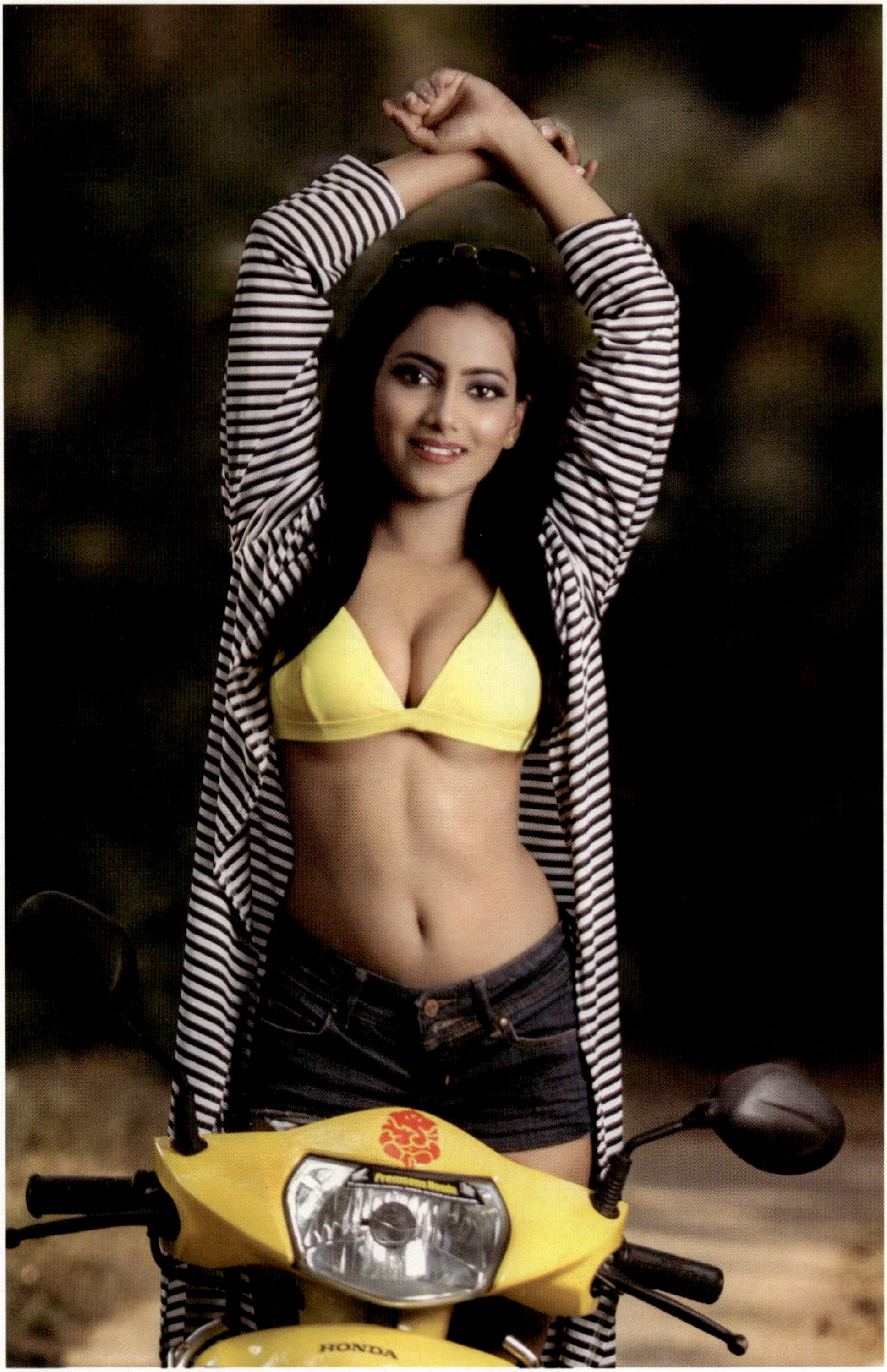

Fig. 24

8. Advanced Camera Features : Active D-Lighting and Picture Control

You always face trouble while shooting a frame consisting of highlights as well as shadows. If you set the exposure for the highlights, you lose details in the shadow areas. If you chose exposure for shadow or dark areas, you lose details in the highlights or brightest area or it gets over exposed. Even you chose Matrix or Evaluative metering mode, the similar problem is faced. Every DSLR camera gives an advanced feature of Active D-Lighting. With proper use of this feature you can get details in the shadow areas as well as details in the highlight areas.

A scene like the one in this figure presents the classic photographer's challenge:

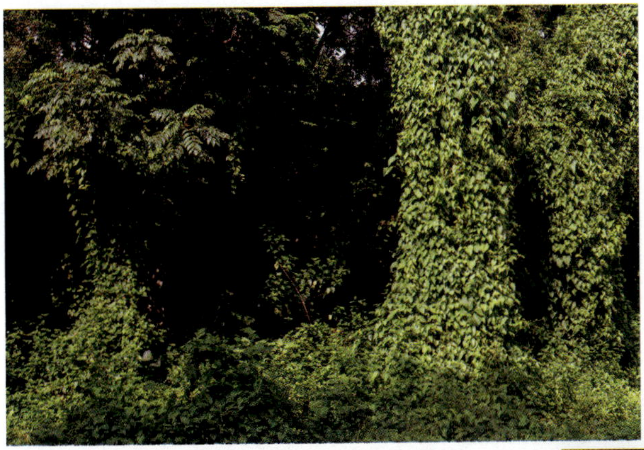

Fig. 1 Without use of ADL

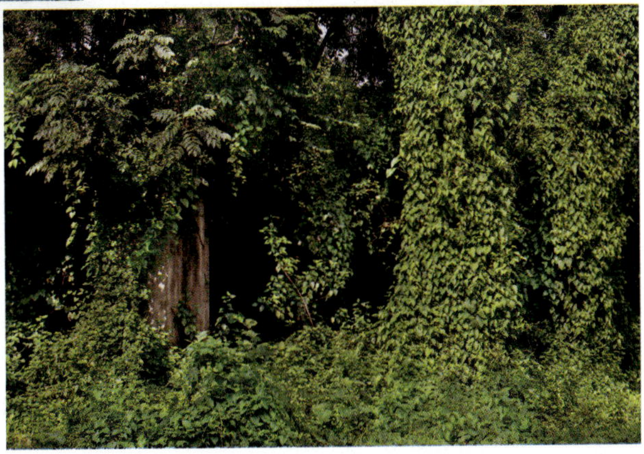

Fig. 2 With use of ADL

In fact, the D in Active D-Lighting is a reference to the term dynamic range, which is used to describe the range of brightness values that an imaging device can capture. By turning on this feature, you enable to camera to produce an image with a slightly greater dynamic range than usual.

In the landscape shown above, turning on Active D-Lighting produced a brighter rendition of the darkest parts of the brick column and green leaves inside, for example, and yet the colour in the brighter part of green leaves didn't get blown out as it did when the image was captured with Active D-Lighting turned off.

Active D-Lighting actually does its thing in two stages. First, it selects exposure settings that result in a slightly darker exposure than normal. This half of the equation guarantees that you retain details in your highlights. After you snap the photo, the camera brightens the darkest areas of the image. This adjustment rescues shadow detail.

It's usually best to keep this option set to Off so that you can decide for yourself whether you want any adjustment instead of having the camera apply it to every shot.

How to set Active D-Lighting

Press the Menu button and chose Shooting Menu. Scroll down to get Active D-Lighting.

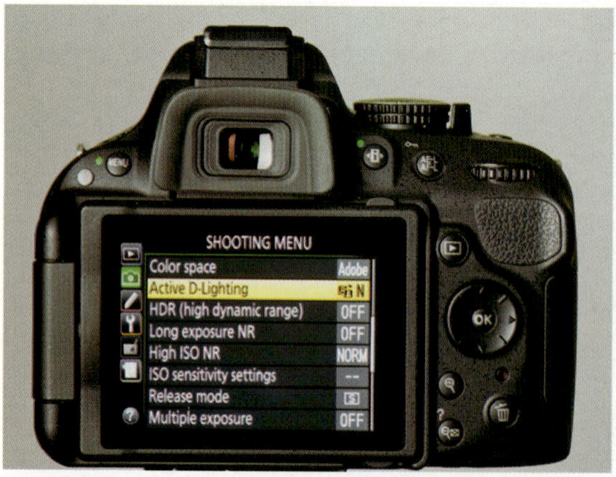

Fig. 3 Shooting Menu-ADL

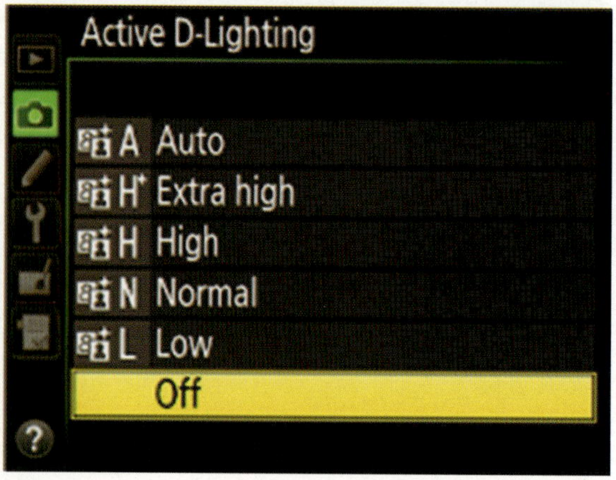

Fig. 3A ADL-options

Before you select ADL ON, you must know the important conditions for its effective use. These are mentioned below:

1. **Metering Mode:** You get the best results in MATRIX metering mode.

2. **ISO:** Active D-Lighting doesn't work when the ISO Sensitivity is set to Hi 1.0.

3. **Exposure Mode:** It works effectively in A and S mode only.

   It's not recommended to use Active D-Lighting in the M exposure mode. In M mode, the camera doesn't change the shutter speed or f-stop to achieve the darker exposure it needs for Active D-Lighting to work.

4. **Outdoor n Indoor Photography:** ADL is used mainly for outdoor photography like landscape, street life, portrait, fashion shoots etc. Apart from natural light, it's useful in indoor also with any constant light source such as porta light, LED, Halogen etc.

To make you very clear about the effects of this feature, I did content shoot of landscape and the portrait in each option of Active D-Lighting.

I did content shoot with my model Madhumita Soren to show the effect of Active D-Lighting.

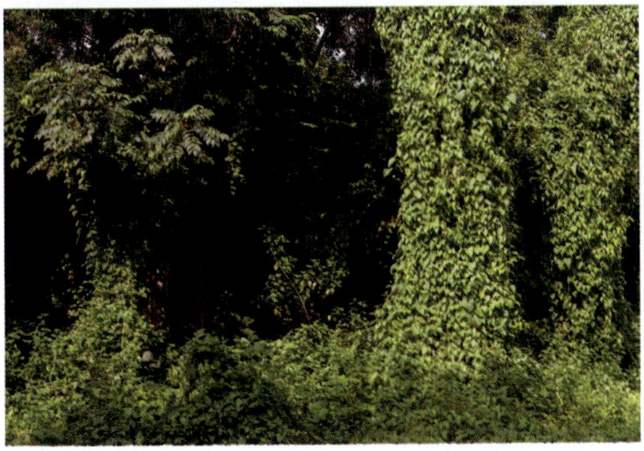

Fig. 4 ADL-off

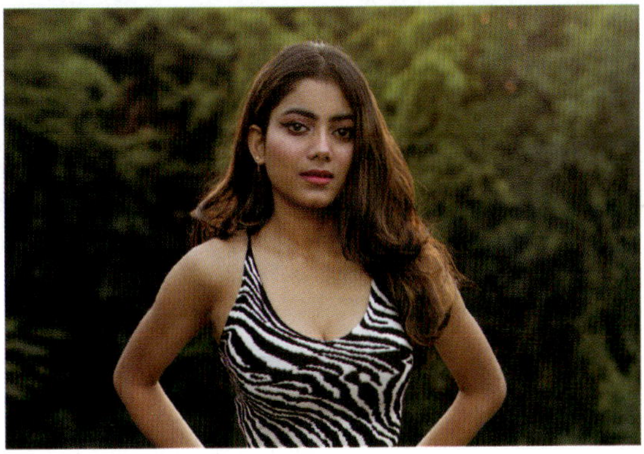

Fig. 5 ADL-off

In ADL OFF option, you can see details are almost lost in dark area of the landscape and the shadow area of the portrait.

In ADL LOW option, you can see details are almost lost like OFF option in dark area of the landscape and the shadow area of the portrait.

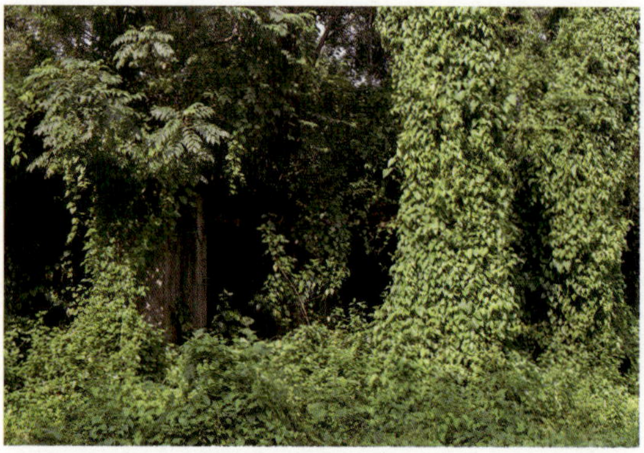

Fig. 6 ADL-Low

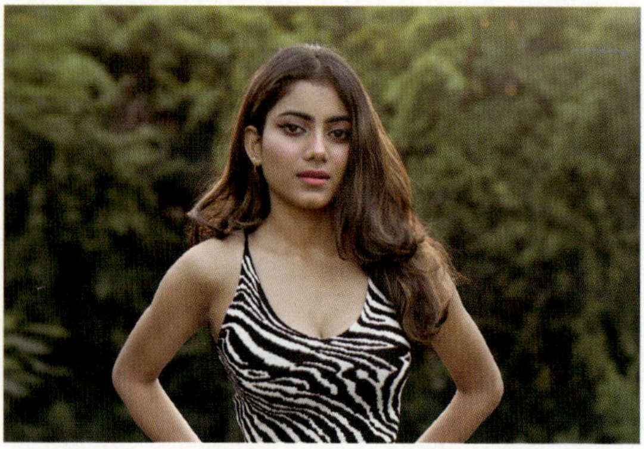

Fig. 7 ADL-Low

In ADL NORMAL option, you can see details are visible in dark area of the landscape and the shadow area of the portrait.

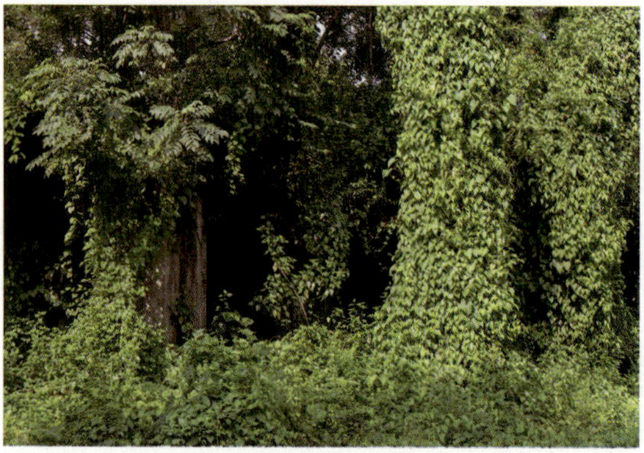

Fig. 8 ADL-Normal

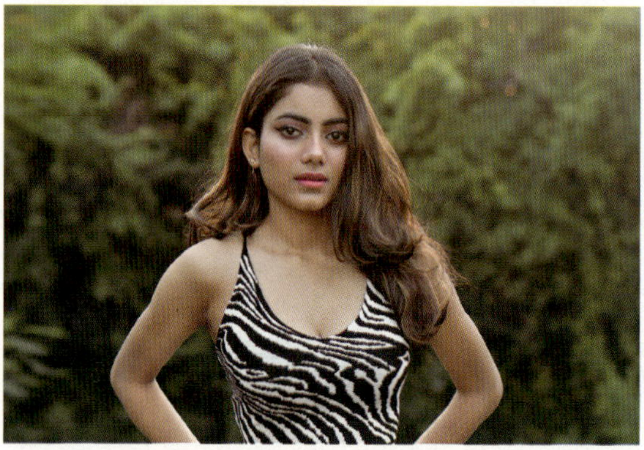

Fig. 9 ADL-Normal

In ADL HIGH option, you can see details are more visible in dark area of the landscape and the shadow area of the portrait.

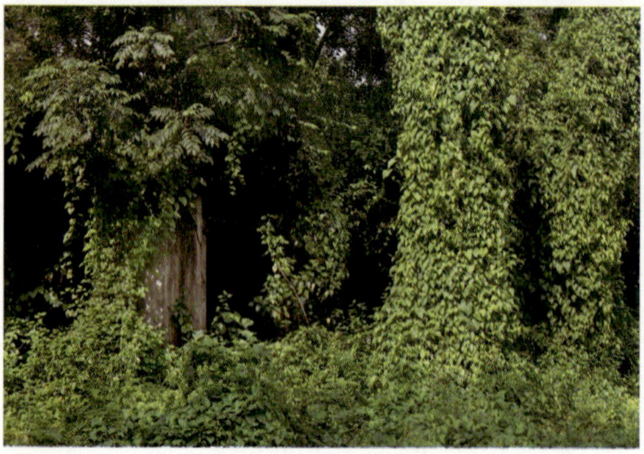

Fig. 10 ADL-High

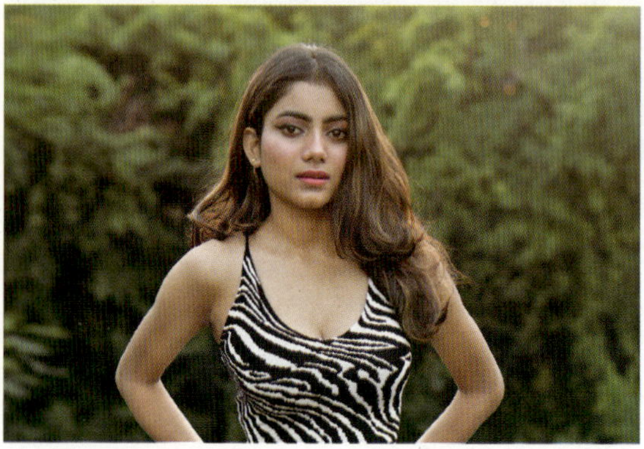

Fig. 11 ADL-High

In ADL Extra High option, you can see details are much more visible in dark area of the landscape and the shadow area of the portrait.

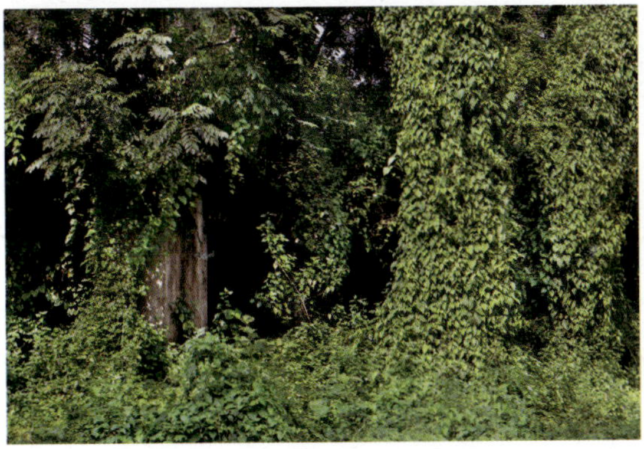

Fig. 12 ADL-Extra High

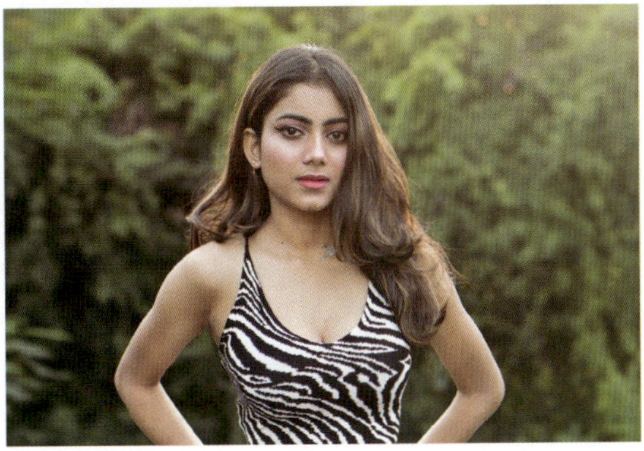

Fig. 13 ADL-Extra High

In ADL AUTO option, you can see details are little visible in dark area of the landscape and the shadow area of the portrait.

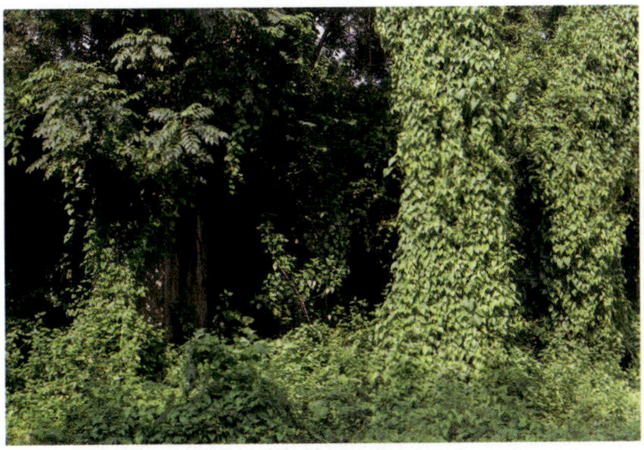

Fig. 14 ADL-Auto

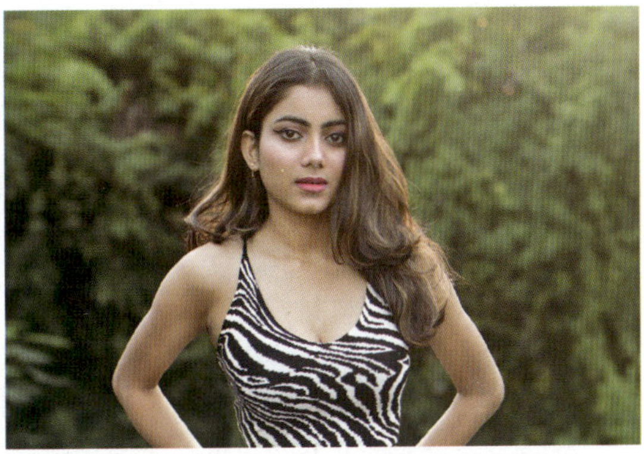

Fig. 15 ADL-Auto

Technical Analysis of ADL Feature

Camera never does any magic. Always there are enough technical reasons of doing a job by the camera. The exif data of each images clicked are being presented below.

I used Nikon D500 DSLR with 50mm, f/1.4 lens, A priority mode, ISO-250, f-2.8, focal length-75mm. In table mentioned below you can see the change in shutter speed as per various options of ADL:

ADL Option	Shutter Speed
ADL OFF	1/200s
ADL LOW	1/160s
ADL NORMAL	1/125s
ADL HIGH	1/100s
ADL Extra HIGH	1/80s
ADL Auto	1/100s

You can see here. ADL mainly changes the f-stop.

Conclusion

So, for portrait shoot it's recommended to keep ADL in off position. In case there is harsh shadow, you can change to High or Extra High option.

If you opt out of Active D-Lighting, remember that the camera's Retouch menu offers a D-Lighting filter that applies a similar adjustment to existing pictures. Some photo-editing programs, including Nikon ViewNX 2, also have good shadow and highlight recovery filters. (In View NX 2, investigate the D-Lighting HS, Shadow Protection, and Highlight Protection filters; the program's Help system explains how to use them.

At A Glance

You can see the effects of all options of Active D-Lighting in the pictures below:

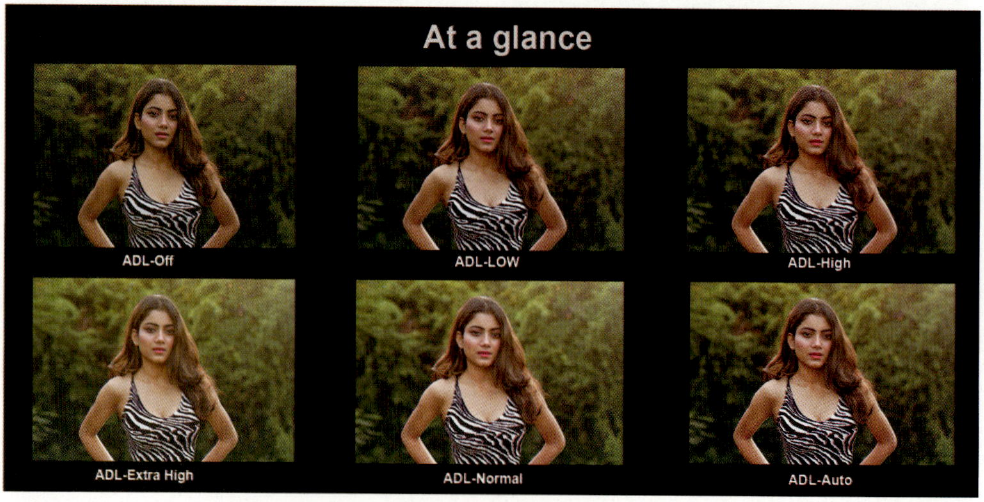

Fig. 16

Picture Control

Picture control is another advanced feature in DSLR cameras. It mainly enhances the picture in terms of Brightness, Contrast, Saturation, Hue and Sharpening.

Go to Shooting Menu, you will get Set Picture Control options. Here we will discuss mainly top three options like Standard, Neutral and Vivid.

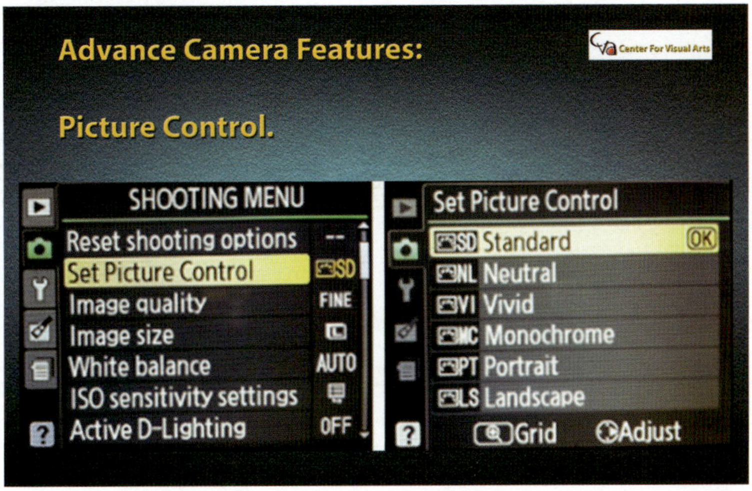

Fig. 17

In every option, you can increase or decrease the amount of Sharpening, Contrast, Brightness, Saturation and Hue to get added enhancement as shown below:

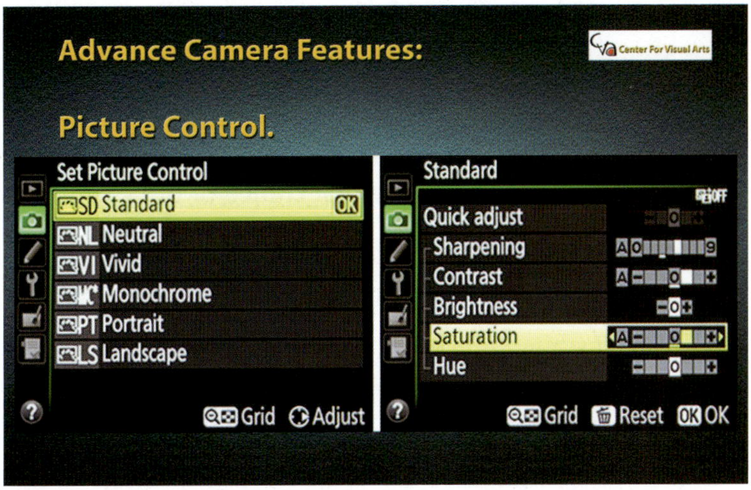

Fig. 18

I did content shoot with my model Prity Kumari to show the effect of picture control.

Standard

Camera does enhancement for balanced results and is recommended for all normal situations. You can see the portrait below. The camera has processed it to some extent for normal use.

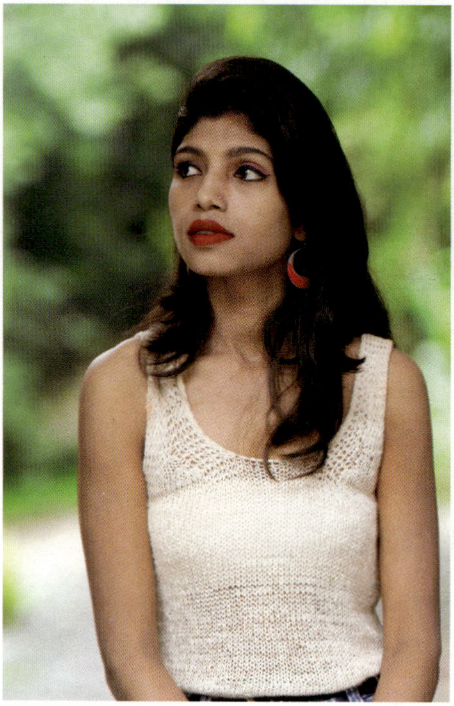

Fig.19 Standard

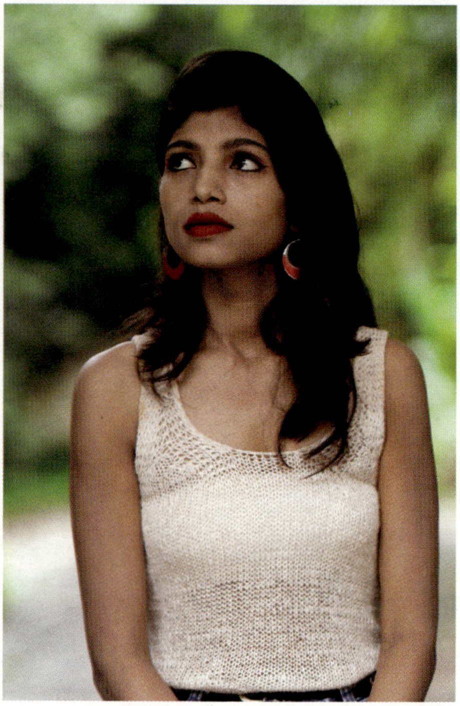

Fig. 20 Neutral

Neutral

Camera does almost negligible enhancement, so you can do the required enhancement as per your choice in post processing. It's the first choice of professional photographers.

You can see the portrait below. The camera has not done much processing. So to get desired tone, colour and sharpening, you can process it during post processing.

Vivid

Camera does quite reasonable enhancement for photoprint effect. It's recommended for the wedding and the press photographers as they do not have much time for post processing.

You can see the portrait below. The camera has processed it to greater extent for ready to use.

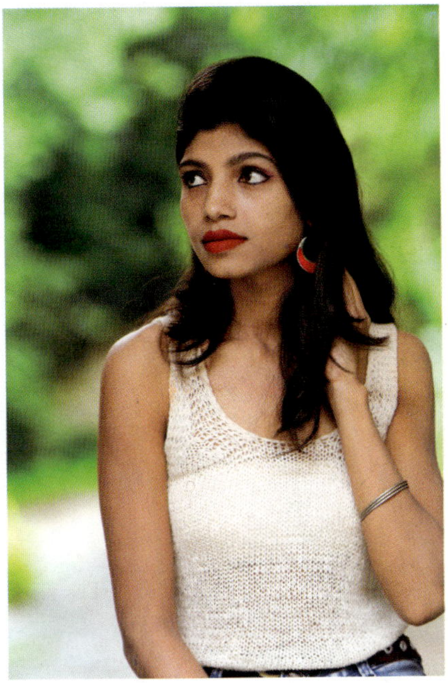

Fig. 21 Vivid

At a Glance

Here you can see all three effects of picture control

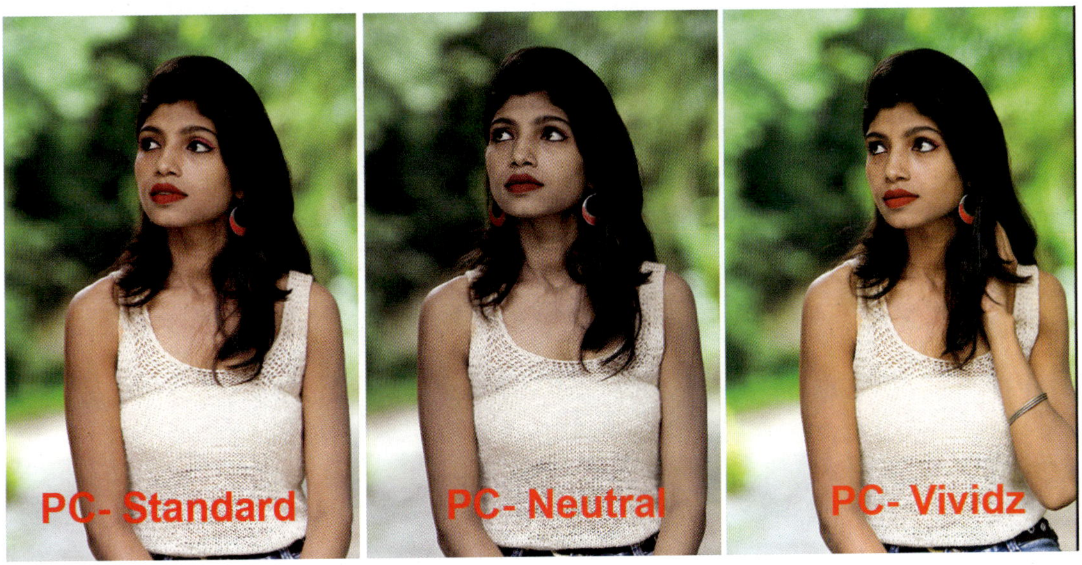

Fig. 22 At a Glance

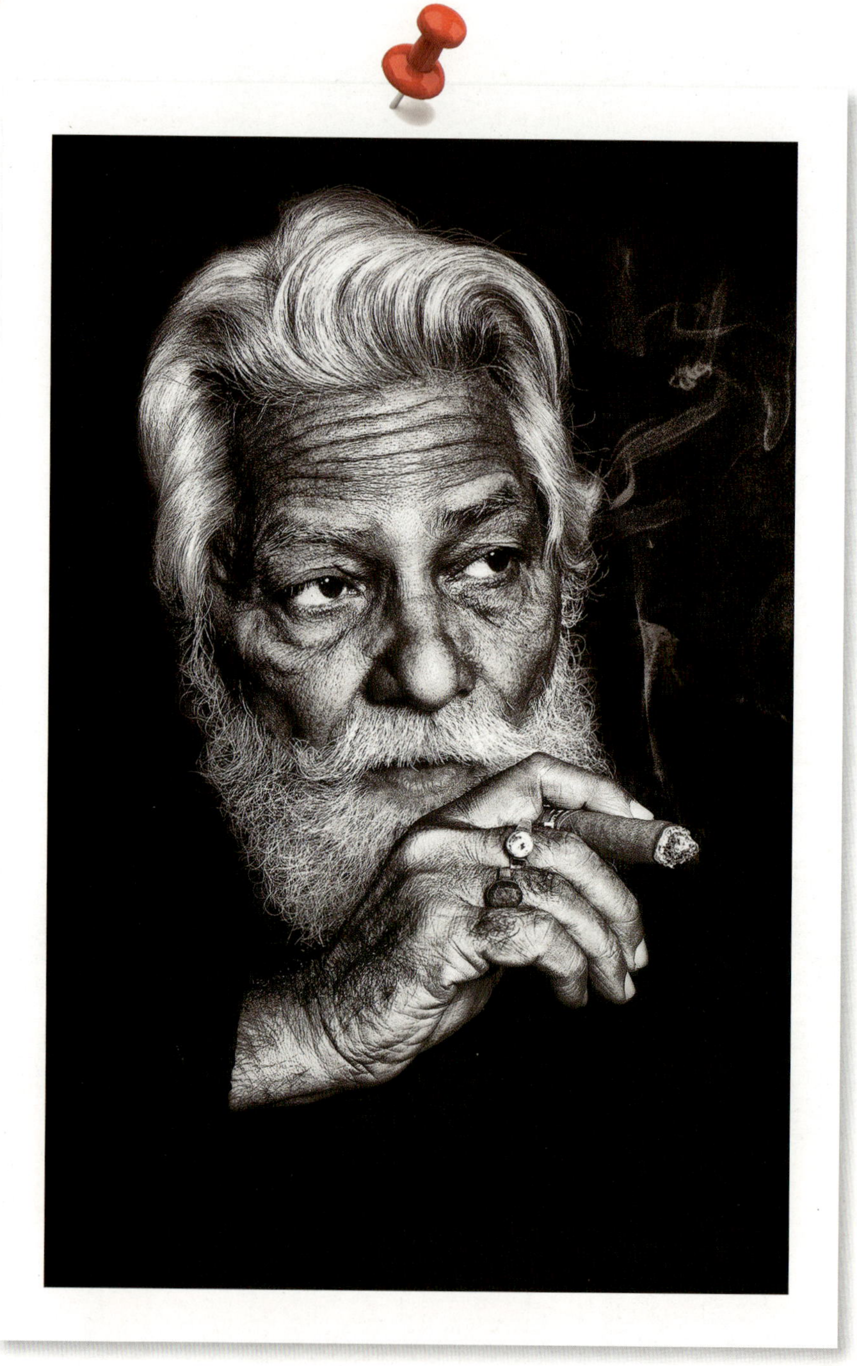

9. Panorama Photography

Panorama photography is a technique of photography, using specialized equipment or software that captures images with horizontally elongated fields of view. It is sometimes known as *"wide format photography"*. The term has also been applied to a photograph that is cropped to a relatively wide aspect ratio.

An image showing a field of view approximating, or greater than, that of the human eye – about 160° – may be termed panoramic. This generally means it has an aspect ratio of 2:1 or larger, the image being at least twice as wide as it is high. The resulting images take the form of a wide strip. Some panoramic images have aspect ratios of 4:1 and sometimes 10:1, covering fields of view of up to 360 degrees. Both the aspect ratio and coverage of field are important factors in defining a true panoramic image.

Types of Panoramas

The different types of Panoramic image are as follows:

1. Wide angle panoramas – anything that looks like a wide angle photograph, which covers less than 180 degrees, whether horizontal or vertical. Wide angle panoramas can even look like regular images, except they are stitched from several photographs and therefore would have more resolution.
2. 180 degree panoramas – panoramas that cover 180 degrees from left to right. These types of panoramas look very wide, covering a large area.
3. 360 degree panoramas – panoramas that cover up to 360 degrees. These panoramas look extremely wide and they cover the whole scene in a single, super wide image.
4. Spherical panoramas – also known as "planets". These are 360 degree panoramas that are converted to a square spherical image using a special post-processing technique.

Camera Equipment Required for Panorama Photography

1. Digital Camera – Any DSLR or Mirrorless camera. It does not matter whether it's a full frame or crop sensor camera.
2. Lens – You can shoot panorama using Fish eye lens, but you will get Distortion and convergence problem. See the images Fig. 1 and Fig. 2:

Both are captured using Tokina 10 – 16mm Fish eye lens. Fig. 1 is a view of Pangong lake and another Fig. 2 is a view of Seol, South Korea.

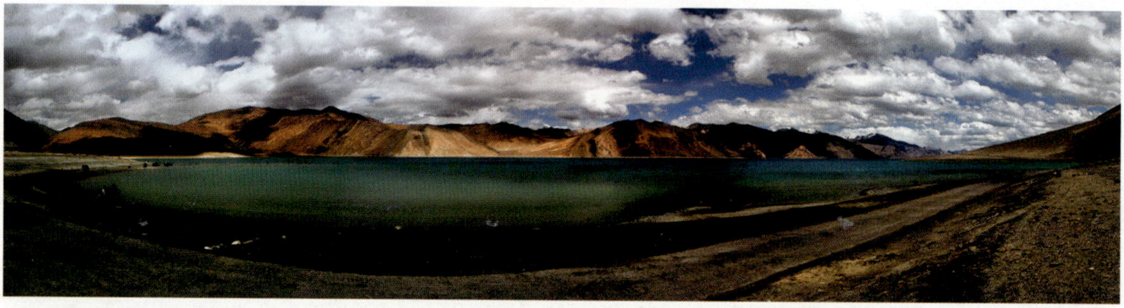

Fig. 1

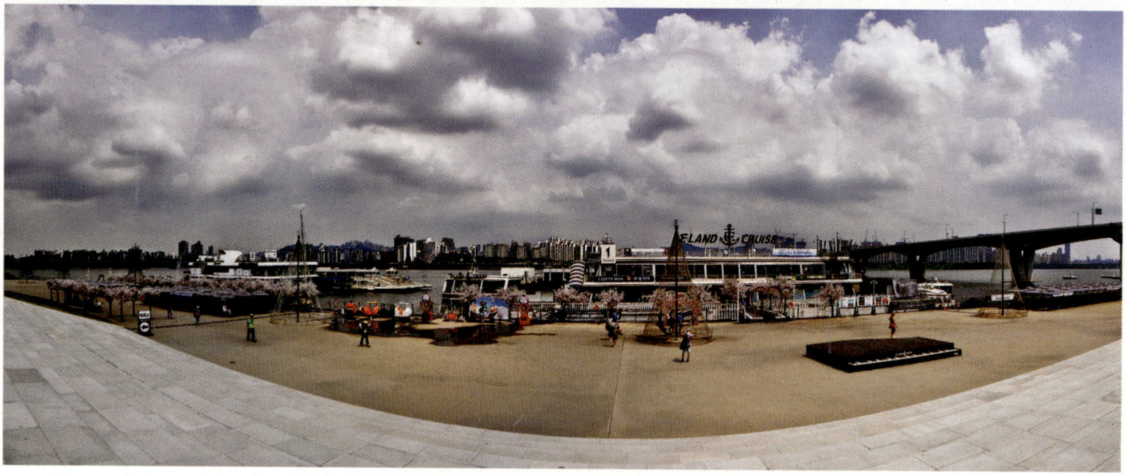

Fig. 2

3. I find zoom lenses to be the most useful for panoramic photography. You can certainly photograph panoramas with fixed/prime lenses, but being able to zoom in and out will give you more options and versatility, especially in difficult conditions where your movements are limited. If you have a DSLR, any wide zoom lens such as Nikon 18-55mm, or Nikon 18-200mm should work perfectly fine. I personally use the Nikon 50mm f/1.4 or normal zoom lens 28-300mm depending upon the distance of the scene from the camera for most of my panoramas.

4. Lens Filters – I recommend taking filters off your lens while shooting panoramas. It is OK to keep a UV filter on. Definitely remove a circular polarizer if you have one mounted on your lens, because it will screw up your sky.

5. Tripod – a tripod is optional, but highly recommended for best results. Any sturdy tripod should work, but make sure that the head is flexible enough for you to be able to pan from left to right with ease. I use Manfroto 190x tripod.

6. Cable Release/wireless trigger – optional, but recommended for capturing shake-free images.

7. Panoramic Setup – For serious and profession photographers use of Pano head is recommended.

Camera Settings

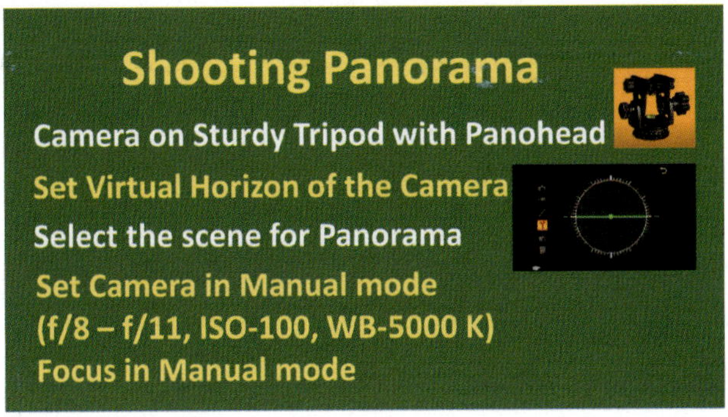

Fig. 3

Shoot in "Manual" mode

Set your lens to Manual Focus

ISO – Don't use "Auto ISO", otherwise the camera could change the exposure between shots if the lighting changes, this would cause unwanted variations in the images

Make sure that "Auto ISO" is turned off and set your ISO to the camera base ISO (either 100 or 200).

Aperture and Shutter Speed – you should set your aperture to at least f/8, preferably f/1. Once you set the right aperture, set your shutter speed based on the meter reading.

Metering – Matrix or evaluative metering is preferred.

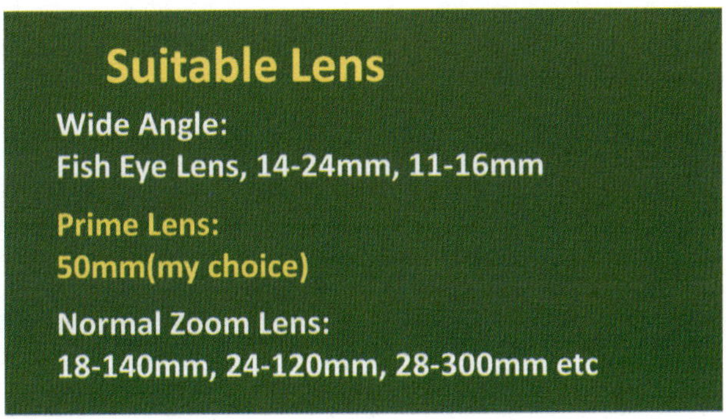

Fig. 4

Shoot in RAW – I always recommend shooting in RAW for best results.

White Balance – set your White Balance to "Auto" when shooting in RAW and change later, if necessary.

Shooting Technique

Set up camera on tripod in a such a way that it can rotate freely on the axis. Watch your scene carefully and decide how much part of the scene you want to cover. Preferably keep camera in vertical orientation.

Focus in the middle of the frame. Then rotate your camera in extreme left of the scene. Take a shot.

Overlap 50% of the frame between first and second frame (See Fig. 5, 6 & 7). Take the second frame and continue till you click the last frame of the scene.

For example I decided to shoot panorama of a scene in Fig. 19 and I captured six frames as shown in Fig. 8 to 13.

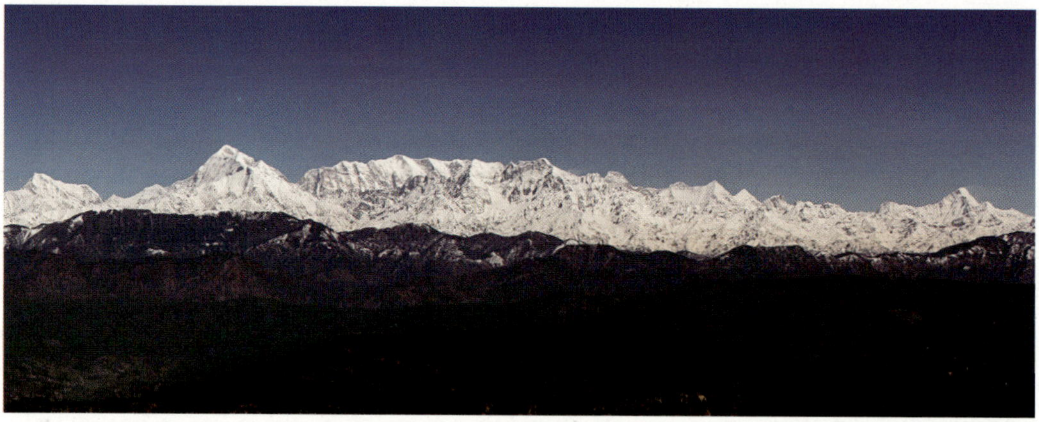

Fig. 19

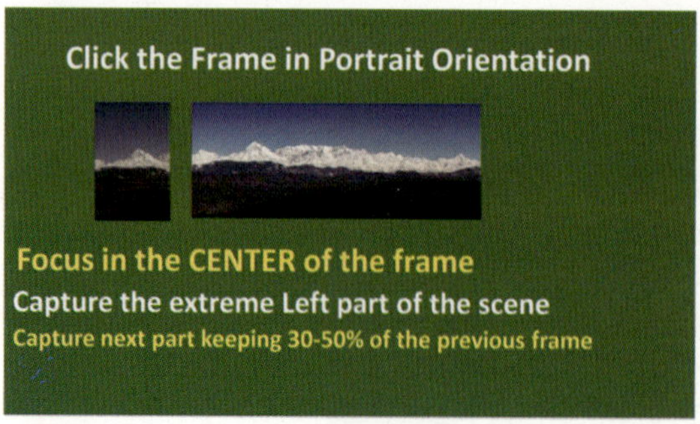

Fig. 5

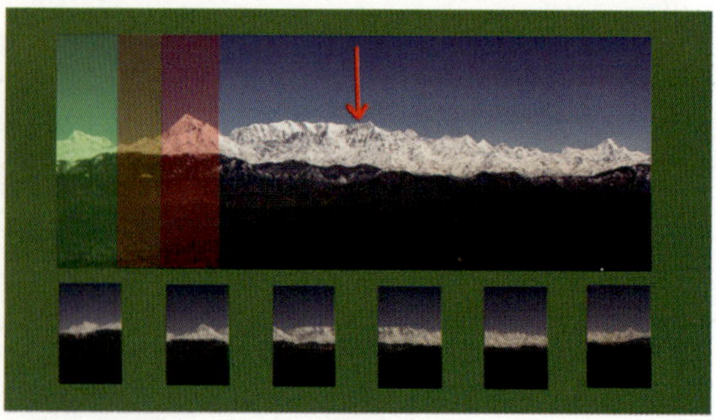

Fig. 6

Overlap your shots by at least 30%

Overlap each image by at least **30%** if you are shooting in landscape orientation
and up to **50%** if shooting in portrait.

By overlapping you will have duplicates of parts of your scene, this will allow the software to stitch the images together better and adjust for the perspective distortion too.

Fig. 7

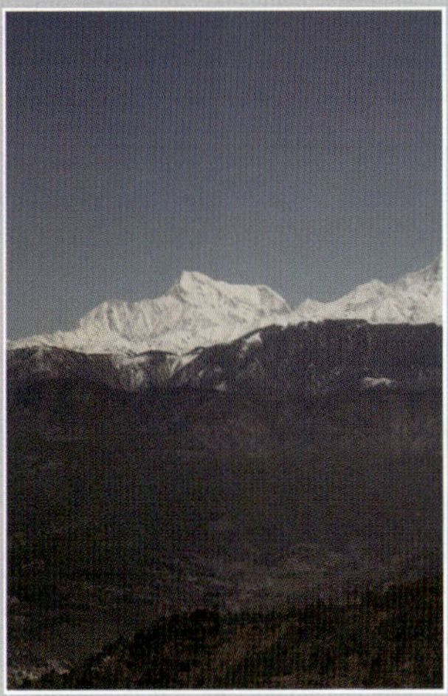

Fig. 8

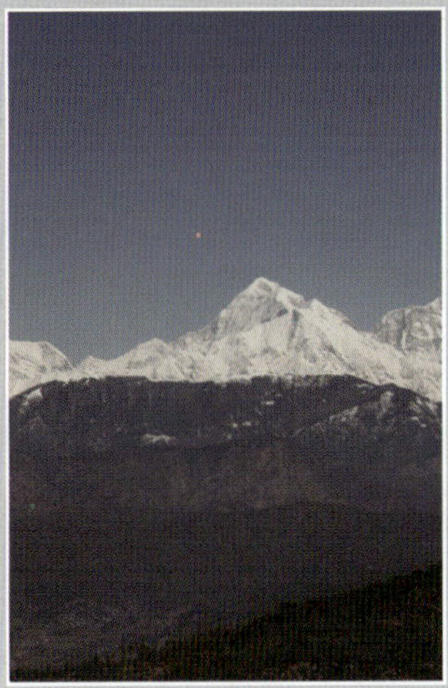

Fig. 9

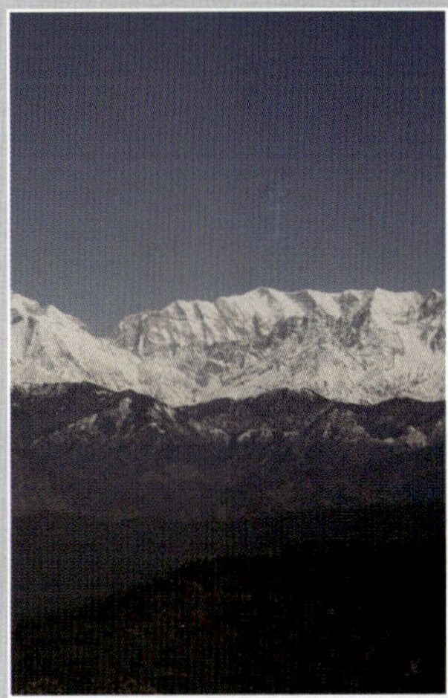

Fig. 10

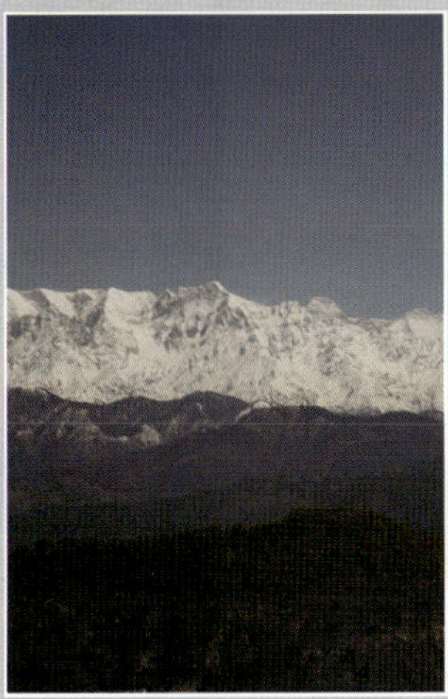

Fig. 11

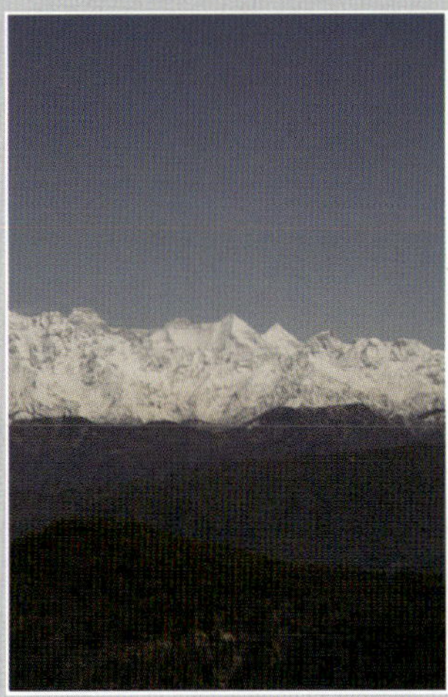

Fig. 12

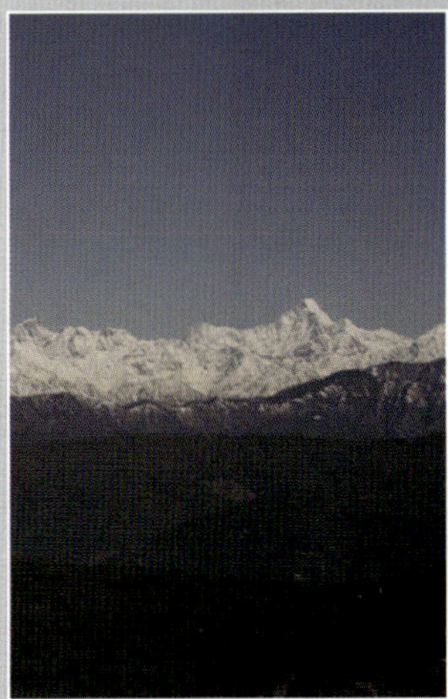

Fig. 13

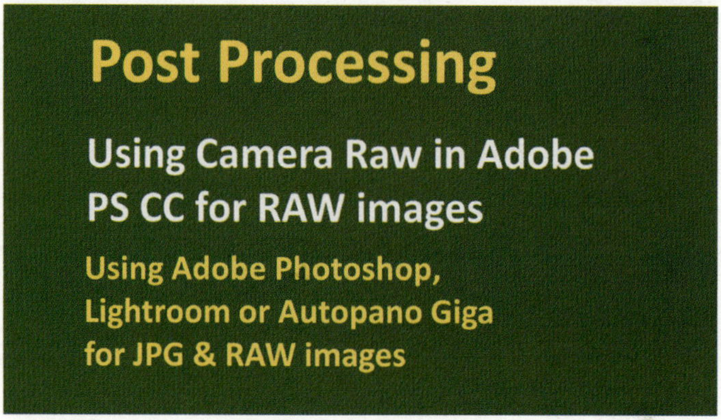

Fig. 14

4.1. Using Adobe Photoshop

Stitching panoramas in Photoshop is super easy. In Photoshop: simply open up Photoshop and then go to "File" - "Automate" - "Photomerge". A dialog box will come up that looks as shown in Fig. 15

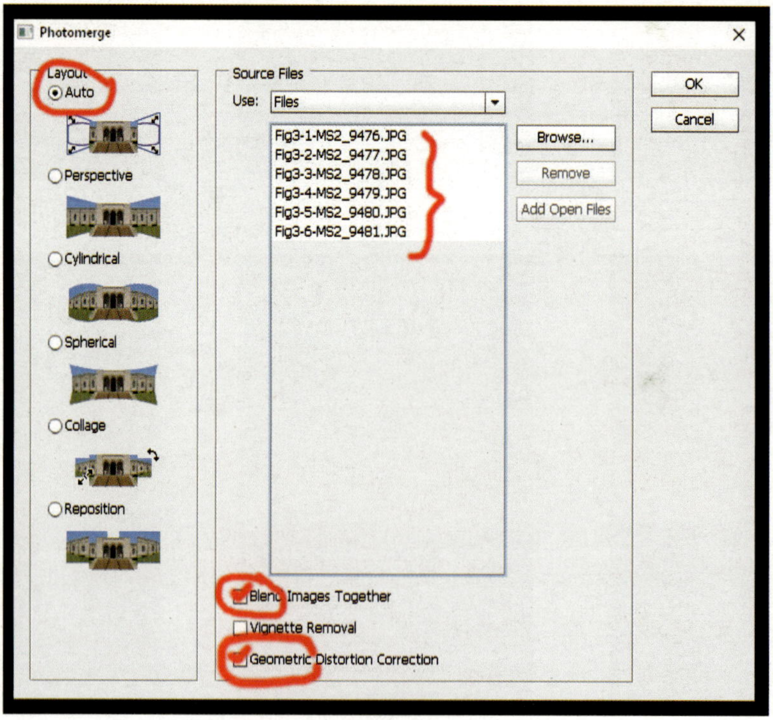

Fig. 15

Simply click "Browse" and select the images to be merged into a panorama. Make sure that "Blend Images Together" and "Geometric Distortion Correction" are checked, then click OK. This will start the stitching process, which can sometimes take a long time, depending on the number of images and their size. Once the process is completed, all you have to do is crop the image and you are all set!

The Process I Use

If you shoot in RAW, the best method of post processing is using advanced feature of Adobe Photoshop CC. I will describe this process in detail.

1. Select all the RAW images. Drag and drop in PhotoshopCC.
2. From the top left pull down menu, click "Select All". Further click "Merge to Panorama". Stitching of images will start and you will get next window as shown in Fig. 16.

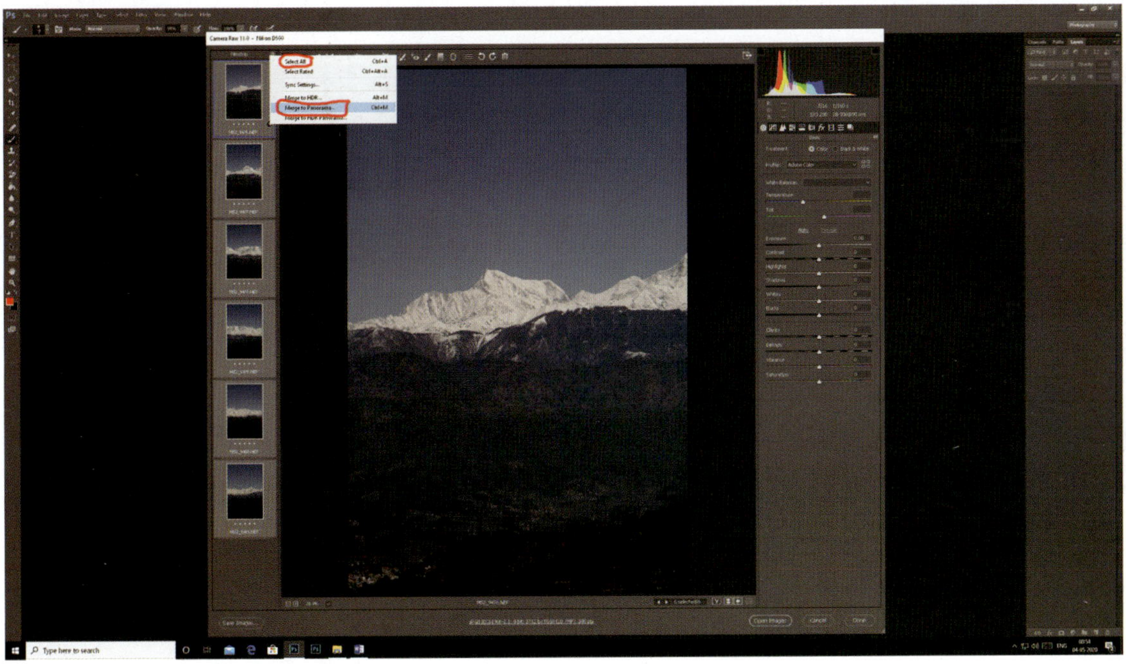

Fig. 16

3. In Projection, try all three options and judge yourself. But "Spherical" option is better. You can tweak "Boundry Wrap" to correct the prospective of your stitched image.
4. In image work flow options tick mark both : "Apply Auto Tone and Colour Adjustments" and "Auto Crop" The software will perform the process fast and accurate.

Finally you click "Merge" and save the Processed Panorama image like shown in Fig. 17 & 18. You will get final panorama as shown in Fig. 19.

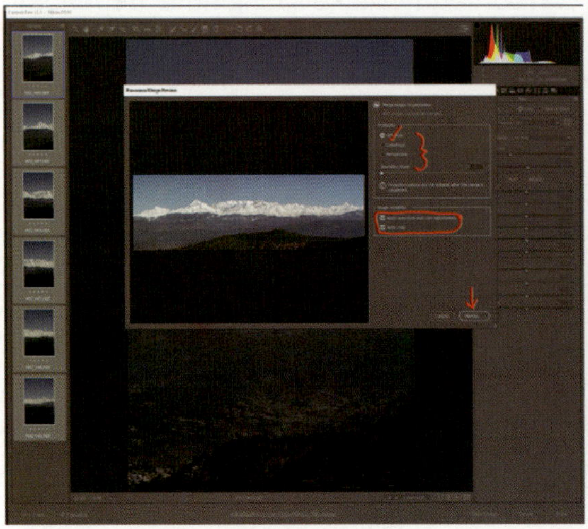

Fig. 17

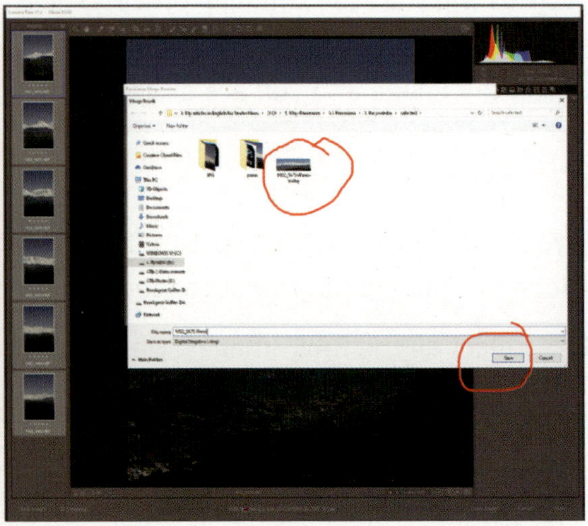

Fig. 18

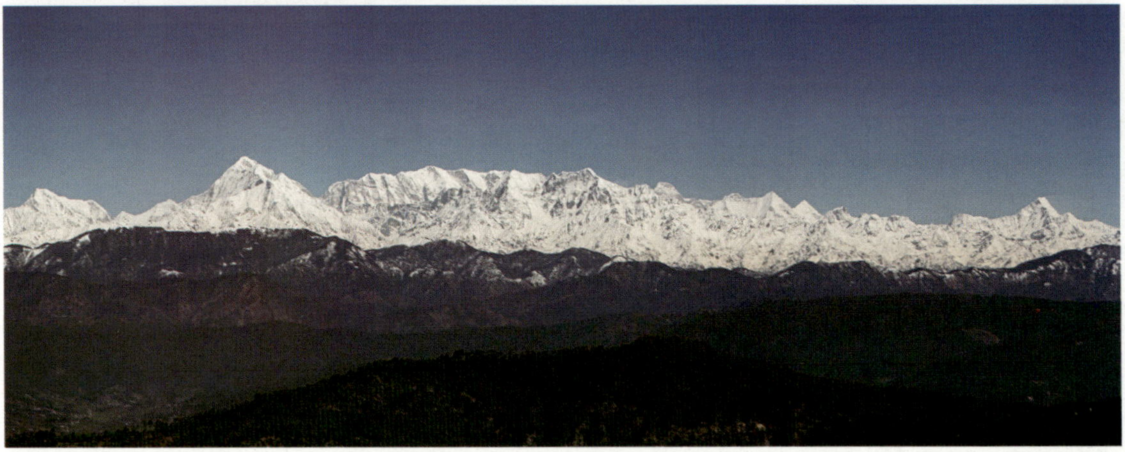

Fig. 19 Final Panorama

Watch youtube tutorial on this topic:

Episode-4-Through The Lens: Panorama Photography - YouTube

10. Effect of Focal Length

The lens plays a vital role in the creation of a beautiful portrait. There's not necessarily a right or wrong lens to use, but rather the most appropriate for the subject and location.

One of the interesting facts I remember from my photography workshops was that "wide-angle lenses are not meant for portraits". Of course, you can always experiment and photograph people with wider focal lengths, but the truth is – it does make them seem a bit distorted in the photos.

Lenses with smaller focal lengths distort the face so it looks thinner, while those over 50mm make it more realistic and wider.

You might already know that an 85mm lens is just about the ideal focal length for shooting portraits—if you're using a full-frame camera. The 105mm is also a good focal length to shoot portraits with, as is the 135mm. The longer the focal length, the more compressed and therefore portraits look more realistic. On the other hand, the shorter the focal length the portrait gets more distorted.

To make the comparison, I shot all the images in an outdoor environment. An Octa softbox used to fill the shadow on the model.

Camera was set in manual mode with the measured exposure of the background at f/8, S-1/250s, ISO-125.

For every change in focal length I tried to maintain the same frame by moving near or farther from the subject.

I used full frame DSLR Nikon D800E with Nikkor 16-35mm for content shoot at 16mm, 24mm n 35mm. Used Nikkor 50mm, f/1.4 for focal length 50mm. Used Nikkor 70-200mm, f/2.8 for focal length 85mm, 105mm, 135mm n 200mm.

All the images are straight from the camera without editing and cropping.

Here are the results:

Close up Portraits

Observe the change in face distortion compared to REAL FACE by changing focal length. Also observe the change in Depth of Field. The wider the focal length the more Depth of Field. Third change to be observed is the compression ratio (distance between the background and the subject). The higher the focal length, more compression.

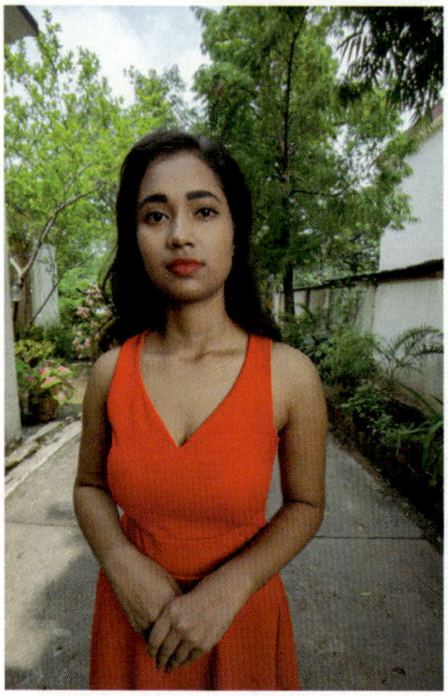

Fig. 1 16mm

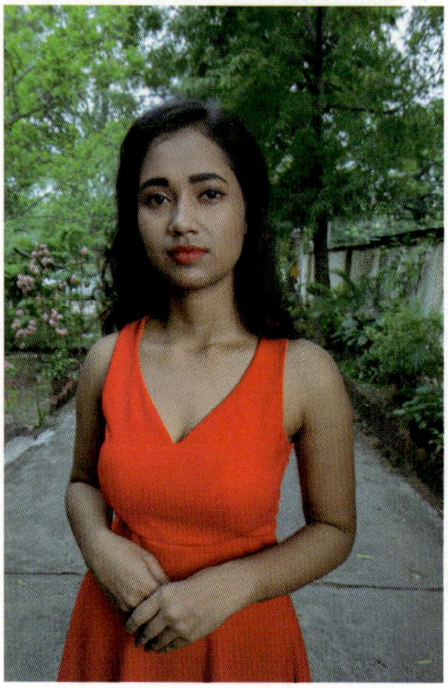

Fig. 2 24mm

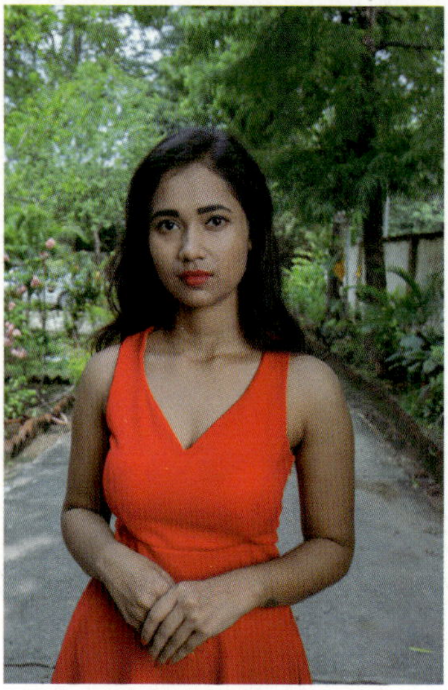

Fig. 3 35mm

16mm

As you can see in Fig. 1 the distortion speaks for itself. This is definitely not a proper focal length for portrait photographers.

24mm

See the effect in Fig. 2 with 24mm. Still not quiet acceptable, but perfect.

35mm

Things are looking a little better now with 35mm in Fig. 3. But still not the best portrait.

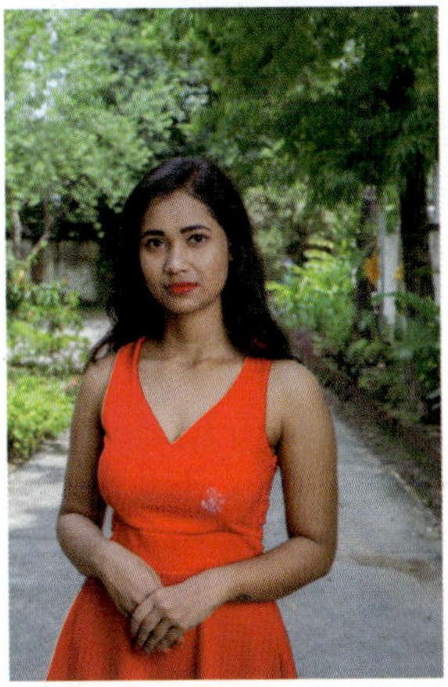
Fig. 4 50mm

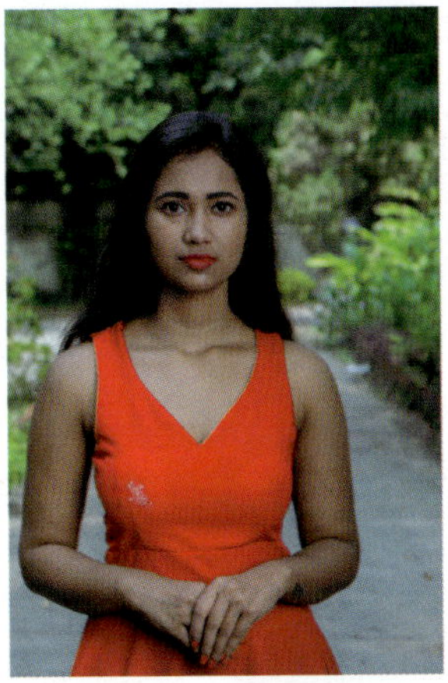
Fig. 5 85mm

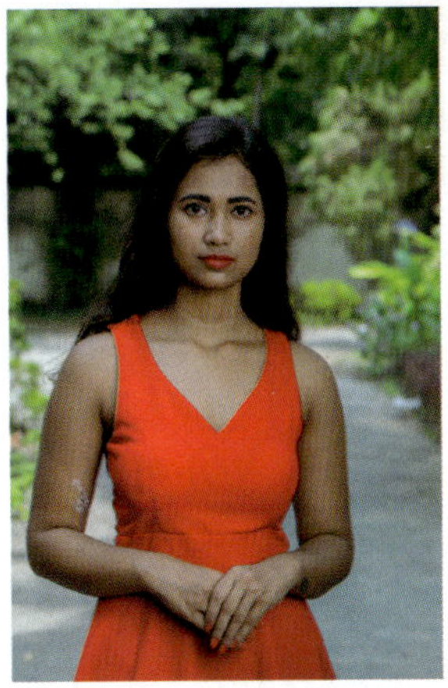
Fig. 6 105mm

50mm

Yes! Finally, with the 50mm prime we start looking at realistic results

85mm

Anything longer than 50mm makes things look even better. The 85mm, for example, produces pretty flattering results.

105mm

Anything above 85mm is considered as a telephoto lens. These lenses essentially compress a subject rather than distort, as wide angle (and ultra-wide angle) lenses tend to do. So, when you move from 85mm to 105mm and beyond, the image gets really compressed.

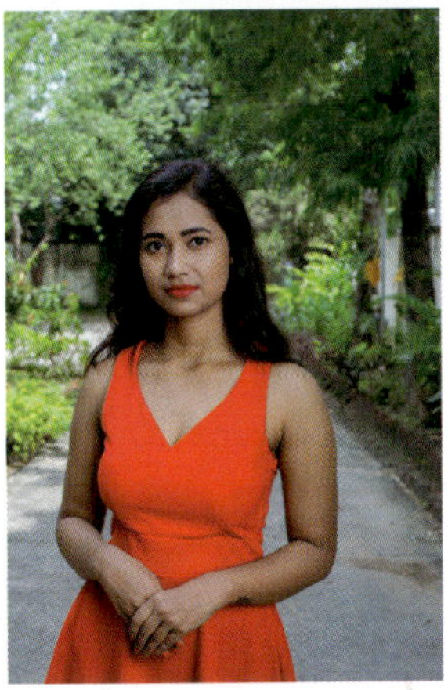
Fig. 7 135mm

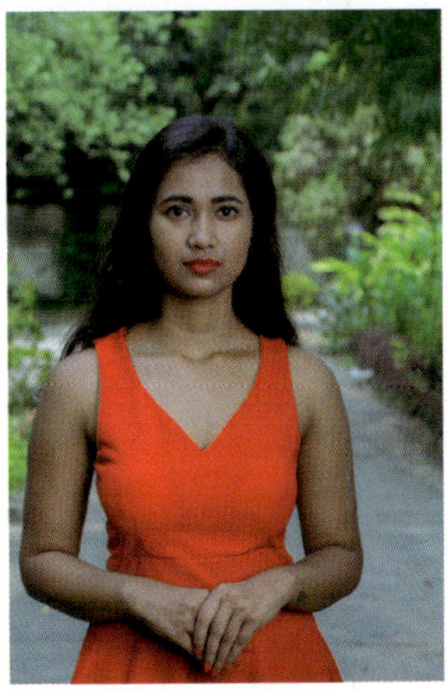
Fig. 8 200mm

Notice there isn't much of a difference between the results at 135mm and 200mm.

Some photographers prefer the 100mm to 200mm focal length range, again for the compression, which is especially important when photographing subjects with larger noses.

It is safe to say that anything from 85mm and beyond is a great lens for shooting portraits.

That's the reason 70-200mm lens is most preferred by professional portrait and fashion photographers.

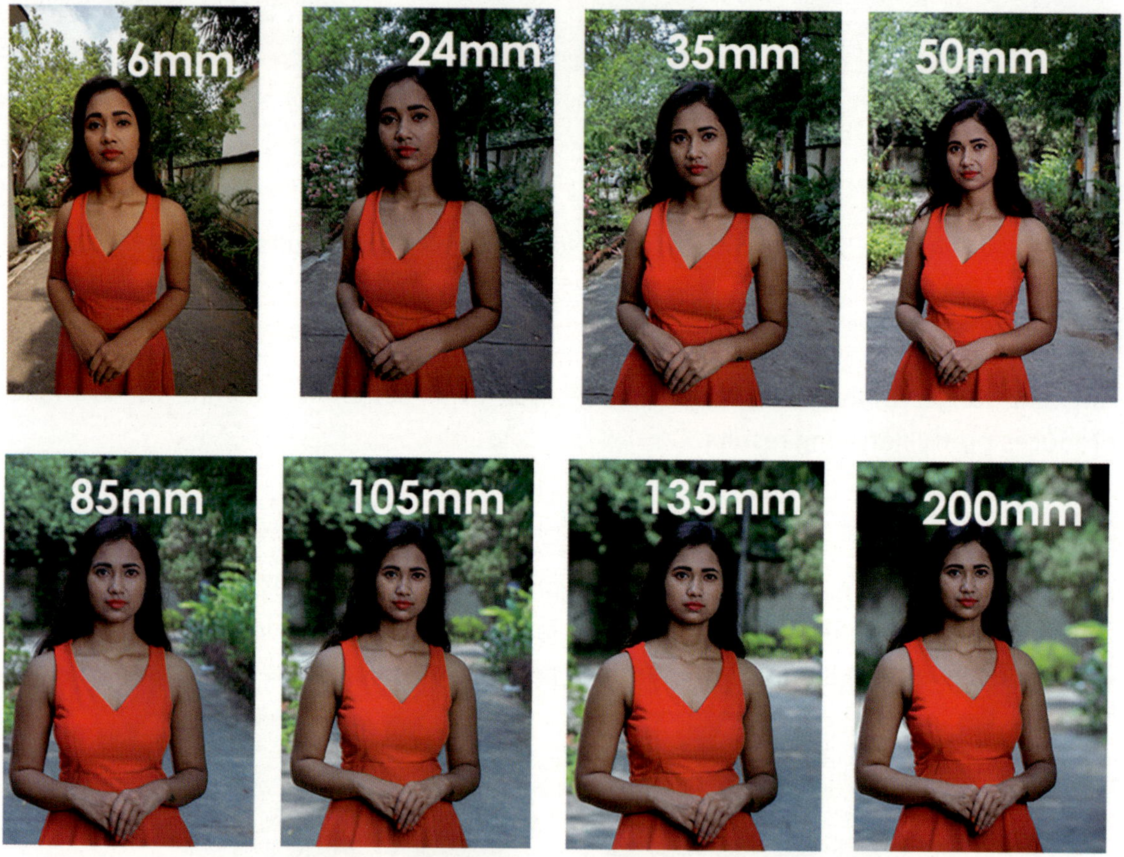

Fig. 8A

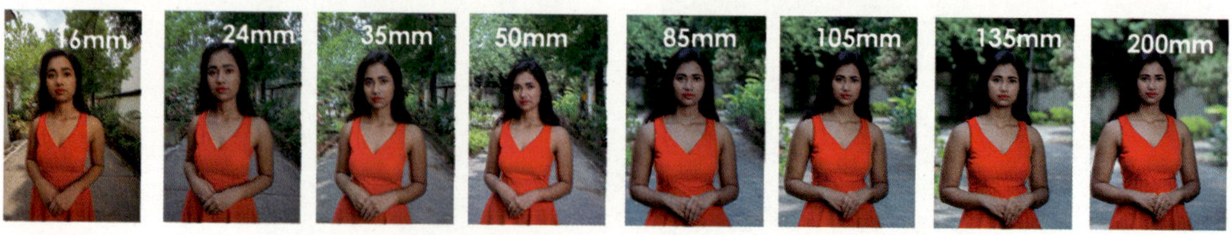

Fig. 8B

Full Length Portrait

Observe the change in distortion by changing focal length. The effect of Depth of field and compression is more prominently visible in case of full length portraits.

Now you can observe the change in Depth of Field much better. The wider the focal length the larger Depth of Field. Third change to be observed more prominently is the compression ratio (distance between the background and the subject). The higher the focal length, more compression.

Here the Depth of field starts getting Shallow and the compression is normal.

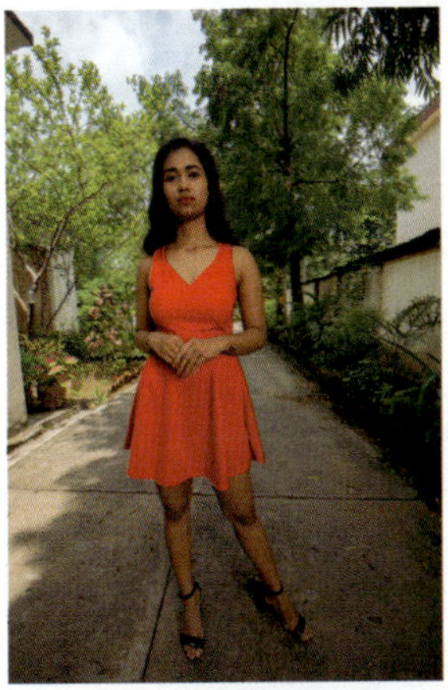

Fig. 9 16mm

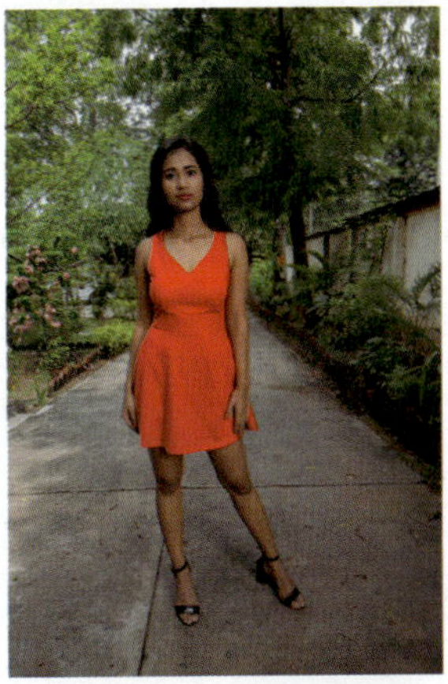

Fig. 10 24mm

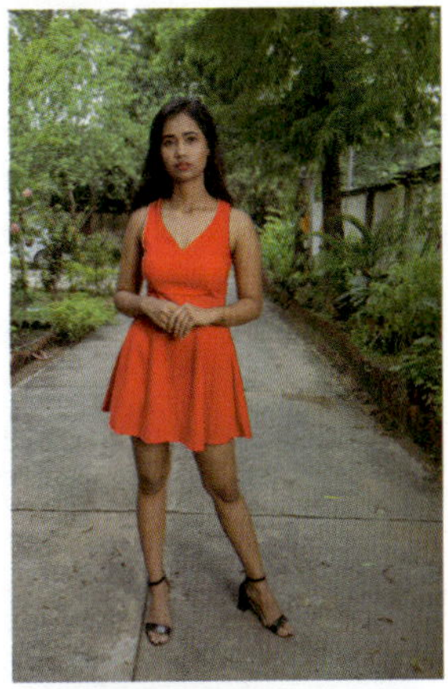

Fig. 11 35mm

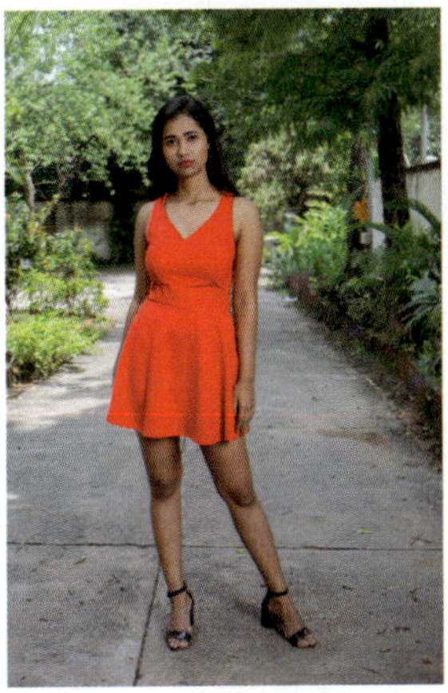

Fig. 12 50mm

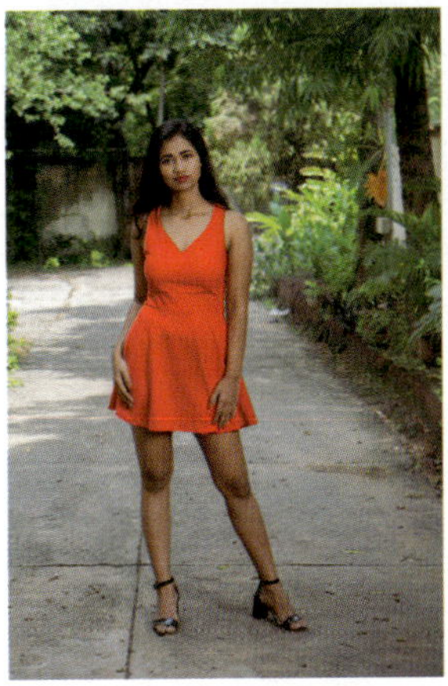

Fig. 13 85mm

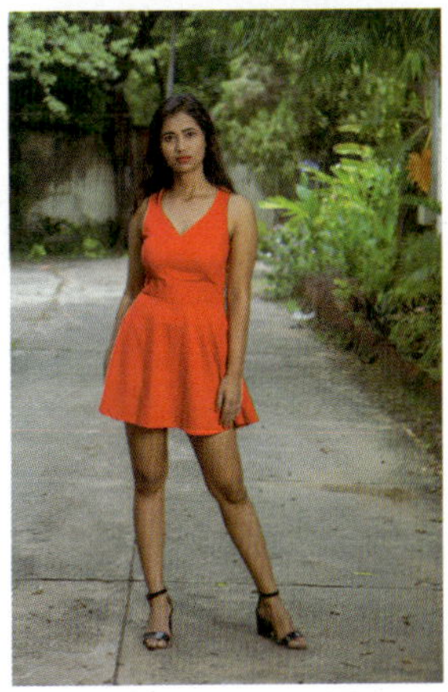

Fig. 14 105mm

50mm focal length Looks like more natural and acceptable portrait, as practically no distortion. The Depth of field as well as compression is normal.

From 85mm, the compression starts getting visible and Depth of field becoming shallow.

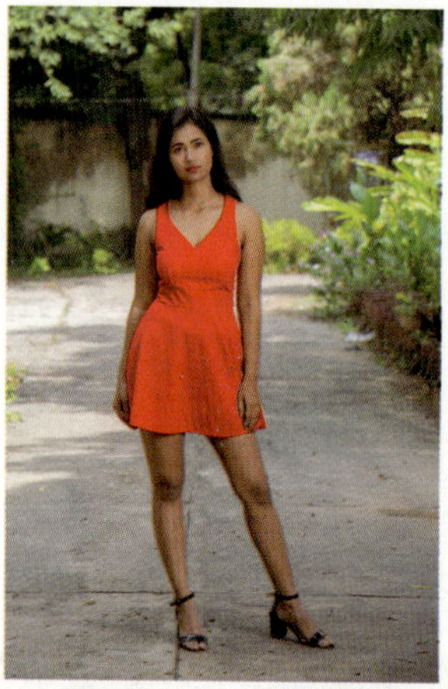

Fig. 15 135mm

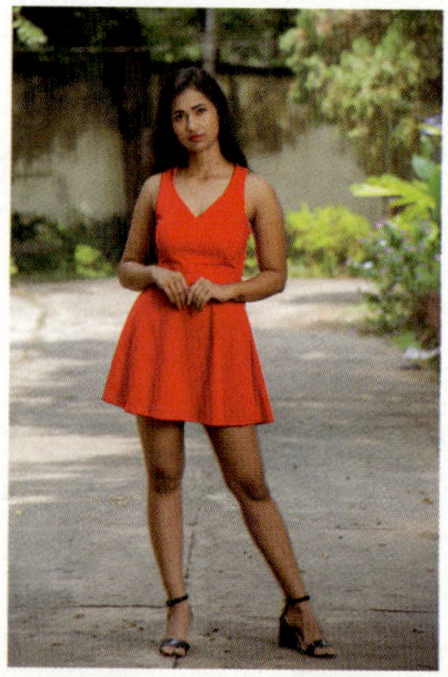

Fig. 16 200mm

Here the Depth of field is shallow with high compression. The focal length 135mm and above looks more attractive and suitable for portraits with shallow Depth of field .

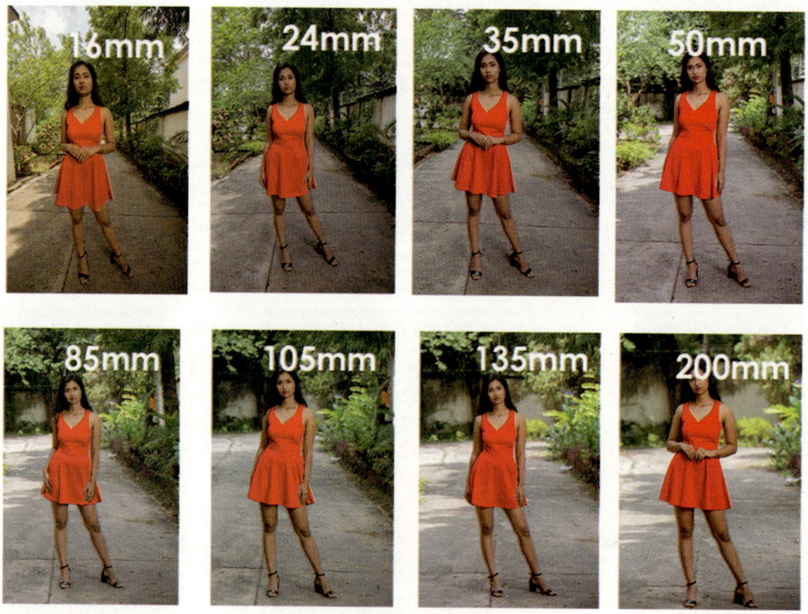

Fig. 17

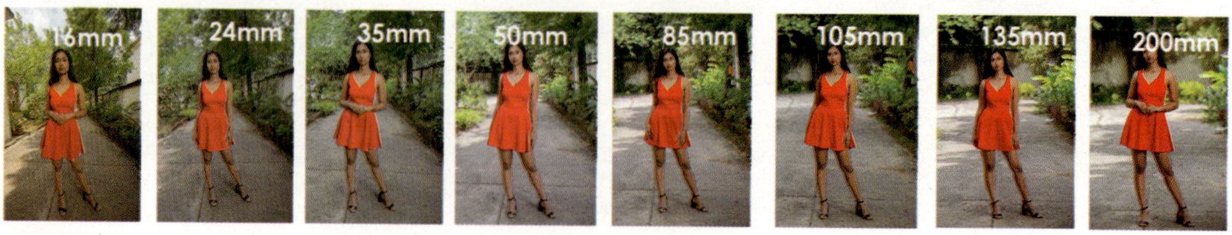

Fig. 18

Wider angle lenses (shorter focal length) require that the portrait be taken from closer (for an equivalent field size), and the resulting perspective distortion yields a relatively larger nose and smaller ears, which is considered unflattering. Wide-angle lenses – or even fisheye lenses – may be used for artistic effect, especially to produce a distorted image. Conversely, longer focal lengths yield greater flattening because they are used from further away. This makes communication difficult and reduces rapport. They may be used, however, particularly in fashion photography, longer focal lengths require a loudspeaker or walkie-talkie to communicate with the model or assistants.

Conclusion: Any focal length 50mm and above is good for portrait whether it is close up or full length. But still wider focal lengths from 10mm to 35mm are magical for fashion portraits if used creatively.

I will give you few examples of creative use of wide angle and fish eye lenses.

Images captured with Tokina 10-17mm Fish eye lens:

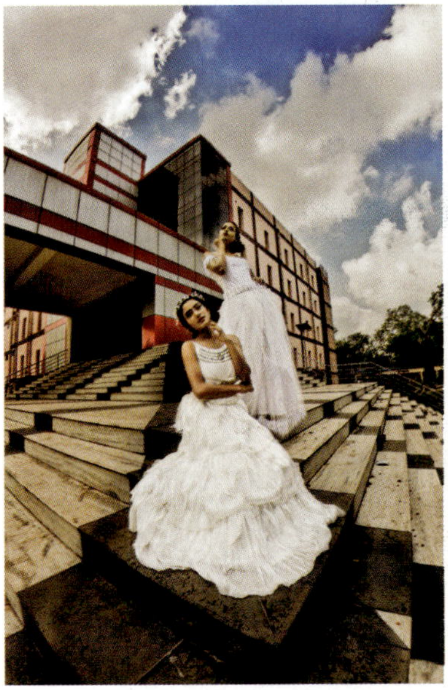

Fig. 19

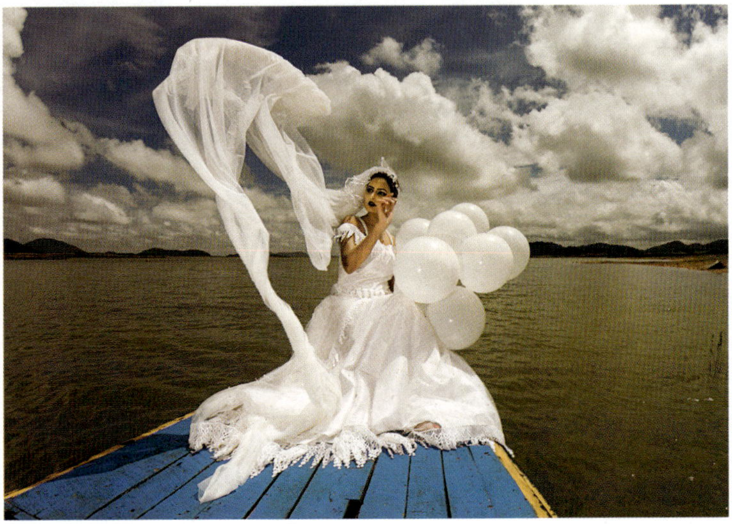

Fig. 20

Finally it's your vision to use lens with any focal length creatively.

Images captured with Nikkor 16-35mm Wide Angle lens:

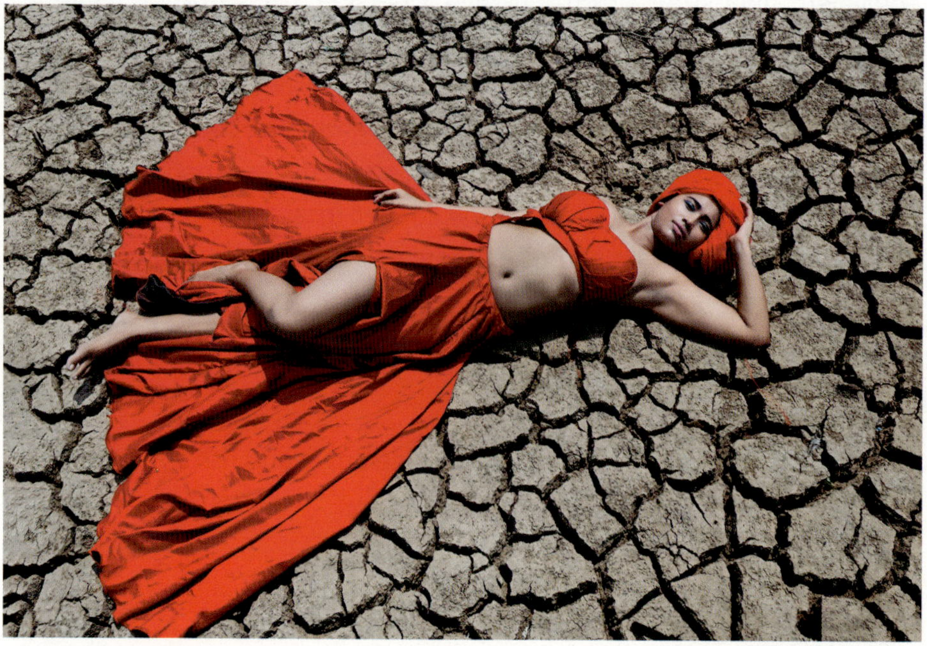

Fig. 21

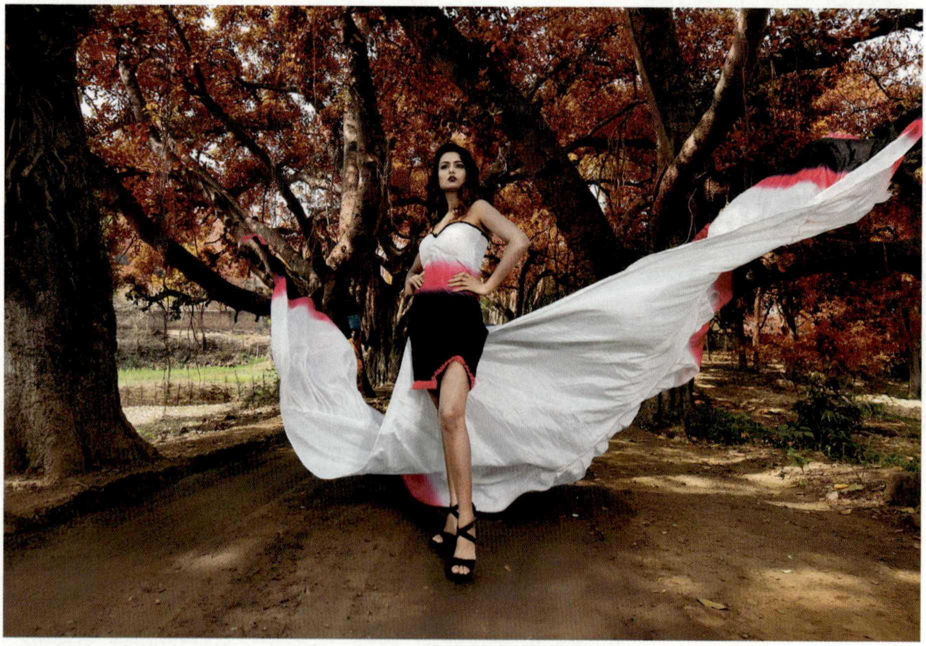

Fig. 22

You can feel the extent of creativity which can be obtained by using wide angle lens.

Images captured with Tokina 10-17mm Fish eye lens:

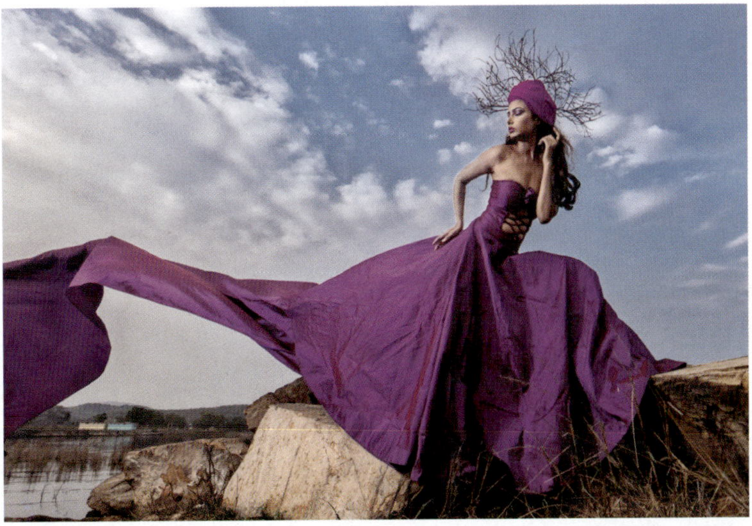

Fig. 23

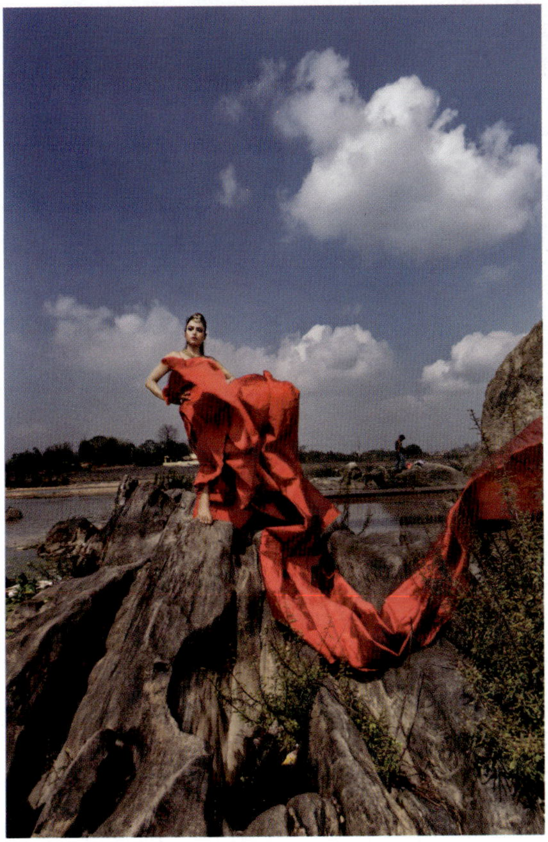

Fig. 24

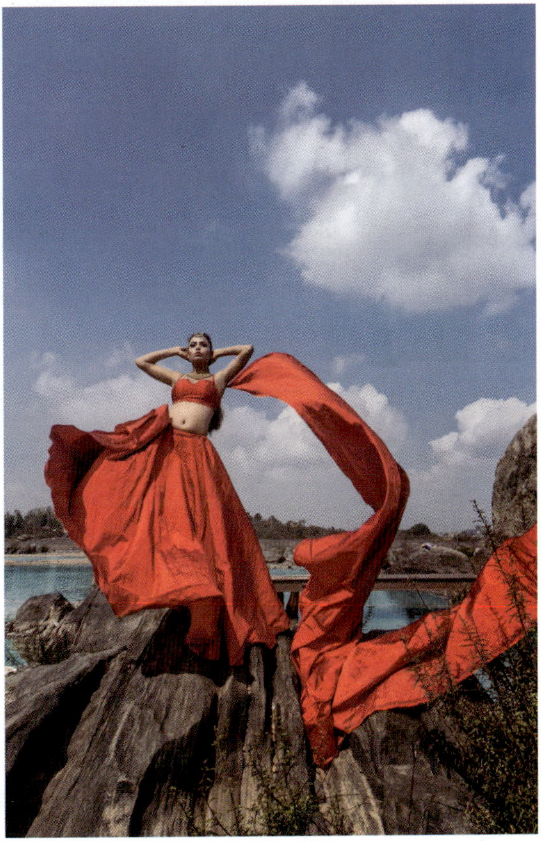

Fig. 25

Images captured with Tokina 10-17mm Fish eye lens:

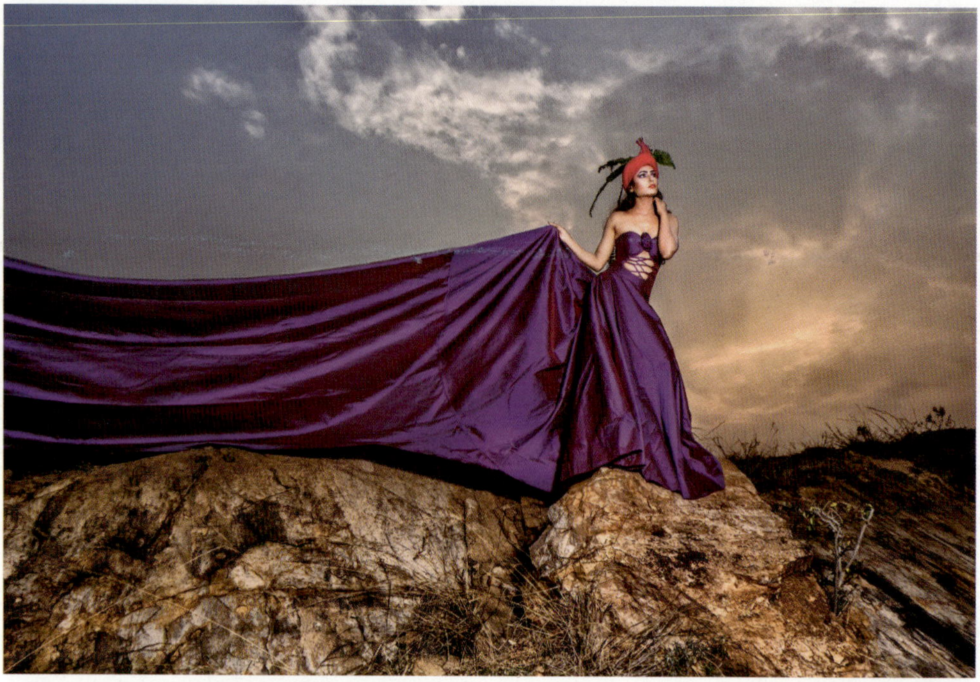

Fig. 26

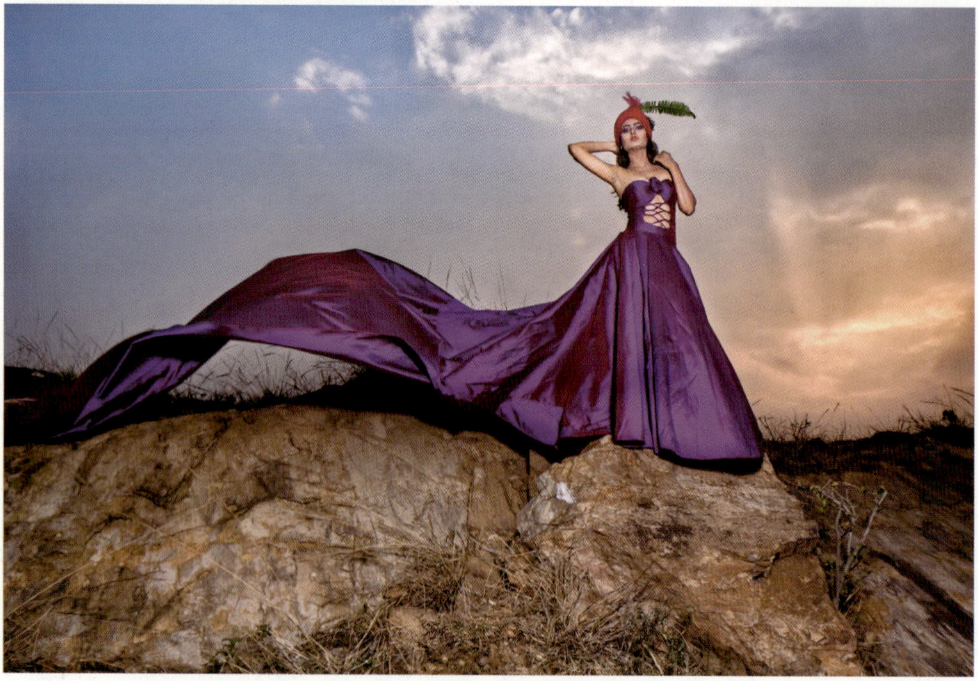

Fig. 27

Images captured with Tokina 10-17mm Fish eye lens:

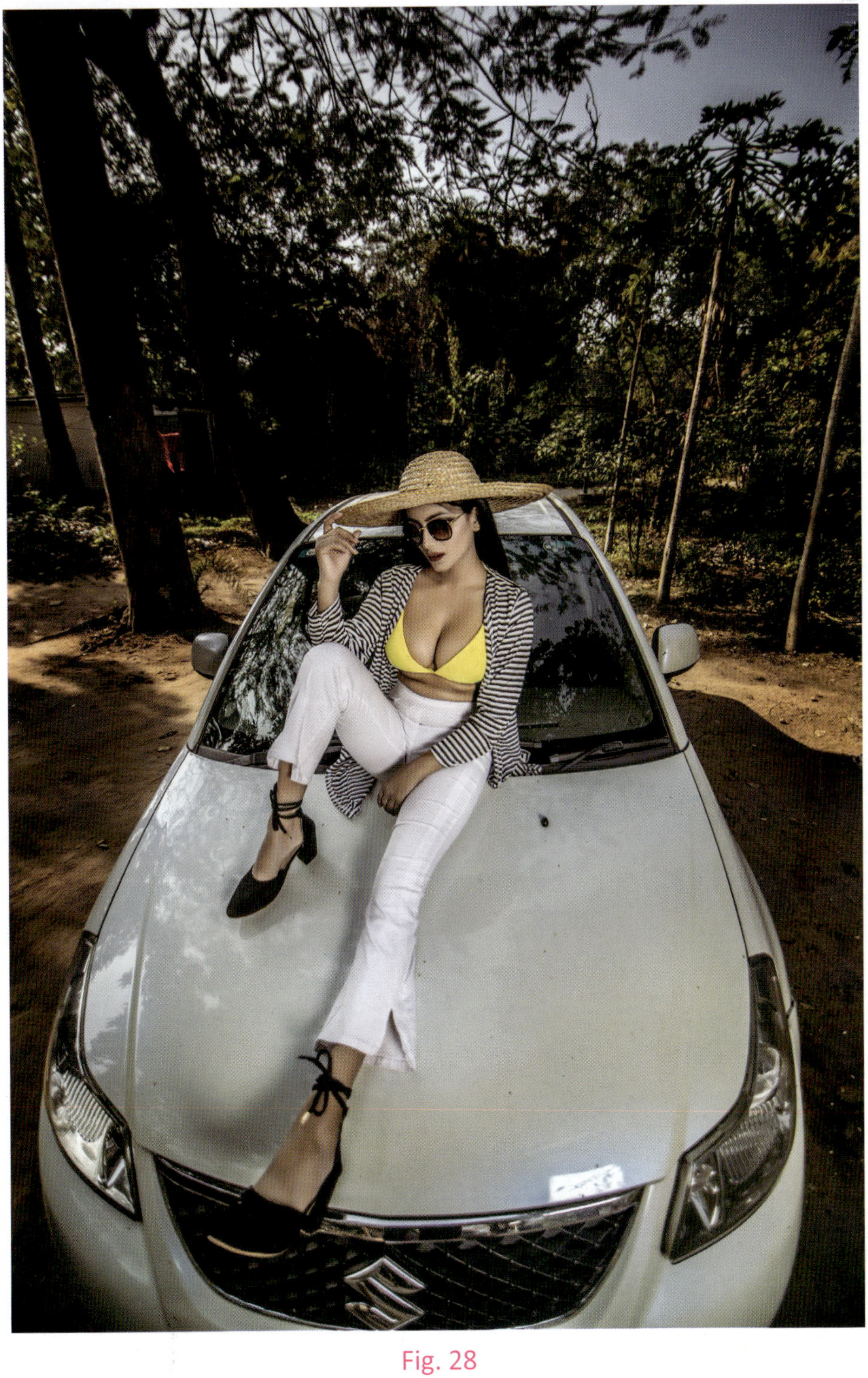

Fig. 28

Images captured with Tokina 10-17mm Fish eye lens:

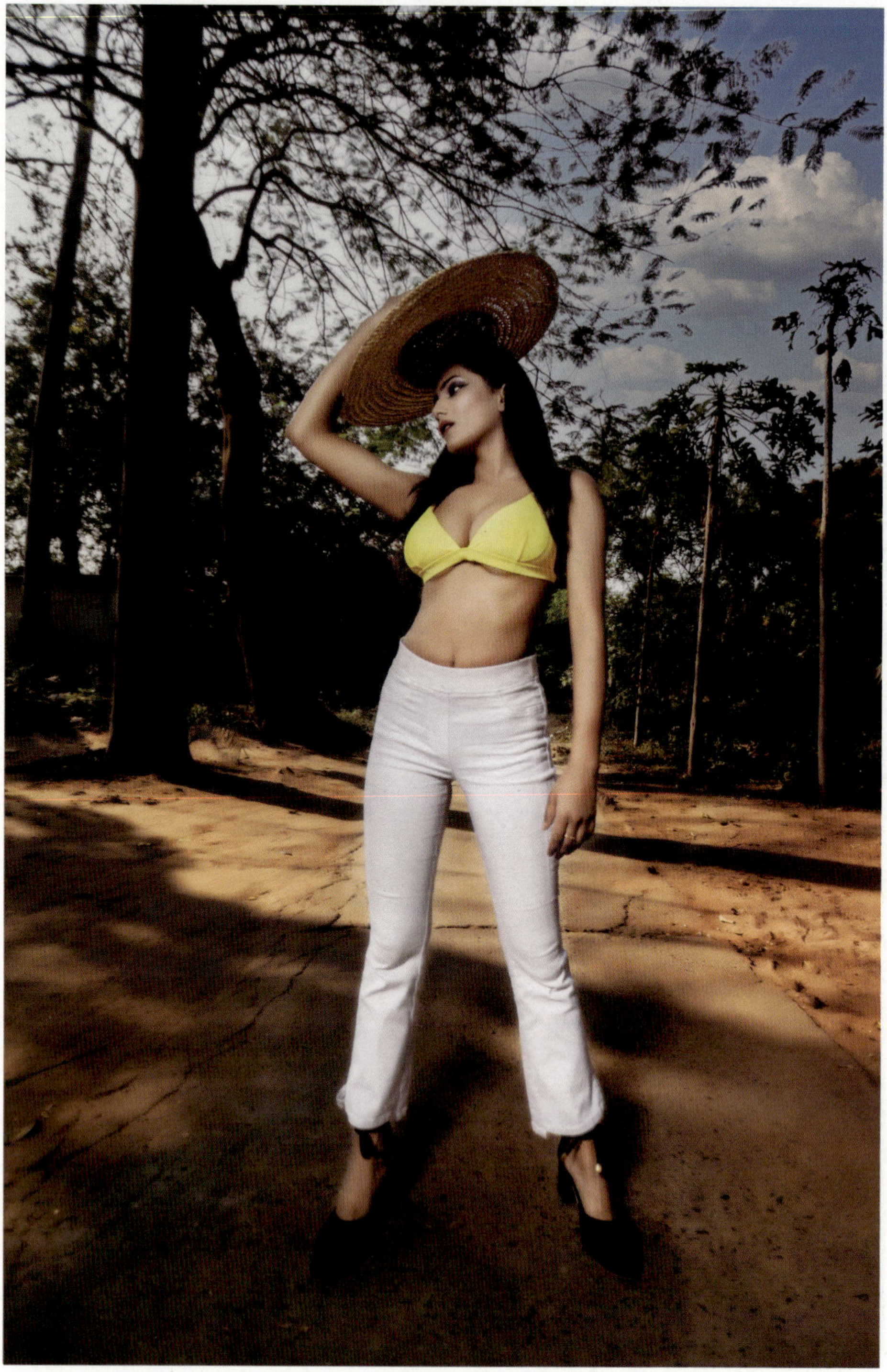

Fig. 29

Images captured with Tokina 10-17mm Fish eye lens:

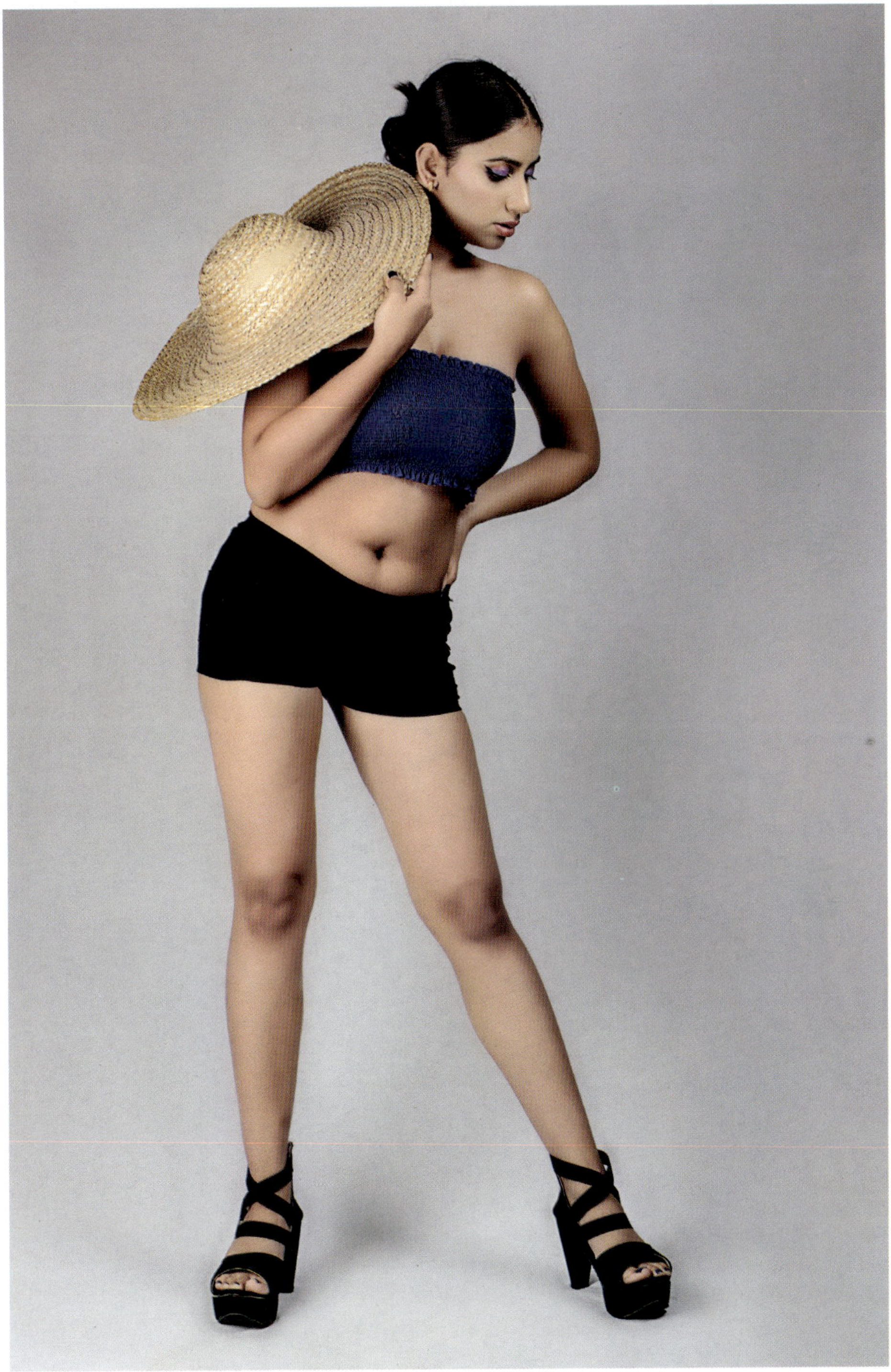

Fig. 30

Images captured with Tokina 10-17mm Fish eye lens:

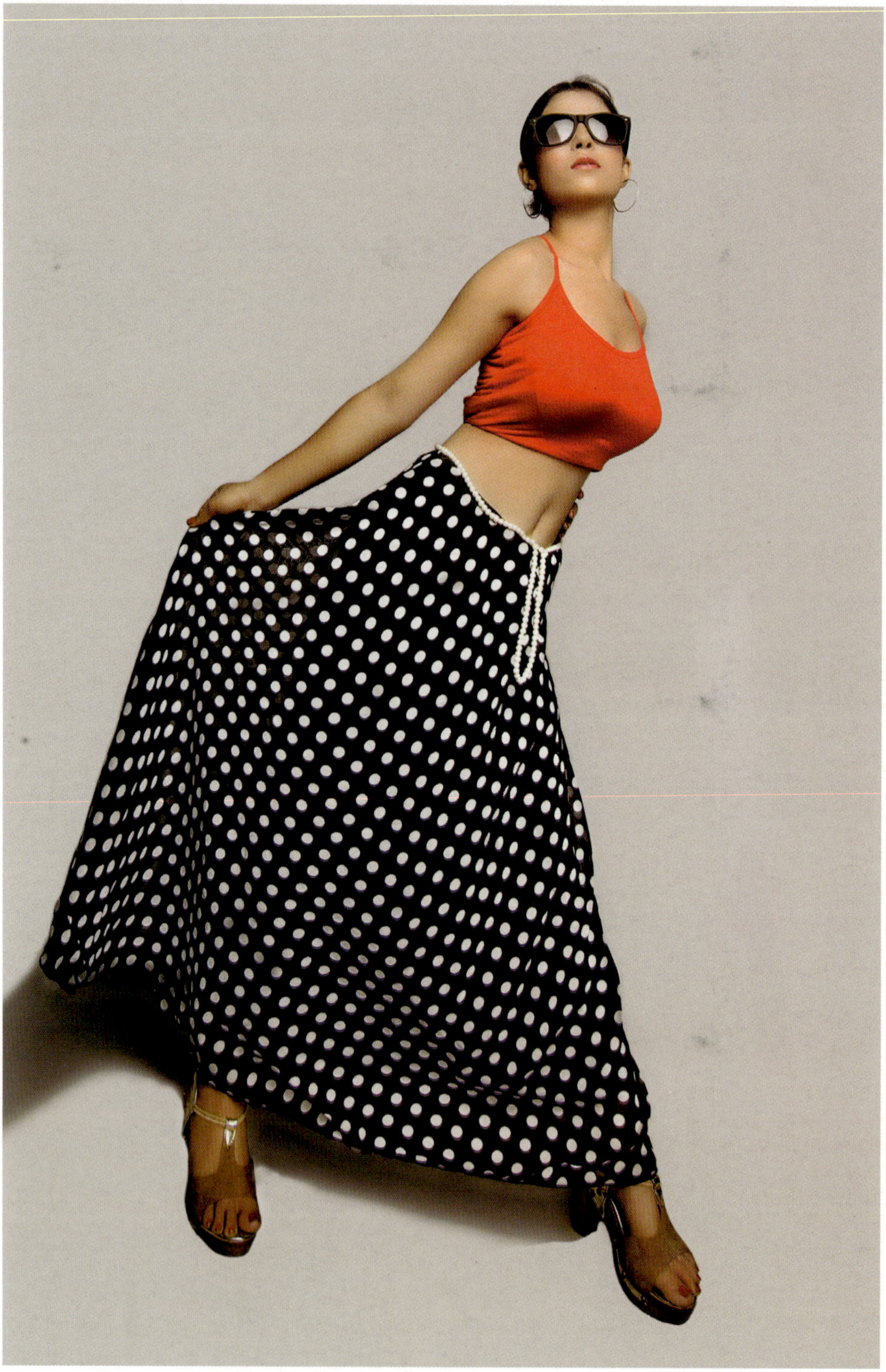

Fig. 31

Images captured with Tokina 10-17mm Fish eye lens:

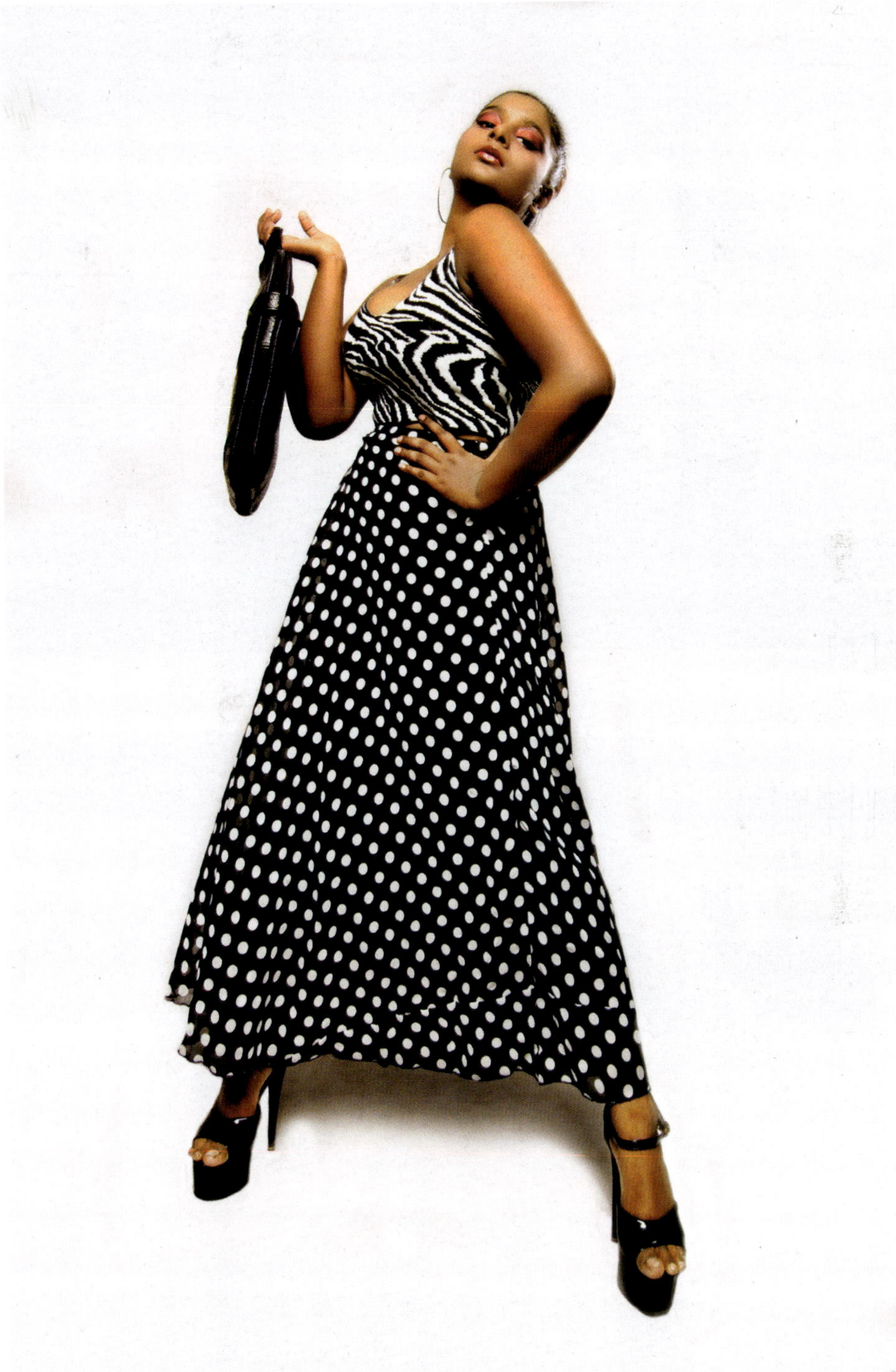

Fig. 32

Images captured with Tokina 10-17mm Fish eye lens:

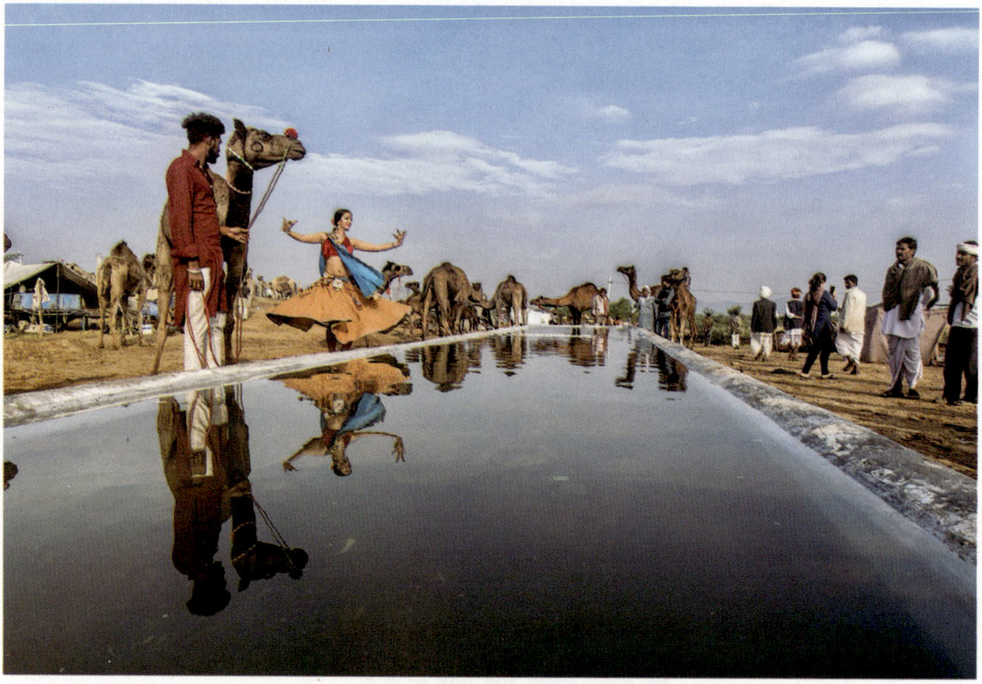

Fig. 33

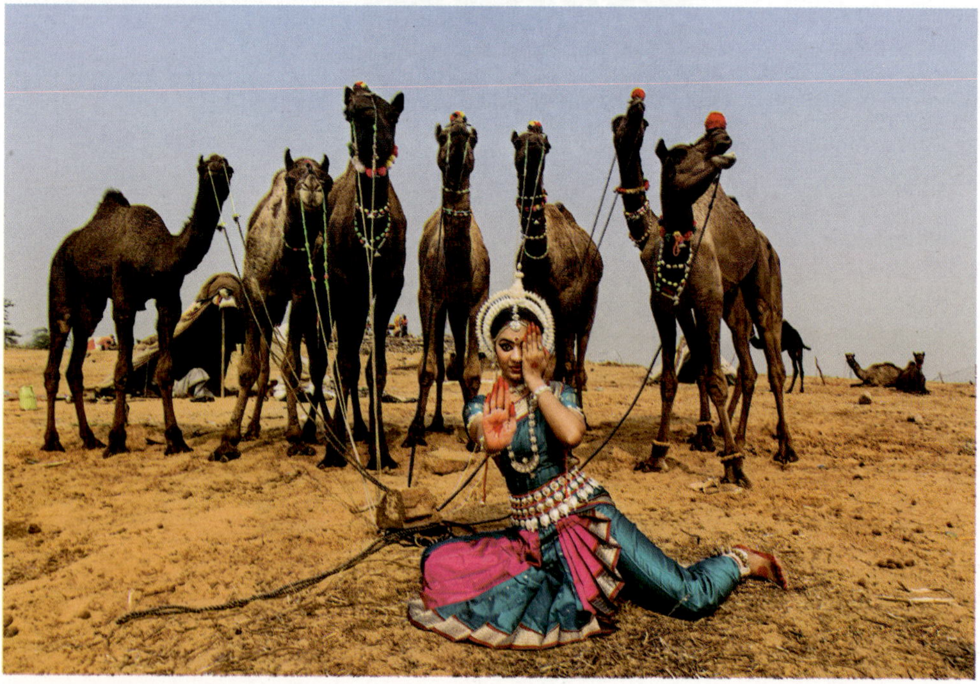

Fig. 34

11. Creative Fashion Photography

Normally we shoot fashion in conventional style with repeated concepts. To make one self recognised as a different fashion photographer, we must be CREATIVE in Vision, shooting techniques and presentation. Here are a few creative concept in Fashion Photography, which I experimented during 2017-18:

Under Water Fashion Shoot

Such fashion photography is very challenging and interesting too. We need to select the camera housing first which should be true waterproof.

Waterproof Camera Housing

1. The most reliable camera housing is one which is dedicated for the camera model. Like MDS-D800 (Fig. 1). It can perform safely upto 100Mts depth. But it is very costly and priced at Rs. 2.3 Lacs.
2. Another cheaper option is the universal camera housing which can accommodate any DSLR camera (Fig. 2). It can work safely upto 30Mts depth and costs Rs. 8000.
3. Third option is GoPro Hero 7 (Fig. 3) which is priced Rs. 37000 and can perform well upto 30 feet depth.

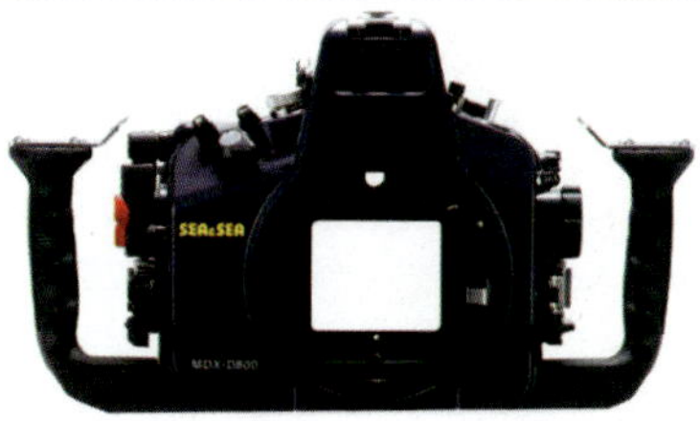

Fig. 1

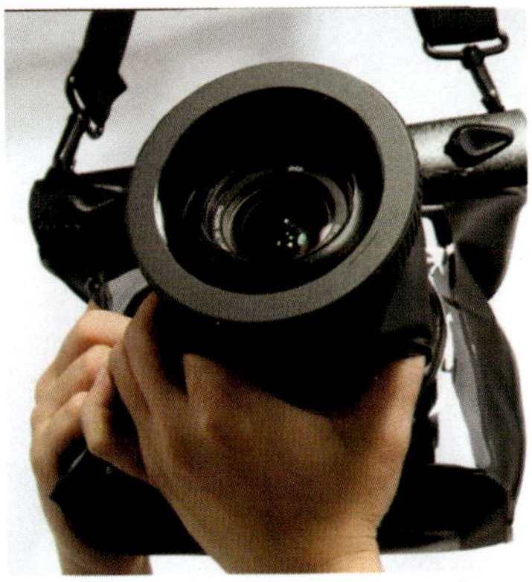

Fig. 2

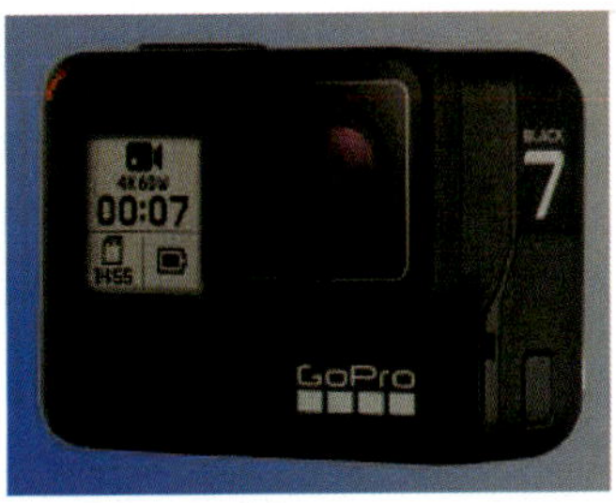

Fig. 3

Important Aspects

Swimming

Both the model and the photographer must know swimming.

Outfit

Outfit should colourful like red, blue, green etc. If we use saari wrapped around the model we can create attractive shapes.

I used the second waterproof housing and saari wrap to shoot first under water fashion in eastern India. See a few (Fig. 4, 5, 6 & 7)

Camera & Lens

Any DSLR preferably full frame. Lens should be wide angle such as 10-17mm, 16-35mm, 14-24mm.

Lighting

Sunny daylight is preferred.

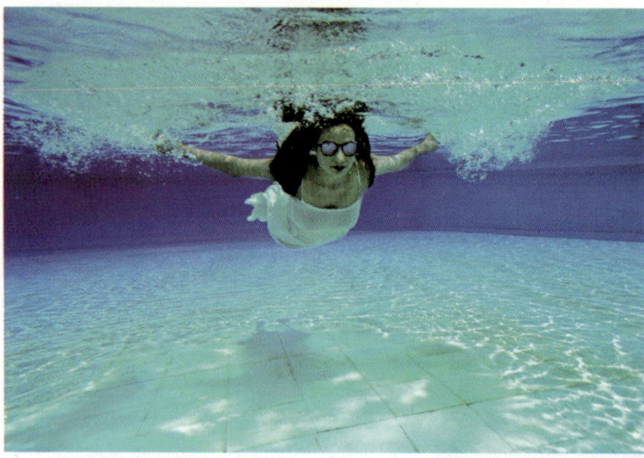

◂ Fig. 4

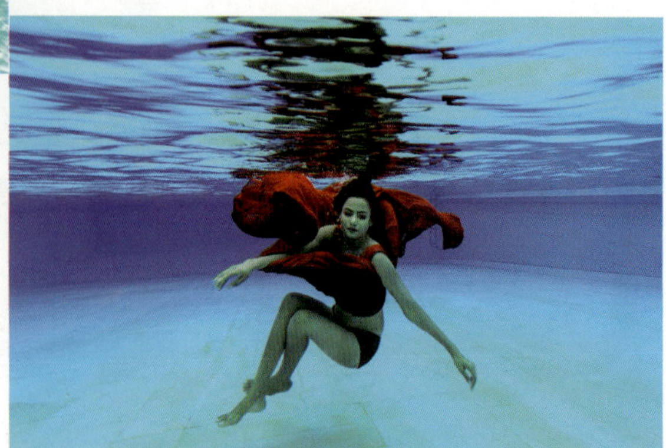

Fig. 5 ▸

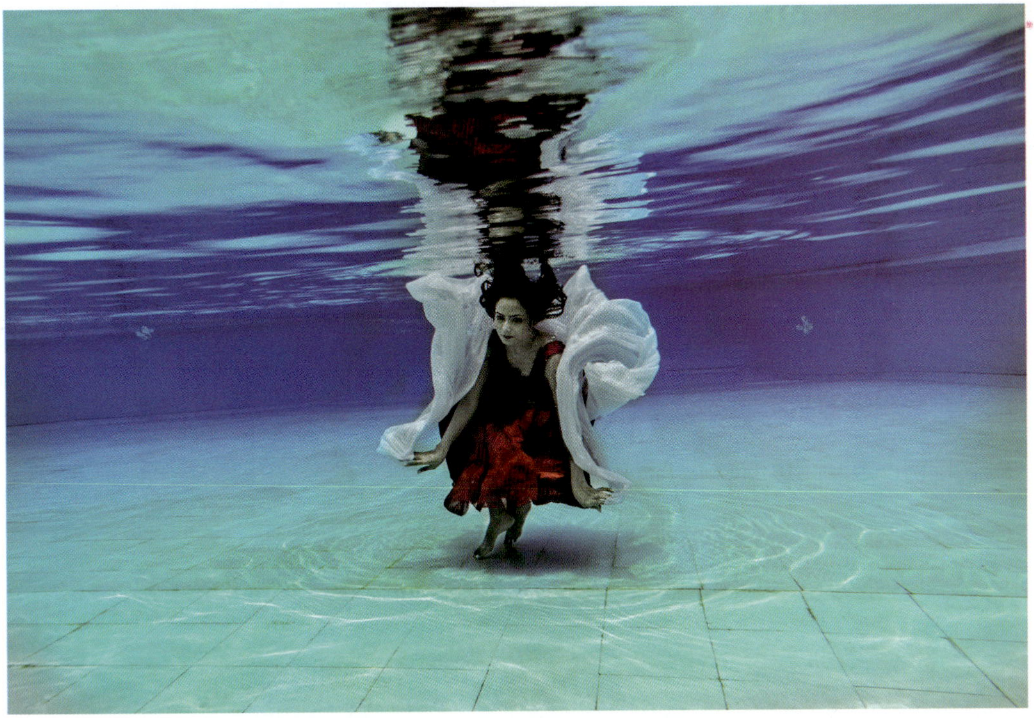

Fig. 6

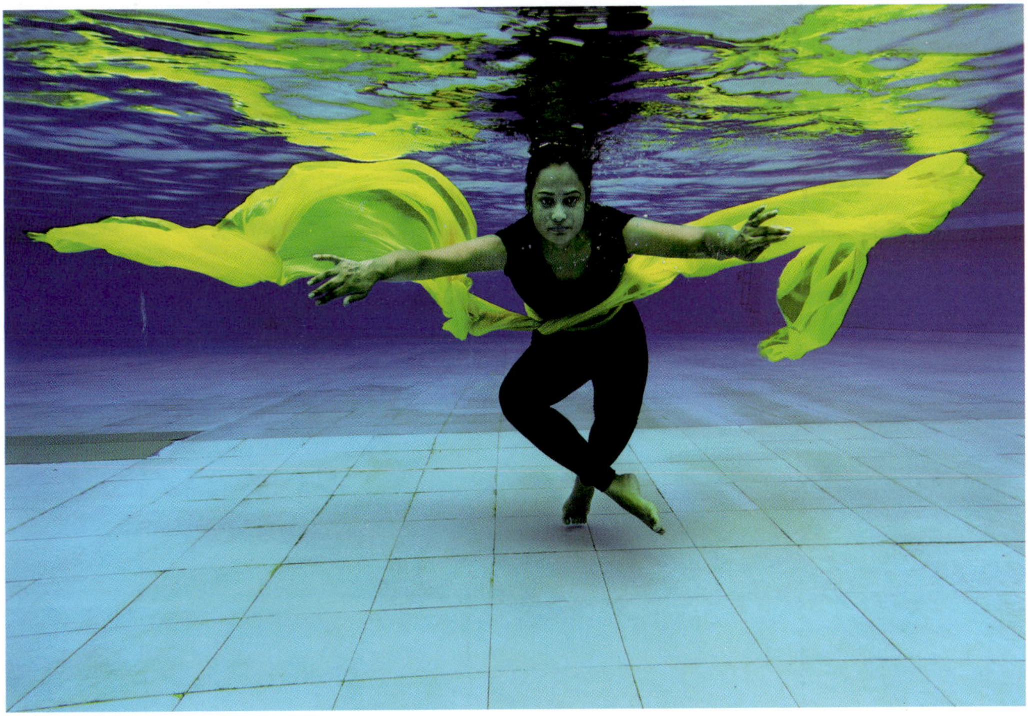

Fig. 7

Milky Bath

Another interesting creative Fashion photography is Milky bath. For such photography a water tank of at least 3'×6' with 2 feet depth is needed. Either mix milk with water or alternatively mix white distemper with water and pour in the water tank.

Lighting

Use just one strobe light preferably Octa soft box from top. Alternatively you can use two rectangular strobe lights placed at 45 degree.

Outfit

Use contrasting colour outfits like red, black etc.

Shooting Angle

Use ladder and shoot from top. Do not forget to use grey card for proper white balance.

Camera & Lens

Any DSLR preferably full frame. Lens 18-105mm, 24-70mm, 50mm etc.

Arrangement

It's very important use proper posing to get beautiful body formation. You can use some probes such as flower, musical instrument etc. You can also spread flower petals in milky water to add more beauty.

I did such creative Fashion shoot with unique composition. See a few images (Fig. 8 to 13)

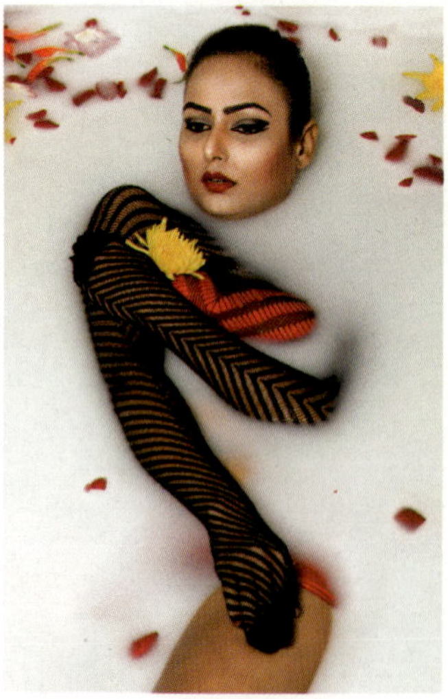

Fig. 8

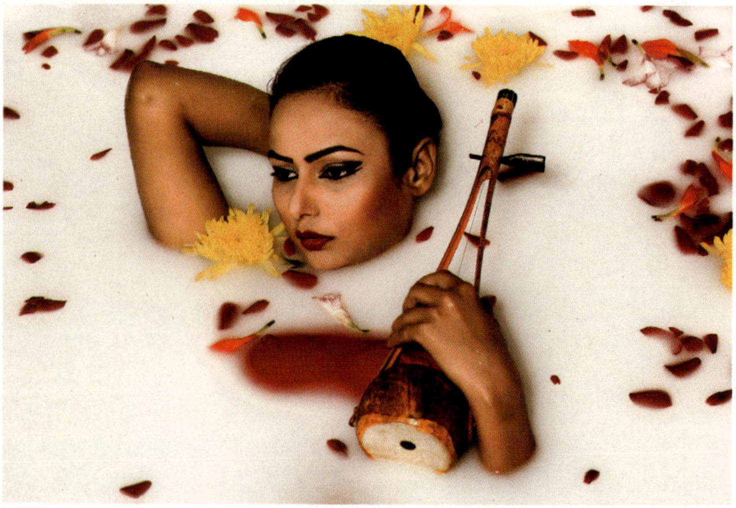

Fig. 9

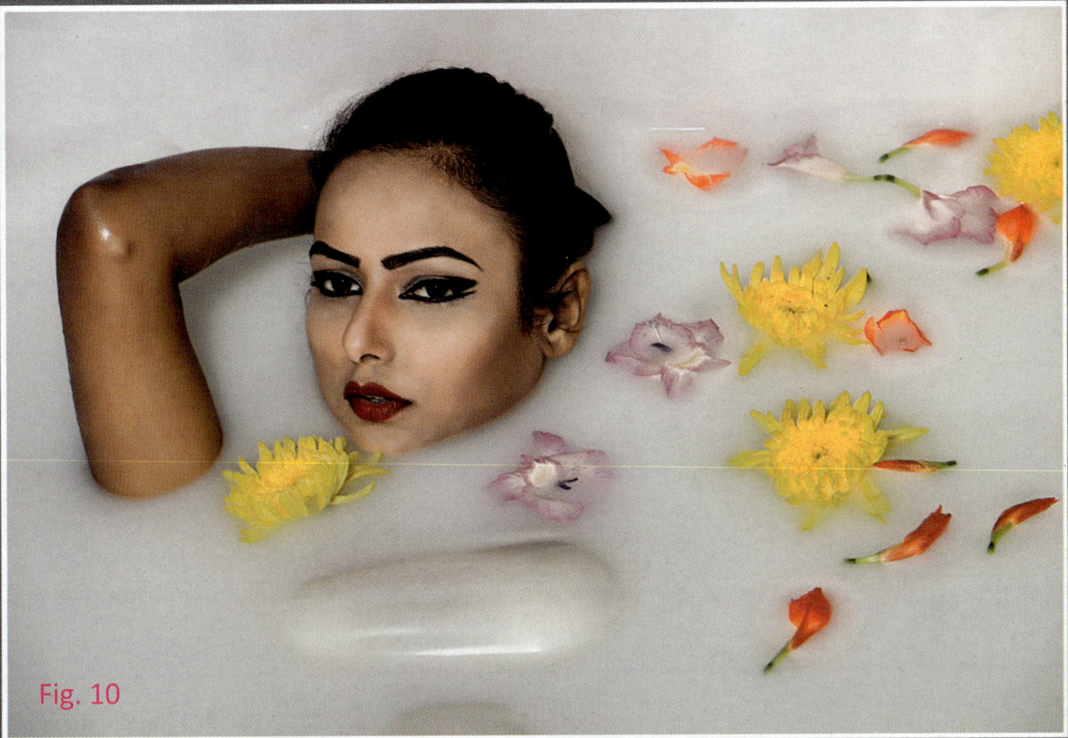

Fig. 10

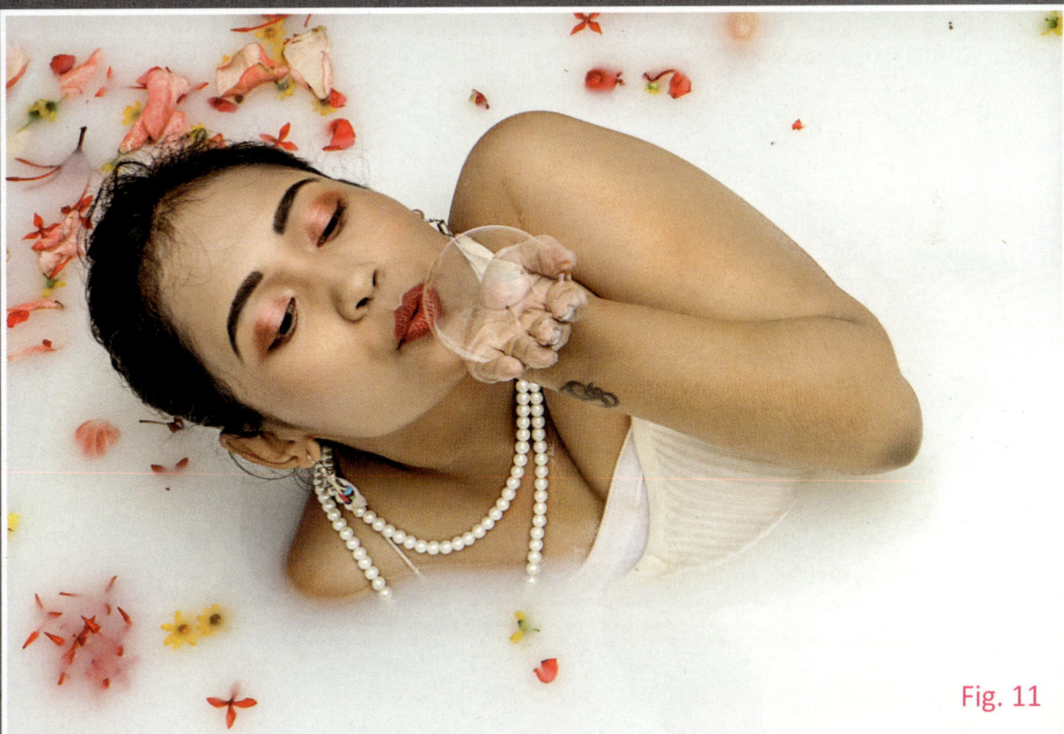

Fig. 11

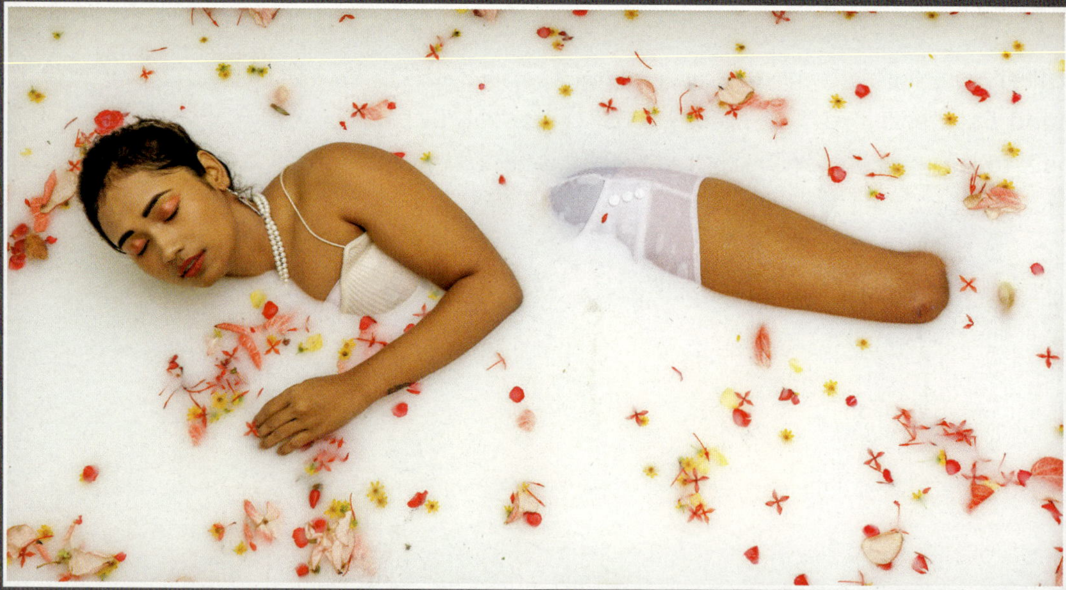

Fig. 12

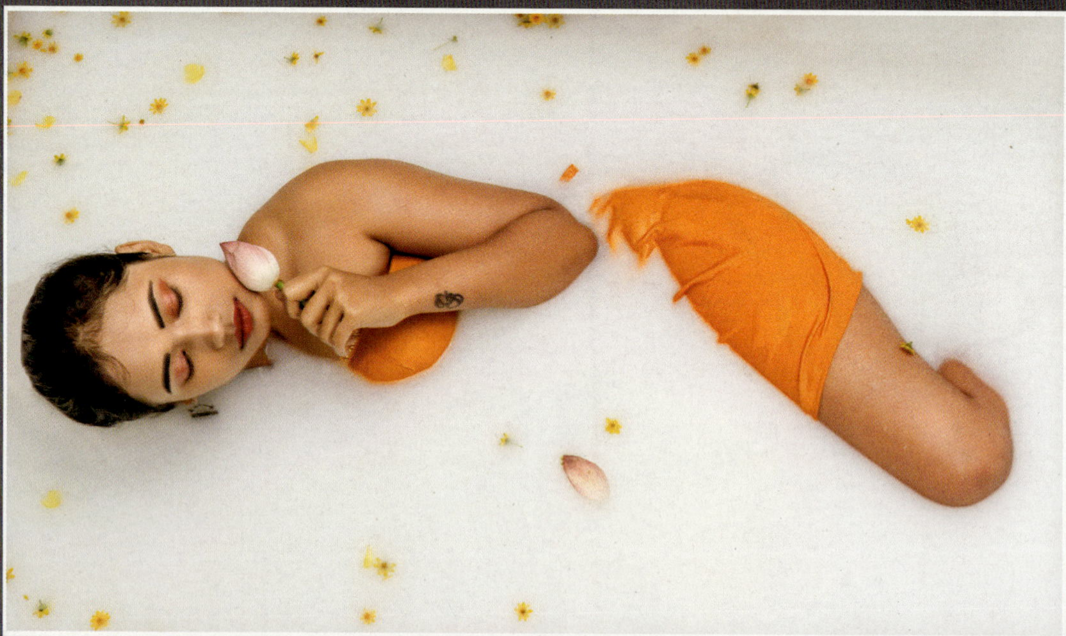

Fig. 13

Honey Bath

Another very interesting creative fashion photography. For this we should use Honey around 5Kgs and large diameter utensil. We can get such utensil from caterer. Ask the model to stand and pose in the middle of the utensil and ask your assistant to pour honey from top.

Lighting

Normal studio lighting like Key light, Fill Light and back light.

Camera & Lens

Any DSLR preferably full frame. Lens 18-105mm, 24-70mm, 50mm etc.

Do not forget to use grey card for proper white balance.

I did such creative fashion shoot. It was not very comfortable for the model, but Priya Jha did well with her required expression and body language. See a few images (Fig. 14 to 20)

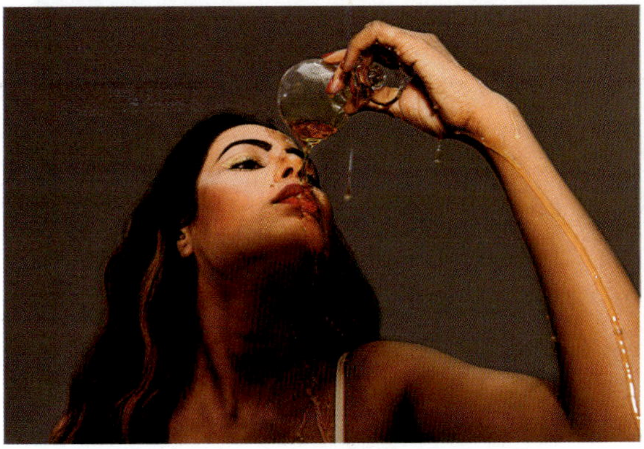

Fig. 14

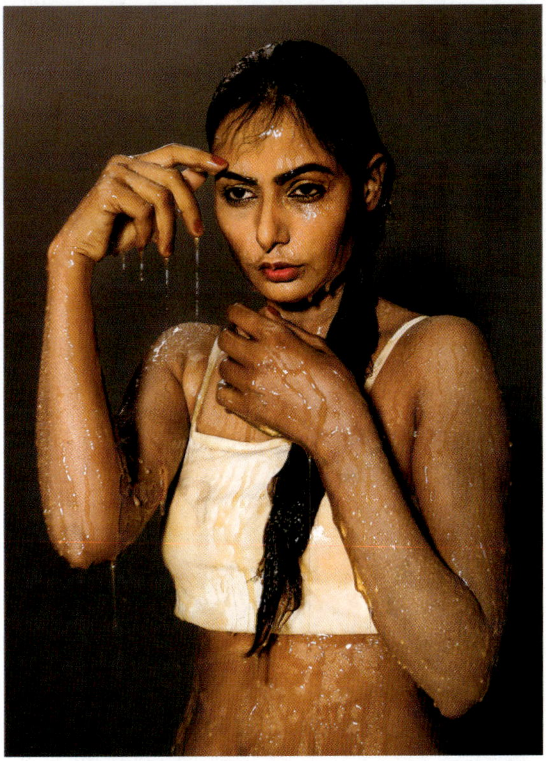

Fig. 15

More Images on Honey Bath

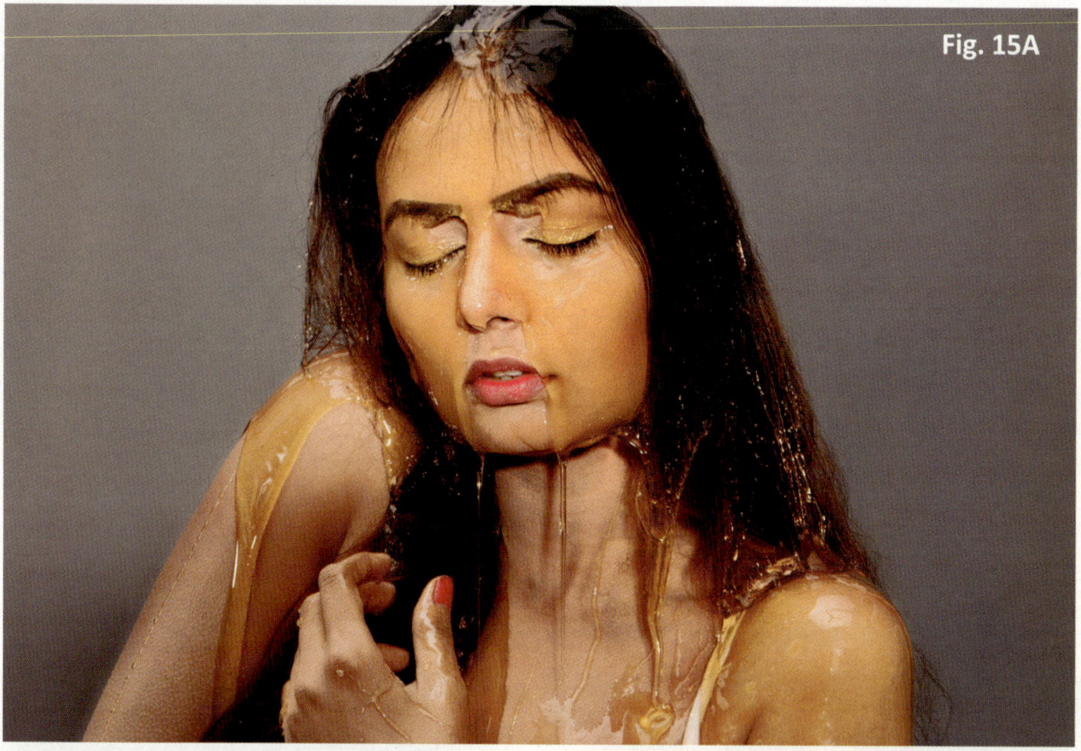

Fig. 15A

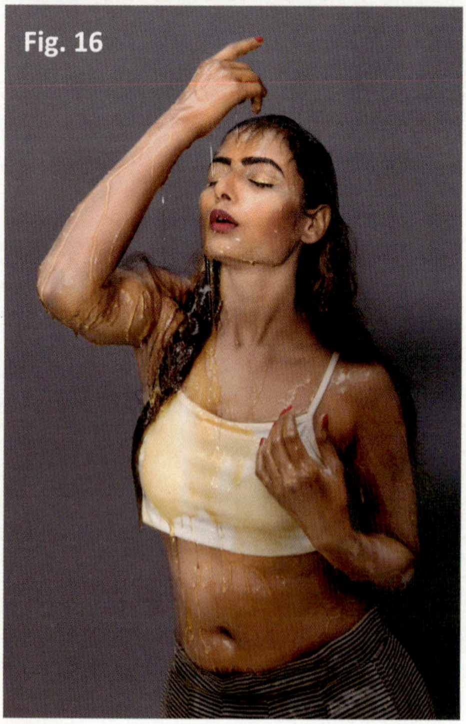

Fig. 16

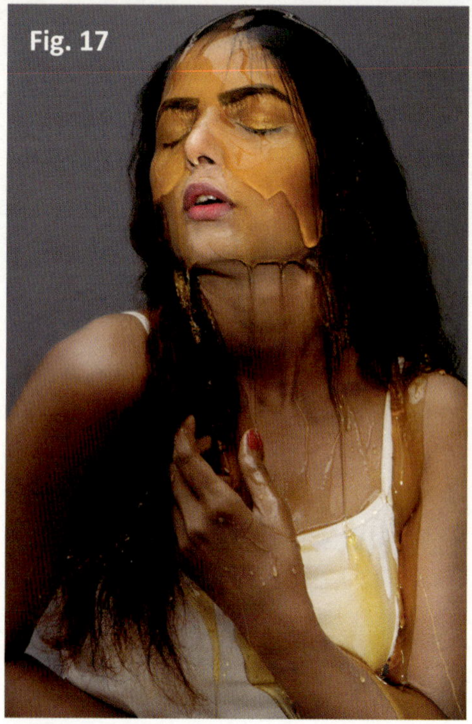

Fig. 17

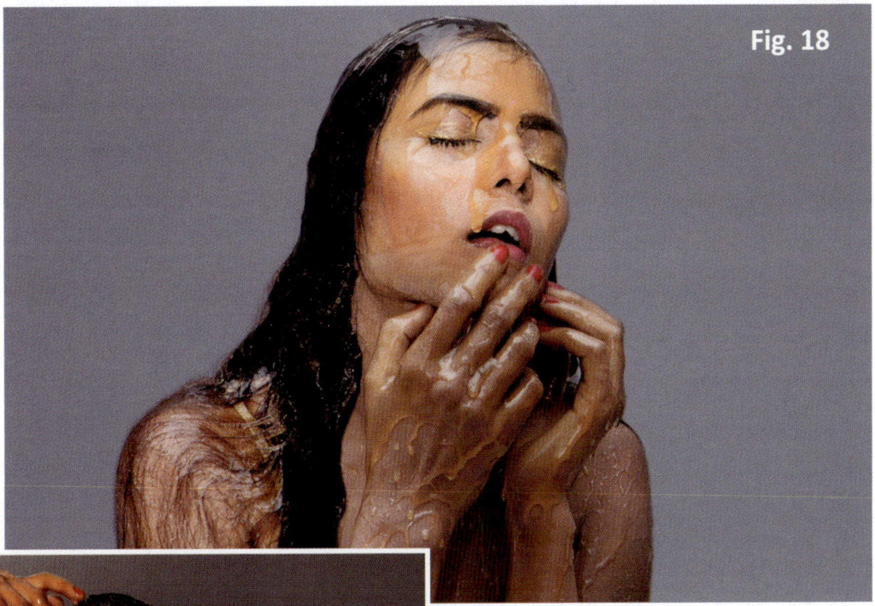
Fig. 18

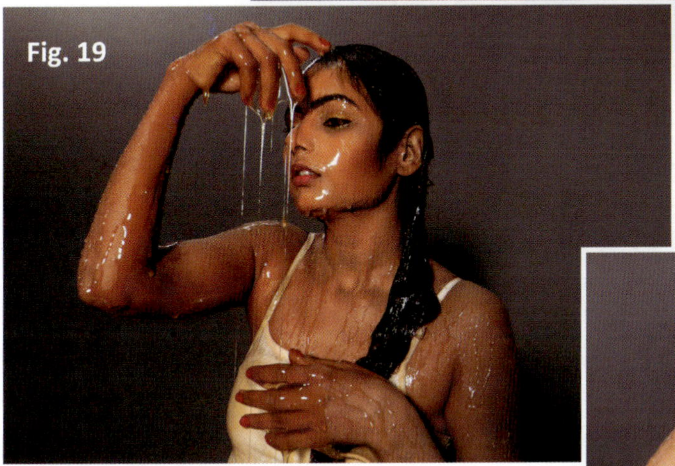
Fig. 19

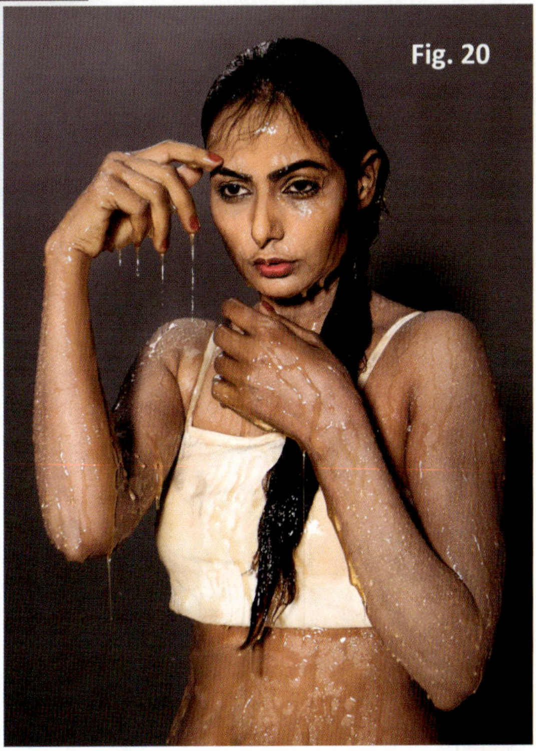
Fig. 20

Street Fashion Shoot

If you watch carefully while walking through the streets, you can find some interesting object to shoot fashion creatively.

I did reiki in my city for two days and located tyre puncture shop, electric poles lying on the side of road and corroded vehicles.

I planned different outfits for each location and did photo shoot in the morning hour 6 to 7AM to avoid disturbance from the general public.

Again this is a new concept and very different.

See few of my images (Fig. 21 to 24B)

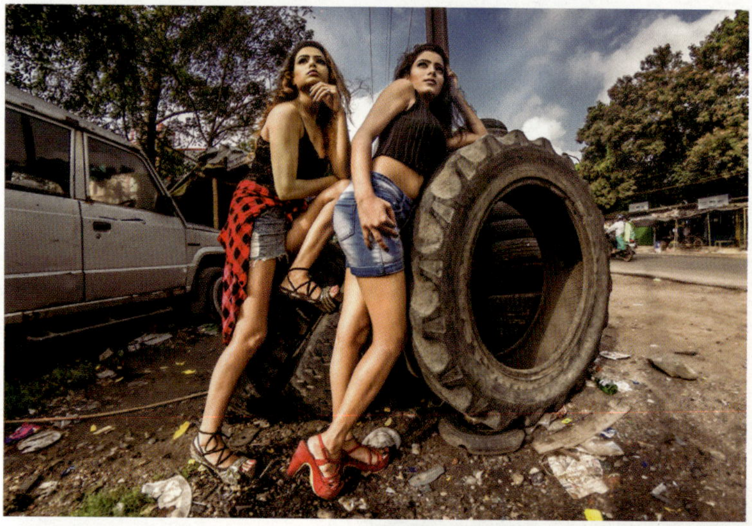

◀ Fig. 21

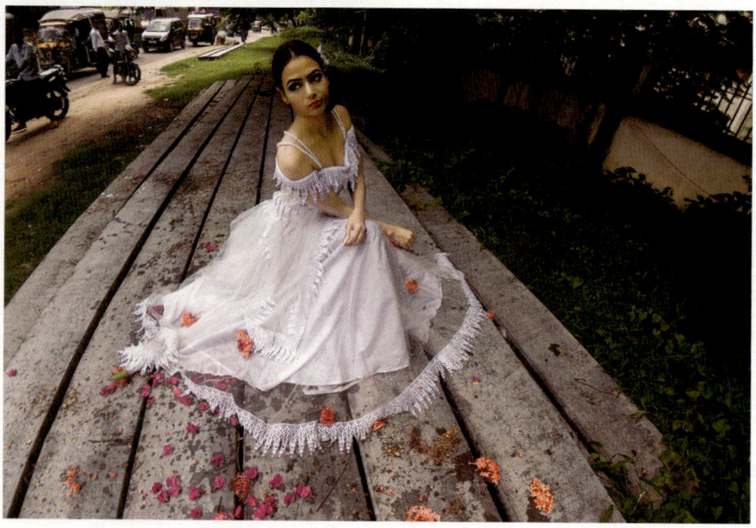

Fig. 22 ▶

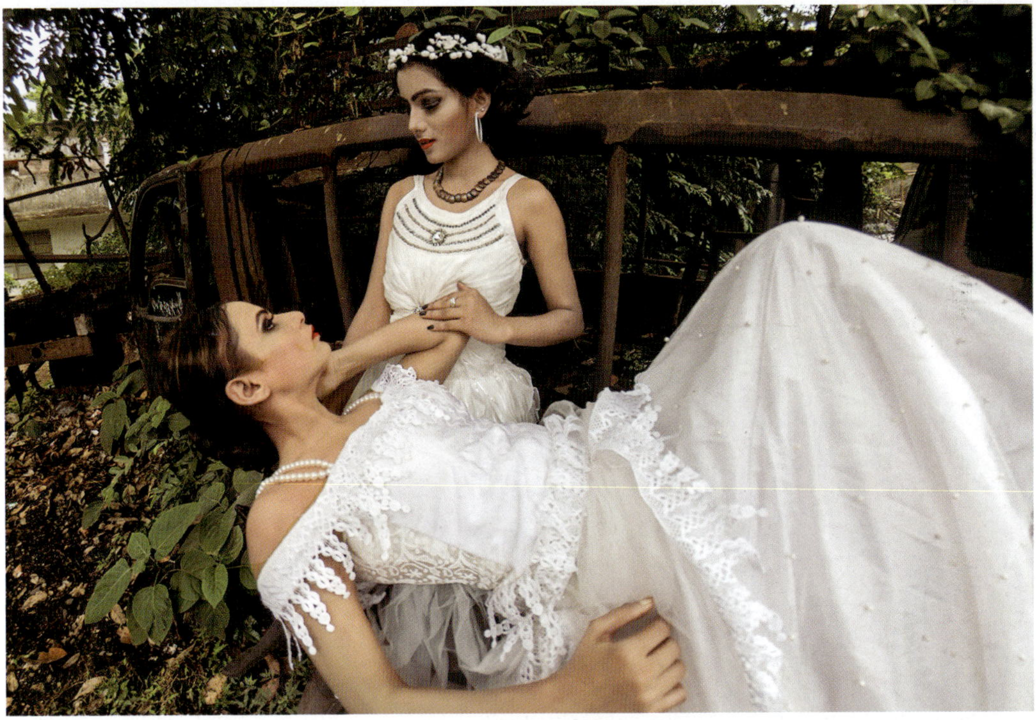

Fig. 23

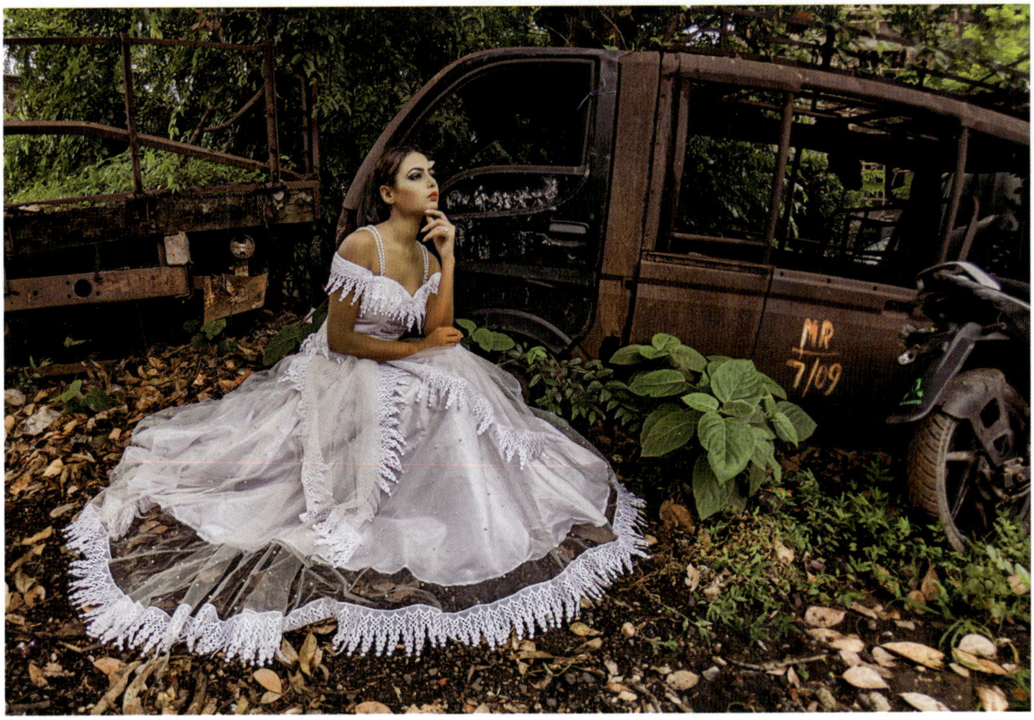

Fig. 24

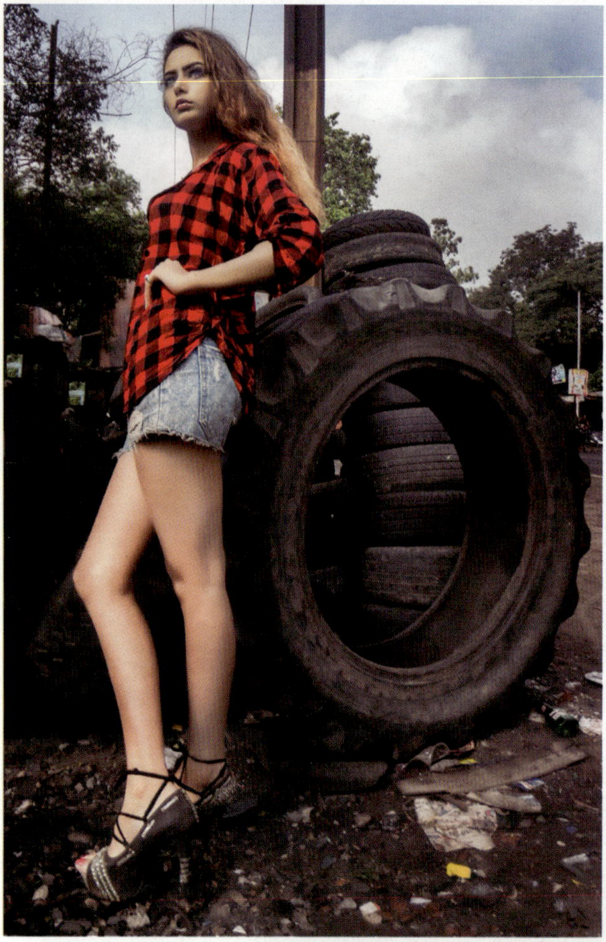

◄ Fig. 24A

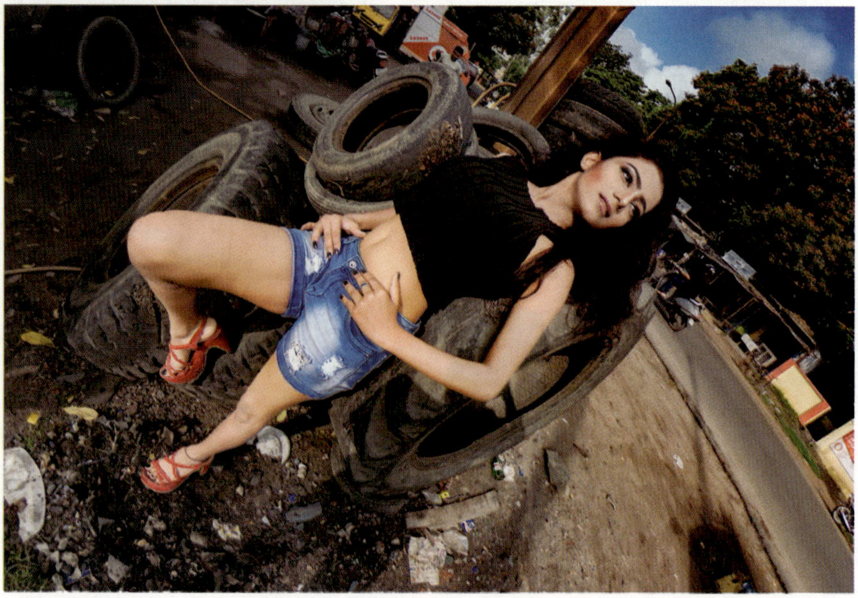

Fig. 24B ►

Colour Splash Photography

Technique

Mix water colour in a bucket filled with water. Use plastic mug to through colour water on the model. Care should be taken to safeguard the eyes of the model. You can use two colours to get colour contrast. High speed continuous mode is very helpful. Do not try indoor. It will spoil the stuffs stored in the studion. Do it outdoor with white backdrop and use two strobe lights from both the sides.

See my shoots from Fig. 25 to Fig. 30.

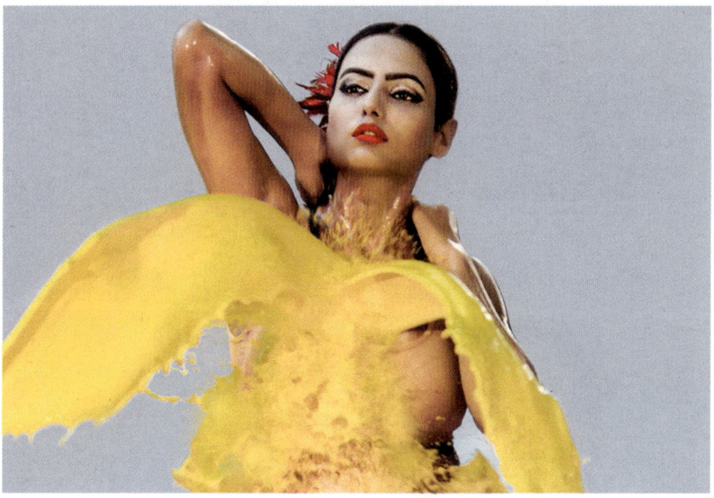

◀ Fig. 25

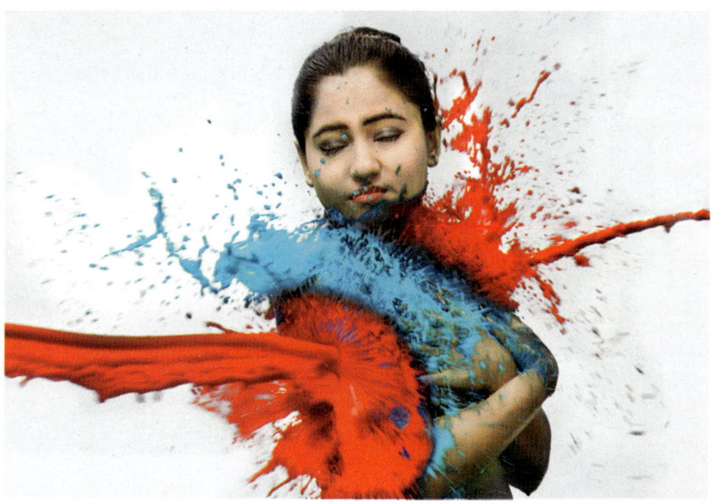

Fig. 26 ▶

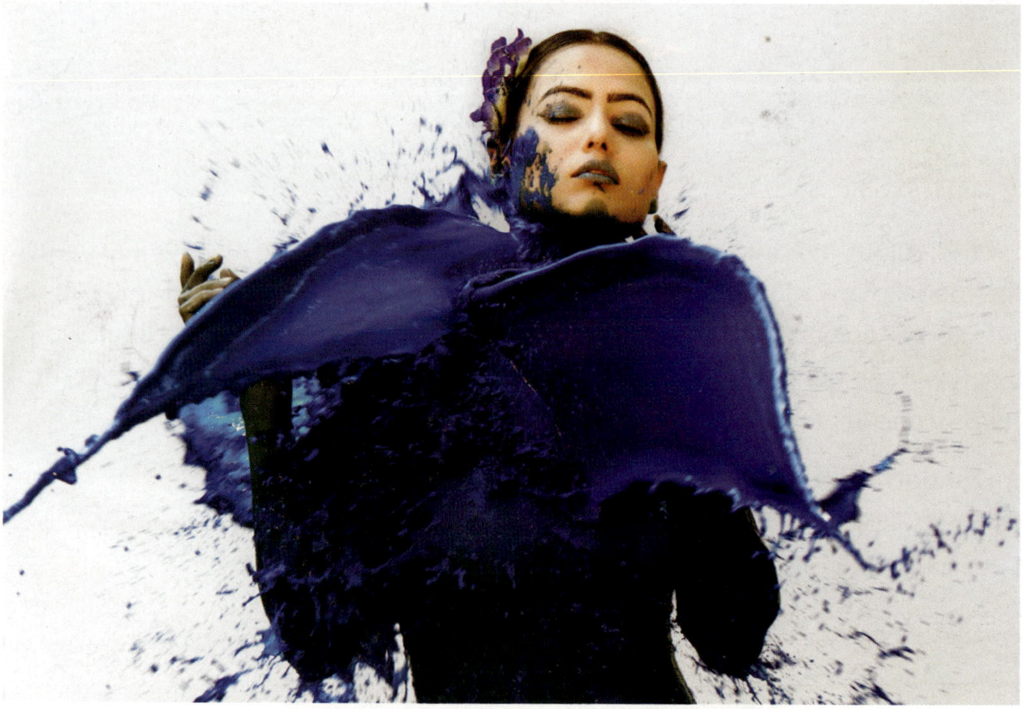

Fig. 27

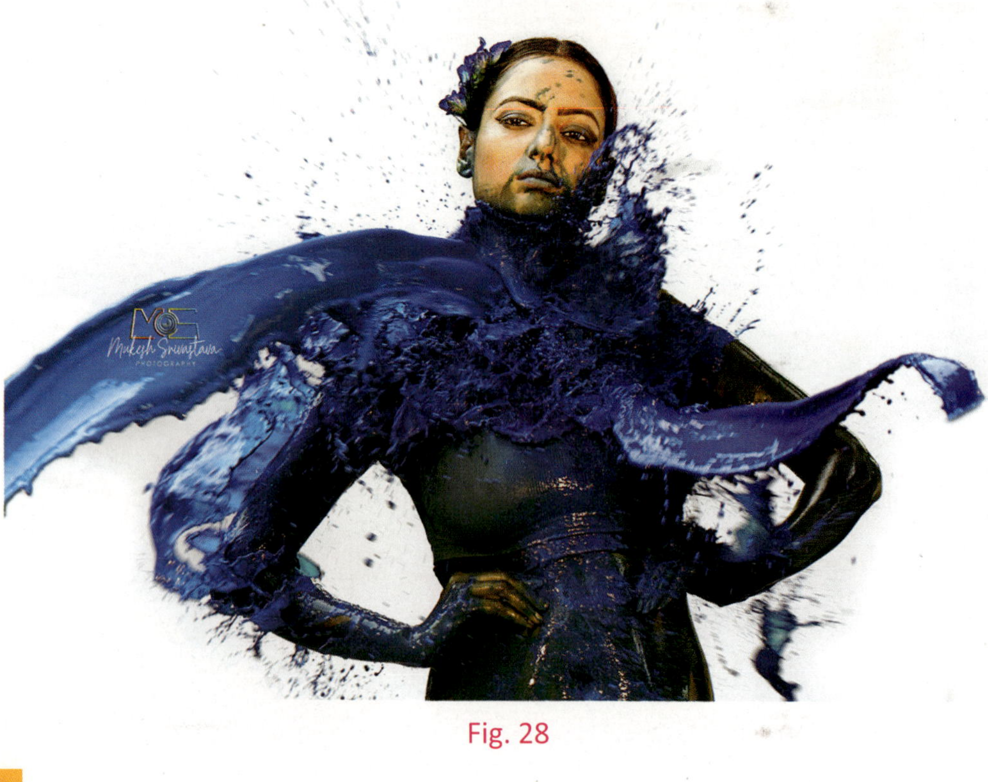

Fig. 28

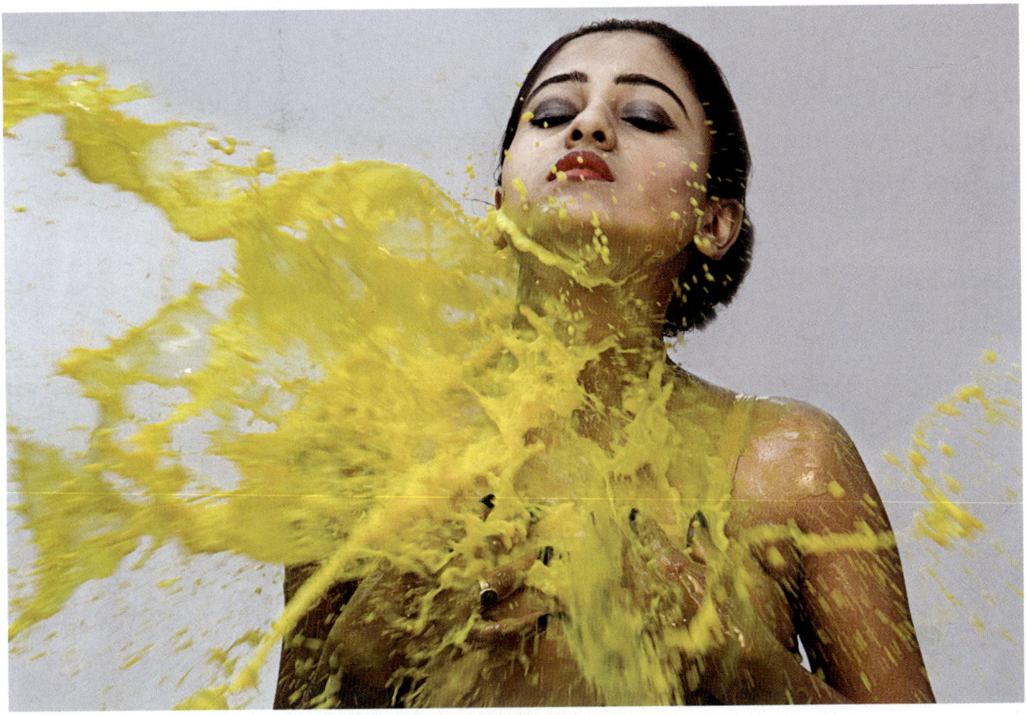

Fig. 29

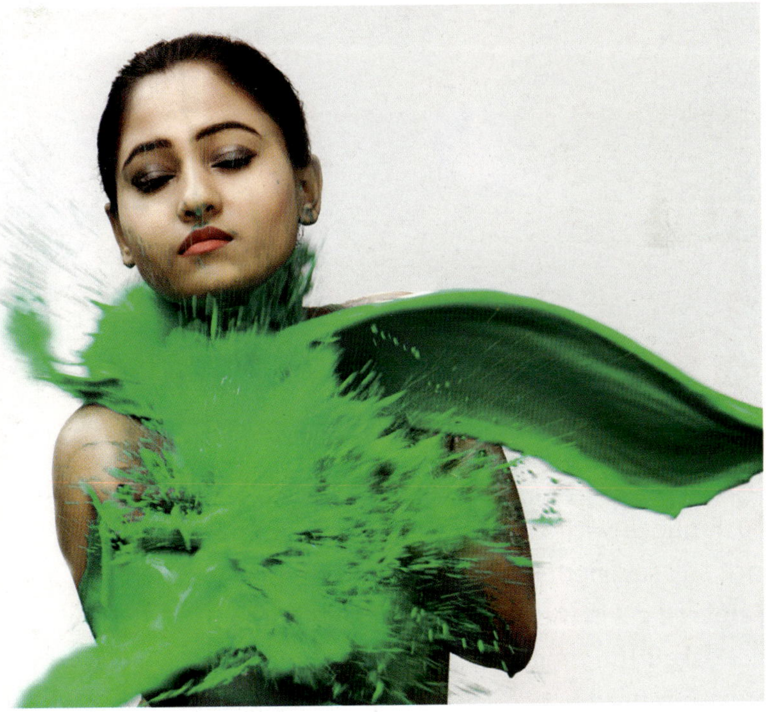

Fig. 30

Creative Fashion with Talcum Powder

I always believe in experimenting in Fashion Photography by using new technique. I thought to use talcum powder to get striking colour effect. I was looking for a model with slim and flexible body. Thanx to Sushma Singh who supported me to accomplish my creative idea.

In the image below (Fig. 31) initially I used single large light source, but I was not very happy. I wanted some punch with colours.

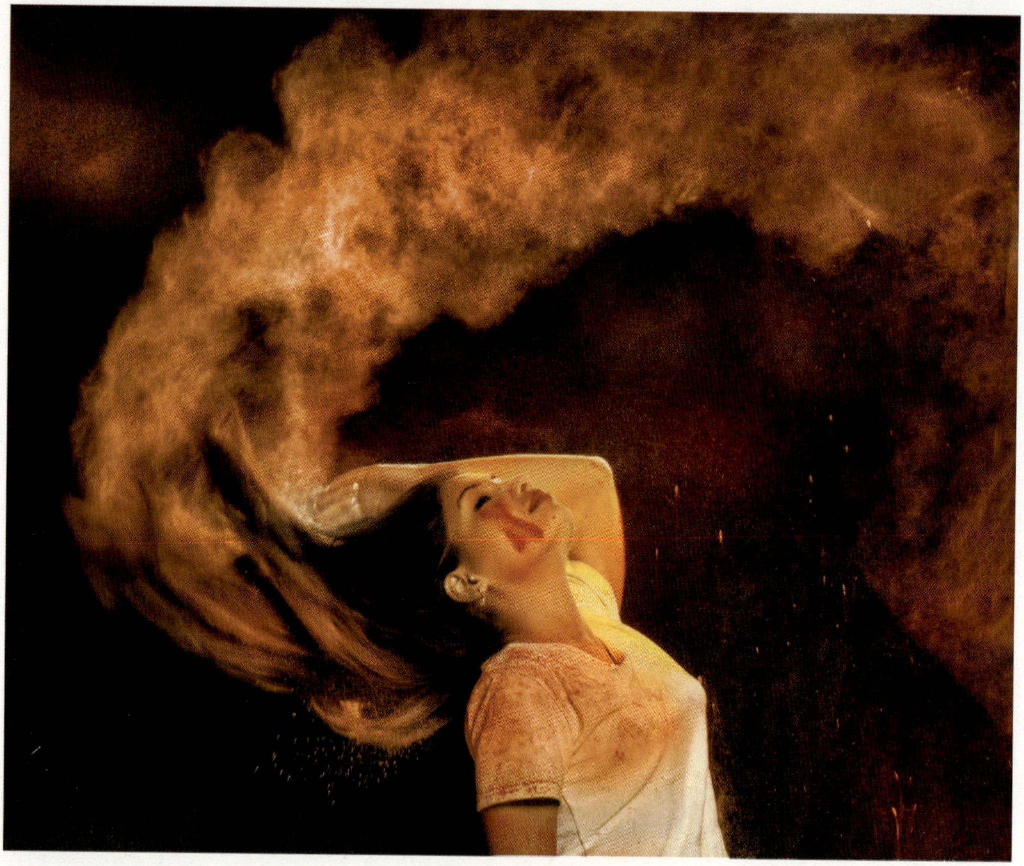

Fig.31

For such punch with colours, I tried with different dry colours to get the punch (Fig. 32). But not still satisfied. Finally I decided to play with light shapers. Placed two snoot with blue and red gel in the left and right side of the back. Kept the large size light shaper from front. I asked the model to through powder after I say 1, 2, 3. She did with perfection. Thanx to her flexible body and dedicated support. See the images (Fig. 33 to 35) on next pages.

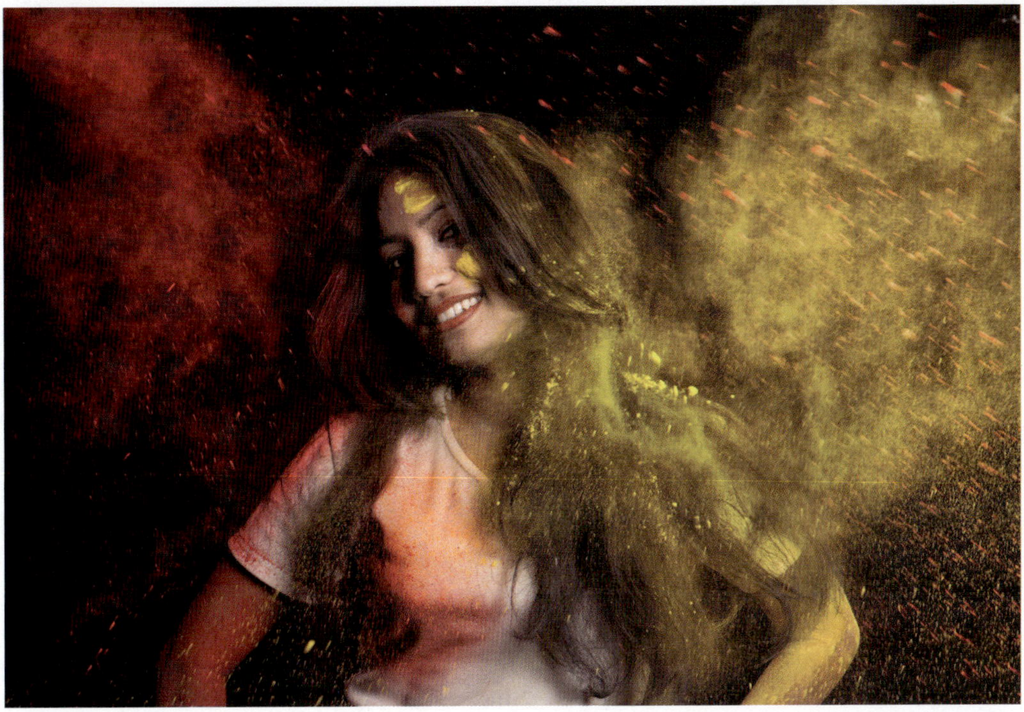

Fig. 32

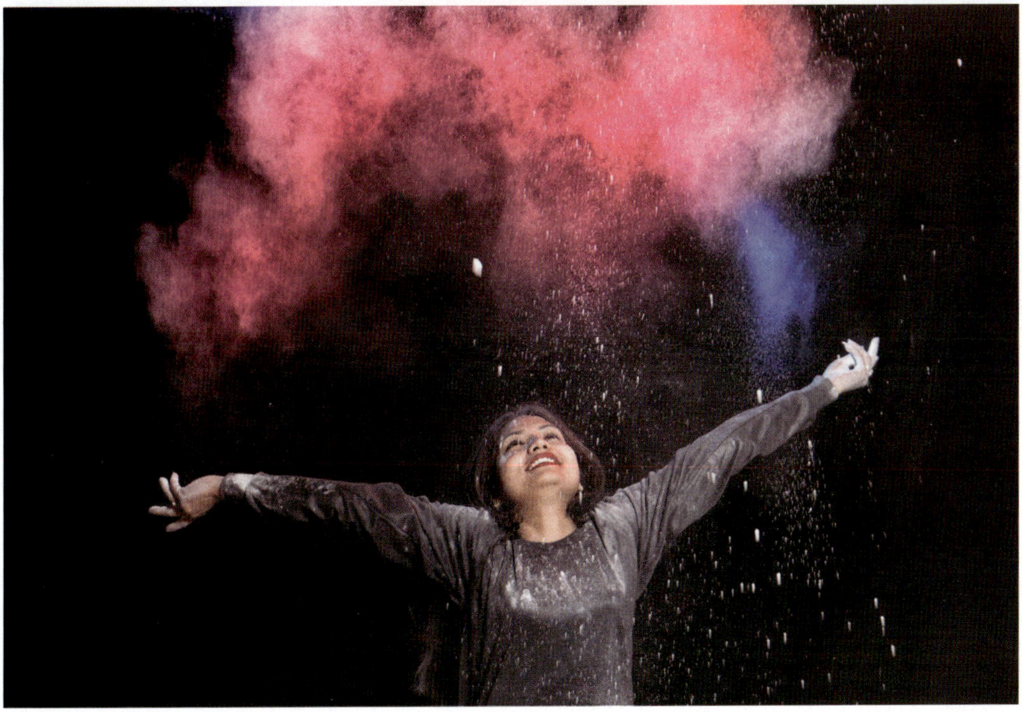

Fig. 33

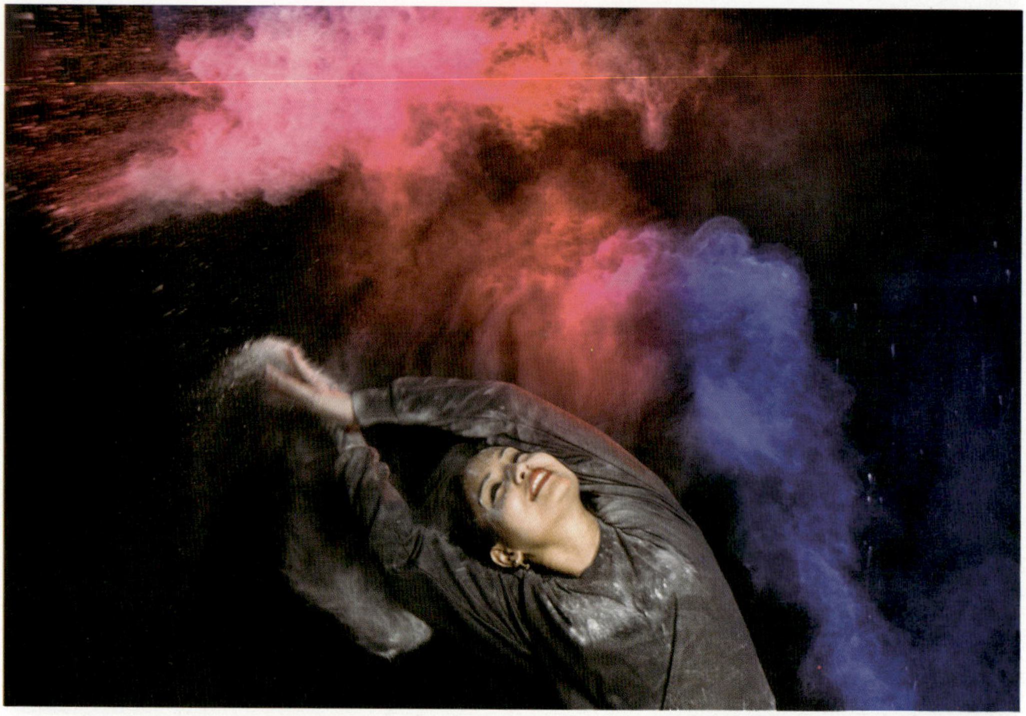

Fig. 34

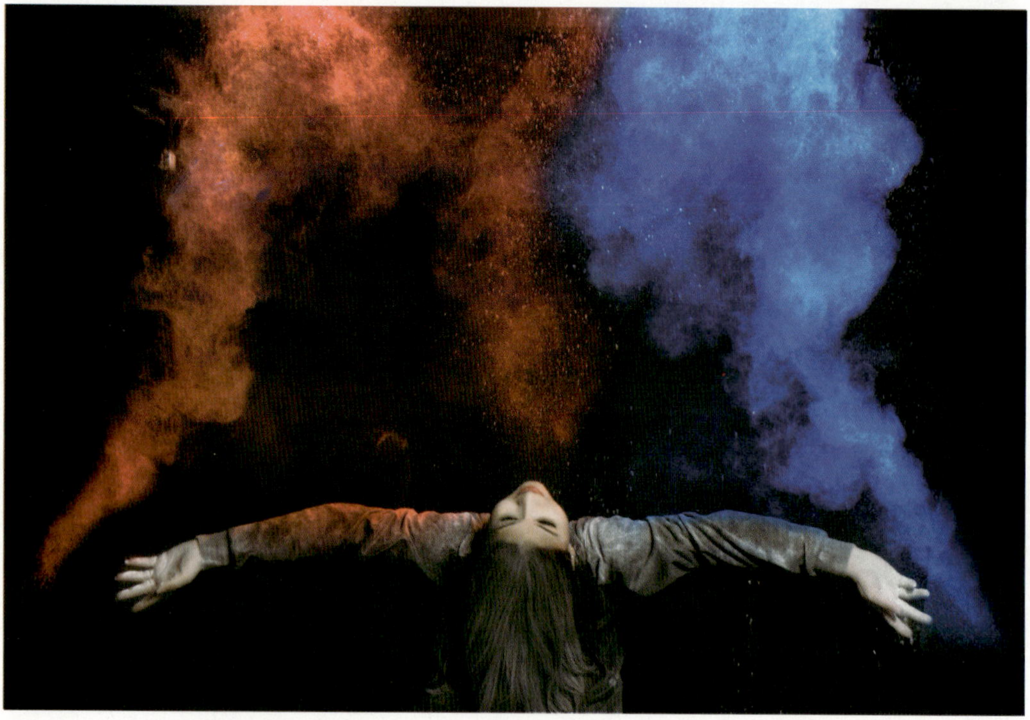

Fig. 35

Creativity with Unique Concept

Always try to pre plan and conceive an unique concept never seen before. That imagination is very important. Pen down your concept. Write detail about lighting pattern, background, costume and supporting items. Selection of proper model as per theme is also very important.

See Fig. 36 to 38. Here I conceived the concept of office girl.

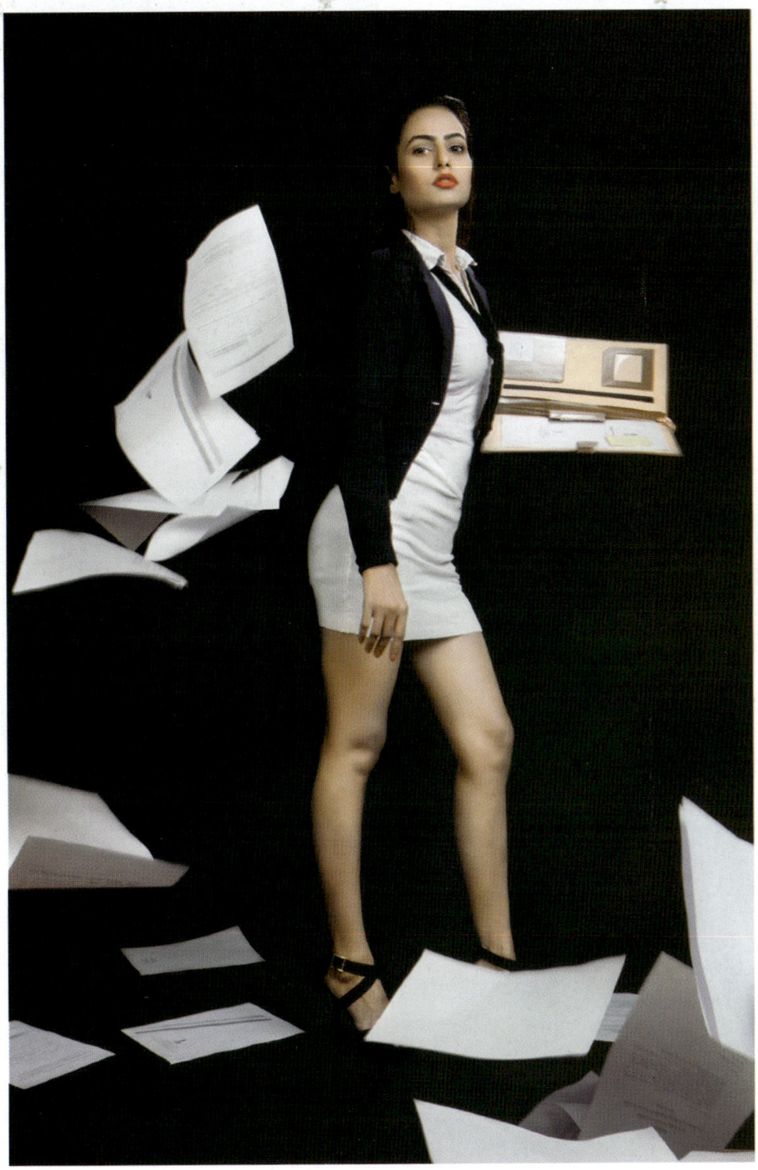

Fig. 36

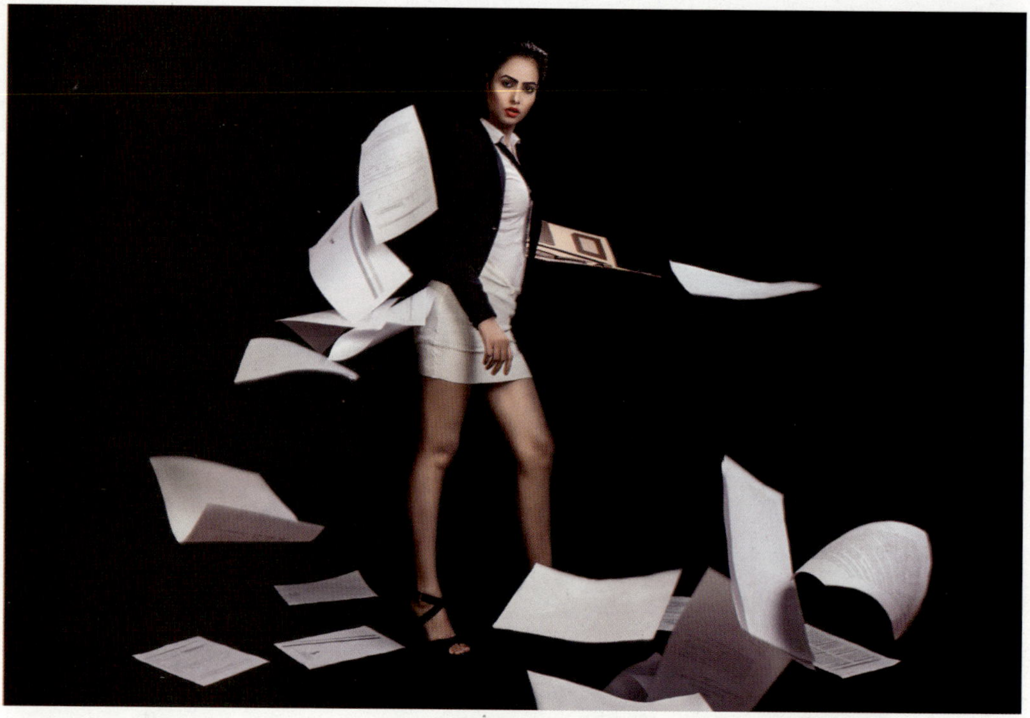

Fig. 37

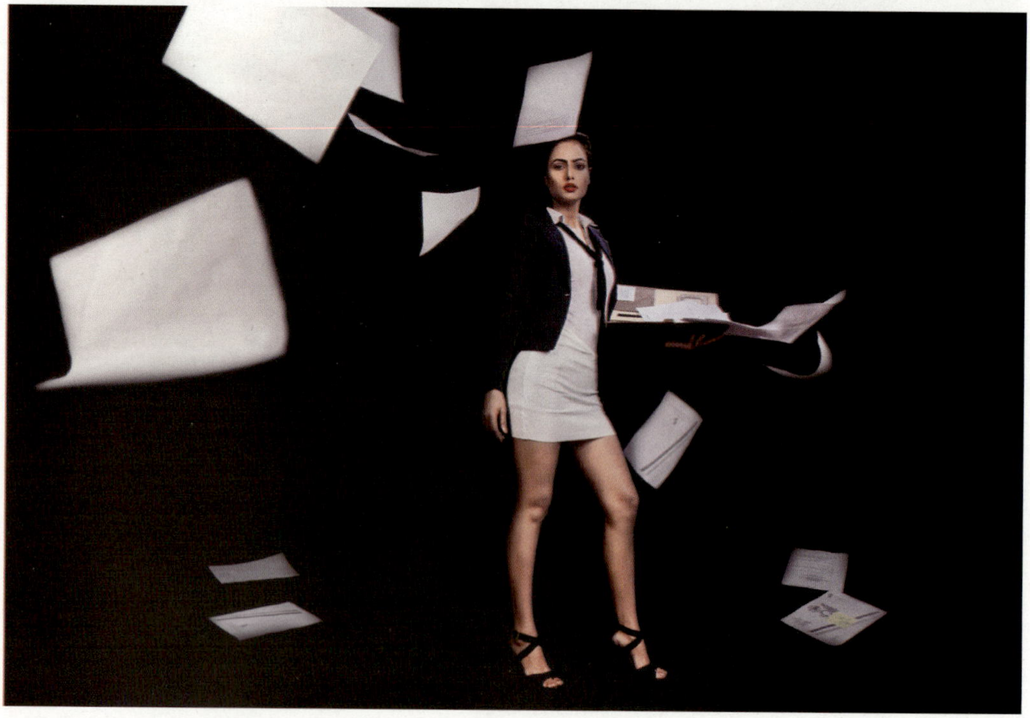

Fig. 38

Creativity with Unique Concept-II

I experimented with an arrangement to shoot two legs coming out of the collar of the shirt. I asked the model to raise legs by putting back on the floor. It is not possible to insert shirt collar in both legs. So, I inserted shirt collar in only one leg and adjusted second leg so that it comes just behind the first leg. It was a challenge for me to create the feeling of actual human chest. So I filled up inner part of the shirt with cotton and got the desired result.

See Fig. 39 & Fig. 40.

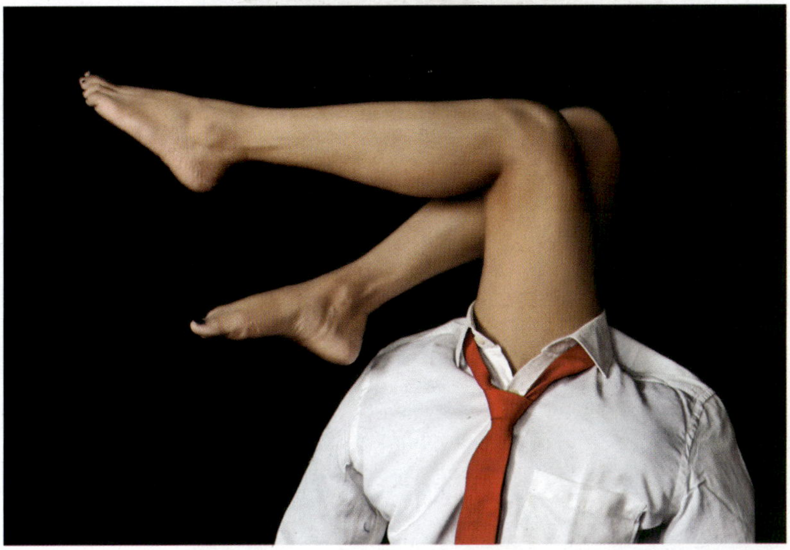

Fig. 39

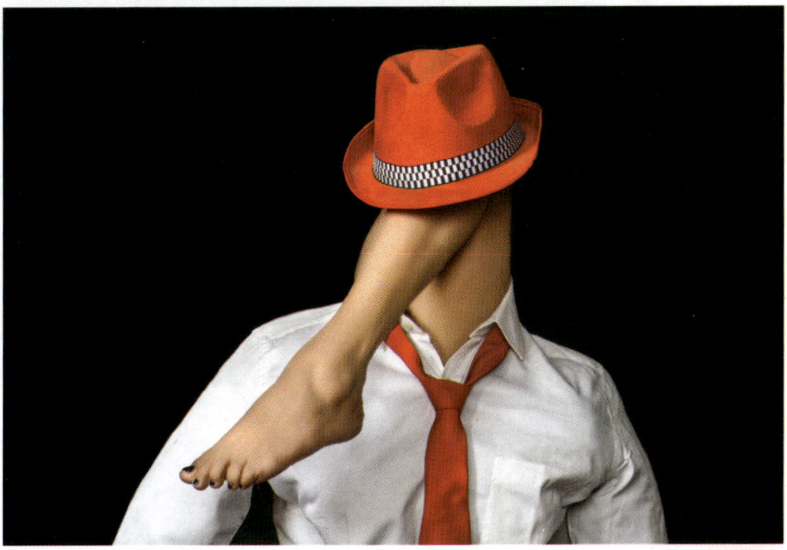

Fig. 40

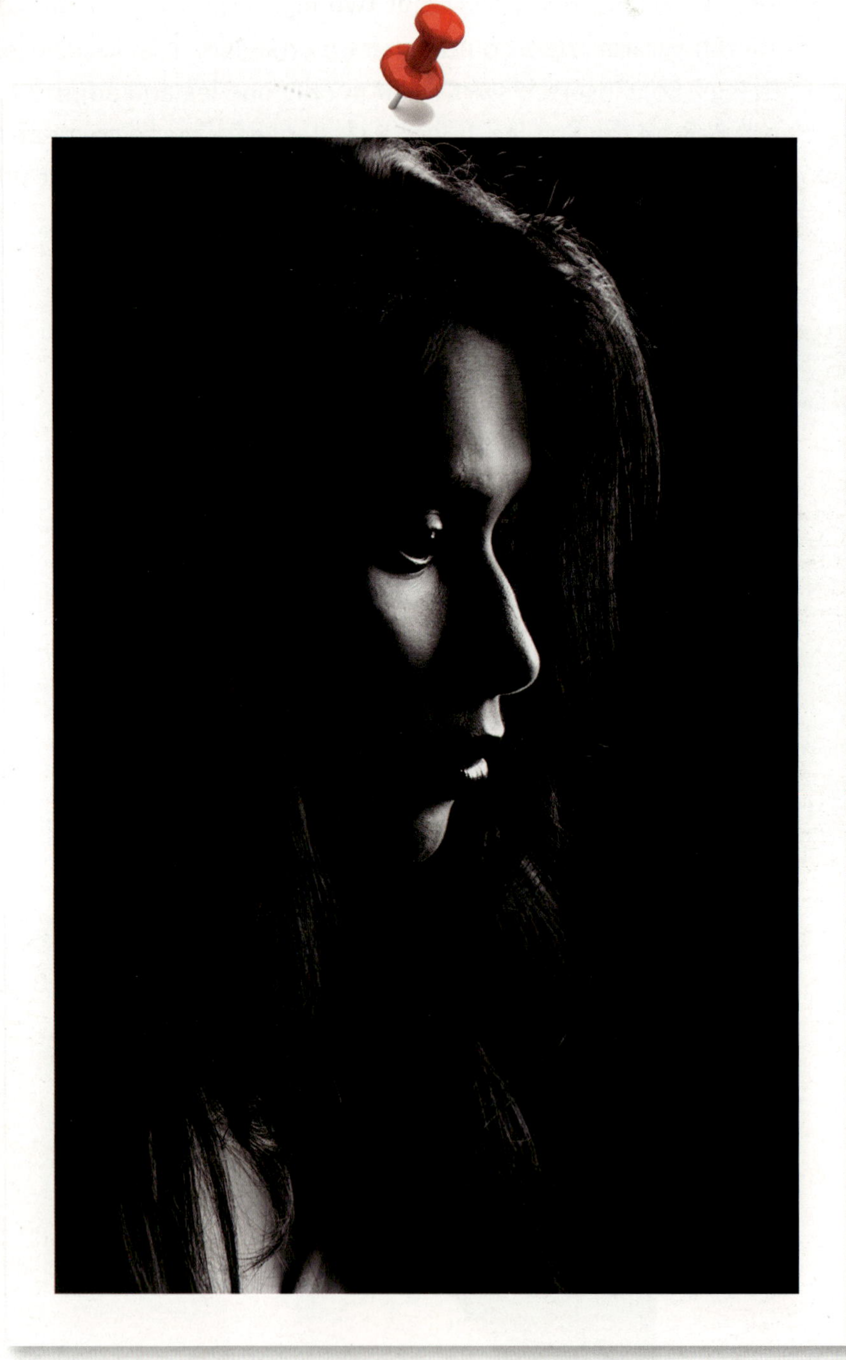

12. Virtual Fashion Photography

During the lockdown period due to pandemic, we all photographers got practically locked inside our houses. We started working in stay home mode. Few photographers were experimenting with table top, Droplet photography. Few were editing images from old stocks. It was also a nice period to update our knowledge and skill by watching photo tutorials and reading articles to learn advanced photography techniques and post processing techniques.

I too did few table top photography during the month of April. In the first week of May, I got the idea of portrait or fashion shoot using video chatting apps. I first searched in google and I got lot of photographers across the globe including few from India were doing such photography using video calling apps such as Face Time, Google Duo, Skype etc. In India Angio Fernandes, Anil Khana, Vasanth Kumar and Sunder Ramu did fashion shoots in stay home mode with models at different locations. Most of them used Face Time video calling app. Others used Google Duo and Skype video calling app. Face Time app is an apple app and works only on iphone or imac. The users of such device in India is hardly 1%, so I did not prefer to use iphone. So, initially I tried few portrait and fashion shoots using google duo and Skype. I did few sessions with Prerna Hazra, Miss Jharkhand in Dhanbad and Meghna Sakshi and Diksha Singh Miss Devghar at Devghar. In both the cases mobile at model's end was hand held. A little shake at model's end was resulting in poor quality of sharp images.

See my initial shoots in stay home mode below (Fig. 1 to 3):

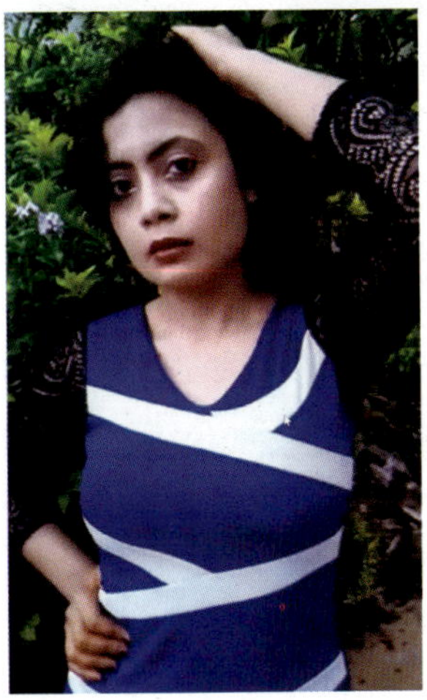

Fig. 1

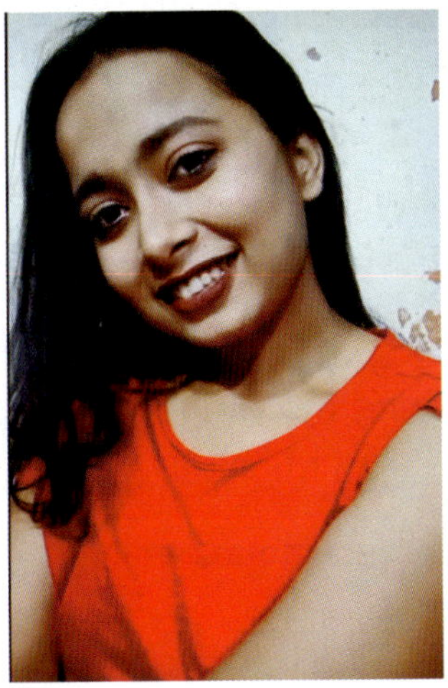

Fig. 2

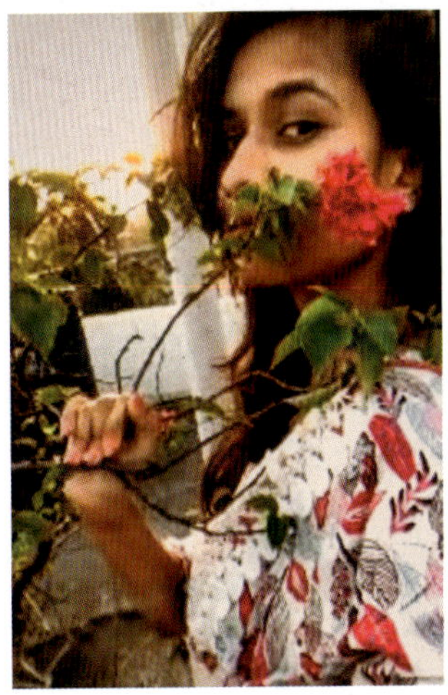

Fig. 3

I was not very happy with the final outputs due to small size display on the computer screen resulting in low resolution and poor quality images. The effect of interlacing due to monitor pixels was also a real problem. Although it could be handled in post processing but would have compromised with the picture quality. So I decided to use mobile holder fitted on the tripod to avoid any shake. Due to lockdown, it was not possible to arrange camera tripod at Devghar and Dhanbad. So, I contacted Sunita Mondal in Kolkata who was having camera tripod fitted with mobile holder. So I decided to go for professional fashion shoots with her.

During photo seminar by Photographers of Uttarakhand on Zoom video conferencing app, I saw pictures of the participants in very large size almost 3 to 4 times larger than video calling apps such as Face time, Google Duo and Skype. So I decided to do professional way of fashion shoot in stay home mode. I studied the technical features of the monitor to know about the role and functioning of pixels. The moment I read that the pixels blinks on and off. Immediately the slow shutter technique struck my mind.

In my first professional shoot with Sunita Mondal I used 1/50s to 1/10s shutter speed setting in my DSLR to capture the model. I asked my model to fit the mobile on a camera tripod so that any shake in mobile is eliminated. Again I asked my model to hold the pose for at least 2 seconds after posing. I started video conferencing with Sunita Mondal using Zoom video conferencing app. I asked her to show few costumes online so that I can select the matching outfits. I also asked her to show interior of her house as well as different locations on her roof top. I selected the right locations in her room as well as on the roof top. I needed a helping hand at model's end and Surajit Das a friend of Sunita Mondal agreed to assist me as assistant photographer at the model's end. I did my first fashion shoot using Zoom app with my technique on 12th May, 2020 inside her home. The output was very close to physical fashion shoot. Even I did not find any pixilation after enlarging my image to 20x30inch print size. This technique of profession photo shoot using Zoom is first in India. The result was very encouraging. See Fig. 4.

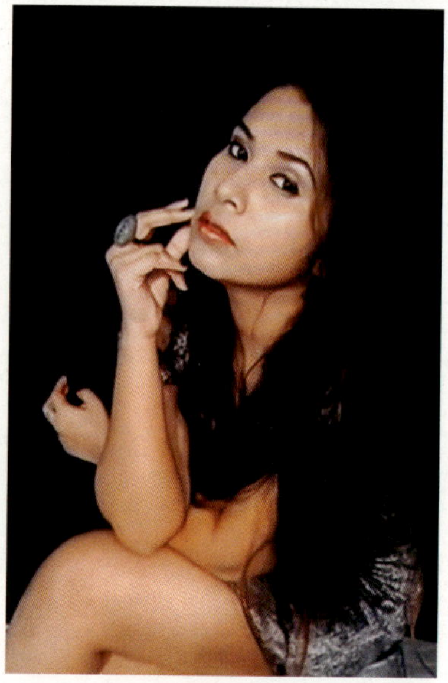

Fig. 4

Finally I got success and kept on doing more and more such fashion shoots in Kolkata with Sunita Miondal.

First of all lets us understand the technique which I adopted.

Technique

The Zoom app must be installed in the photographer's computer as well as in the mobile of the model. Mobile with the higher resolution camera (16MP, 32MP) is preferred at model's end. The mobile must be tightly fitted with the holder mounted on the camera tripod. The model is asked to pose as directed by the photographer at the selected location. Now to get a proper frame, the help of assistant photographer or any person is very important. As desired by the photographer, the assistant at model's end will raise, lower or rotate the mobile till the perfect frame is achieved. The set up shown in Fig. 5 & 6 is self explanatory.

Let's enjoy the professional fashion shoot in stay home mode with Sunita Mondal using Realme Pro mobile at model's end and Nikon D500 at the photographer's end in Fig. 7 to 15.

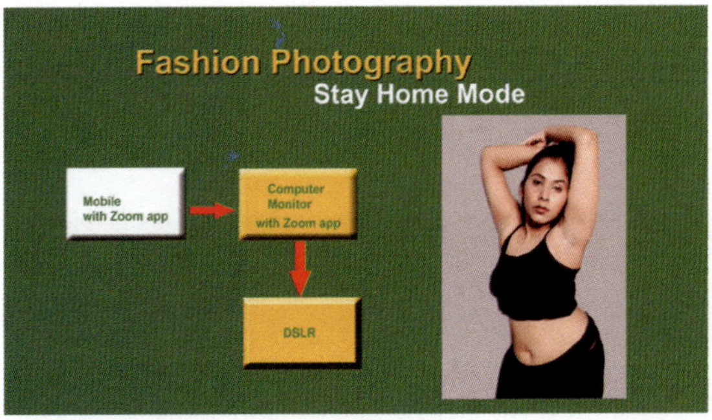

Fig. 5

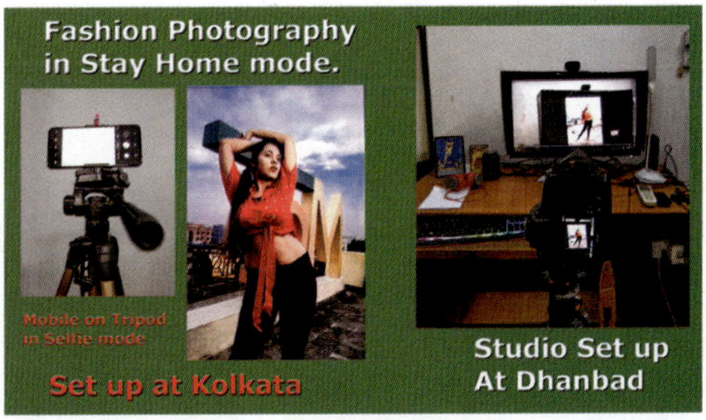

Fig. 6

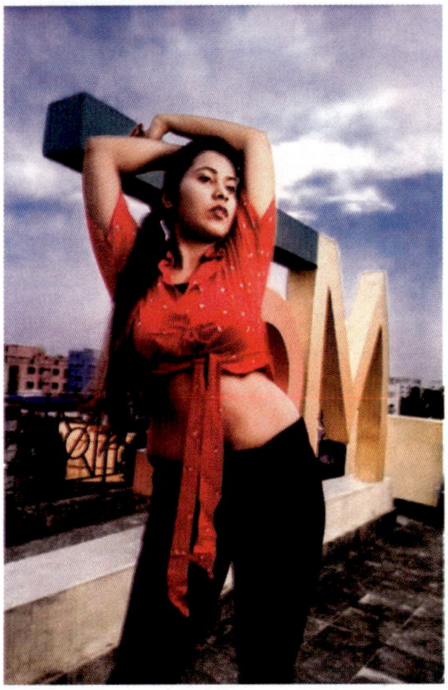

Fig. 7

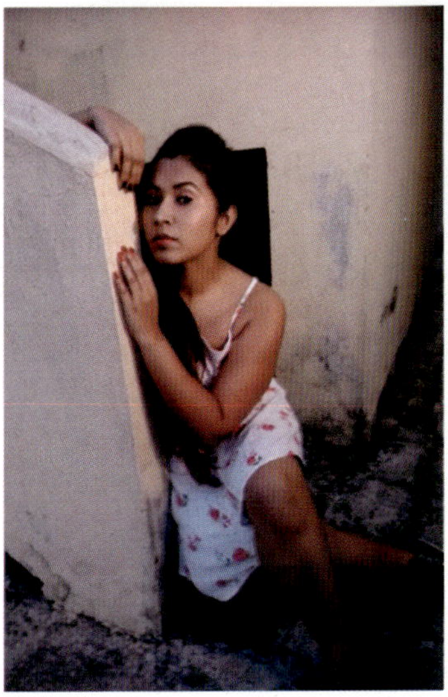

Fig. 8

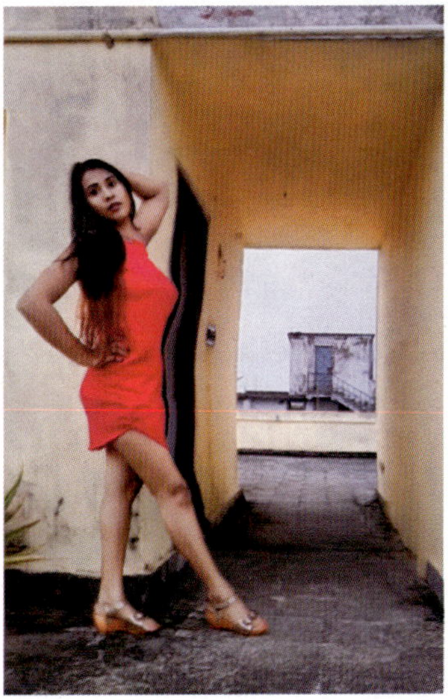

Fig. 9

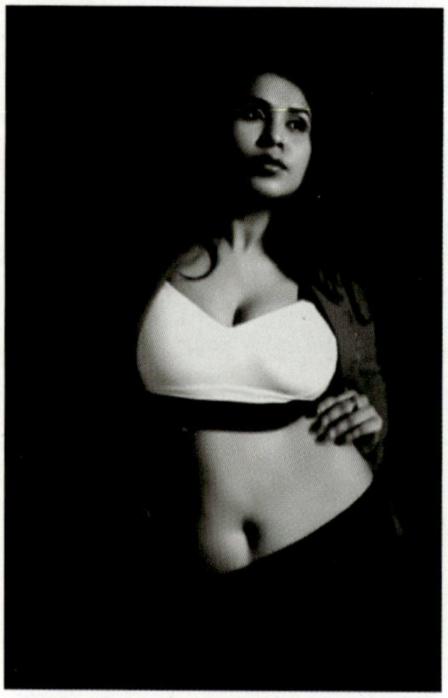

Fig. 10

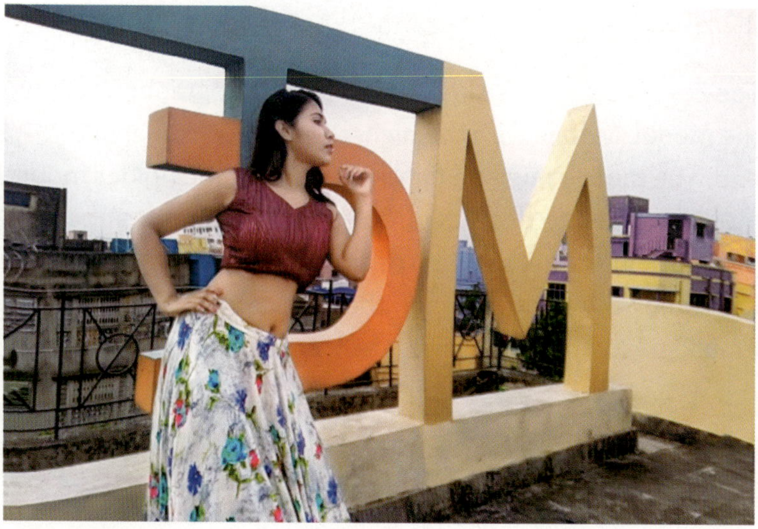

Fig. 11

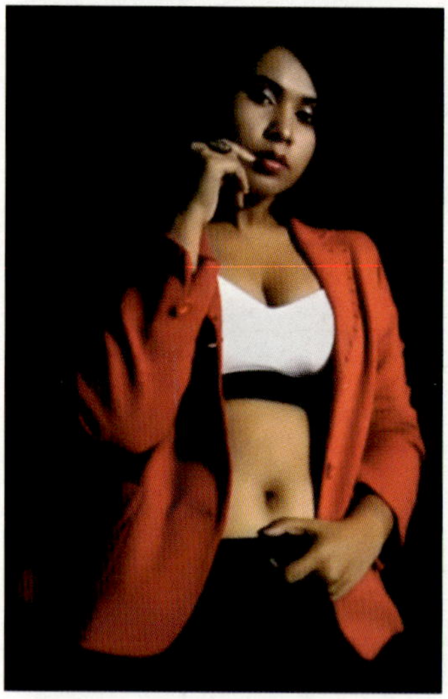

Fig. 12

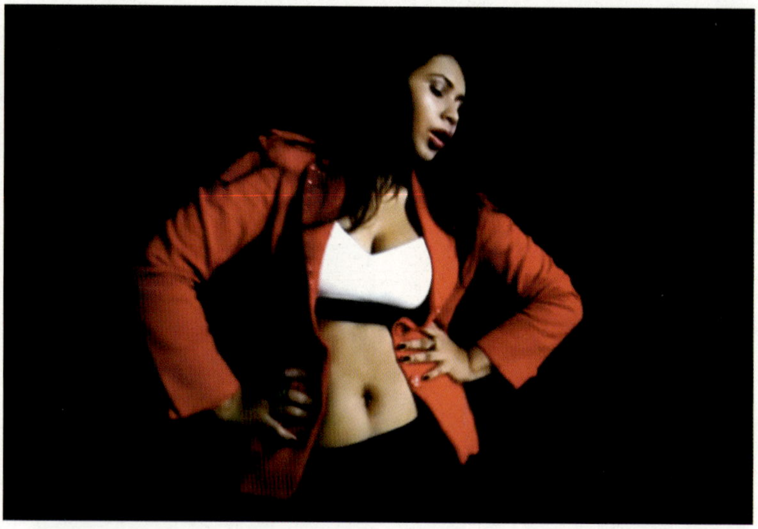

Fig. 13

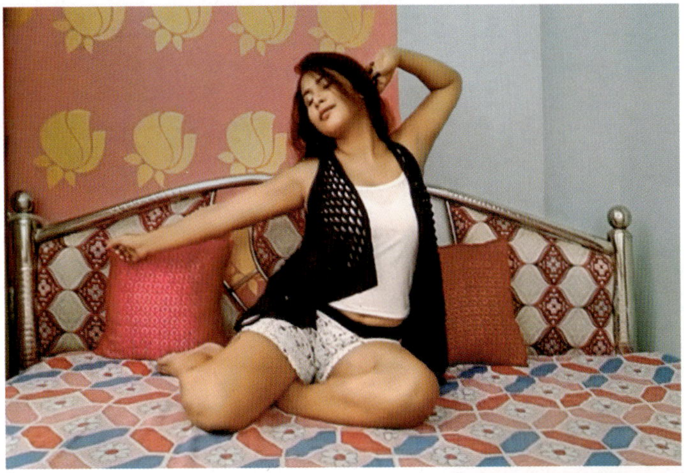

Fig. 14

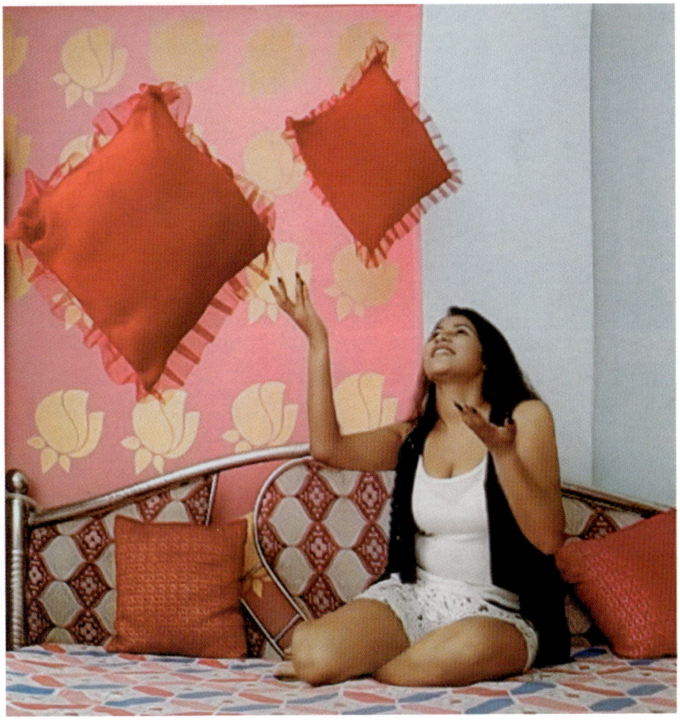

Fig. 15

I made a photo tutorial on this subject and uploaded on you tube on 16th May, 2020 so that other photographers can learn and use this technique. You can watch this tutorial by scanning the QR code mentioned here.

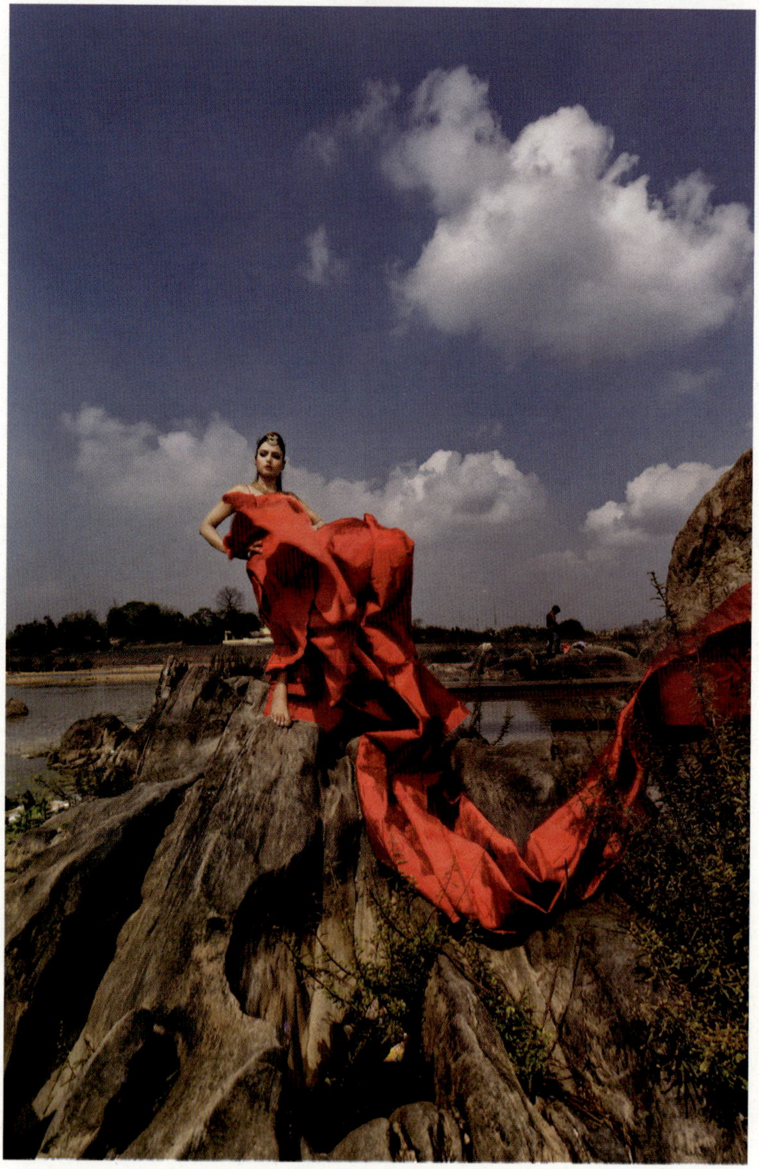

13. Experiments with Body Forms

It's very interesting while visualising the body form with alphabets, geometrical forms & design elements. Use of creative lighting pattern is very important for such experiments.

Thanx to Loannis Lykouris whose works were my source of inspiration.

I selected models with beautiful figure and flexible body. Thanx to Veronica Alfraid and Bipasha Dutta to support me in such experiments with body forms.

Lighting

This is very important to use creative light to get body forms pop up. You can use either single large octa or two lights placed at 45 degree in the back of the model.

Fig. 1

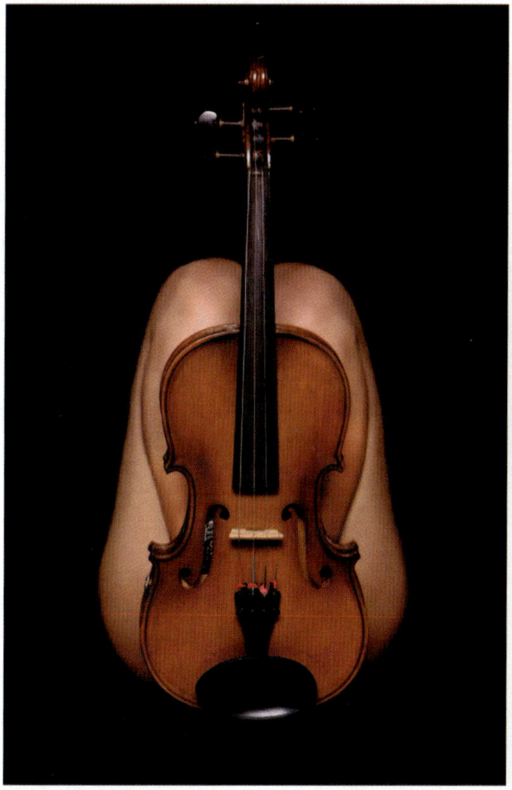

Fig. 2

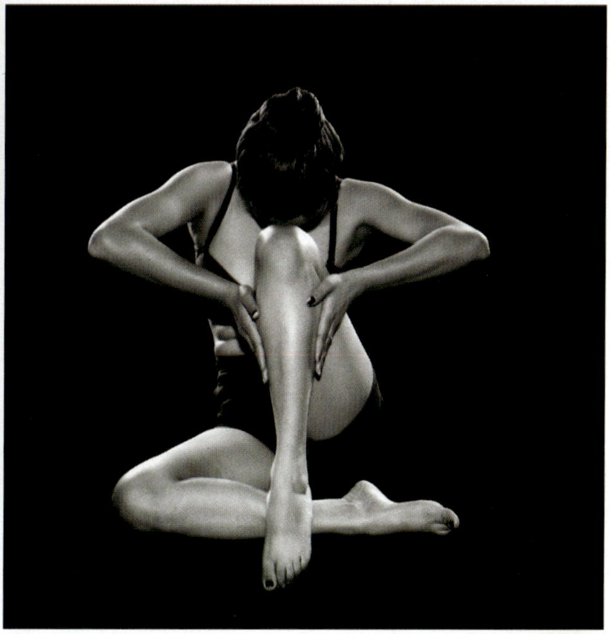

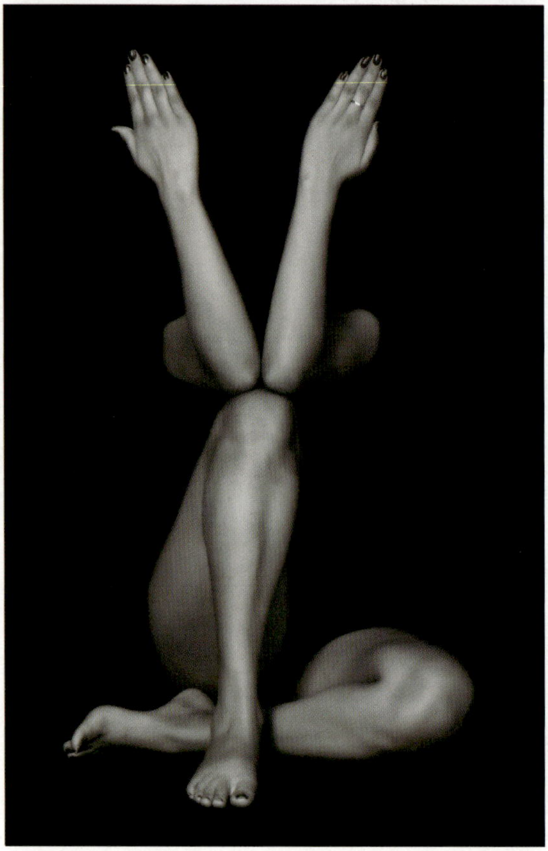

Fig. 3

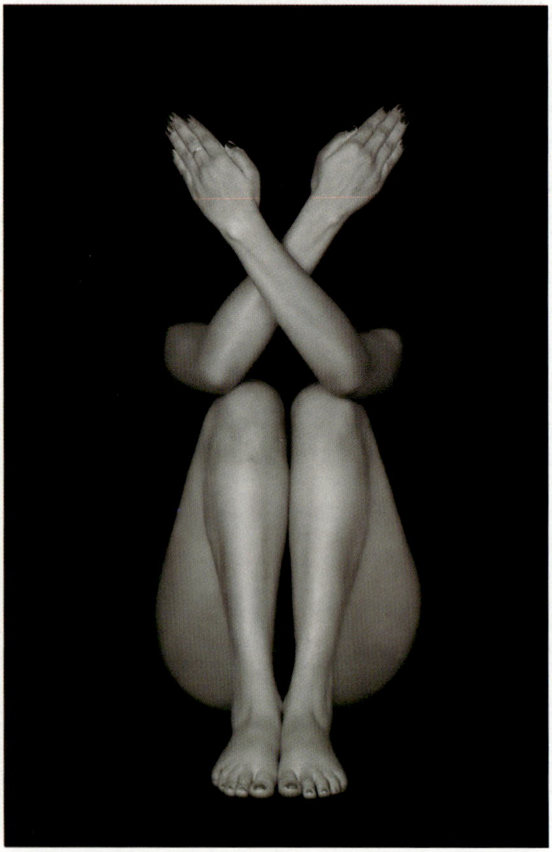

Fig. 4

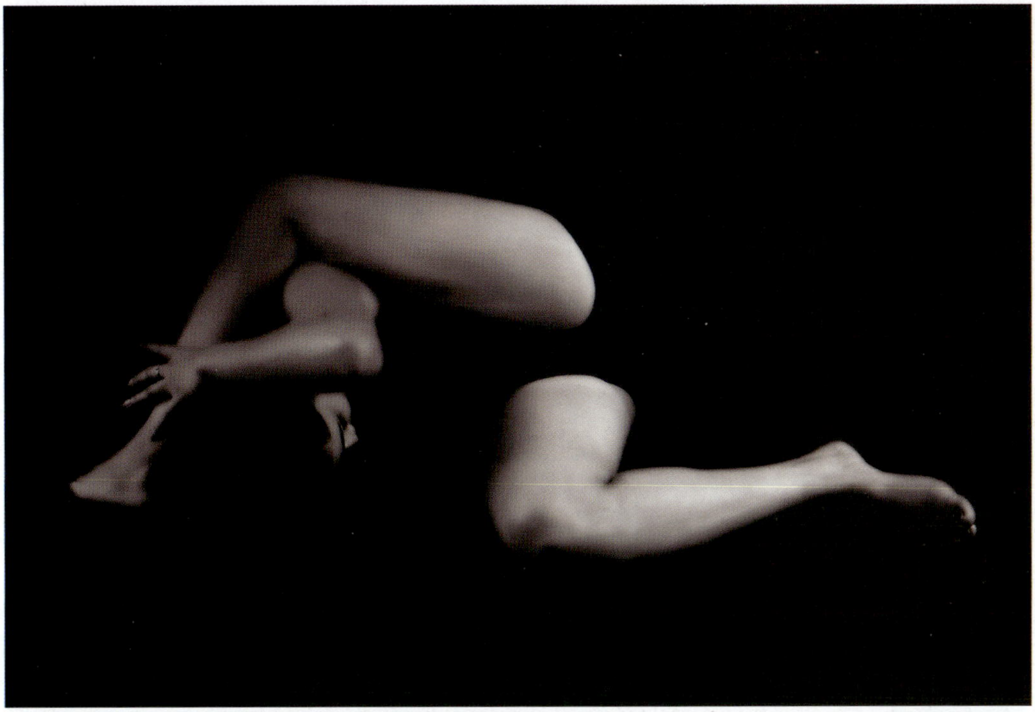

Fig. 5

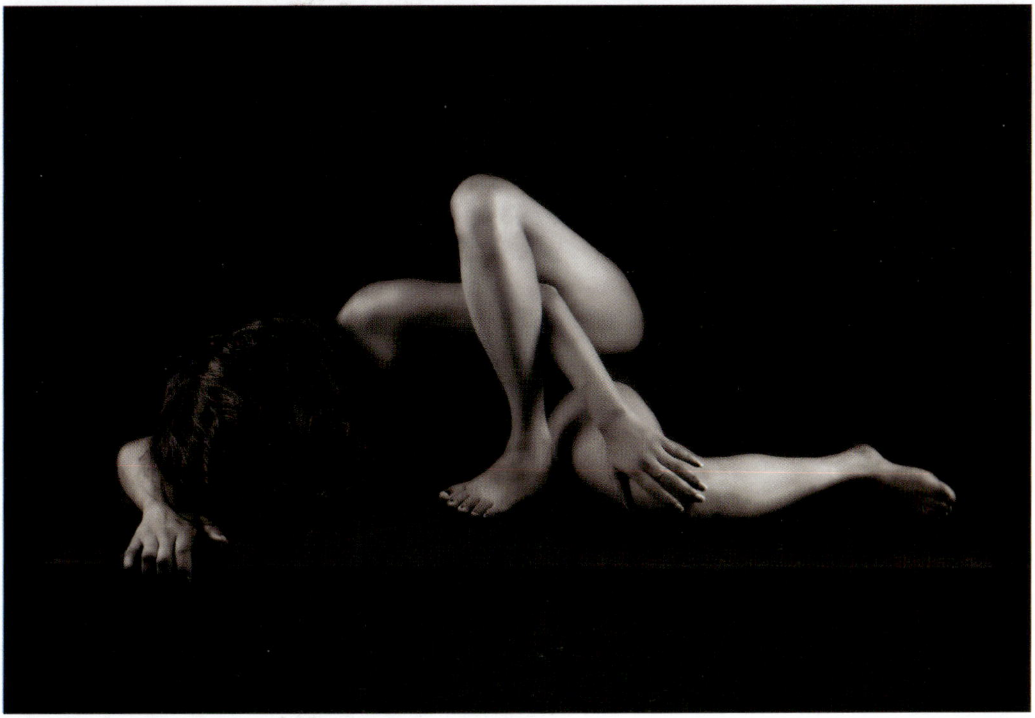

Fig. 6

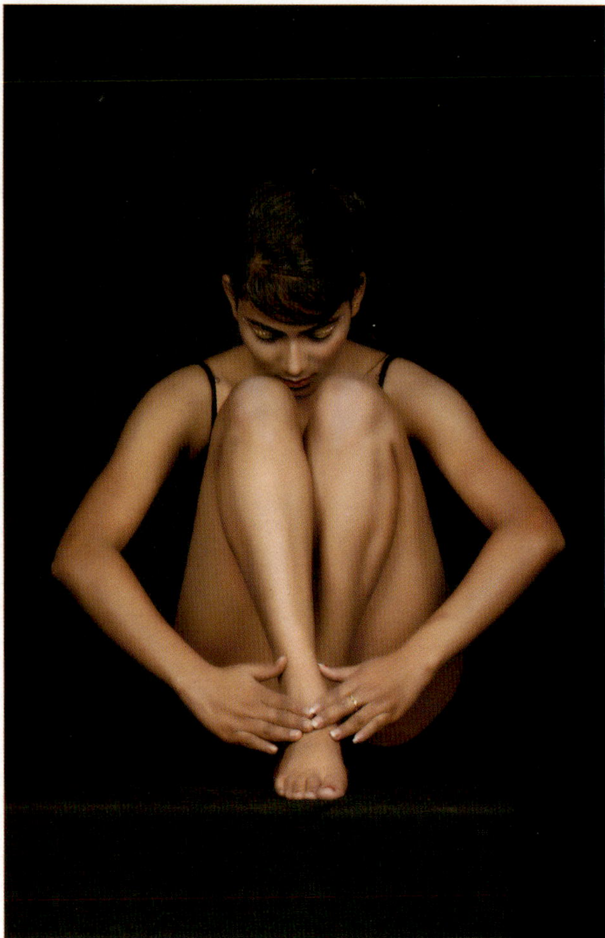

◀ Fig. 7

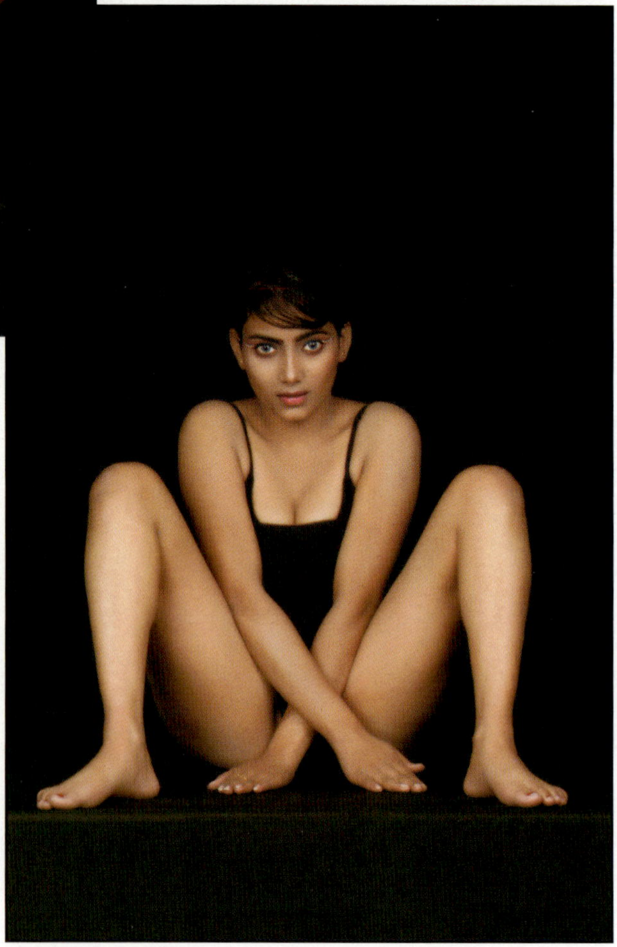

Fig. 8 ▶

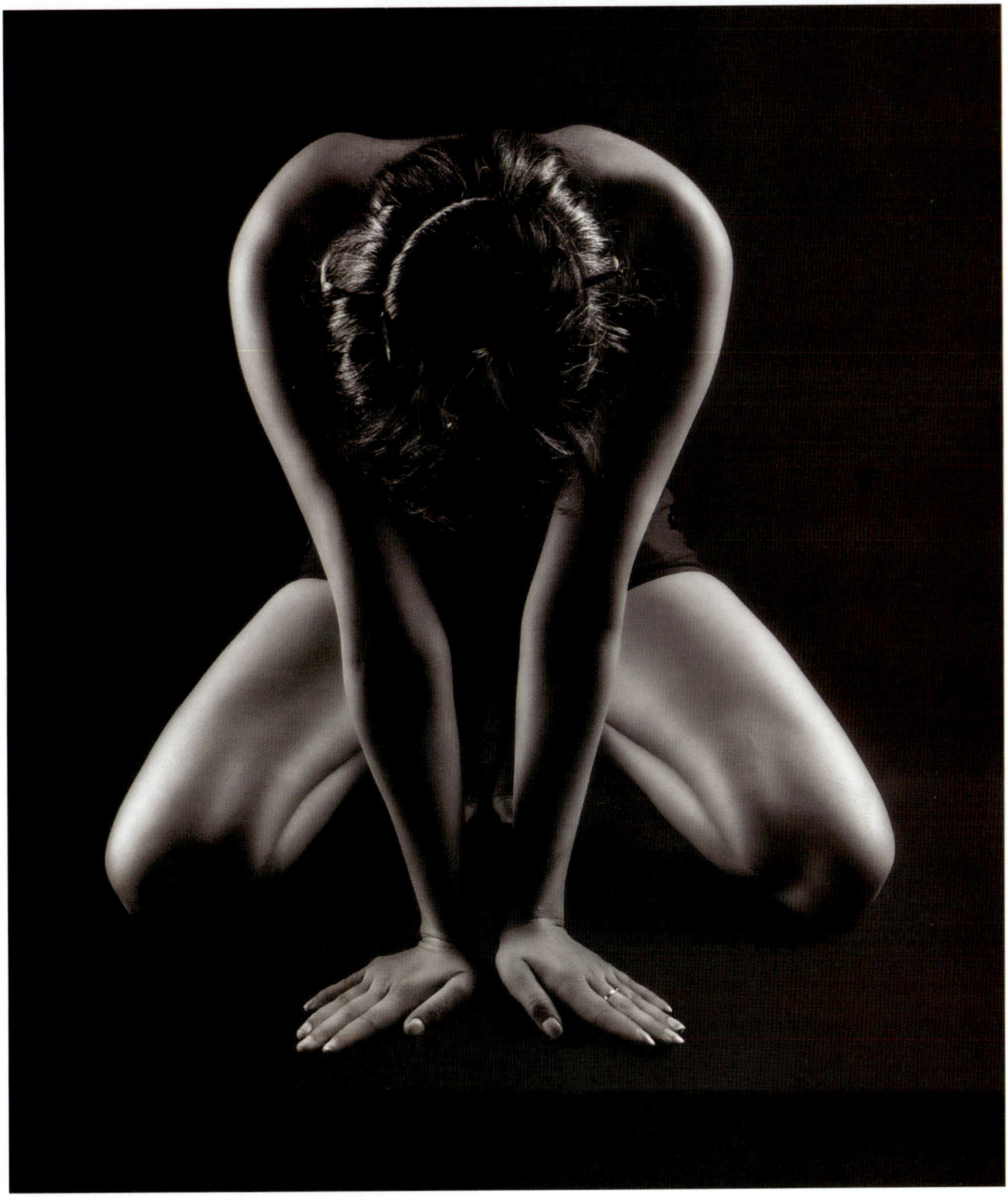

Fig. 9

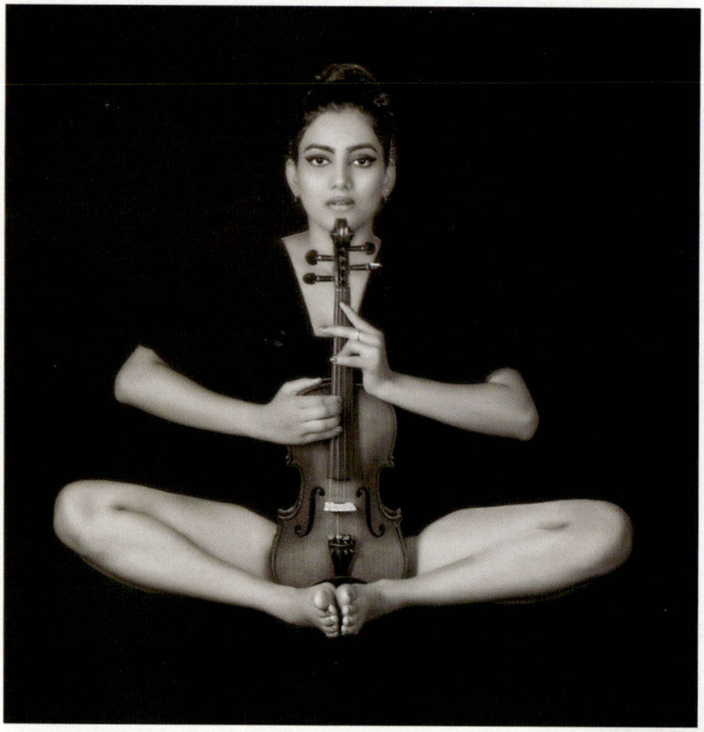

Fig. 10

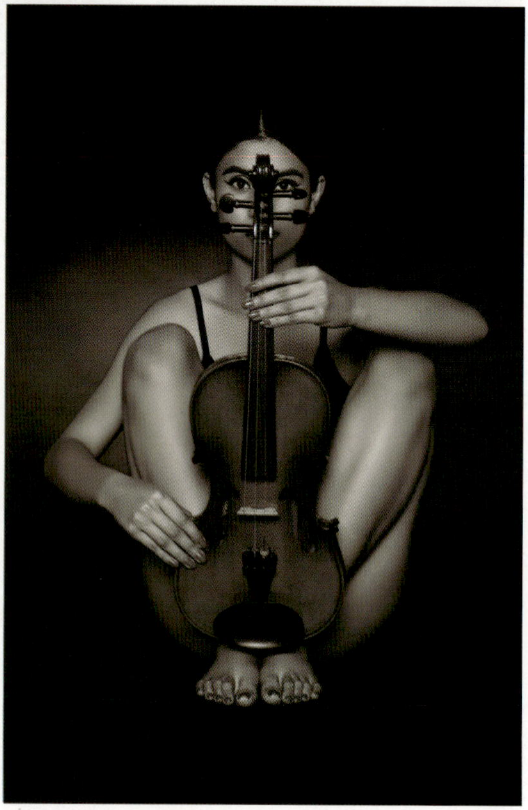

Fig. 11

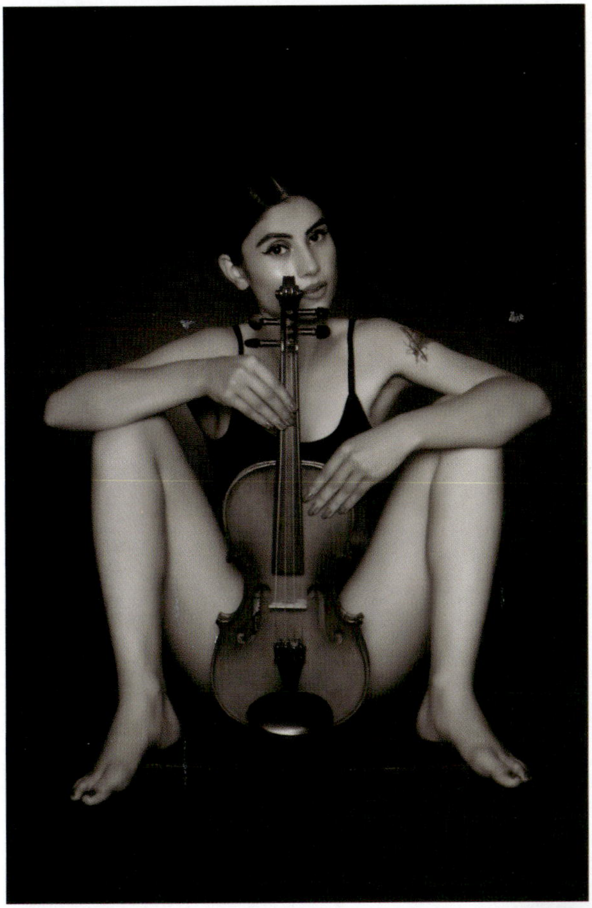

Fig. 12

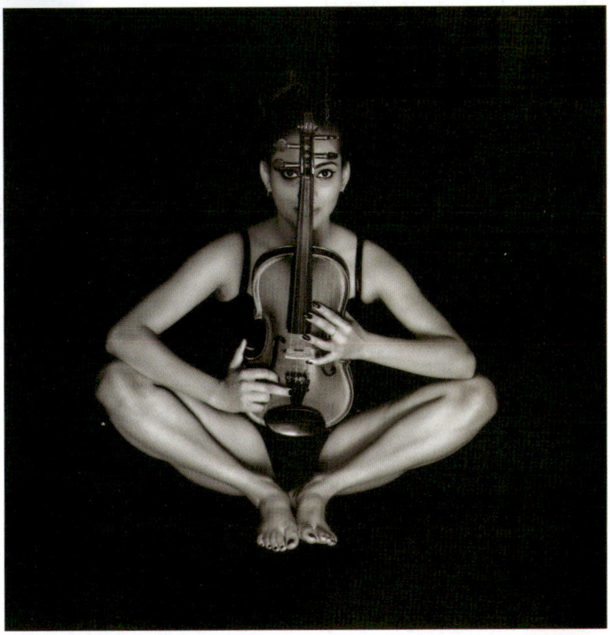

Fig. 13

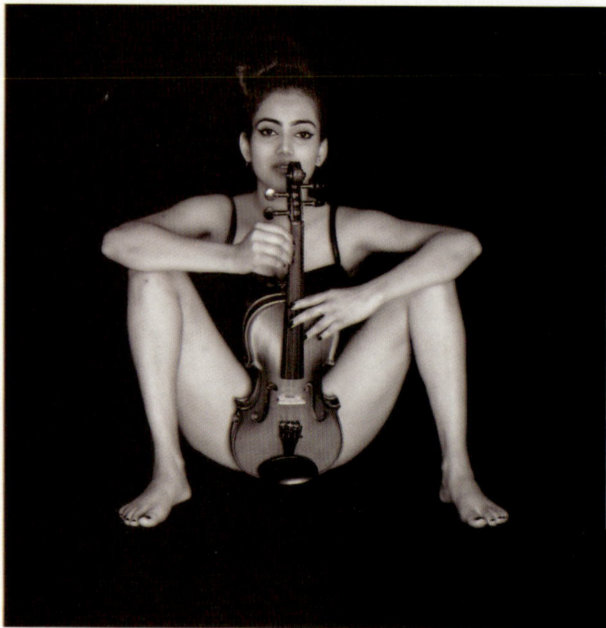

Fig. 14

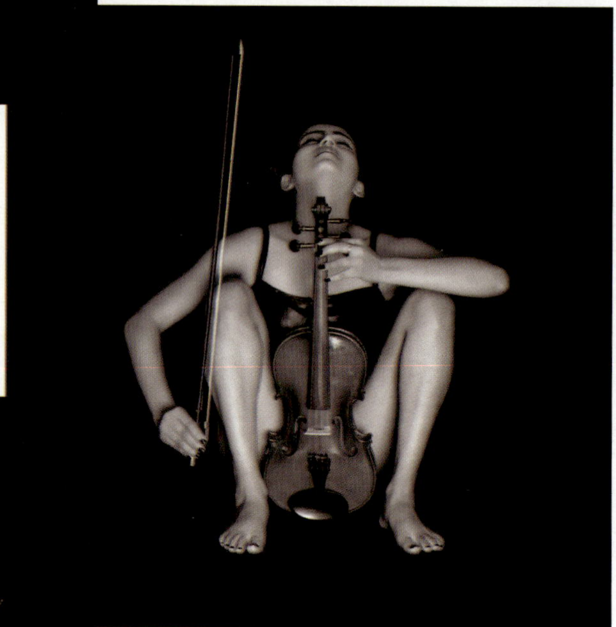

Fig. 15

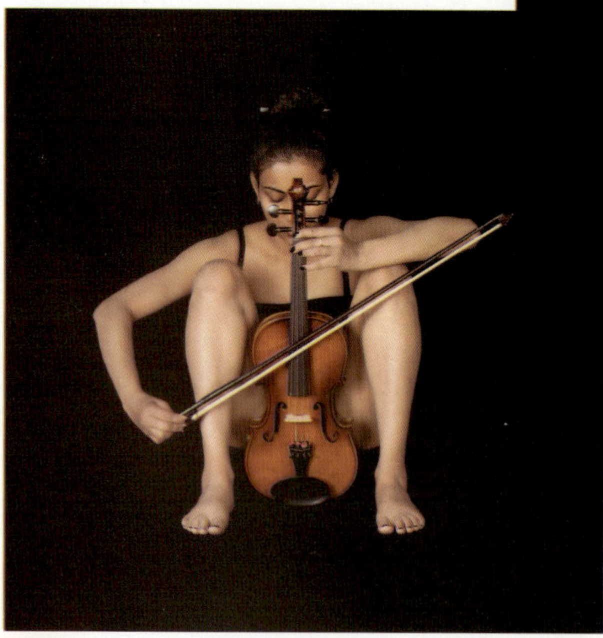

Fig. 16

14. Art of Wine Glass

In 2009 the idea of creating art using wine glasses came to my mind. I planned and got the technical inputs from my Guru Ms. Susan of Holland. I observed her works and created my own. The main technique here is the use of computer monitor as a light source. Rest is your creativity to arrange glasses to create a frame with variety of forms and geometrical shapes.

Technique

Create a wall paper of your creative idea and place it on the desk top. Keep in mind the theory of light i.e. reflection and refraction. This plays most important role in creating rim light and attractive back ground to suit your imagination.

Place a toughened glass or a mirror in front of the monitor (LCD monitor). Place wine glasses of different shapes and sizes to create attractive geometrical forms.

Use of tripod is a must. Place your camera preferably with prime lens. I used 105mm macro lens for more precision. Set aperture value from f/8 to f/11. Do not use f/16 or f/22. This will create chromatic abrasion.

Focus at the edge of the glass. You can use focus stacking technique described in the chapter 4 to get better DOF.

Arranging glasses is up to your creativity and imagination. This is the most part in such advanced photography.

One of my image of art of wine glass got image of the year award from PSA in 2015 (Fig. 1)

Got Image of the year award from PSA in 2015

Fig. 1

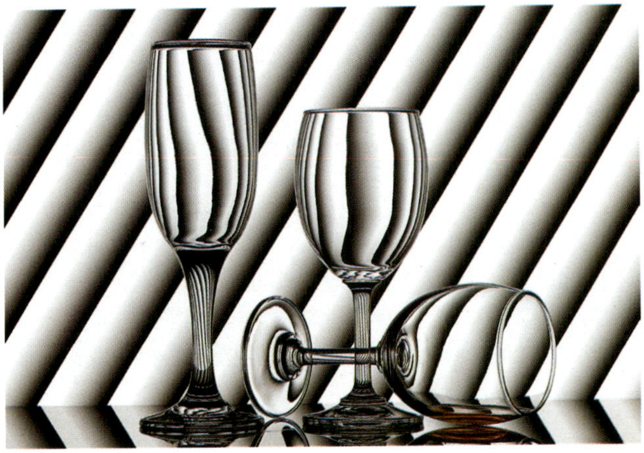

For art of wine glass at Fig. 1 I created a wall paper in photoshop and used as desktop background shown in Fig. 2.

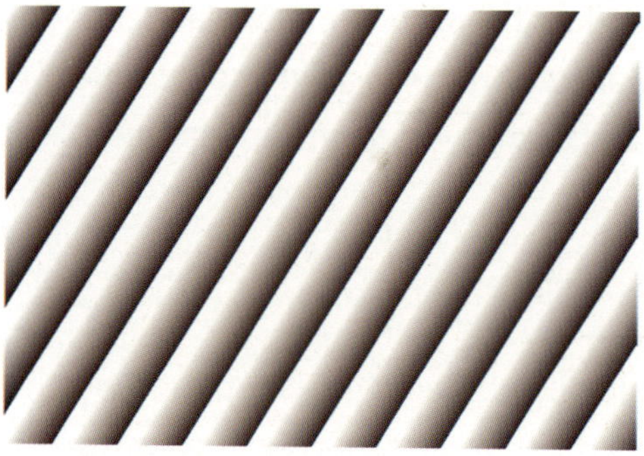

Fig. 2

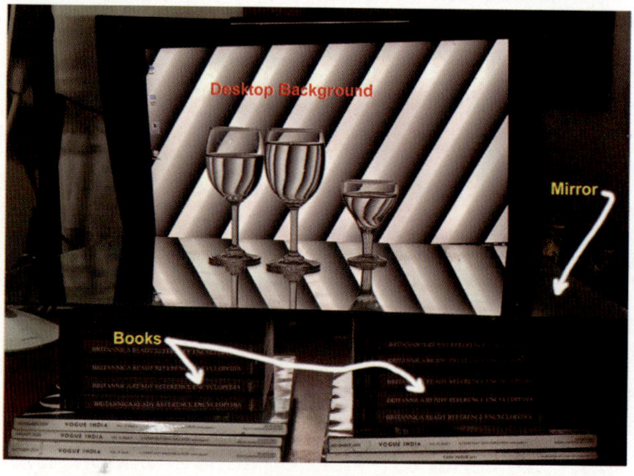

Fig. 2A

Set Up

The room must be dark. See the Fig. 2A. Set your wall paper as desktop background (Shown as red). Keep few books to place the Mirror or any dark glass (shown as white arrow). Place the wine glass empty or filled with water or any liquid. Arrange glasses as per your creativity.

See the Fig. 3. Keep your camera on tripod. Set aperture f/8 to f/11. ISO as minimum as possible. Frame the subject as per your vision and click.

See the final output in Fig. 3A after cropping and little post processing.

See Fig. 4 to Fig. 11 shot with this technique.

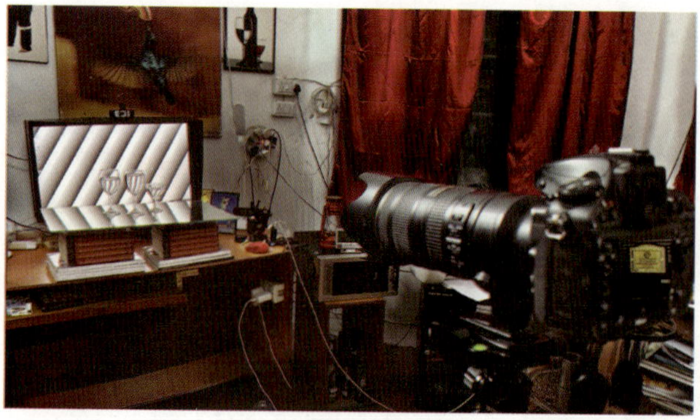

Fig. 3

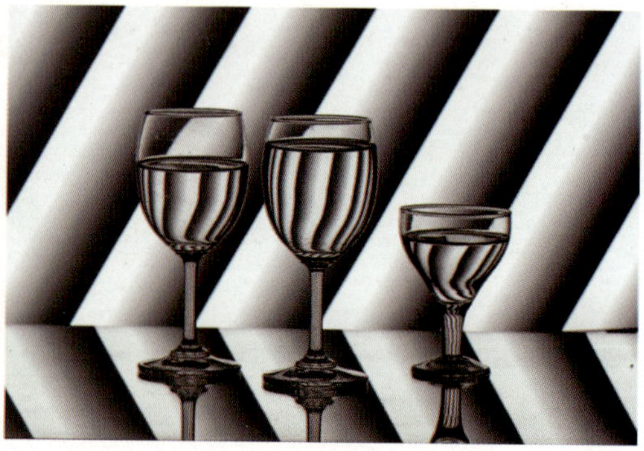

Fig. 3A

See the effect of rim light in Fig. 4 to Fig. 5.

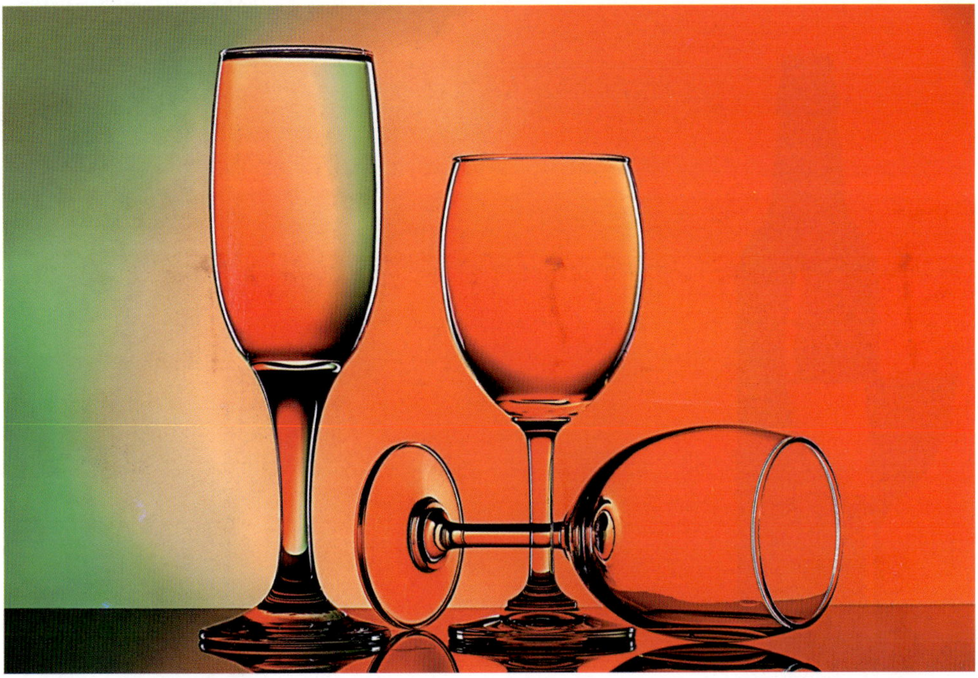

Fig. 4

With added texture in Post processing.

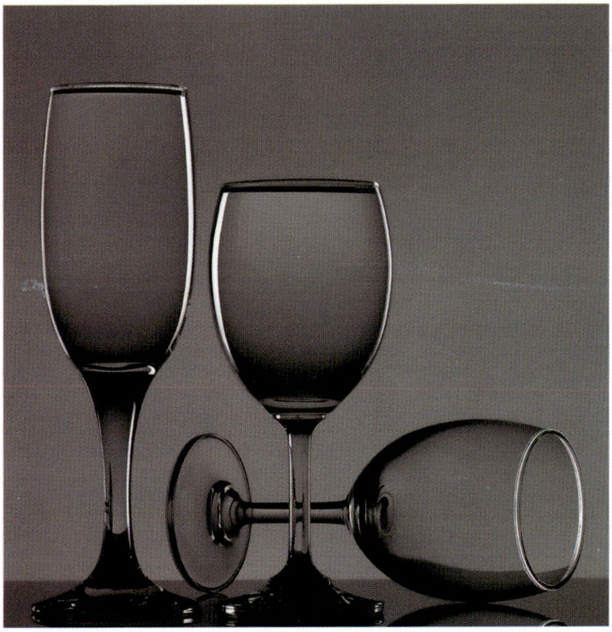

Fig. 5

With proper arrangement you can get very interesting geometrical forms. (Fig. 6 to Fig. 11)

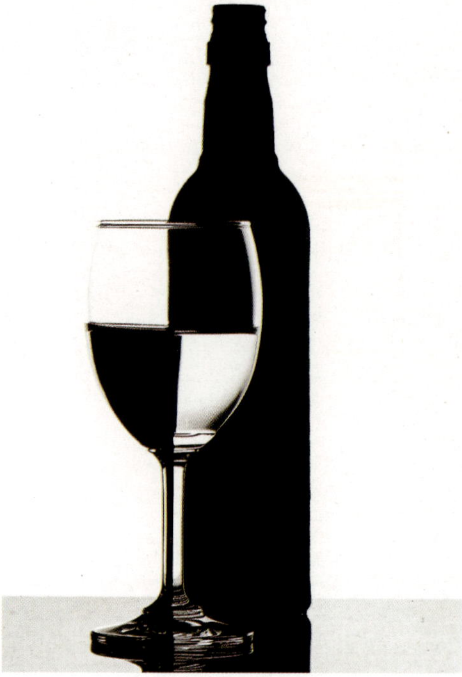

Fig. 6

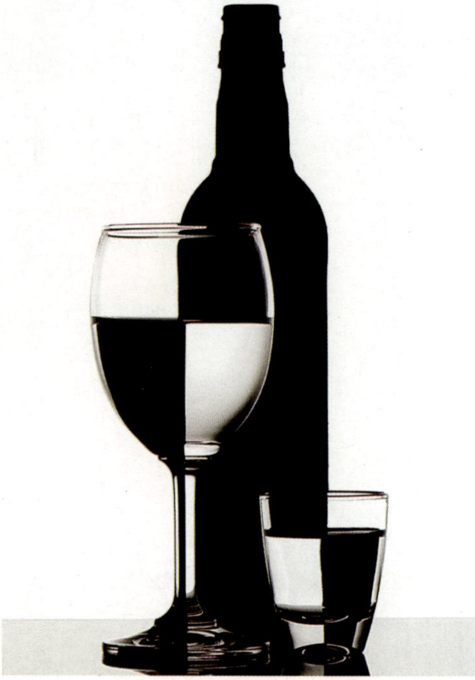

Fig. 7

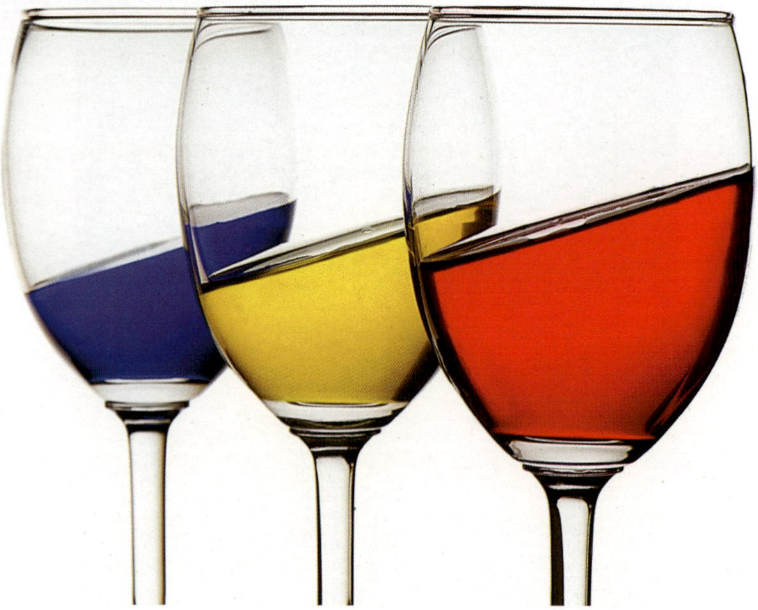

Fig. 8

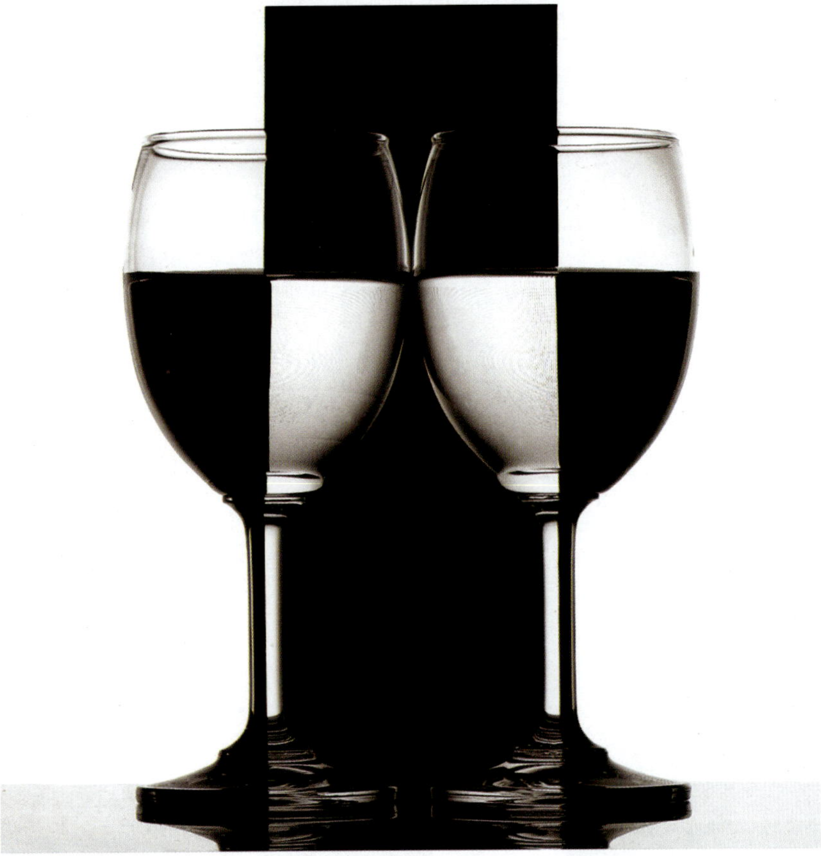

Fig. 9

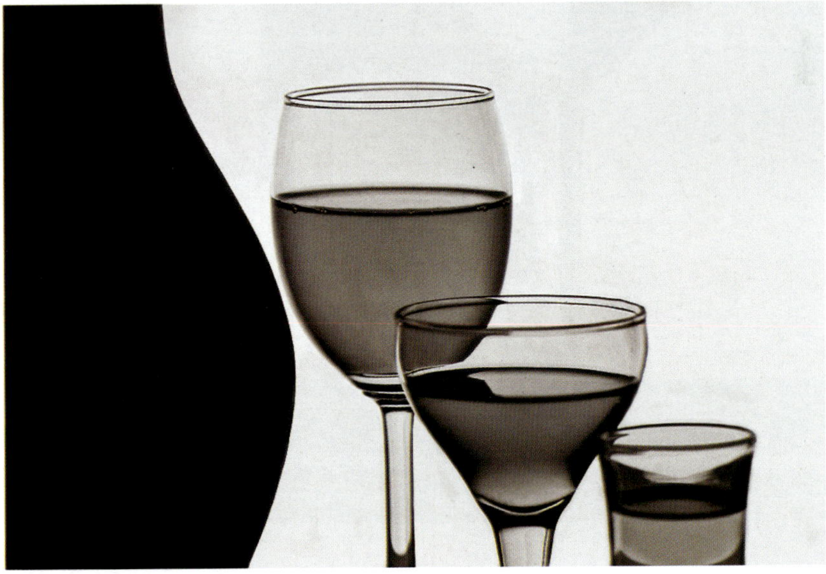

Fig. 10

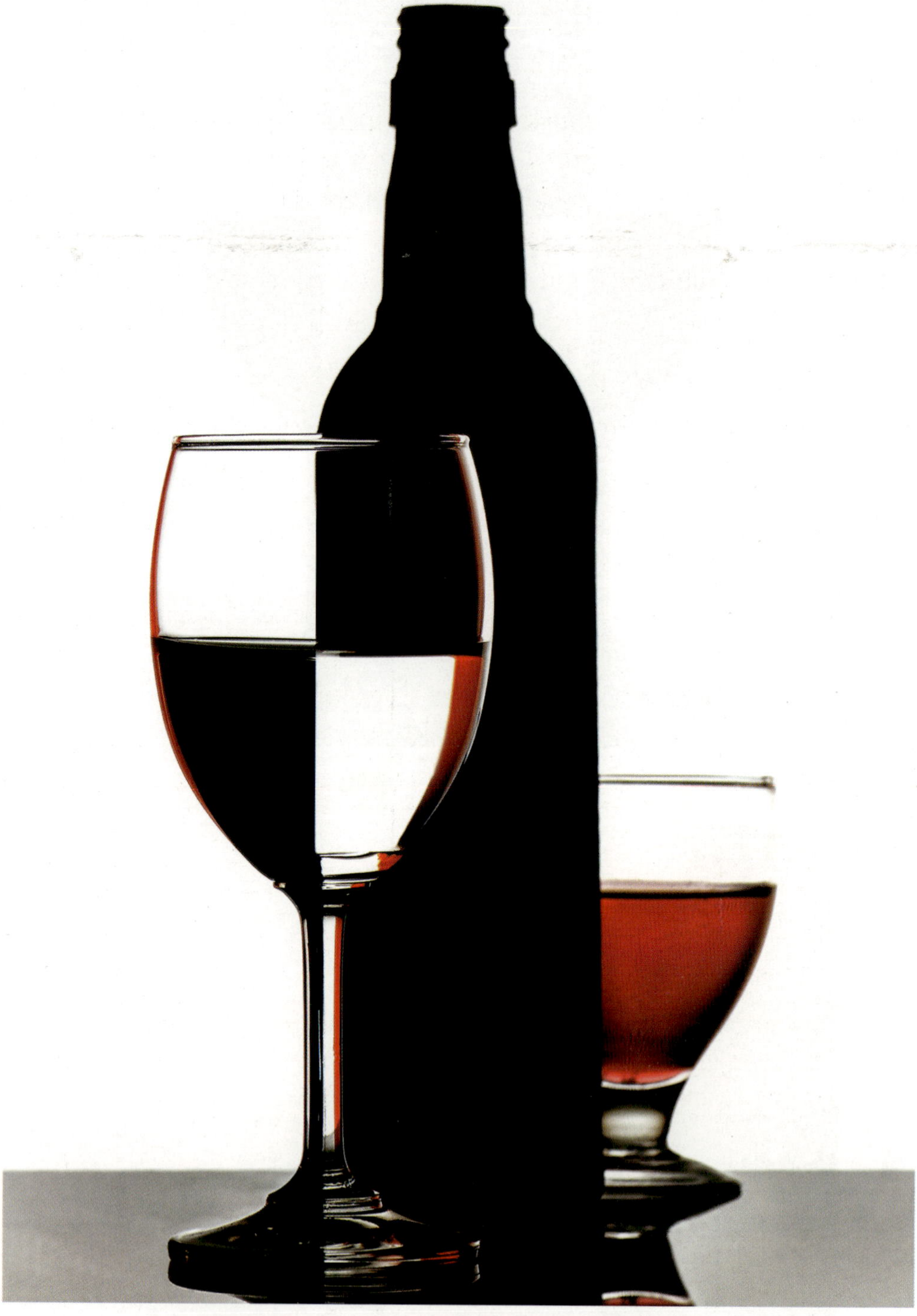

Fig. 11

15. Time Lapse Photography

There are many ways of capturing a series of images to use for creating time lapse movie. Setup your camera on a sturdy tripod and set the camera to take a photo every two to five seconds over 10 to 30 minutes. Select a location to get moving objects in the frame. Such as people walking on the street or vehicles moving on the road. You can also select a landscape if clouds are moving in the sky, you can create drama in the time lapse movie.

You can do this in various ways:

1. Use in camera Time Lapse Photography or Time Interval Shooting feature (Fig. 1 to Fig. 3).

If you use time lapse feature, you need to set interval say 5 seconds and duration say 10 minutes. Camera will click and give you a time lapse movie output. You need not to process in Photoshop or any movie software.

If you use time interval feature of the camera or external intervalometer, you will get set of images clicked at every 5 second interval and 10 minutes duration. You need to process these images in photoshop or any video editing software.

I will describe the option of using time interval feature or intervalometer in detail.

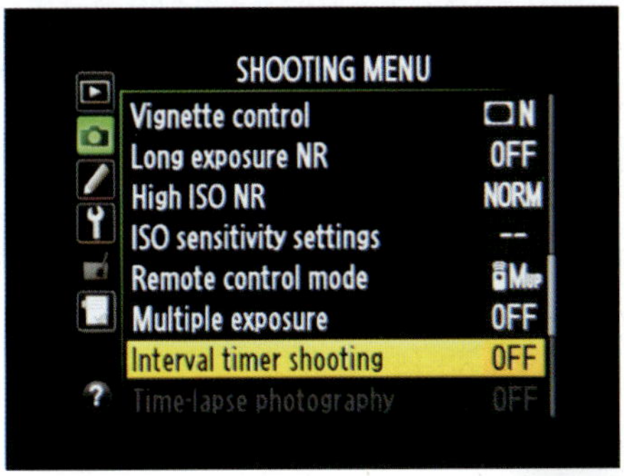

Fig. 1

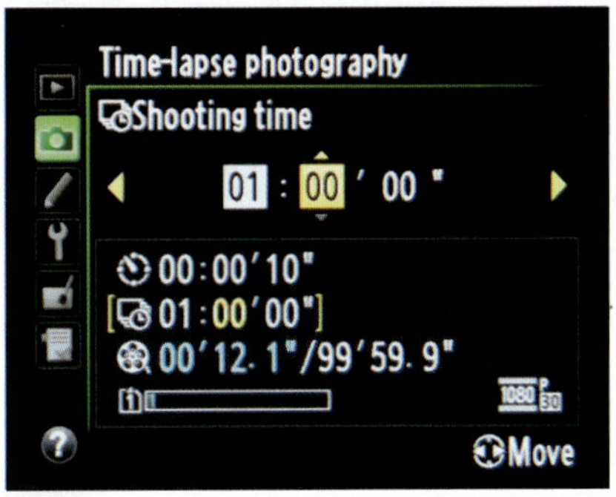

Fig. 2

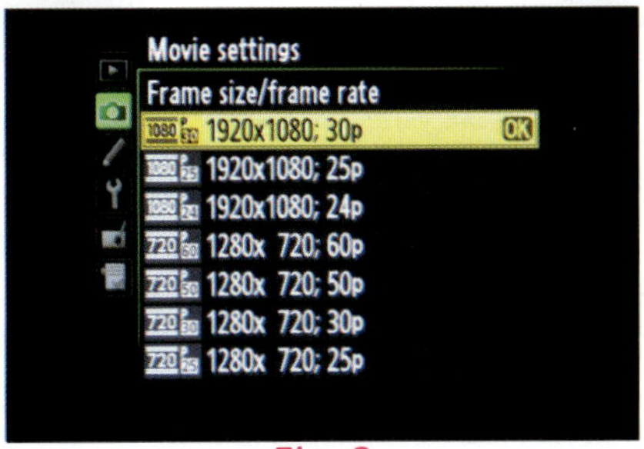

Fig. 3

2. If your camera does not have time interval feature, use intervalometer (Fig. 4 & Fig. 5)

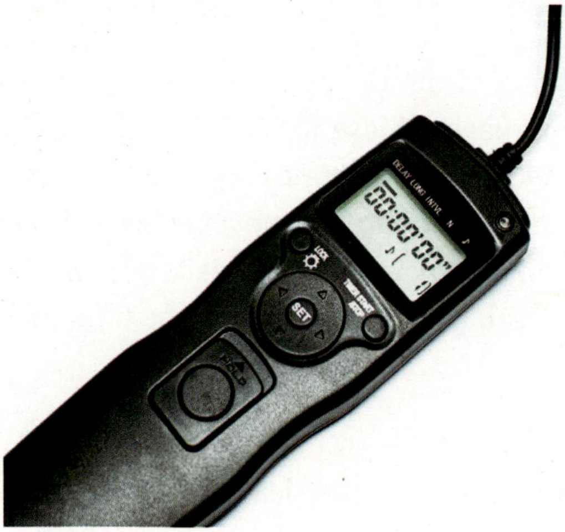

Fig. 4

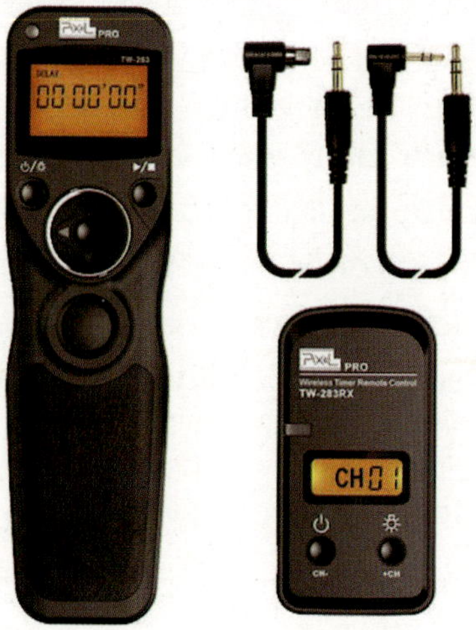

Fig. 5

3. you can also click manually using remote trigger device.

Procedure

I visited Zanskar Valley in September 2021. Planned to shoot time lapse at Gonbo Rangjon, an iconic location in Zanskar valley, Laddakh, India. Kept the tents as fore fround. Used Pixel Pro Intervalometer. Used Nikon D500 with Tokina 10-17mm lens. Set the intervalometer to click the camera every 5 second for number of shots 300.

After downloading the image, I processed RAW images in Photoshop 2022.

Editing RAW Images

Drag and drop all 300 images in photoshop. Select the first image, edit it and copy the edited parameters. In the next step select all images and paste the copied parameters. All 300 images will gett uniformly edited. Save all image in JPG format in a separate folder.

Post Processing JPG Images for Time Lapse

In Photoshop go to File and Open. (File > Open) Go to the folder with 300 images and select the first one in the sequence. In the same window, before you press Open, make sure you check the box that says "Image Sequence" which is located left bottom (Fig. 6).

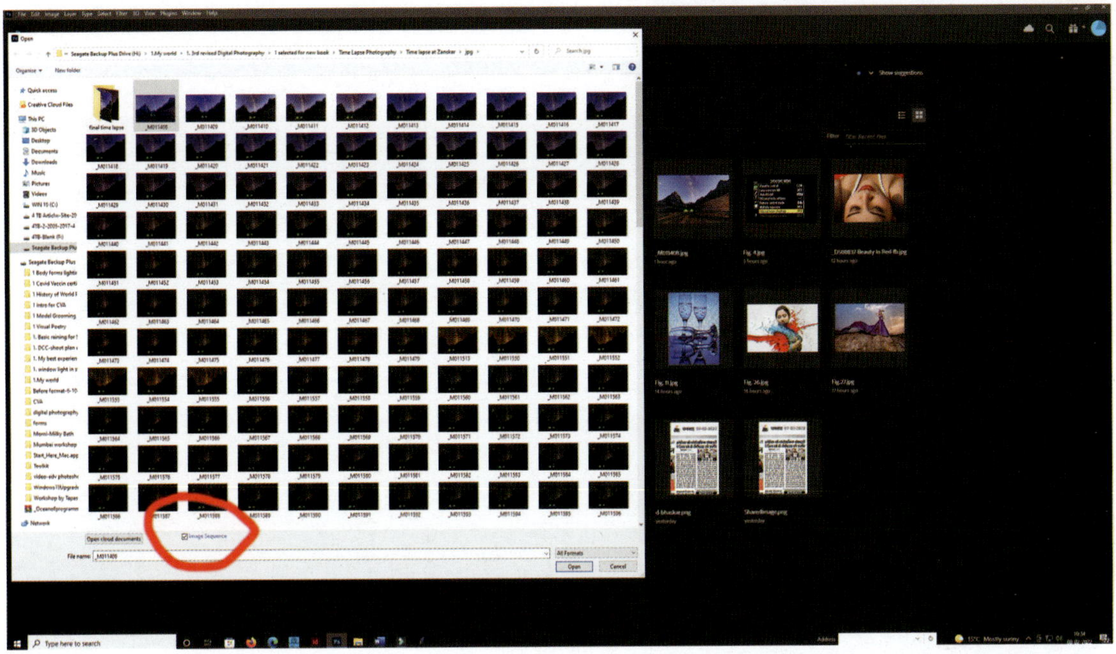

Fig. 6

Once you have checked it, select Open. Before Photoshop opens them, a new window will come to select frame rate (Fig. 7). I selected 24 frames per second. This can be changed in later stage too.

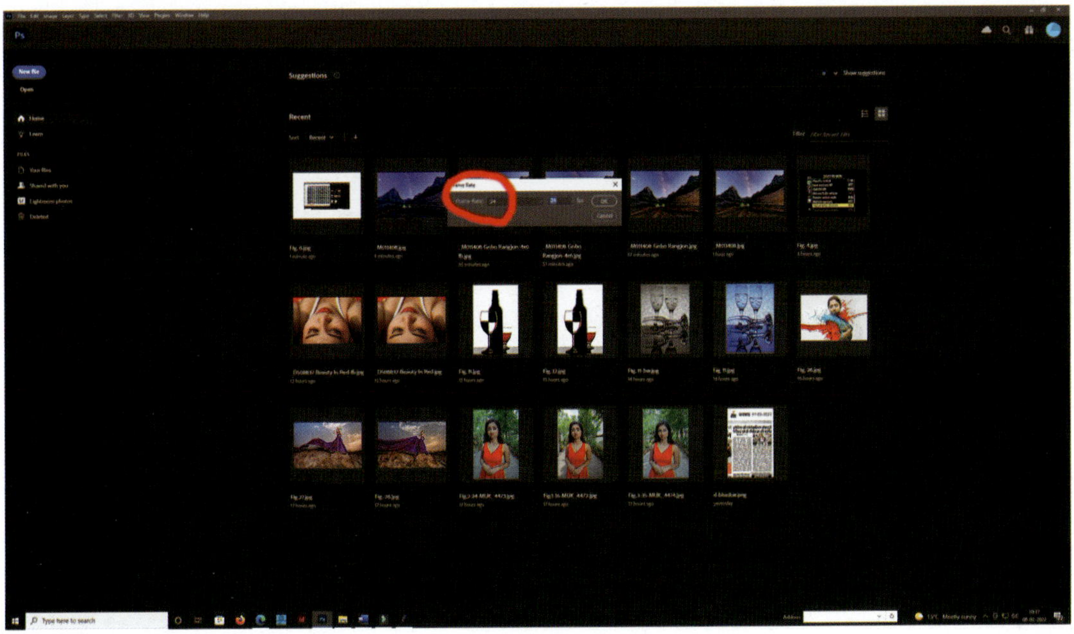

Fig. 7

To make it a time lapse you need to open another window in the Photoshop main window. Go to main menu at the top, and pull down to select "Timeline" (Fig. 8)

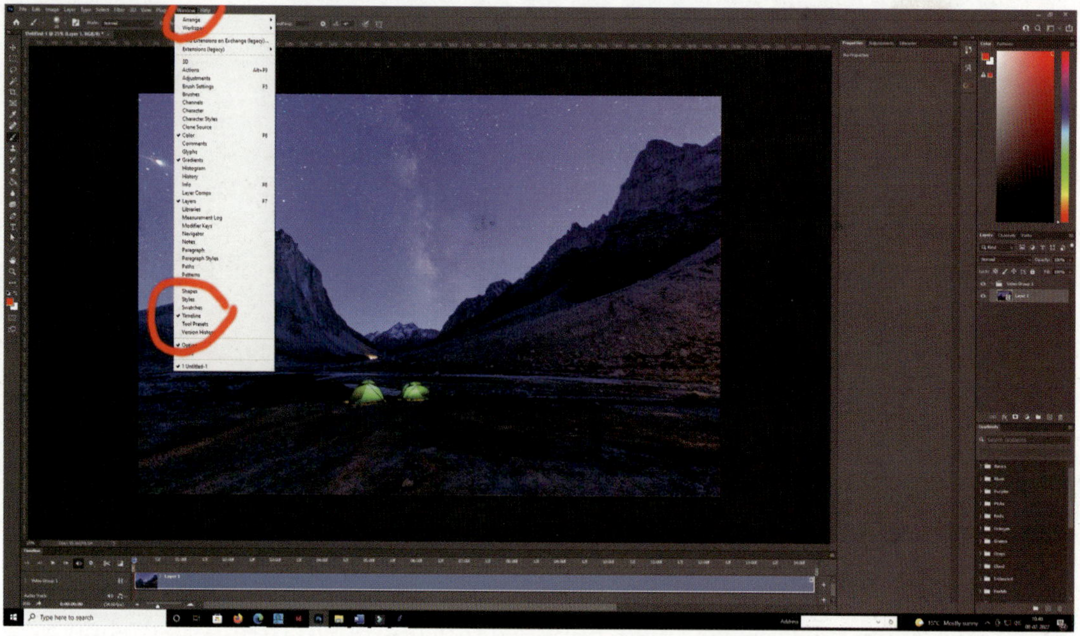

Fig. 8

You will see a new window appear down the bottom. Look at the image shown in Fig. 9.

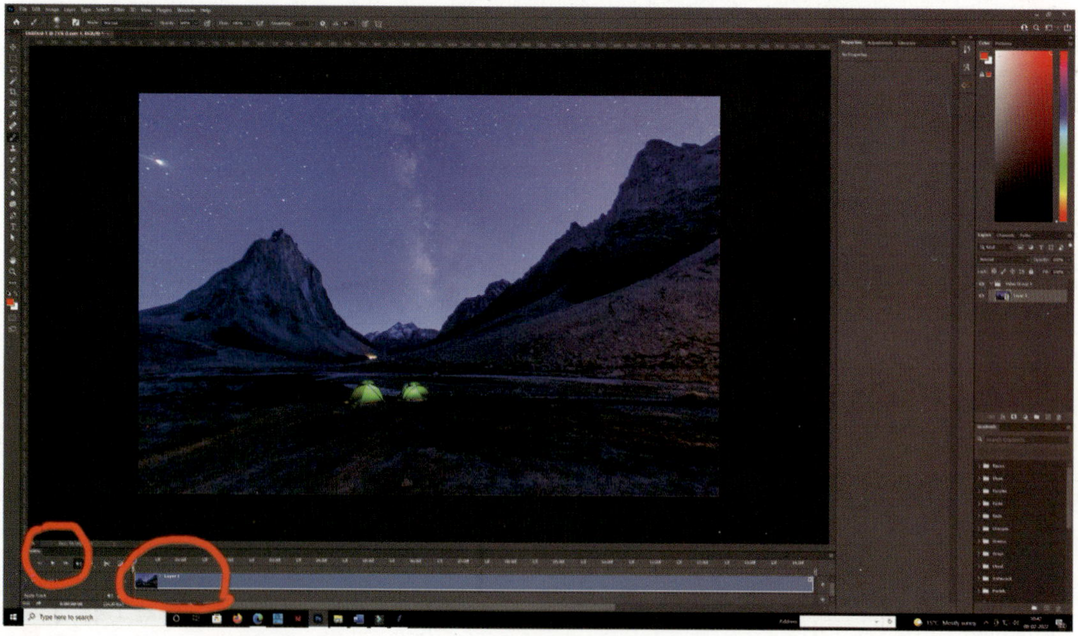

Fig. 9

Next press the play button you will see your time lapse run.

If you want to change the Frame Rate this is the time to do it. In the Timeline Window, up in the right corner, you should be able to see a down arrow with lines next to it, click on that and a drop-down menu will appear. Go down and select "Set Timeline Frame Rate" (Fig. 10).

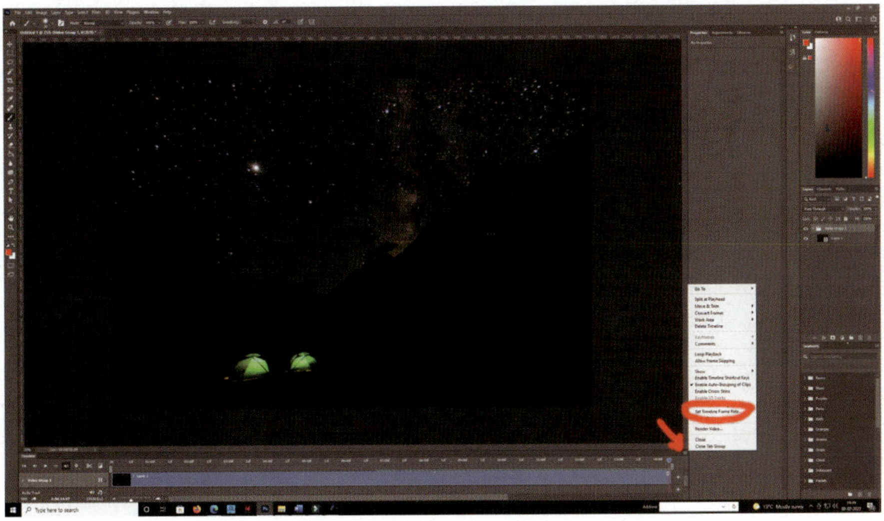

Fig. 10

Next go to File, then select Export. In the drop down menu choose Render Video. (File > Export > Render Video- Fig. 11)

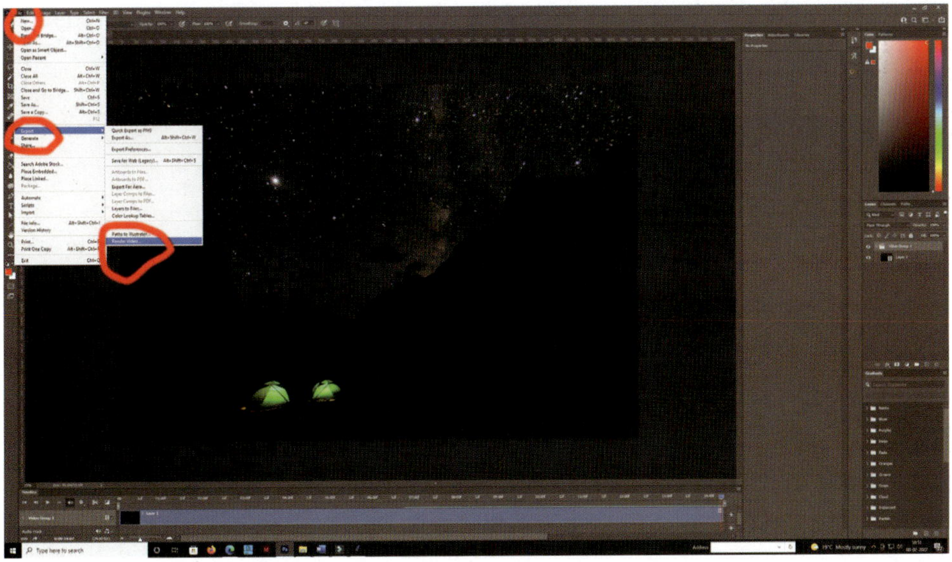

Fig. 11

After initializing, the Render Video window will come up. In this Window you can name your video and decide in what format you want it saved (Fig. 12).

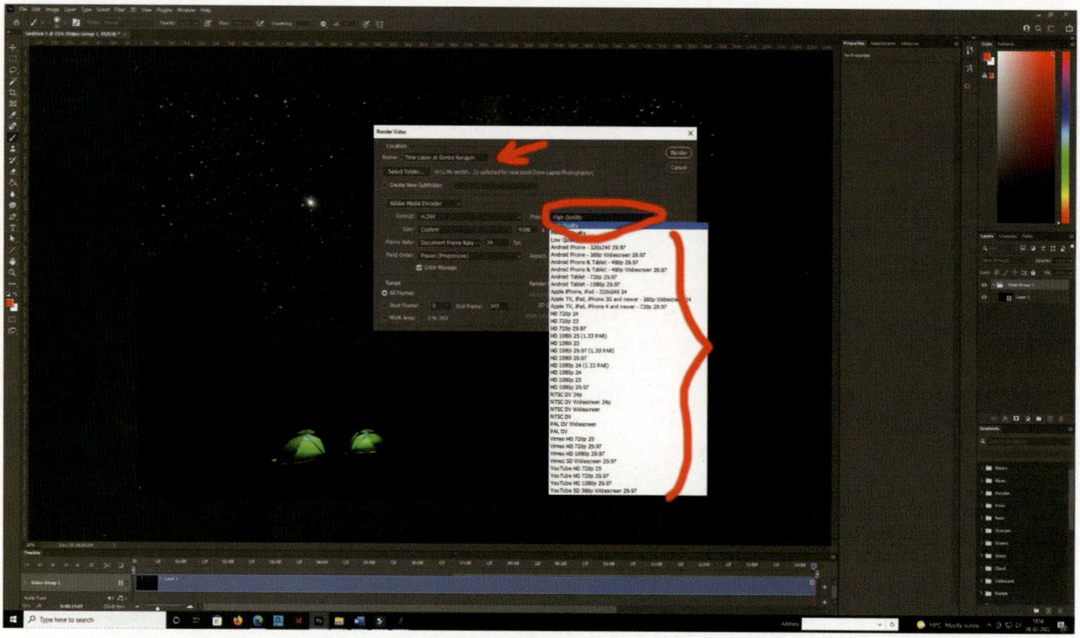

Fig. 12

Set it on one of the HD settings and you will get an MP4 video. Save this MP4 Time Lapse movie. If you need you can process this MP4 file in video editing software like Adobe Premiere Pro or Filmora to enhance colour etc. You can add audio file here as background music. I used Filmora to adjust colour and audio. You can enjoy the time lapse video by scanning the QR code shown as Fig. 13 below:

Fig. 13

16. Image Management

Image management is very important, and becomes even more so with every picture you shoot. Without proper management, your images could be lost or destroyed, and tracking existing images could be a cumbersome, onerous task.

Proper image management begins with setting up an organized system, and includes having a clear, hierarchical folder system. This system has to extend from when you first transfer images to your hard drive, to managing your edited images. It is also important to be aware of proper backup storage techniques.

Better if you keep a dedicated internal hard disk only for your photographs - no other files, no programs - just your photographs.

Create one folder each for every year of photographs you have - this will be your primary filing level. Then create sub folder for the month of your shooting. Further create a sub folder for the date and location of your shooting. That's it.

For security of your image data, make a back up copy in a portable hard disk. Further, you can save the data in the cloud too for better security.

See the flow chart of image management system on next age.

One of my image of art of wine glass got image of the year award from PSA in 2015 (Fig. 1)

Image Management System

↓

Dedicated hard disk for Photos (Say My Photos)

↓

Create folder year wise. (Say 2011)

↓

Create sub folder for Month (say January)

↓

Create sub folder for Shooting date & Location (say 10.1.11-model shoot)

↓

Transfer your images shot on that day

↓

Create "Edited" sub folder

↓

Edit the selected images and save in the Edited sub folder

↓

Tag every images in Adobe Bridge

↓

Make a back up another portable hard disk

↓

Make third back up in the cloud and store like film negatives.

Fig. 1

17. Ready Reckoner Table

A chart showing Types of Picture to shoot and important settings of the camera such as Metering mode, Priority modes such as A, P, S, M based on my own experience is as below:

Note: This is just to start shooting. You can experiment further.

BDE (Basic Daylight Exp.) = 1/ISO @ f16

Type	Metering	Priority	Aperture	Exposure	Remarks
Close up Portrait	Center weighted	A/M	1.4 to 11	——	
Landscape	Matrix/ Evaluative	A/M	8 to 16	———	
Landscape (Sunrise/ Sunset)	Spot (Sky)	M	8 to 16	———-	Use GND filter
Fire Works	Matrix/ Evaluative	M	8	10-30sec	Use Tripod
Water Fall	Matrix/ Evaluative	M	8 to 11	1/8 to few seconds	For Streaks & Milky flow
Landscape (Moonlit)	Matrix/ Evaluative	M	8 to 11	2 to 5 minutes	
Landscape (Stars)	Matrix/ Evaluative	M	8 to 11	15 to 30 minutes	Follow rule 500/600
Motion (Freezing)	Matrix/ Evaluative	S/M		1/250s 1/500s 1/1000s 1/4000s	People Horse etc Car/train Birds
Tracking shots (From one moving vehicle to Another)	Spot/ Matrix		—	1/8s, 1/15s ets.	
Panning Shots (Swing camera to give panoramic effect or follow subject)	Matrix/ Evaluative S/M	S/M	——	1/8s, 1/15s ets.	Prefocus on closer point. Follow subject. Continue moving camera after shutter release.

Type	Metering	Priority	Aperture	Exposure	Remarks
Static Camera Moving Subjects (Swinging palm tree, Flowers etc.)	Spot	S/M	——-	1/8s, 1/4s, 1/2s	
Creative Technique (Zooming + slow shutter speed) (a) **Lower to higher focal length gives outwards streaks.** (b) **Higher to lower focal length gives inward streaks.**	Spot	S/M	——-	1/4s, 1/2s	
Creative Technique (Moving camera in an arc)	Spot	S/M		1/4s to 1s	Focus on main subject & move camera in an arc.
Night shots (Traffic & streaks)	Matrix/ Evaluative	S/M	—-	1/10s, 1/30s	
Raining	Matrix/ Evaluative	S/M		1/25s, 1/30s	

18. Advanced Lighting System & Patterns

Advanced Lighting System

There are certain lighting rules to achieve the WOW factor in a portrait. You will get complete details with the visual presentation below.

Lighting System-1 with single softbox and reflector

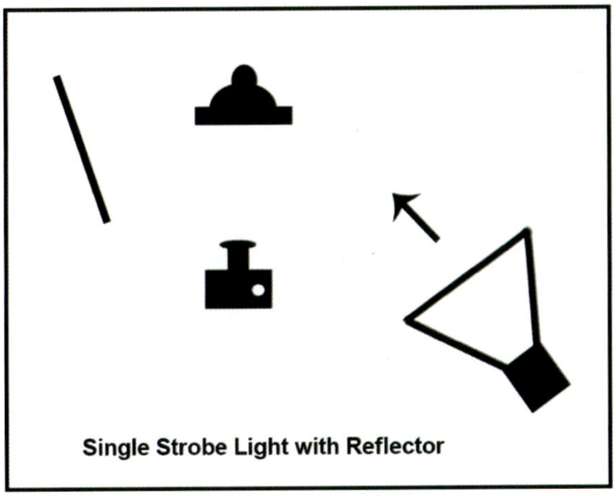

Fig. 1

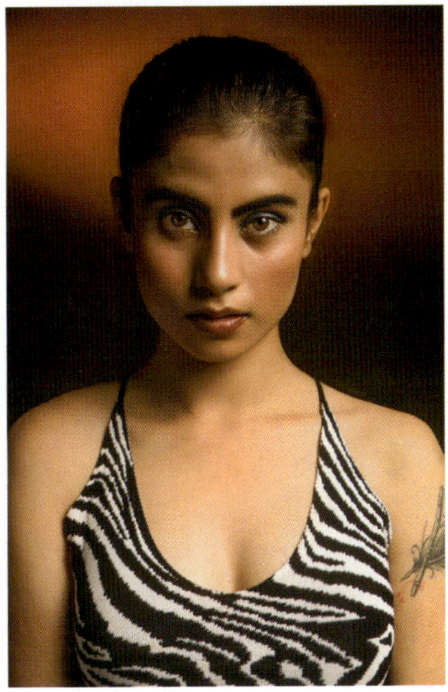

Fig. 2 Used single soft box and reflector

Set Up

Place the model at a distance of 3 feet to 5 feet from the background. Put the light to the right or left of the camera and raise at 45 degree from the nose of the model.. This is the key light. Keep very close to the model to get soft light. Use the biggest softbox you have, and have it quite close to the subject. Use reflector preferably mounted on a stand to fill the shadow. This will work like a Fill light. See Fig 1 & 2.

Lighting System-2 with two softboxes

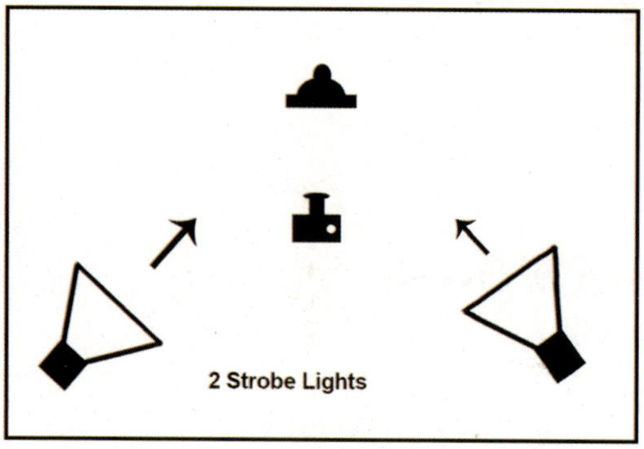

Fig. 3 Used 2 lights

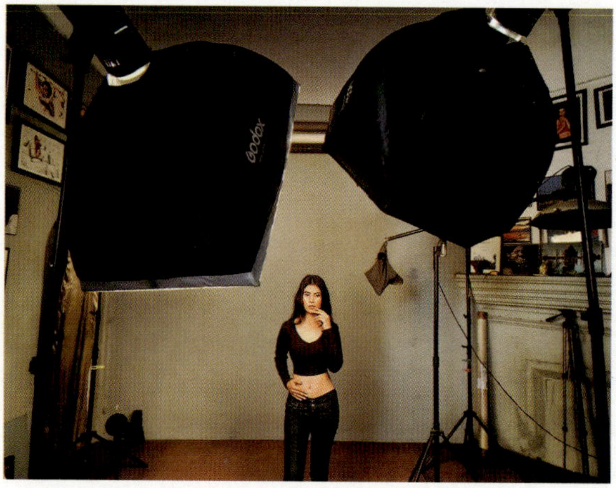

Fig. 4

Set up

Place two softboxes at an angle of 45 degree to get three-dimensional image (Fig.3, 4, 5 & 6) Alternatively two lights at 30 degree (Fig. 5). Keep the light intensity ratio of 1 : 4 or 1 : 5 to get soft shadow.

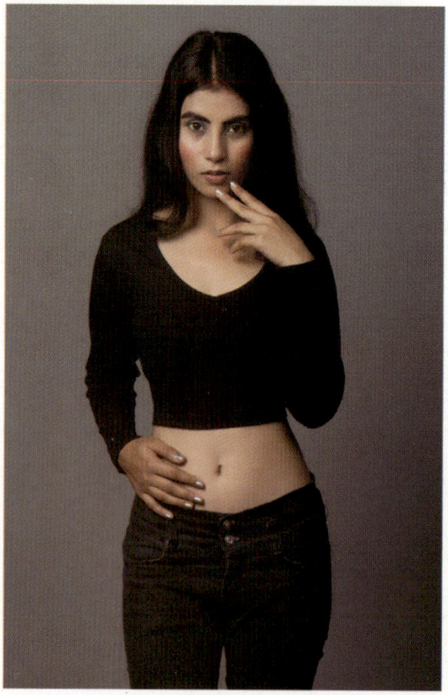

Fig. 5 Used two soft boxes. At 45 degree

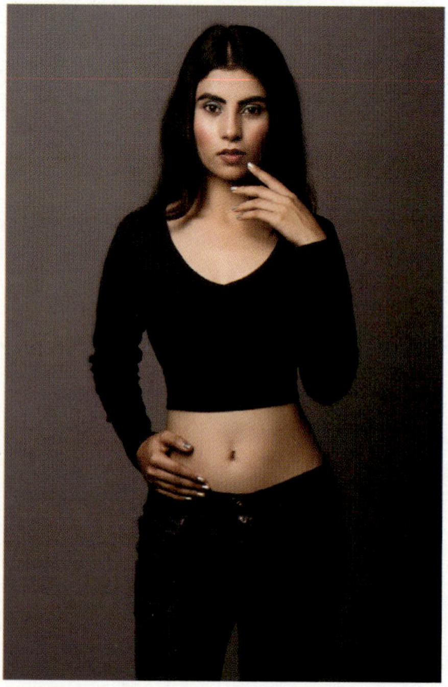

Fig. 6 Used two soft boxes. At 30 degree

Lighting System-3 with three softboxes:

Same as with two lights, but with the third light to lighten the background. (Fig. 7 & 8).

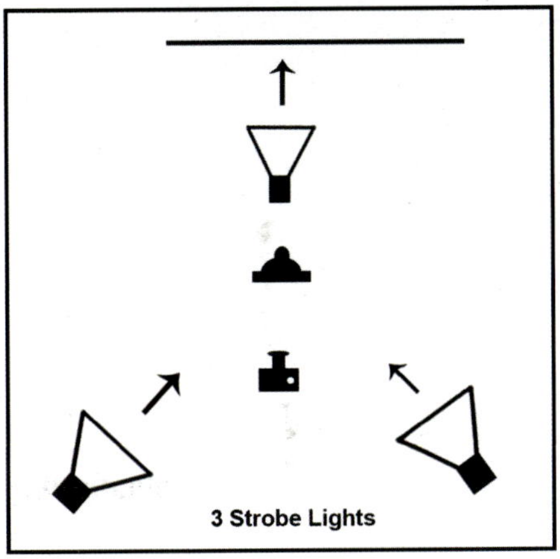

Fig. 7

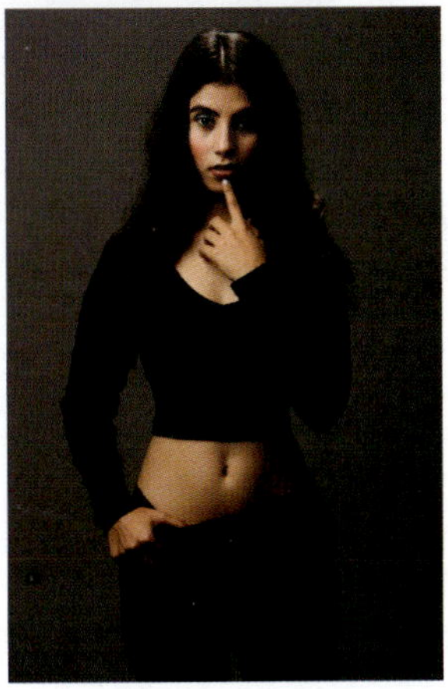

Fig. 8 Used three soft boxes

Lighting System-4 with three softboxes and hair light

Set up

First softbox is positioned at camera level.

Second softbox is positioned at an acute angle from around 3 mts height.

The hair of the model is lighted from varndoor or round softbox with honeycomb (Fig. 9).

The third softbox is positioned to lighten the backdrop. Used blue gel for the backdrop lighting. (Fig. 10 & 11)

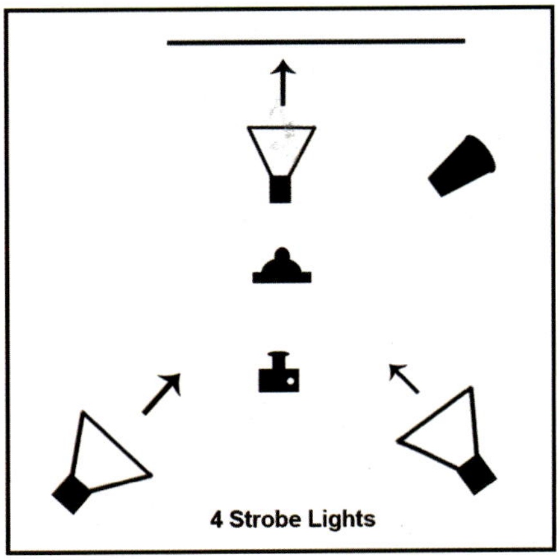

Fig. 9

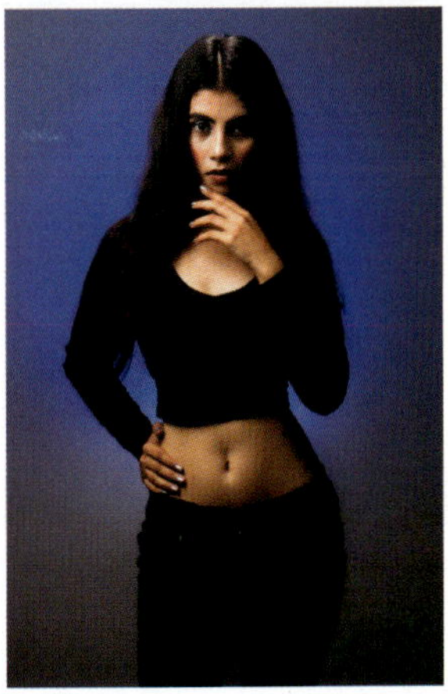

Fig. 10 Used four strobe lights

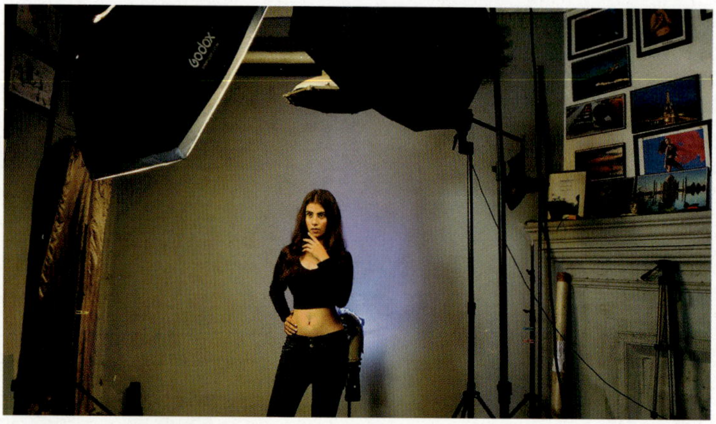

Fig. 11 Used four strobe lights

Advanced Lighting Patterns

Butterfly Lighting

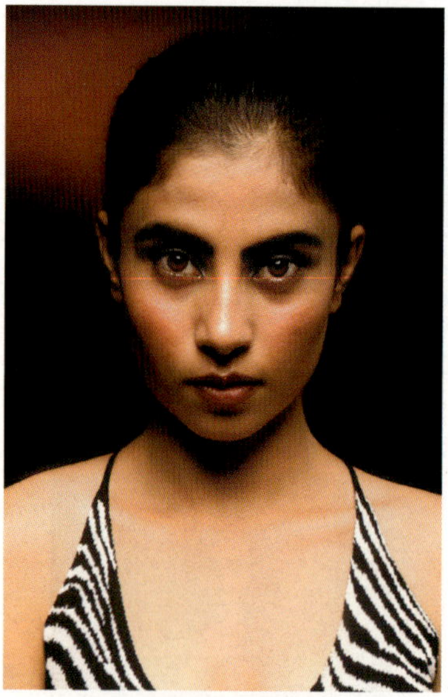

Fig. 12 Butterfly Lighting

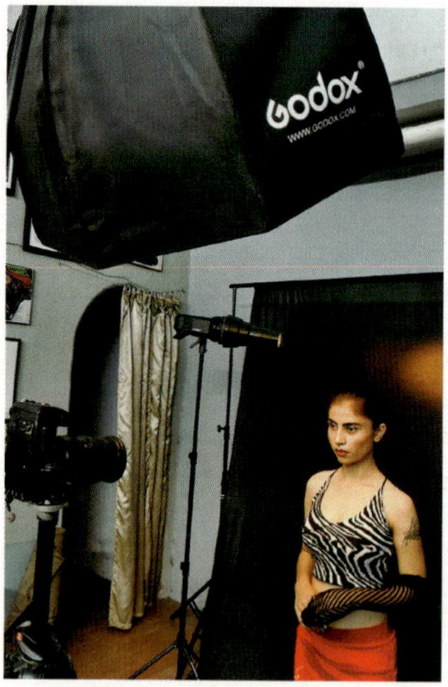

Fig. 13

The name comes from the shadow under the subject's nose, which looks slightly like a butterfly.

Butterfly lighting has also been known as "Paramount" lighting and "Hollywood" lighting because it has been frequently used to light movie stars. It's a form of lighting that's very glamorous and tends to slim down the face (thanks to the heavy shadow under the subject's chin). So you'll often find it used in fashion portraits and on professional glamour shoots.

I recommend using butterfly lighting only on subjects that want that intense result, one that highlights cheekbones and emphasizes angles. For this reason, butterfly lighting is great when working with professional models, but less good for family portraits, corporate headshots, and the like.

Set up

Place a light above and in front of the subject, pointed downward so that it lights the face from above. A good starting point is a 45-degree downward angle (though you can experiment with different options, and get different results depending on your subject's facial features). See Fig. 12 & 13.

If you'd like to make the setup slightly more refined, you can place a reflector or a low-powered second light under the subject, pointing upward. This will punch up the shadowy areas, but you have to be careful not to dispel them completely; if you lose the shadows, then you'll get much flatter and less dramatic results.

Loop Lighting

Loop lighting is one of the most popular lighting patterns out there, and one that looks great on pretty much anyone.

Here's what loop lighting looks like in action:

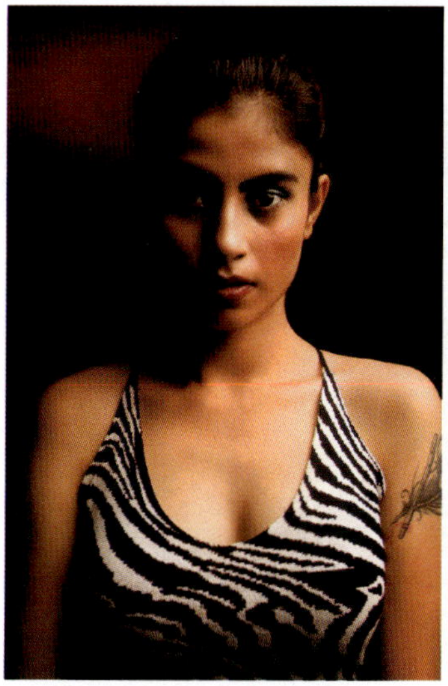

Fig. 14 Loop Lighting

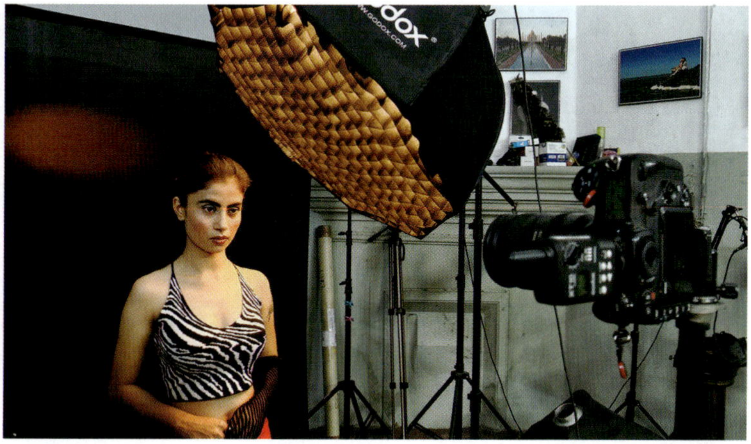

Fig. 15

Do you see the slight shadow of the subject's nose? That's the distinguishing feature of loop lighting. You should see a shadow that falls across the face, without creating a true triangle of light on the subject's cheek (more about that in the next section!). See Fig 14 & 15.

As you can see, loop lighting creates some shadows–but not especially strong shadows. This is what makes loop lighting so all-around useful, because it adds depth to the shot without creating dark, moody, dramatic shadows. So you can use it in pretty much any scenario, and it'll get you flattering results every time.

To create loop lighting, you'll want to take your main light and place it out in front of the subject and off to the side slightly (at about 20 to 35 degrees from straight ahead). You'll also want to put the light up slightly, so that it's pointing downward at the subject.

(You'll need to play around with these angles, because it will depend on your subject's face.)

Once you've achieved the basic loop lighting look that you're after, you're free to add a second light on the opposite side of your subject, in order to boost the light on the opposite side of your subject's face. Note that this will give you a slightly flatter, less dramatic result, which works just fine (as long as this is what you're after).

However, if you'd prefer a very dramatic look, more dramatic than even the most intense loop lighting can provide, I recommend trying out Rembrandt lighting:

Rembrandt Lighting

Rembrandt lighting is named after the Dutch painter Rembrandt, thanks to his frequent use of this particular lighting pattern for moody, three-dimensional portraits. It results in images like this (Fig. 16 & 17)

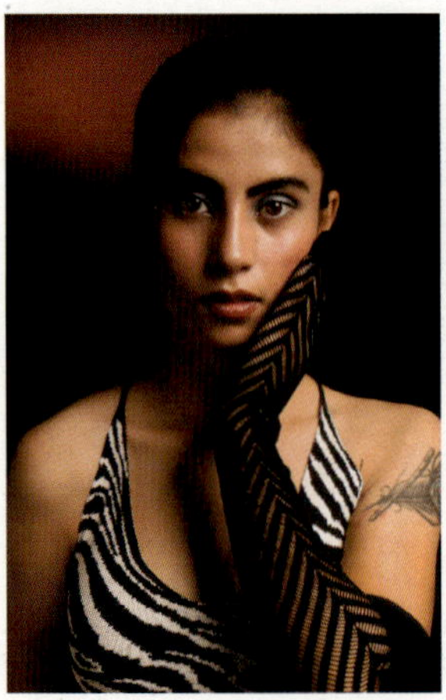

Fig. 16 Rambrandt Lighting

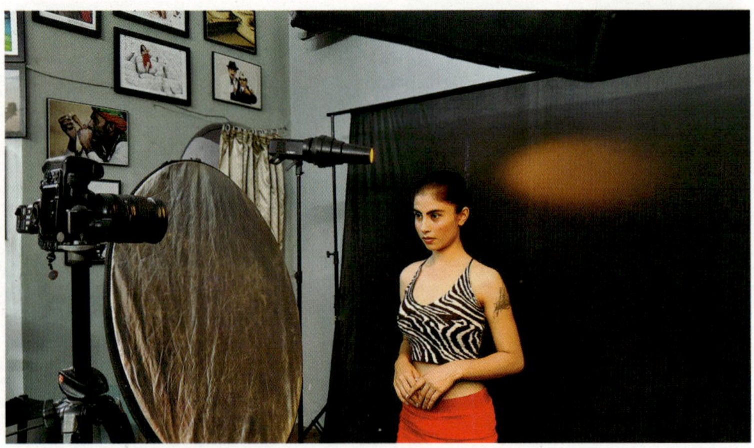

Fig. 17

Do you see the triangle under the subject's eye? That's the distinguishing feature of Rembrandt lighting (and it's what distinguishes Rembrandt lighting from loop lighting, above).

Rembrandt lighting is great for really sculpting out your subject's features and achieving a dramatic look, while also keeping things detailed and relatively well-lit.

Here's how it works:

First, place your main light around 45 degrees out and 45 degrees down (it should be above your subject's eyeline).

Play with these angles a bit, because you need to make sure you have the triangle on your subject's cheek.

If you're after a dramatic look, you can leave things as they are and start taking photos.

But if you're looking to soften the level of contrast, then add a second (lower-powered) light on the other side of the subject. You'll want to play with the positioning and strength, because you don't want to overpower the shadows; instead, you want to keep them in place while lessening their effect somewhat.

Personally, Rembrandt lighting is a favorite of mine. It's slightly moody, yes, but it also creates wonderfully three-dimensional images. So I recommend testing out Rembrandt lighting whenever you get the chance!

Split Lighting

Split lighting isn't the most popular lighting pattern out there, but it's very useful when you're looking for powerful, ultra-dramatic results. It looks like this (Fig. 18 & 19):

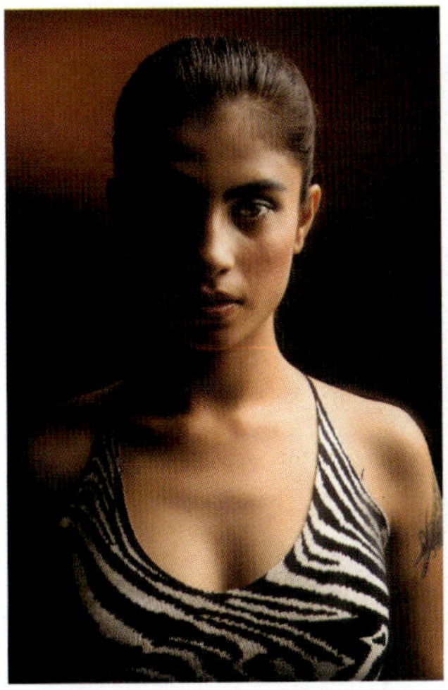

Fig. 18 Split Lighting

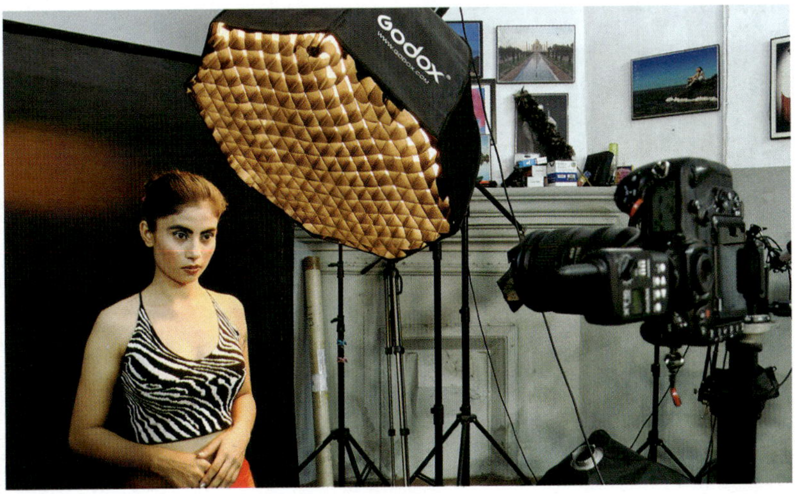

Fig. 19

As you may have guessed, it's so named because of how it splits the subject's face in two halves: a light half and a dark half.

Now, split lighting is very easy to create:

Just put the light source off to the side of the subject (at a 90 degree angle from their line of sight), and have them look straight ahead.

You'll get a perfect split, where half the face is dark and half is light.

Obviously this isn't ideal for standard portraits–but if you're doing glamour photography, or you're attempting to convey a very dramatic feel, split lighting can work well.

Note that you can always tone down the drama by placing a reflector or a second light on the opposite side of your subject (to reduce the strength of the shadows).

But, as with any fill light, you have to exercise caution. Too much, and you'll lose the beautiful effect you were after in the first place.

Short Lighting

Remember how I said some so-called "lighting patterns" are really more "compositional patterns"?

Short lighting is one of those.

You see, short lighting has less to do with the lighting pattern you use, and more to do with the angle of the subject relative to your camera.

Let me explain

Short lighting is when you photograph the subject with the darker side of their face angled toward the camera. Like this (Fig. 20 & 21):

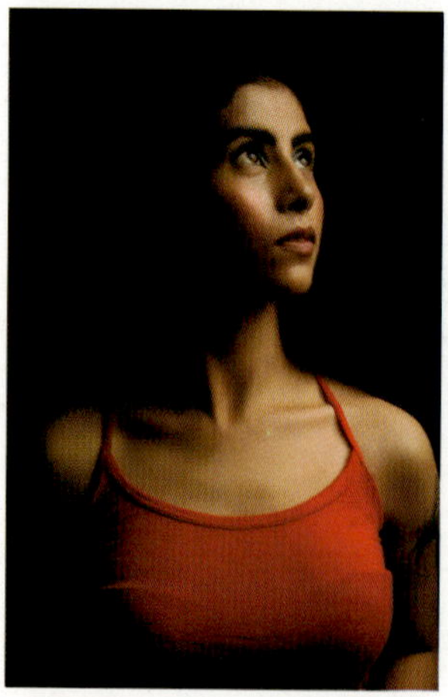

Fig. 20 Short Lighting

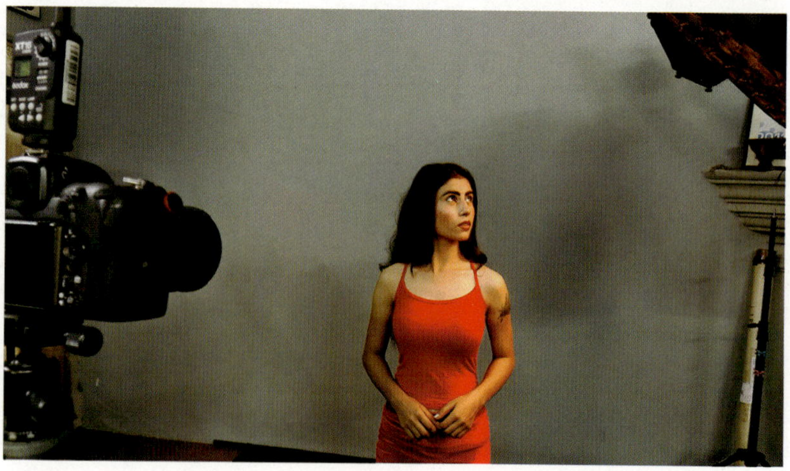

Fig. 21

As you can see, the lighter portion of the face is angled away, and the shadowy portion of the face is pointed toward the camera.

That's short lighting.

Now, short lighting does depend somewhat on lighting patterns, because you can really only use it with a sidelit pattern such as Rembrandt lighting, loop lighting, or split lighting.

(Otherwise, you won't have a good amount of shadow area to work with, and without shadows there's no way to distinguish between the well-lit and shaded portions of the face.)

So to use short lighting, simply set up the way you would when doing Rembrandt lighting, loop lighting, or split lighting.

Then position yourself (the photographer) on the side of the subject opposite the light, and take some photos!

As you've likely noticed, short lighting is very dramatic (because it offers up heavy, very noticeable shadows.) It also has a slimming effect, because the shadows make the face appear narrower, which is why it's good for photographing subjects with wider faces.

Broad Lighting

Broad lighting is the opposite of short lighting.

Instead of photographing the side of the face that's in shadow, you photograph the side of the face that's well-lit. See Fig. 22 & 23.

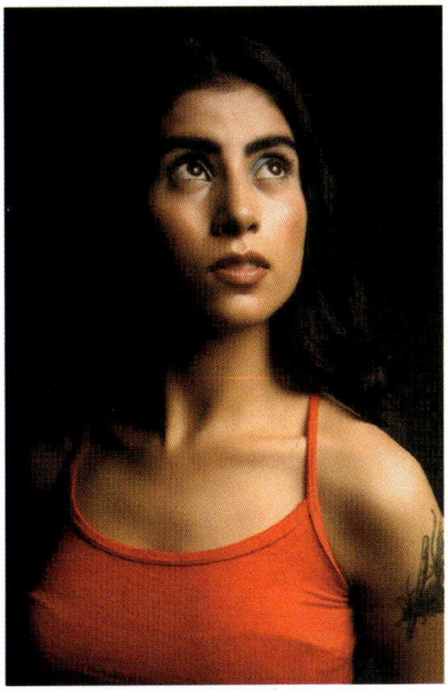

Fig. 22 Broad Lighting

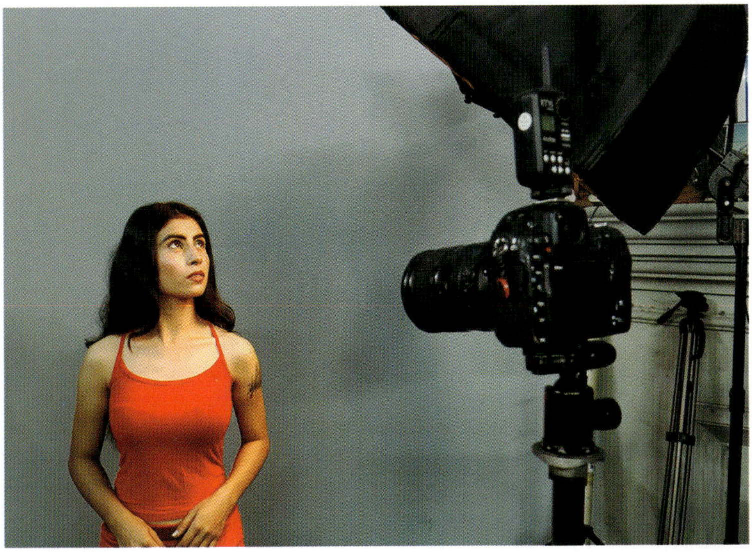

Fig. 23

But in every other way, broad lighting is the same.

So to set it up, simply use a Rembrandt lighting setup, a loop lighting setup, or a split lighting setup (remember, you need shadows!).

And then stand on the side of the subject with the light.

Note that broad lighting is known for its ability to widen faces, so it works well when dealing with narrow-faced subjects (but less well when your subject has a wide face).

You can also use broad lighting to hide aspects of your subject's face, such as blemishes; just make sure you light the part of the face without the blemishes.

19. Glossary

A

Aberration: Imperfections in the image formed by a lens. These include spherical aberration, curvature of field, coma, astigmatism, curvilinear distortion (also known as barrel or pincushion distortion) and chromatic aberration. Chromatic aberration, for example, can be corrected by using special ED lens elements.

Adobe Photoshop: The leading professional image-editing program for your computer.

Adobe Photoshop Album: A program that enables you to view one or several of your images at the same time, all in one easily navigated workspace.

Adobe Photoshop Elements: A less expensive version of Photoshop with fewer of the ultra-high-end features the professional version includes.

Anti-aliasing: A process that smoothes the rough edges or jaggies in images by creating partially transparent pixels along the boundaries that are merged into a smoother line by our eyes.

Aperture: An opening made by an adjustable diaphragm, which permits light to enter the camera lens and reach the image sensor.

Aperture-priority: A semi-automatic exposure mode; the photographer sets the aperture, and the camera selects the appropriate shutter speed to produce a good exposure.

Auto Mode: A digital camera mode in which both the aperture and shutter speed are set automatically.

Autoexposure: A feature that puts the camera in control of choosing the proper exposure settings.

Autofocus: A camera setting that allows the camera to choose the correct focus distance for you, usually based on the contrast of an image or set by a mechanism, such as an infrared sensor, that measures the actual distance to the subject.

AF Metering Field: Spot or area in the frame marking the position where the autofocus system takes readings to set the focus.

Aperture: Mechanism within the lens that controls the amount of light entering the camera. The aperture not only influences image brightness but also regulates _depth of field. Most cameras are equipped with an iris aperture that can be freely adjusted or set according to pre-selected values.

Aperture Priority: In this mode, the user can adjust the aperture and the camera automatically selects the best shutter speed for the exposure. In most cameras, the Aperture Priority mode is denoted by the letter "A". _Shutter Priority.

Aspherical Lens Literally: not spherical. Normally lenses are shaped like part of a sphere (a single continuous curve) on both surfaces. Aspherical lenses have at least one surface which is not a continuous curve, i.e. it is made up of many complex curves. Being more difficult to manufacture than spherical lenses, they are sometimes used in good quality wide-angle and zoom lenses to correct aberrations.

Auto Bracketing: Using this mode, a series of shots – each adjusted to a different exposure value – is taken in quick succession. This is very useful in tricky lighting conditions where it is difficult to assess the settings. After all shots have been taken, the best may be selected and the others deleted. (_Exposure correction).

Autofocus (AF): Automatic focus adjustment. There are basically two main AF methods: the focus detecting method (or passive autofocus) usually employs a _CCD and works by evaluating the amount of contrast or the phase difference in a scene. Distance metering (or active autofocus) utilises an (infrared) light emitter and receiver in a triangular surveying system. Alternatively, the camera may use ultrasound (sonar) and measure the time taken for the sound signal to return. This data is converted by a microprocessor into information about distance and thereby enables the automatic focusing of the lens.

B

Backlighting: A lighting effect produced when the main light source is located behind the subject. Backlighting is also a technology for illuminating an LCD display from the rear, making it easier to view under high ambient lighting conditions.

Bracketing: Taking a series of photographs of the same subject at different settings to help ensure that one setting will be the correct one.

Bulb Mode Long _exposure mode. In bulb mode, the shutter stays open as long as the release is held down. This allows exposure times of several minutes or even hours. However, in some models the bulb mode is limited to a number of minutes regardless of how long the release is held.

Denoted by the letter "B" on most cameras.

Burst Mode Another term for sequence mode or continuous shooting.

Byte _Binary data packet made up of 8 _bits. A byte can represent values between 0 and 255. It can depict any of 256 symbols, numbers or colours. In the computer field, larger byte size is described using the prefix letter for the abbreviation of the exponent of 2. Therefore:

1 kilobyte = 1 KB = 1,024 bytes

1 megabyte = 1 MB = 1,048,576 bytes

1 gigabyte = 1 GB = 1,073,741,824 bytes

1 terabyte = 1 TB = 1,099,511,627,776 bytes

C

Calibration: The reciprocal balancing or tuning of input and output devices to achieve a matching value. In this way, the colours on a monitor can be matched with the printer's colours. (_Colour management).

Card Adapter Device in which the memory card can be inserted for transferring the data on a memory card between a _PC Card slot and disk drive to the computer.

Card Reader/Writer Device that accepts memory cards and, through connection to a computer, allows data to be transferred between the media and PC.

Cast When a colour of one type is in excess in a picture, such as too much yellow or red. Often appears if the wrong _white balance setting is used.

CCD Charge-Coupled Device. A light sensitive semiconductor that converts received light into voltage according to the level of brightness. It is used as a _chip or line sensor in digital cameras and _scanners. (_progressive CCD, _video CCD).

CD-ROM Compact Disc Read-Only Memory. A "read only" CD-ROM can hold up to approximately 650 or 700 MB of data, e.g. pictures and text.

CD-R Compact Disc Recordable. CD on which data can be saved (at intervals if desired) but not deleted. Besides the standard size of 12cm diameter, smaller versions of 8cm are also available.

CD-RW Compact Disc Rewritable. Compact disc that can be re-written around 1,000 times. Besides the standard size of 12cm diameter, smaller versions of 8cm are also available.

Centre-weighted Average Metering A form of average exposure metering which places more emphasis on readings taken at the centre of the frame, making it less prone to being influenced by dark or light subjects at the edge of the frame.

CF _CompactFlash.

Cloning: The process of copying one area of a digital photo and "painting" the copy onto another area or picture.

Close-up Lens: A lens add-on, resembling a filter, that allows you to take pictures at a distance that is less than the closest-focusing distance of the prime lens alone.

CMOS Complementary Metal Oxide Semiconductor. Light sensitive chip. Unlike in _CCDs, the pixel elements on the CMOS are read individually.

CMYK Cyan, Magenta, Yellow, and Key/Black. These are the printer colours used to create colour prints.

Colour Depth This refers to the maximum number of colours that can be recorded by digital cameras and scanners or that can be displayed by graphics cards. A true colour representation can be achieved at a colour depth of 8 bits for each of the three primary colours, which gives a 24 bit colour depth. The 8 bits per primary colour can give 256 levels for each of those colours, which when multiplied together amounts to 256 (red) x 256 (green) x 256 (blue) = 16,777,216 colours that can be displayed. High-end scanners, graphics cards, etc. provide a minimum colour depth of 24 bit.

Colour Management The calibration of all peripheral devices that feature in the production of colour images (monitors, scanners, colour _printers etc.). For example, by using a colour management system, the data from a scanner is converted into values for a standard colour range. The data is then arranged so that the printer can produce good colour prints.

Colour Noise The incorrect reproduction of colour in an image, e.g. coloured dots on an area which is supposed to be pure white.

Color Saturation: The purity of color; the amount by which a pure color is diluated with white or gray.

Colour Space Refers to a model that specifies how colour information is represented. It defines a multidimensional space where the various dimensions represent intensity values.

Colour Temperature Describes the spectral energy distribution and thereby the colour quality of a light source. The temperature of a colour is given in Kelvin (K). It is important to choose the correct colour temperature so that a subject can be photographed in its true colours. Most digital cameras can be automatically or manually set between a range of around 3,000K to 8,000K.

Compact Digital Camera Smaller dimensions and reduced weight make these easy to handle models ideal for travel and everyday use.

Compact Flash Card Rewritable removable memory or function card developed by SanDisk in 1994. In contrast with SmartMedia or xD-Picture Card technology, it has a built-in controller. The newer CF type II (CF/2) cards are 5mm thick, the CF type I are only 3.3mm thick.

Complementary Colours Any two colours, such as cyan and red, yellow and blue or magenta and green, that when mixed together give white or grey.

Compression In order to store digital pictures economically, the image data is compressed. However, compression often causes a reduction in picture quality. The most common compression format is JPEG.

Composition: The arrangement of the main subject, other objects in a scene, and/or the foreground and background.

Continuous Auto-Focus: A mode in which the camera updates focus when the subject moves as long as you continue pressing the shutter button halfway.

Converter/Lens converter Lens extension that increases or shortens the focal distance. (Macro-converter, tele converter, wide-angle converter)

CPU Central Processing Unit. The main processor of a PC (personal computer).

D

Depth of Field The distance between the closest and most distant points at which a subject appears to be in focus, without changing the focus setting of the lens.

Depth of Focus The distance, forwards and backwards, through which the film plane (or CCD surface) can be moved while still maintaining an acceptably sharp focus of a set subject, without altering the focus setting of the lens.

Digital Opposite of analogue. Digital information is made up of a limited number of gradations (e.g. 256 colours, 8 bit). The change from one digital element to the next is always "step by step" and not continuous.

Digital Camera Usually captures images with the help of a CCD or CMOS chip. The image data received is then saved to special memory cards or other storage media such as SmartMedia, xD-Picture Card, CompactFlash, Memory Stick, SD Card, and MMC Card.

Digital Zoom This achieves a zooming effect by calculating (or interpolating) the available image data. Picture quality is reduced when a digital zoom is used.

Display LCD; TFT, CRT

Distortion Misrepresentation of an image. Wide-angle lenses normally produce more distortion than tele lenses.

DNG (Digital Negative) Open _file format developed by Adobe for camera RAW files.

Dot The smallest raster element of an image.

Dot Pitch Used with monitors, it indicates the distance between individual _dots. The smaller the distance between dots, the sharper the image.

Download Describes the process of receiving data, usually via either a mailbox, the internet or another device like a digital camera to a PC

Dpi Dots per inch (1 inch = approx. 2.54cm). A measuring unit in printing to describe the geometric resolution of an image.

Driver A small program that allows communication between the application program and a certain device, for example a printer or digital camera.

DSLR _Digital _single lens reflex camera.

DVD+R/DVD-R Recordable DVD.

DVD-RAM Rewritable storage medium which, unlike other writable DVDs, does not require separate burning software but can only be read and written to by special DVD-RAM-compatible drives. The medium is treated like a regular _hard drive. The big advantage of DVD-RAM is the increased level of data security.

DVD-ROM Digital Versatile Disc. A standard for CD-ROM with a much greater capacity (e.g. 9.4 GB) than a regular CD-ROM.

E

ED Lens Lens made of special glass with extra low dispersion characteristics.

Electronic Viewfinder The electronic viewfinder consists of a small LCD which displays the picture seen through the lens, just like with a regular SLR. This is achieved with the help of the CCD which continually sends the captured image information to the electronic viewfinder. As a result, composition is much easier because the photographer is shown the very same image seen by the camera. Furthermore, shooting data, such as picture number and settings, may also be displayed here.

Email A worldwide electronic mail system. Digitised data can be sent almost immediately throughout the world via telephone lines using only a PC. Every email user has his or her own internationally distinct address where he or she can be reached electronically. Files, such as digital pictures, can be sent with any email message.

Exif Exchangeable image format. A standard for image files created with digital cameras and other input devices. Exif files can be either uncompressed TIFF or compressed JPEG images and can hold data about the camera and settings employed. Using special programs, the information saved can be shown. Exif 2.2 saves even more information, such as the shooting mode, white balance and flash settings used. Compatible printers can then intelligently apply this data to produce optimal printed results.

Exposure During exposure, the sensors on the CCD (or chemicals on the film) are subjected to light for a certain amount of time.

Exposure Control Describes how the shutter speed and aperture are controlled by the camera. This can be either automatic (fully automatic, programmed auto or scene mode), or semi-automatic (Aperture Priority, Shutter Priority) or manual (full manual control of the aperture and _shutter).

Exposure Compensation Conscious deviation from the value ascertained by the light meter. The change can be made manually (under and overexposure)

Exposure Meter Light meter

Exposure Time The length of time for which the shutter is open.

Exposure Value (EV): EV settings are a way of adding or decreasing exposure without the need to reference f-stops or shutter speeds. For example, if you tell your camera to add +1EV, it will provide twice as much exposure by using a larger f-stop, slower shutter speed, or both.

Extension Tube: A camera attachment that moves your camera lens farther from the sensor, enlarging the image captured by the camera. Also called a lens extender.

F

File A set of data that has been arranged according to specific rules. Files are managed in the computer by the _operating system and can be stored long-term on an external storage medium.

File Format Describes the contents of files. Common file formats include <txt> for a text file, <eps> (Encapsulated PostScript) for PostScript, and <tif> for "TIFF"-images.

Fill-in Flash A flash mode that is particularly useful when shooting a subject in front of a strong light source or bright background. Normally, because of the backlight, the subject would be in shadow.

However, the flash provides the additional illumination to ensure a well-lit subject.

Filter: 1. A transparent, usually coloured sheet of glass or plastic that can be placed in front of a lens to create a certain effect. 2. An option in an image editing program that enables certain adjustments to the picture, e.g. colour and brightness or sharpening. (Imaging software).

Fisheye Special mode featured in some cameras where the shot is saved as though it were taken with a fisheye lens, providing a very surreal, artistically distorted result.

Fisheye Lens Having a viewing angle of 180°, these lenses can provide a very surreal image. Can be divided into diagonal types, which provide a frame-filling picture, and circular lenses which project a round image on the frame.

Fixed Focal Length When the camera's lens has a set focal length, optical zooming is not possible.

Fixed Focus Fixed focus cameras do not have autofocus or manual focus systems. The focus and aperture have been set so that everything within a certain distance is captured clearly. However, the drawback is that they do not have a very close focusing range and they only have a small aperture.

Flash Produces a large amount of light for a brief moment to illuminate the subject. Modern flashes work with gas discharge tubes. Computerised camera flashes can measure and automatically control their intensity by means of a sensor directed at the subject.

Flash Duration The period for which the flash tube emits light. This can be from around 1/250 to 1/40,000 of a second depending on the amount of light required.

Flash Range The distance needed to be covered by the flash to give the subject optimal illumination. This can be calculated using Lambert's law. As the distance from the light source is doubled, only a quarter of the original amount of light will reach the subject. (—'Guide number)

Flash Synchronisation Coordinates the opening of the camera's 'shutter with the time and duration of the —'flash. Some cameras allow you to synchronise the beginning or end of the exposure time ("first curtain" and "second curtain" flash respectively).

Focal Length The distance between the point of focus of a subject at infinity and the rear nodal point of the lens. For a simple lens (a single lens element) it is the distance from the centre of the lens to the point where an infinitely distant object is brought into focus. A compound lens (such as that fitted to a modern camera) would produce an image the same size as a single lens element of the same focal length, but the compound lens could be closer to, or further from the point of focus. The "standard" focal length gives an image impression roughly corresponding to the human eye (about 50mm in a conventional film camera and about 7mm in a digital camera with a 1/3" —CCD).

Focal Plane The place in the body of the camera where the film or CCD is placed, perpendicular to the lens. This is the point at which the image is formed inside the camera. Also known as the film plane.

Focusing Adjusting the position of the lens elements to bring the image into focus, i.e. so that it is clear and sharp.

Format In computers as well as digital cameras writable storage media such as floppy and hard disks as well as —removable storage media and some types of —CD-Rs need to be formatted. During the process they are prepared to accommodate the respective —operating system's file system, so data can be written to and read from the medium correctly. Format may also refer to the type of file, such as —JPEG, —TIFF or DOC. In photography the format or size of the film or the image sensor has a major bearing on the angle of view of a lens. Format is also used to describe the two dimensional size of an image. In film cameras, the photos typically have a ratio of 3:2 (Format: 36 x 24mm). With digital images, the ratio is normally 4:3 but can be changed to 3:2 in some cameras. For prints, the format means the size of the print out, such as 9 x 13cm, 10 x 15cm, 13 x 18cm.

Front Curtain Sync: The default kind of electronic flash synchronization technique. The flash fires at the beginning of the exposure — in the instant that the first curtain of the focal plane shutter finishes its movement across the film or sensor plane.

F-stop: Refers to the size of the camera aperture. A higher number indicates a smaller aperture. Written as f/2, f/8, and so on.

G

Gamma A process whereby contrast values are optimised.

GB -Gigabyte.

GIF Graphic Interchange Format. A compressed image -file format with a maximum of 256 colours. Often used on the -internet, especially for simple graphics and animation.

Gigabyte 1 gigabyte = 1,024 -megabytes.

GPS Global Positioning System. The GPS receiver uses satellites allowing you to determine the exact longitude, latitude, and height above sea level anywhere on earth.

Graphics Card Component of a computer that is necessary to display an image on the monitor screen.

Grey Scale A scale of shades ranging from white to black. Devices that can only display data in black and white translate colour differences into various shades of grey.

H

Halo Artifacts These are visible as light/dark outlines or halos near edges. Halos artifacts become a problem when the light and dark over and undershoots become so large that they are clearly visible at the intended viewing distance.

Hand-held Exposure Meter External exposure meter. (reflected-light metering, incident-light metering).

Hard Drive/Disk Device for the permanent storage of programs and information that remain after a computer has been turned off.

Hardware All actual physical computer components such as the computer itself and peripheral devices like monitor, mouse, printer, digital camera, etc.

HDD Hard Disk Drive. (—Hard drive)

Highlights – The brightest parts of a photo.

Histogram This shows the distribution of tones for a particular image. With some cameras, the histogram can be used in real time or after capture. The histogram is particularly helpful for recognising incorrect —exposure.

Hot Shoe – An interface for attaching flashguns (or accessories like flash adaptors) to cameras, usually found on the top of the camera. It has two metal brackets and normally one or several electrical contacts in the centre to allow communication between the camera and flash. If it has no contact, this is an accessory shoe. The flash also features a hot shoe contact and normally a locking mechanism to prevent it falling out of the shoe.

Hot Spot: A bright area in a photograph that come from reflections on eyeglasses or unevenly spread lighting.

HQ Resolution High Quality resolution. Description for high digital photo quality using the camera's maximum resolution with a high level of compression.

HTML HyperText Markup Language, a file format used in the World Wide Web.

http Hypertext transfer protocol: transmission format and communica.

I

ICC Profile An ICC (International Color Consortium) profile describes the colour range of a device that processes colour (like -scanners), displays colours (such as monitors), or produces colours (-printers). The ICC profiles for each of these devices help ensure that colour reproduction is consistent. (-Colour management).

Image Compression – In order to store digital pictures economically, the image data must be compressed. However, compression often causes a reduction in picture quality.

Image Editing Describes software that allows the user to view **software** and alter digital images. A commonly used image editing program is Adobe Photoshop.

Image Sensor: A digital camera's solid-state capture device, made up of a grid-like arrangement of red-, green-, and blue-sensitive elements.

Image Stabiliser Either opto-mechanical or electronic system that helps prevent camera shake to ensure sharp, clear results even at high magnifications (long focal lengths).

Upon detecting any unintentional movement of the lens, the system compensates optically or electronically to keep the subject steady.

Infrared: Using film, a filter, or a censor that is sensitive to infrared light and also blocks visible light. The effect produces a dreamlike effect, with dark skies and brightly colored foliage.

Interpolation Calculating non-existent image data from captured image data. Interpolation is used by all digital cameras to determine colour data from neighbouring sensors. (The reason: a sensor can only record one colour.) Interpolation can also be used to increase (or decrease) an image's resolution. The quality of the resulting photo depends on the capabilities of the -'algorithm used. It is important to remember, interpolation cannot produce detail that has not been captured.

ISO International Organization for Standardization, which was responsible for combining the old ASA and DIN film speed standards into the current ISO system (-'Film sensitivity).

J

JPEG Joint Photographic Experts Group. The de facto standard for image compression in digital imaging devices, which enables different levels of compression to be selected. Because brightness information is more important than colour data, most pixels only store the brightness information. When the JPEG file is opened, the missing colour data is automatically calculated from the existing information. (—MPEG).

JPG File ending for —JPEG files.

K

KB — kilobyte.

Kbit/s Kilobits per second. The number of —kilobits transmitted per second. (—Baud)

Kbyte — kilobyte.

Kelvin Scale Temperature scale beginning at absolute zero (approx. –273° Celsius = 0 Kelvin). Therefore Celsius values can easily be converted into Kelvin by adding 273 degrees to the Celsius value. (—Colour temperature)

Kilobit 1 kilobit = 1,000 —bits.

Kilobyte 1 kilobyte = 1,024 —bytes.

L

LAB LAB colours consist of a luminance or brightness component and two chromatic components.

Laser Printer A printer that uses a laser beam to project characters and graphics onto a drum, which then electrographically transfers the image, using toner, onto paper. Laser printers are known for their high quality reproduction and printing speed.

Layer: A way of managing elements of an image in stackable overlays that can be manipulated separately, moved to a different stacking order, or made partially or fully transparent.

LCD Liquid Crystal Display. LCDs are commonly used in calculators, watches, digital cameras, notebook computers, flat-panel monitors and projectors.

LED A Light Emitting Diode is often used as an indicator lamp.

LED Printer As opposed to —'laser printers, the printed image is not brought on to a drum by a laser beam, but by a row of densely located light diodes.

Lens Transparent glass or plastic that has been formed and polished to form a certain shape, usually spherical. When a beam of light reaches the area between the air and the lens, a part of this light is always reflected. The remaining light passes into the lens and alters its propagation direction, i.e. the light is refracted. The incorporation of various lenses (converging and diverging lenses) creates a 'lens system. When optimally arranged, they allow the subject to be presented correctly on the 'image plane.

Lens Adapter Adapter between the end of the camera's lens and the lens converter. A step-up-ring is also a type of lens adapter.

Lens Hood Made from metal or plastic, the hood fits on the end of the lens to shade the front lens element from incidental light, which could otherwise cause reflections, glare and ghosting.

Lens System Group of —'lenses (sometimes just one lens) that enable the sharpest and brightest pictures to be taken. Often simply referred to as the lens or objective.

There are various lenses available such as —'wide-angle, normal, —'macro, and —'tele with fixed focal distances as well as —'zoom lenses with adjustable focal distances.

Light Intensity A measure of light energy from a light source measured in —'candela. (—'Flash).

Light Meter To ensure correct exposure, most analogue and digital cameras feature an automatic light meter. Internal or external cells measure light intensity and convert the information into an electrical signal. This is then used by the camera to set the right shutter speed and aperture for the relevant light conditions.

Live Preview An alternative to framing the shot through the viewfinder. The image sent through the lens to the image sensor is displayed directly on the camera's LCD. Whereas most compact digital cameras have been equipped with Live Preview functionality for many years, this feature has now for the first time entered the DSLR domain with the Olympus E-330.

Lossless Compression: A file-compression scheme that doesn't sacrifice any vital image data in the compression process. Lossless compression tosses only redundant data, so image quality is unaffected.

Lossy Compression: A compression scheme that eliminates important image data in the name of achieving smaller file sizes. High amounts of lossy compression reduce image quality.

Luminance Another word for brightness.

M

Mac Abbreviated name of the Apple Macintosh computer. This computer is often used for graphics applications and -image processing.

Mac OS The Apple Macintosh computer's operating system.

Macro Converter Lens attachment that permits fascinating detailed close-up shots. (-Tele converter, -wide-angle converter)

Macro Lens A lens (usually for SLRs) that is designed to be highly optically corrected especially for close- focusing and reproduction work. A macro lens will normally give a maximum reproduction ratio of the subject of around 1:10 to 1:1 on the focal plane (without additional extension).

Macro Mode A special camera setting allowing the camera to focus closer than normal, giving detailed close-up photographs of small objects.

Macro Lens: A lens that provides continuous focusing from infinity to extreme close-ups, often to a reproduction ratio of 1:2 (half life-size) or 1:1 (life-size).

Marquee: The dotted outline that results when you select a portion of your image; sometimes referred to as marching ants.

Masking: In an image editor, selecting an area of an image to prevent that area from being modified accidentally.

Mass Storage – USB Mass Storage Class.

Matrix Metering: Also called multizone metering. A metering mode that calculates exposure based on the entire frame.

MB – megabyte.

Megabyte 1 MB = 1,024 -kilobytes.

Megapixel 1 megapixel = 1 million -pixels.

Memory Stick A removable memory medium developed by Sony.

Metering Mode: Refers to the way a camera's autoexposure mechanism reads the light in a scene.

MF Manual Focus.

Microdrive A miniature hard drive developed by IBM that fits the -'Compact Flash Type II format. To record images to a Microdrive, a digital camera not only needs to be compatible with Compact Flash Type II, but also electronically compatible (able to provide the power required and have the necessary firmware.)

Micro Processor The programmable -'chip controlling the computer. It is composed of either one or more integrated circuits.

Midtones: Parts of an image with tones of an intermediate value, usually in the 25 to 75 percent range.

MMC – 'Multimedia Card.

Modem Word derived from Modulation and Demodulation. A device which transforms digital data into analogue signals in order to send the information through a telephone line.

Monochrome A picture in only one colour or in black and white.

Modeling Lights: Incandescent lamps built into a studio flash that give you a preview of exactly how the light from the flash will look.

Modular Belt System: A belt that can hold a variety of photography equipment.

Monopod: A one-legged support, or unipod, used to steady the camera.

Multiple Auto-focus: A setting that allows the camera to find more than one area of contrast to focus on.

Multiple-exposure: A technique in which a small aperture gives you a long exposure, allowing your subjects to move within the frame during shooting, which creates a photo that looks like it has been exposed more than once.

N

Noise Unwanted variations or disturbances that reduce the amount or quality of information in a signal. In digital imaging, noise is a term used to describe the visible effect of interference on the CCD sensor. It appears as unwanted colour spots on images – especially those taken at night with a slow shutter speed. (—'Colour noise).

Noise Reduction In noise reduction mode, the camera takes two shots: the normal shot and one with the same exposure time but with the shutter closed. It is then able to determine the areas of an individual image that are susceptible to noise and compensates for this.

O

Opacity: The degree to which a layer allows layers beneath it to show through.

Optical Real Image Viewfinder – A viewfinder system that produces a virtual image, correct way round and right way up. Separate to the camera's main lens, it gives a representational view of the image to be taken. (compare -Single Lens Reflex Camera.)

Optical Zoom -Zoom lens.

Overexposure When a shot receives too much light so that the photo is too bright and the colours are bleached out. (-Underexposure).

P

Panorama: A broad view, usually scenic. Some digital cameras also have a panorama mode used with software to stitch the images together.

PictBridge: Standard for the communication between printers and cameras. With the help of PictBridge, the images can be printed directly from the camera to the printer without requiring a computer.

Pixel: Short for picture element. The basic building block of every image.

Polarisation Filter: A filter that blocks polarised light waves when turned to oppose the plane of polarisation of those waves. Light is polarised when reflected by a non-metallic surface (glass, water, etc.). By blocking those waves, the filter effectively reduces the amount of reflection. Use of the filter also increases colour saturation, making blue skies appear even bluer, for example.

ppi: Pixels per inch. A value to denote the resolution of digital images.

Primary Colours The three basic colours red, green and blue to which the human eye is primarily sensitive. These three colours are used in the additive system of colour reproduction. (—Additive colour mixing)

Prosumer Camera Term to describe a camera with features of professional models that also appeal to the consumer.

R

RAW: RAW files are the actual data taken directly from a digital camera's image sensor. They have not been processed by the camera at all. This means they are the purest image file possible in digital photography. Often, quite correctly, the terminology "digital negative" is used to scribe them. Different camera manufacturers have different names for their own RAW files. For example, Canon uses the digital photography terminology "RAW", Nikon uses different digital photography terminology - "NEF". They are incompatible with each other. Whereas every computer can show JPEG images, RAW files need specific software. This is always supplied by the manufacturer when you purchase a digital camera. It is also easy to obtain on the Internet too.

Rear Curtain Sync: An electronic flash synchronization technique in which the flash fires only when the second (rear) curtain of the focal plane shutter begins to move at the end of the exposure.

Red Eye: An effect from flash photography that appears to make a person or animal's eyes glow red. Caused by light bouncing from the retina of the eye.

Red-eye Reduction A —'flash mode. Dim light causes the pupils of the eyes to widen. This can lead to the well known red glow in the eyes when a flash is fired as the light may reflect from the blood vessels on the retina. That's why most cameras offer a red-eye reduction mode. In this setting, the camera fires a number of flashes, or one single long one, before the actual flash. This causes the pupils' diameter to shrink, reducing the possibility of red-eye.

Reflected Light Metering Method of 'exposure metering by which the amount of light reflected from the subject is measured. ('Incident light metering, 'Digital ESP/ selective multi-zone metering, 'light metering, 'spot metering, 'centre-weighted average metering)

Removable Lens —'Lens that is not permanently fixed to the camera and can be removed and replaced by another lens.

Removable Memory: Memory card that may be inserted into and taken out of the camera. Examples are 'xD-Picture Card, 'SmartMedia and 'CompactFlash.

Resolution: Measurement of the image detail ('ppi, 'dpi) that a device can capture or reproduce. With a monitor or printer, the resolution describes the number of 'pixels that can be shown. When used with devices for image capture, such as digital cameras or scanners, the resolution refers to the number of pixels that record the image. The result is given in ppi (often dpi although not strictly correct is used instead) or the horizontal and vertical total of pixels (e.g. 2,272 x 1,704, equivalent to 4 million pixels). In general, it can be said that the higher the resolution, the better the quality.

RGB – Red, Green, Blue – the three primary colours for additive colour mixing

Rule of Thirds: A way of mentally dividing your picture horizontally and vertically into thirds, then placing important subject matter where these lines intersect.

S

Scene Mode: Modes for certain types of shots. In a scene mode, the camera automatically selects the best parameters (such as -'aperture, -'shutter, -'flash mode, etc.) for the type of scene in question. Typical scene modes include night scene, landscape, portrait, sport.

SD Card –'Secure Digital Card

Secondary Colours: A colour produced by combining any two -'primary colours. Common secondary colours are cyan, magenta and yellow, which are often used in the -'subtractive colour mixing system as colours for printing inks.

Shutter: Either mechanical and/or electronic shutters are possible. Mechanical systems can use a leaf (or iris) shutter or curtain shutter. In digital cameras a third alternative is also possible: the electronic shutter. This works by activating and then deactivating the —'CCD so that no further light can be recorded, regardless of whether light is hitting the CCD. The shutter controls the exposure time, which can range from thousandths of a second to several minutes or more. Fast shutter speeds freeze action, slow speeds are more suited to stationary subjects. A tripod is recommended for slow exposure shots to avoid camera shake. (—'Aperture)

Shutter Priority: In this mode, the user can adjust the —'shutter speed manually and the camera then selects the —'aperture setting for the best exposure. Often described as "S" mode on the camera.

Single Lens Reflex Camera: Camera type that directs the image coming in through the —'lens into the viewfinder by means of a mirror and prism/mirror system. When the —'shutter is released the mirror swings out of the way to allow light on the image plane. The picture seen through the viewfinder is almost 100% identical to the resulting photo.

Slow Synchronisation: Flash mode that uses a slow —shutter speed in combination with a —flash. Since the duration of the flash is far shorter that the selected shutter speed, the flash fires at either the beginning (first curtain) or end (second curtain) of the exposure time. Because the fired flash freezes action in the foreground while capturing background scenes in low light conditions with slow shutter speed, the slow synchronisation mode can produce particularly attractive, atmospheric shots. (The night scene mode found in some cameras acts in a similar fashion.)

SLR —Single Lens Reflex.

SmartMedia Card: SmartMedia cards are small (45mm x 37mm x 0.76mm) and light (approximately 2g) storage media. The controller is located in the drive instead of being incorporated in the card to allow simple construction. (—xD-Picture Card)

Soft Focus: Image effect offered by some digital cameras where the contours in the image are gentle but the shot is not actually out of focus.

Spot Metering – Exposure metering method where the exposure reading is taken from the centre of the frame. This is often used when working with backlight. (-Digital ESP/selective multi- zone metering, -reflected-light metering, -light metering).

sRGB: Abbreviation for "small RGB". The aim of sRGB is to allow different devices to produce colours that look as natural as can be without too much effort. For this to be possible, these devices have to support sRGB. Then, ideally, the colours in a print produced by an sRGB compatible printer should resemble those that were displayed on the sRGB monitor. Step-Up-Ring-'Lens adapter, with which a filter/conversion lens with a wider diameter than that of the camera's lens is attached.

Studio Flash: Stationary, high power —'flash that is mostly used by advertising and fashion photographers. Normally consisting of simply a flash tube and pilot lamp that shines continuously to enable the user to check the exposure, they have no automatic metering system and must be adjusted manually. Studio flashes can be equipped with diverse accessories, such as softboxes, filters, reflectors, Fresnel lenses etc. to achieve special lighting or effects. These flash systems are generally much more powerful than compact flashes and their output is measured not by a —'guide number but by watts per second (Ws). Models over 400 Ws usually have to be powered by an external power source. The studio flash is connected to the camera via an —'x-synchronisation cable. If several flashes are used, the other units are activated by an activation light from the first flash unit.

Super Macro: This special feature lets you focus on objects that are only a short distance from the lens – sometimes just 2cm away. As such, it is perfect for capturing detail in very small objects, such as jewellery, flower petals or insects.

T

Tele: Short for telephoto lens. A lens that offers a narrower angle of view than the standard lens for a given format, e.g. focal lengths above 50mm for the 35mm format, or above 25mm for the FourThirds format. Typical characteristics include a narrow field of view (around 30° or less depending on focal length), short depth of field and the flattening of perspective between objects (i.e. near and distant objects appear closer together) (-'Wide angle, -'zoom.)

Tele Converter Lens attachment that extends the focal length. (-'Macro converter, -'wide-angle converter).

TFT: Thin Film Transistor. TFT displays are used in notebooks as well as in digital cameras from OLYMPUS.

Thumbnail: The miniature representation of a digital image that usually serves as a preview in -'image editing programs.

TIFF: Tagged Image File Format. A specific, high quality -'file format used for the storage of -'digitised images.

Tripod: Stand to which the camera can be attached to hold it steady, especially during slow exposure shots where camera shake must be avoided. While tripods have three legs, many professionals use single legged monopods to help support long telephoto lenses, giving them more manoeuvrability for action shots.

True Colour Describes the colour output on a monitor or printer. Requires at least 16 million colour nuances.

TTL Metering Through The Lens metering.

TTL Flash Metering With —TTL flash metering, the flash light and ambient light is measured through the lens so the intensity of the flash can be set. All work is done by the camera so the flash does not need any metering cells or control circuits. Also, no manual adjustments are necessary.

U

Underexposure: When a shot does not receive enough light with the result that the picture is too dark.

Underwater Cases: These are special cases that let you take your camera diving with you. Make sure you have a case designed especially for your camera and that you look after the case, especially its seals, as described in the manual. For -'DSLR underwater photography additional -'underwater lens ports as well as underwater housings for external flash units are required.

Underwater Lens: Water-tight cases for -'DSLR interchangeable lenses used in combination with DLSR -'underwater cases for underwater photography.

Unsharp Masking Often abbreviated to USM. Describes an image sharpening process. The quality of the result depends on the characteristics of the -'algorithm used.

Update: An updated version of a -'software program or the -'firmware (e.g. of a camera).

Upgrade: A new improved version of -'hardware or -'software that is already available.

Upload: Process of copying a file from a computer to a remote computer. Opposite of download.

USB: Universal Serial Bus (USB) enables the effortless connection of -'peripheral devices without the need to install cards into the computer or reconfigure parts of the operating system. The most important advantages are: the support of -'Plug and Play, -'hot plugging, automatic configuration of external devices upon connection (no re-start necessary), faster data transfer and the possible operation of up to 127 devices from a single port. USB 2.0 comes in three different speeds: Hi-Speed (480 MB it/s), Full-Speed (12 MBit/s) and Low-Speed (1.5 MBit/s). A further benefit of USB 2.0 is backward compatibility with existing USB technology, so older devices will still work with USB 2.0 at the original speed of the USB 1.1 specification. Newer, Hi-Speed USB-compliant devices will profit from the much faster data transfer speed of USB 2.0.

V

Vignetting: Fading off the sides of a picture into plain white or black instead of having abrupt edges. Also unintentional loss of brightness at the edge of the image. -Wide-angle lenses are particularly susceptible. However, the problem can be more or less avoided by removing the elements causing the effect, such as a filter with a frame that is too large or an ill-fitting -lens hood.

W

White Balance: The adjustment of a digital camera to the respective type of light (-colour temperature) such as daylight, overcast, tungsten, or fluorescent light for even truer colours, or alternatively, to create a different, striking effect.

Wide Angle: A lens that offers a wider angle of view than the standard lens for a given format, e.g. focal lengths below 50mm for the 35mm format, or less than 25mm for the FourThirds format. Typical characteristics include a wide field of view, from around 60° and up to 180° (-fisheye lens) depending on focal length, large depth of field and the deepening of perspective between objects (i.e. near and distant objects appear farther apart.) (-Tele, -zoom.).

Wide-angle Lens attachment that reduces the -focal length. **Converter** (-Macro converter, -tele converter).

Z

ZIP: 'File format used for data compression.

ZIP-Drive: A device that allows the storage of up to 750 -'MB of data.

Zoom Lens: A type of lens that allows the photographer to vary the angle of view of a scene. By adjusting the focal length the degree of image magnification can be altered. The focal length markings on the lens give an indication of the range of the zoom; e.g. 35-1 05mm* would be a 3x zoom giving a good range from medium wide-angle to short telephoto angles of view. Some cameras offer a 1 0x magnification (e.g. 38-380mm*), giving a high magnification for capturing distant objects in close-up. When using such high magnifications it is important to hold the camera steady to achieve good sharp results, especially in low-light conditions. If necessary, brace the camera against a fixed object or use a -'tripod. (* refers to a 35mm camera equivalent focal length) (-'Tele, -'wide angle, -'digital zoom, -'focal length).

How to Showcase Your Works:

You should upload your works on a free online galleries so that other photographers in the world can see your work and give you the honest feedback. You will also get an opportunity to see others works and get inspiration. In this way, you will improve your photography gradually. Here are a few free online galleries. I am also an active member in all these galleries.

Free Online Galleries:

www.redbubble.com

www.bluecanvas.com

www.ngm.com

www.kodak.com

www.natgeo.com

Stock Photography:

In case you want to sale your images, you can upload your images to the stock photography sites. A few populay sites are mentioned below:

1. *www.stock-photos.com*
2. *www.dreamstime.com*
3. *www.shutterbugs.com*
4. *www.imagekind.com*
5. *www.shutterstock.co.in*
6. *www.imagesbazaar.com*
7. *www.fotolia.com*
8. *www.alamy.com/*

List of Photography Magazines, Books and Important Websites

1. Photography Magazines:

Smart Photography

Publisher: Next Gen Publishing Ltd.

Website: *www.nextgenpublishing.net*

Better Photography
Publisher: Infomedia 18 Ltd.
Website: *www.infomedia18.in*

Asian Photography
Publisher: Special Audience Publications Pvt. Ltd.
Website: *www.asianphotographyindia.com*

Popular Photography
Website: *www.popphoto.com*

Digital SLR Photography
Website: *www.digitalslrphoto.com*

Digital Photographer
Website: *www.dphotographer.co.uk*

Photo Techniques
Website: *www.phototechmag.com*

Photo Plus
Website: *www.myfavouritemagazines.co.uk/*

Amateur Photographer
Website: *www.amateurphotographer.co.uk*

Photo Pro Magazine
Publisher: Bright Publishing Ltd.
Website: *dppro. co.uk*

Photography Monthly
Publisher: Archant Limited
Website: *archant.co.uk*

Professional Photographer
Publisher: Archant Limited
Website: *archant.co.uk*

Photoshop Creative
Publisher: Imagine Publishing Ltd.
Website: *imagine-publishing.co.uk*

Outdoor Photographer
Website: *www.outdoorphotographer.com*

Photolite
Website: *www.photolife.com*

Master Photography
Website: *www.masterphotography.co.uk*

2. Books

Teach Yourself Photography
Author: Lee Frost
Publisher : Hodder & Stoughton
ISBN: 0 340 74272 0

PC Multimedia Handbook
Author: David Dick
Publisher: Dumbreck Publishing
ISBN: 09514 848 X

Creative Digital Photography
Author: Michael Busselle
Publisher: David & Charles
ISBN: 0 7153 11549

Freelance Photographers' Market Handbook 2003
Author: John Tracey and Stuart Gibson
Publisher: BFP Books
ISBN: 0 907297 536

The Digital Photographers' Handbook – landscapes and Cityscapes
Author: Simon Joinson
Publisher: Roto Vision
ISBN: 2 88046 655 5

The Complete Guide to Digital Photography
Author: Michael Freeman
Publisher: Themes Hudson
ISBN: 0 500 54246 5

Beginner's Guide to Adobe Photoshop
Author: Michelle Perkins
Publisher: Amherst Media
ISBN: 1 58428 071 9

Landscape Photography
Author: Michael Busselle
Publisher: Roto Vision
ISBN: 2 88046 370 X

Digital Camera Solutions
Author: Gregory Georges
Publisher: Muska & Lipman Publication
ISBN:0-9662889-6-3

Teach Yourself Digital Photography
Author: Peter Bargh
Publisher: Hoddar Headline
ISBN:0-340-86749-3

The Complete Guide to Close-up & Macro Photography
Author: Paul Harcourt Davies
Publisher: David and Charles
ISBN:0-7153-0800-9

The Photographer's Guide to the Studio
Author: Roger Hicks & Frances Schultz
Publisher: David and Charles
ISBN:0-7153-1234-0

50 Fast Digital Camera Techniques
Author: Gregory Georges, Larry Berman & Chris Maher
Publisher: Wiley Publishing Inc
ISBN:0-7645-2500-X

Digital Night Low-Light Photography
Author: Tim Gartside
Publisher: The Ilex Press Ltd.
ISBN:1-904705-63-4

Digital Photography
Author: John Ellis
Publisher: The Ilex Press Ltd.
ISBN:1-84509-277-5

Shoot Like a Pro
Author: Julie Adair King
Publisher: McGraw-Hill/Osborne.
ISBN:0-07-222949-7

Mastering Composition and Light
Author: The Kodak Library of Creative Photography
Publisher: Time-Life Books.
ISBN:0-86706-211-8

Learning From Expert
Author: The Kodak Library of Creative Photography
Publisher: Time-Life Books.
ISBN:0-86706-239-8

Make Color Work for You
Author: The Kodak Library of Creative Photography
Publisher: Time-Life Books.
ISBN:0-86706-205-3

3. Shopping on the Internet

www.flipkart.com

www.amazon.com

www.Jessops.com

www.warehouseexpress.com

www.dcpro.com

www.digitalcameracompany.com

www.ebay.in

www.dabs.com

4. Manufacturers' Websites

Digital cameras :

Canon – *www. canon.co.in.*

Casio – *www.casio.com/Cameras*

Fuji – *www.fujifilm.com*

Kodak – *www.kodak.com/global/en/digital/easyShare/*

Leica – *www.leica-camera.com/index_e.html*

Minolta – *www.minoltaeurope.com./pe/digital_photography.html*

Nikon – *www.nikon-image.com./eng/Lineup/index.html*

Olympus – *www.olympur.co.uk/consumer/digimg/home.cfm*

Pentax – *www.pentaxeurope.com/web/online/cam/index.html*

Ricoh – *www.ricoh-cameras.co.uk/*
– *www. Ricohpmms.com./dc/index.html*

Sumsung – *www.sumsungcamerausa.com/*
– *www.sumsungcamera.co.uk/*

Sony – *www.sonystyle.com/home/dept.jsp?hierc=96828deptid=9682*

Memory Cards

Sandisk – *www.sandsick.com*

Lexar – *www.lexarmedia.com*

Crucial – *www.crucial.com*

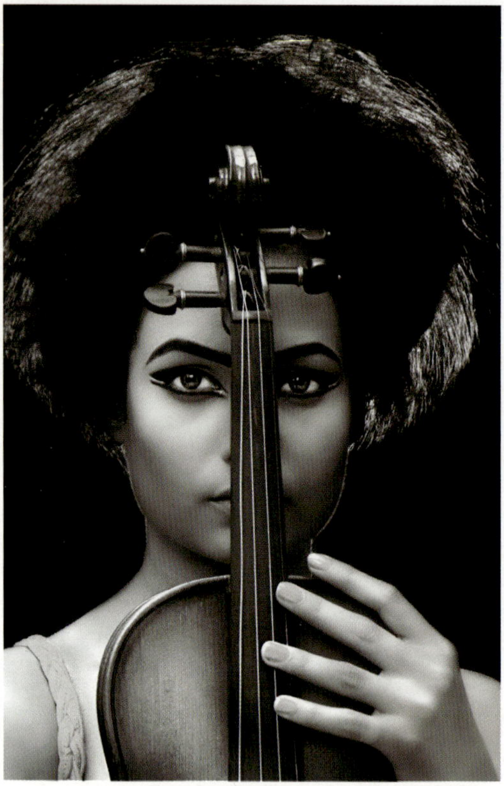

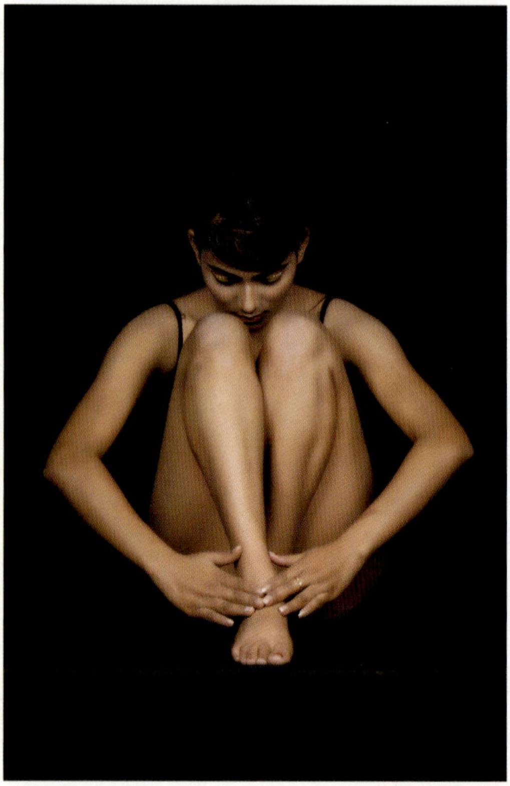

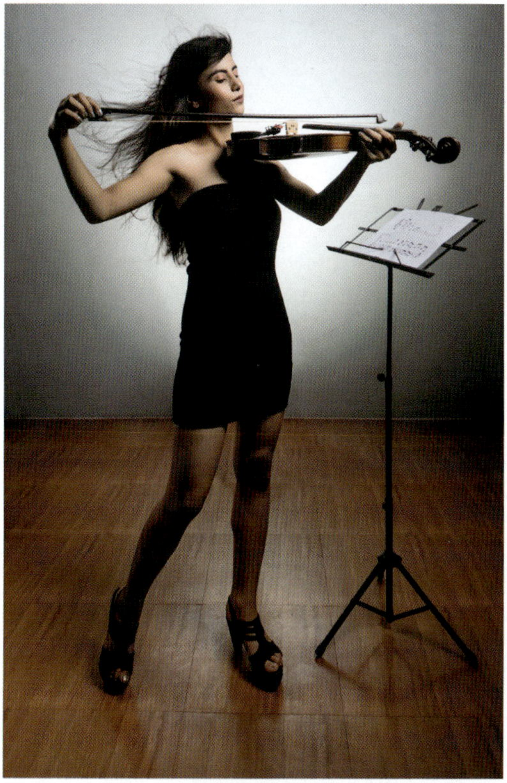

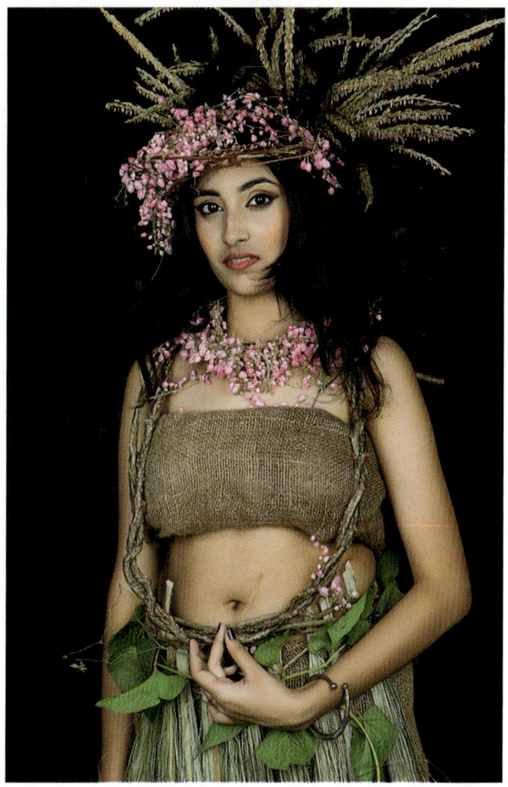

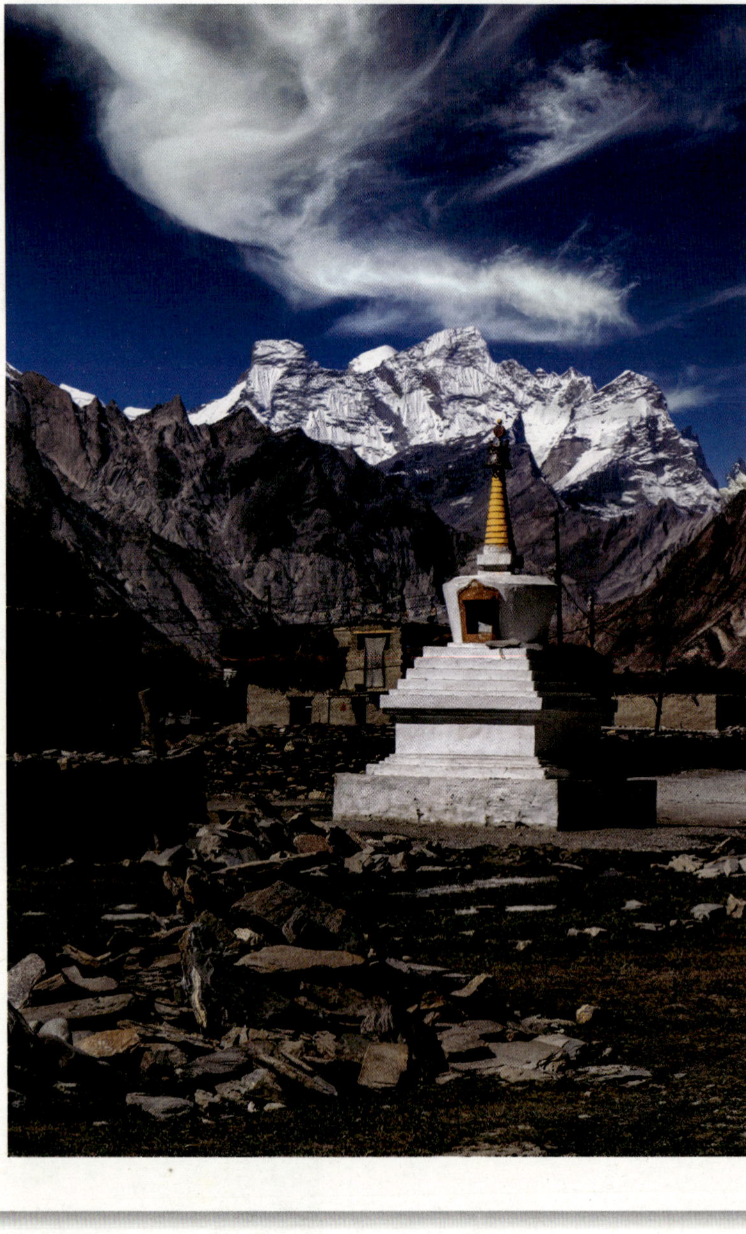